T0298532

"This book gives an invaluable guide to cybersecurity in discrete event systems, from modeling and synthesis of cyberattacks to design of resilient supervisors. A must-read for researchers and students, this book seamlessly blends resilient supervisors with smart attackers, starting a new and comprehensive approach to one of the most challenging problems in cybersecurity."
Prof Feng Lin, *Wayne State University, Fellow of IEEE*

"This book provides a timely and systematic analysis for smart attacks and resilience for better cybersecurity from the perspective of discrete-events and provides excellent theoretical insights on how smart attacks might leverage on existing supervisory control logics to inflict damage to systems without being detected easily and how such attacks could be prevented by properly designed supervisory controls. Enjoy your reading and digestion of the first, interesting and inspiring monograph on cybersecurity research!"
Prof Sam Shuzhi Ge, *National University of Singapore, Fellow of IEEE, Fellow of IFAC, Fellow of IET*

"This book provides comprehensive coverage of a framework for modelling cyberattacks and developing defence (as well as attack!) strategies in the context of discrete event systems. Rong Su, who has been working on discrete event systems for more than two decades, provides an elegant description of the recent work of his group on discrete event system cybersecurity. This is a well-motivated and quite thorough exposition, ranging from smart sensor attacks to resilient supervisory control strategies! I highly recommend this book to anyone interested in cybersecurity aspects in finite state dynamic systems."
Prof Christoforos Hadjicostis, *University of Cyprus, Fellow of IEEE*

"Cybersecurity is no doubt one of the most important subjects and has been affecting everyone on this planet on a daily basis. This book provides a nice introduction to this subject in the framework of discrete event systems (DES), addressing smart cyberattacks and suitable/effective defence techniques against them. It presents mathematically rigorous concepts, methods, and theory as well as many practically useful algorithms for this complex and important subject. The insights provided in the book are expected to benefit researchers and practitioners not only in the DES community but also in much broader communities of control, communication, networking and cyber-physical systems. Hence, I highly recommend this book to all who have a genuine interest in cybersecurity."

Prof Mengchu Zhou, *New Jersey Institute of Technology, Fellow of IEEE, Fellow of IFAC, Fellow of AAAS, Fellow of CAA, Fellow of NAI*

"This excellent book introduces a comprehensive array of formal approaches essential for cybersecurity analysis and defence, drawing inspiration from the cutting-edge theoretical advancements in discrete event systems."

Prof Alessandro Giua, *University of Cagliari (Italy), Fellow of IEEE, Fellow of IFAC*

Cybersecurity of Discrete Event Systems

This book describes analysis and control against smart cyberattacks in discrete event systems (DES). This is the first technical DES book to provide a thorough introduction to smart cyberattacks on supervisory control systems modelled by regular languages or finite-state automata and possible resilient defence methods against smart cyberattacks.

"Smart attacks" cannot be detected by the supervisor until an irreversible process toward ensured damage occurs. An attack may be conducted either in the observation channel (i.e., the supervisor's input of the supervisor) or in the command channel (i.e., the supervisor's output) or both simultaneously. Therefore, defence strategies against these attacks are urgently needed. Rong Su provides a comprehensive overview of the latest theories and includes empirical examples to illustrate concepts and methods. By centering on what information is available and how such information is used, the readers are provided with methods to evaluate the cyber vulnerability of a given system and design a resilient supervisor against relevant smart attacks. This book comprises two sections. Firstly, Su introduces the required concepts and techniques related to DES and supervisory control. Then he introduces different types of smart attacks that intercept and manipulate information in sensor and command channels in a standard closed-loop control system. Secondly, he presents resilient defence strategies against relevant types of attacks.

By focusing on a conceptual introduction and systematic analysis, this book provides a solid theoretical foundation for future exploration by researchers and graduate students who are interested in cybersecurity research, not necessarily limited to those in the DES community. To illustrate the practical relevance of this research, realistic examples are used throughout this book. Readers are recommended to have a background in formal language theory.

Rong Su, PhD, is a Professor at the School of Electrical and Electronic Engineering and Director of the Centre for System Intelligence and Efficiency at Nanyang Technological University. He earned a BE degree at the University of Science and Technology of China and an

MAS degree and a PhD degree at the University of Toronto. Dr. Su is a senior member of IEEE and an associate editor for *IEEE Transactions on Cybernetics*, *Automatica* (IFAC), *Journal of Discrete Event Dynamic Systems* and *Journal of Control and Decision*. Dr. Su is prolifically published and has received several best paper awards, such as the 2021 Hsue-shen Tsien Paper Award from the IEEE/CAA *Journal of Automatica Sinica* and the Best Paper Award at the 15th International Conference on Advanced Systems in Public Transport (CASPT2022). He is an IEEE Distinguished Lecturer for the IEEE Robotics and Automation Society.

Cybersecurity of Discrete Event Systems

From Smart Attacks to Resilient Defence

Rong Su

CRC Press
Taylor & Francis Group
Boca Raton London New York

CRC Press is an imprint of the
Taylor & Francis Group, an **informa** business

Designed cover image: Binary code with cyberattack and magnifying lens on black background

First edition published 2025
by CRC Press
2385 NW Executive Center Drive, Suite 320, Boca Raton FL 33431

and by CRC Press
4 Park Square, Milton Park, Abingdon, Oxon, OX14 4RN

CRC Press is an imprint of Taylor & Francis Group, LLC

ISBN: 978-1-032-36810-8 (hbk)
ISBN: 978-1-032-36812-2 (pbk)
ISBN: 978-1-003-33388-3 (ebk)

DOI: 10.1201/9781003333883

Typeset in CMS
by codeMantra

To my three angels: Gabriel, Michael and Raphael,
and my beloved wife Lijuan.
You are my source of strength and courage,
and my safe haven for inner tranquility.

Contents

Preface   xiii

List of Contributors   xvi

Symbols   xvii

CHAPTER   1 ▪ Introduction to Cybersecurity in Discrete
              Event Systems   1

1.1   INTRODUCTION   1

1.2   MOTIVATION EXAMPLES OF CYBERATTACKS   4

      1.2.1   Stuxnet – The First Known Cyber Weapon   4

      1.2.2   SQL Injection Attack   8

1.3   OVERVIEW OF DES CYBERSECURITY RESEARCH   11

1.4   PRELIMINARIES ON SUPERVISORY CONTROL
      THEORY   16

      1.4.1   Languages and Finite-State Automata   17

      1.4.2   Supervisory Control   23

PART I   Modeling and Synthesis of Smart Attacks

CHAPTER   2 ▪ Smart Sensor Attacks   31

2.1   INTRODUCTION   31

2.2   A SMART SENSOR ATTACK PROBLEM   34

      2.2.1   A Non-Deterministic Sensor Attack Model   34

      2.2.2   An Automaton Realization of a Sensor Attack   37

      2.2.3   A Smart Sensor Attack Model   44

2.3   SYNTHESIS OF A SMART SENSOR ATTACK   46

2.3.1   Procedure for Supremal Attack Language   56

2.4   SYNTHESIS OF AN SSA-ROBUST SUPERVISOR   59

2.5   CONCLUSIONS   66

CHAPTER   3 ▪ Smart Sensor-Actuator Attacks   67

3.1   INTRODUCTION   68

3.2   A LANGUAGE FRAMEWORK   69

3.2.1   The Concept of Sensor-Actuator Attack   70

3.2.2   The Concept of Smart Sensor-Actuator Attack   74

3.2.3   Weighted Sensor-Actuator Attack   78

3.3   AN FSA-BASED MODELING FRAMEWORK   79

3.4   SUPREMAL SMART LEAN SENSOR-ACTUATOR ATTACK   83

3.5   SUPREMAL MINIMUM-WEIGHTED SMART
SENSOR-ACTUATOR ATTACK   91

3.6   CONCLUSIONS   100

CHAPTER   4 ▪ Smart Attacks with Unknown Supervisor   102

4.1   SYNCHRONIZED ATTACK   102

4.2   NONSYNCHRONIZED ATTACK   108

4.2.1   Deployment of Non-Synchronized Attack   118

4.3   CONCLUSIONS   121

PART II   Modeling and Synthesis of Resilient Supervisors

CHAPTER   5 ▪ Resilient Supervisory Control against Smart
Sensor Attacks   125

5.1   INTRODUCTION   126

5.2   MOTIVATION – ATTACK OF NAVIGATOR   128

5.3   SMART SENSOR ATTACK   131
5.4   A SUFFICIENT AND NECESSARY CONDITION
      FOR ATTACK EXISTENCE   135
5.5   SUPERVISOR RESILIENT TO SMART SENSOR ATTACKS   138
5.6   DECIDABILITY OF EXISTENCE OF SUPERVISOR
      RESILIENT TO SMART SENSOR ATTACKS   149
5.7   CONCLUSIONS   159

CHAPTER   6 ▪ System Vulnerability Analysis via
            Attack Model Reduction   161

6.1   INTRODUCTION TO SUPERVISOR REDUCTION   162
6.2   PRELIMINARIES   165
      6.2.1   Procedure of Synthesis of Feasible Supervisors   166
6.3   INFORMATION FOR CONTROL EQUIVALENCE   169
6.4   INFORMATION DETERMINING REDUCTION
      EFFICIENCY   178
6.5   IDENTIFYING SYSTEM VULNERABILITY VIA
      ATTACK MODEL REDUCTION   187
      6.5.1   Sensor Attack Constraint Model   188
      6.5.2   Command Execution Model   192
      6.5.3   Sensor Attacker Model   193
6.6   CONCLUSIONS   197
NOTES   198

CHAPTER   7 ▪ Supervisor Obfuscation against Smart
            Actuator Attacks   199

7.1   INTRODUCTION   200
7.2   PRELIMINARIES   203

7.3　SMART ACTUATOR ATTACK – AN INSIGHT VIEW　203

7.4　COMPONENT MODELS AND PROBLEM
　　　FORMULATION　212

7.5　MAIN IDEA OF SOLUTION METHODOLOGY　218

7.6　BEHAVIOR-PRESERVING STRUCTURE CONSTRUCTION　219

　　　7.6.1　Equivalent Behavior Computation　219

　　　7.6.2　Feasible Control Commands Completion　220

　　　7.6.3　Structure Refinement　223

7.7　SYNTHESIS OF OBFUSCATED SUPERVISORS　228

　　　7.7.1　Identification of Covert Damage Strings　228

　　　7.7.2　Pruning of Illegal Control Commands　235

　　　7.7.3　Synthesis of Obfuscated Supervisors　238

7.8　CONCLUSIONS　246

NOTES　247

Bibliography　248

Index　261

Preface

"Internet gives us access to everything; but it also gives everything access to us."

– James Veitch

We are in an era of networks. Every year billions of new devices are connected to the global network. This unprecedented connectivity makes cybersecurity an issue that affects everyone on this planet. According to USA Cybersecurity & Infrastructure Security Agency (CISA), *cybersecurity is the art of protecting networks, devices, and data from unauthorized access or criminal use and the practice of ensuring confidentiality, integrity, and availability of information.* In a report by Steve Morgan [1], the estimated cybercrime damage cost the world $3 trillion in 2015 and is expected to reach $10.5 trillion annually by 2025. It is critically important to develop suitable knowledge and technology to ensure cybersecurity.

This indisputably important subject has been drawing lots of attention from both industry and academia. Researchers in the discrete-event system (DES) community are not immune to this curiosity. A DES can be defined as a group of agents that influence their own or any other agent's state transitions by conducting relevant actions (or events). For each specific instance of a DES, each agent's state space could be either discrete or continuous, and each action (or event) could be either asynchronous or concurrent and could take either no time or some time before finishing. DES theories can be used for system modeling, analysis, control and performance optimization, and have found applications in many areas such as manufacturing, logistics, communication and transportation. However, research on cybersecurity analysis and resilient control has only recently become popular in the community, due to its growing importance. This book aims to present a suite of latest frameworks that describe several types of smart cyberattacks and corresponding defending strategies via resilient supervisory control. Some key questions to be answered in this book include, e.g., what are smart sensor and/or actuator attacks, how to identify the existence of a smart attack in a given closed-loop system, does there exist a resilient supervisor against ALL possible smart attacks of a certain type, and in case an answer to the previous question is positive, how to synthesize one such resilient supervisor.

The idea of smart attacks introduced in this book was first conceived in February 2016, when I visited Stephane Lafortune at University of Michigan. My original plan was to discuss with Stephane and Feng Lin, who was also there for a short visit, about networked DES control. Due to some reason, the discussion was forked into cyberattacks, as Stephane was collaborating with some brilliant researchers such as Lilian Kawakami Carvalho and Raymond Kwong on supervisory control against actuator enablement attack, which later appeared in WODES2016. Compared with the existing works, the key novelty of this new concept of smart attack is to associate an attack with certain characteristics of intelligence in order to distinguish it from indigenous uncontrollable events like faults that cause system functional changes. Some commonly used characteristics of intelligence include *covertness* (or *stealthiness*) and *feasibility of damage infliction* - the former describes the capability of an attacker to hide an attack from being detected before (irreversible) damage can be inflicted, and the latter captures the desirable attack consequence, either guaranteed damage or a chance play.

After imposing such characteristics of intelligence, this line of research becomes much more intrigue than fault diagnosis or opacity analysis, which have been actively studied in the DES community. A system designer basically needs to play two antagonistic roles simultaneously. On one hand, the designer needs to put himself in an attacker's shoes about what can be done to identify most vulnerable system assets and maximize damage to a target system with minimum costs; on the other hand, the designer needs to think from a defender's viewpoint about how to ward off such smart attacks. Ultimately, the goal is to enhance system resilience against cyberattacks. But only after we fully understand an opponent's best moves, we can come up with the best defense measures.

Since the idea of smart attack was conceived in 2016, there have been many follow-up works. Some fundamental questions such as decidability of existence of smart sensor attacks, existence of resilient supervisors against smart sensor attacks, and existence of smart actuator attacks have been satisfactorily answered, which however rely on an assumption of having perfect prior knowledge about a target system. Recently, new results have started to appear that rely on learning system behaviors to gain required knowledge about a target system, upon which attack or defense schemes could be synthesized. Are we able to see more fruitful results on computationally feasible cybersecurity solutions adopted by industry in the next few years? I feel positive about this.

This book is based on inspiring ideas from several past publications jointly written with my current and former PhD students Ruochen Tai, Liyong Lin, and Yuting Zhu. I had so many wonderful moments when discussing with them. Some early idea on smart actuator attacks was conceived when Sander Thuijsman from Eindhoven University of Technology (TUE) visited me at Nanyang Technological University for an 11-week training program in early 2018. Our collaboration led to a conference publication at ACC'19, together with his supervisor Michel Renier. My deep gratitude goes to Joao Carlos Basilio, Christoforos Hadjicostis, Stephane Lafortune, and Feng Lin for their constructive comments and suggestions in the past few years when we worked together on different occasions such as a book project with Basilio and Christoforos, and a tutorial session at IEEE CDC'22 with Christoforos, Stephane and Feng. I would also like to express my deep gratitude to Walter Murray Wonham, who, as my MASc and PhD thesis supervisor, brought me into the DES community and equipped me with all necessary knowledge and tools, without which this book would never be possible. I will also use this opportunity to thank Andrew Stow from CRC Press who provided me with this book project and, with many other staff at CRC Press like Kasturi Ghosh, has been patiently working with me to make the whole preparation journey an unforgettable memory for me.

Finally, I would like to express my deepest gratitude to my wife Lijuan and three children, Gabriel, Michael, and Raphael, for their continuous support and encouragement, without which this project would never even start.

Rong Su

Nanyang Technological University, Singapore

October 2023

Contributors

Liyong Lin
School of Electrical and Electronic Engineering
Nanyang Technological University
Singapore, Singapore

Ruochen Tai
School of Electrical and Electronic Engineering
Nanyang Technological University
Singapore, Singapore

Yuting Zhu
School of Electrical and Electronic Engineering
Nanyang Technological University
Singapore, Singapore

Symbols

SYMBOL DESCRIPTION

Σ	finite alphabet	$En_{\mathbf{G}}(s)$	enabled events after s in $\mathbf{G}$
Σ^*	monoid with concatenation	$L(\mathbf{G})$	closed behavior of $\mathbf{G}$.
ϵ	empty string	$L_m(\mathbf{G})$	marked behavior of $\mathbf{G}$.
Σ^ϵ	alphabet $\Sigma \cup \{\epsilon\}$		
Σ_o	observable alphabet	$UR_{\mathbf{G},\Sigma}(x)$	unobservable state reach in $\mathbf{G}$ from x
Σ_o^ϵ	$\Sigma_o \cup \{\epsilon\}$		with events in Σ
Σ_{uo}	unobservable alphabet		
Σ_c	controllable alphabet	V	supervisory control function
Σ_{uc}	uncontrollable alphabet		
		$V/\mathbf{G}$	controlled plant automaton
$\Sigma_{o,a}$	attackable observable alphabet	S	supervisory control function
$\Sigma_{c,a}$	attackable controllable alphabet	$S/\mathbf{G}$	controlled plant automaton
Γ	control pattern set	$\mathbf{S}$	supervisor automaton
$\sigma \in \Sigma$	event σ from Σ	A_s	sensor attack function
$\|s\|$	length of string s	$\mathbf{A}_s$	sensor attack automaton
$s^\uparrow$	last event of string s		
$s \leq t$	prefix substring s of t	A_c	actuator attack function
st	concatenation of s and t	$\mathbf{A}_c$	actuator attack automaton
$L \subseteq \Sigma^*$	language L from Σ		
$En_L(s)$	enabled events after s in L	$\mathbf{BT}$	bipartite supervisor automaton
$\overline{L}$	prefix closure of L	$\mathbf{BT}^{\mathbf{A}_c}$	bipartite supervisor automaton under attack
$\mathbf{G}$	plant automaton		
$En_{\mathbf{G}}(x)$	enabled events at x in $\mathbf{G}$		

CE	command execution automaton	$P_{\Sigma,\Sigma'}$	natural projection
CE$^{\mathbf{A}_c}$	command execution automaton under attack	P_o	natural projection to Σ_o^*
		$P_{o,a}$	natural projection to $\Sigma_{o,a}^*$
BPS	behavior preserving structure	$|A|$	Cardinality of set A
		$\mathbb{N}$	natural number set
BPNS	nondeterministic **BPS**	$\mathbf{G} \times \mathbf{S}$	parallel composition
BPNS$^{\mathbf{A}_c}$	attacked **BPNS**	$L_1 \| L_2$	synchronous product
M	dynamic mask automaton	$f_1 \circ f_2$	composition of functions
E	edit automaton	$\wedge$	logic AND
I	intruder automaton	$\vee$	logic OR

CHAPTER 1

Introduction to Cybersecurity in Discrete Event Systems

1.1 INTRODUCTION

According to Merriam-Webster [8], "*a system is a regularly interacting or interdependent group of items forming a unified whole*". If we adopt this generic concept of system, then a discrete-event system (DES) can be defined as *a group of agents that influence their own or any other agent's state transitions by conducting relevant actions (or events)*. For each specific instance of a DES, each agent's state space could be either discrete or continuous, and each action (or event) could be either asynchronous or concurrent and could take either no time or some time before finishing. Regarding forms of inter-agent interactions, they could be either *behavior oriented*, where detailed steps of an interaction are specified, or *function oriented*, where the consequence, rather than procedure, of an interaction is modeled. One example of a behavior-oriented agent interaction can be found in parallel composition of formal process models such as calculus of communicating systems (CCS) by Robin Milner [9], where each interaction includes a sending action and a receiving action. One example of a function-oriented agent interaction can be found in parallel composition of finite-state automata [3,10], where a single event execution triggers all agents

DOI: 10.1201/9781003333883-1

(modeled by automata) that permit this event to make state transitions simultaneously. Occasionally, we also use discrete-event dynamical system (DEDS) in the monograph to refer to a DES whose transitional behavior (partially) depends on time, which could be considered either as one special event or part of some prerequisite conditions that trigger a state transition. According to Ref. [2], almost all man-made systems contain some components that can be described by DES, such as software systems, manufacturing systems, communication systems, logistic systems, and transportation systems.

In a general sense, cybersecurity is the practice of protecting systems, networks, and programs from digital attacks, which aim at accessing, changing, or destroying sensitive information; extorting financial benefits from users; or interrupting normal operational processes. There are many different types of cybersecurity based on concerned assets such as network security, cloud security, endpoint security, mobile security, IoT security, application security, and zero trust. The corresponding cybersecurity threats have also evolved for several generations, triggering continuous advancement of cybersecurity measures. For example, in the late 1980s, virus attacks against standalone computers inspired the creation of the first antivirus solutions. As cyberattacks began to come over the Internet, the firewall was developed to identify and block them. Later, exploitation of vulnerabilities within applications caused the mass adoption of intrusion prevention systems. As malware became more targeted and able to evade signature-based defenses, anti-bot and sandboxing solutions were necessary to detect novel threats. The latest generation of cybersecurity threats uses large-scale, multi-vector attacks, making advanced threat prevention solutions a priority. The systems and control community mainly focus on application-based cybersecurity threats, aiming to identify vulnerability of existing application functions and design suitable defense measures [49,131,132, 137–140,167–173].

In this monograph, we focus on one specific type of application-based cyberattack cast in a DES framework, where an attacker aims to inflict damage on a target system by disrupting its control loop. This could be achieved either by intercepting and changing the controller's input signals (such as sensor measurements or operational references or requirements) or by intercepting and changing the controller's output

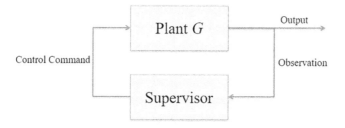

Figure 1.1 The Ramadge-Wonham supervisory control architecture.

signals (such as control commands or state feedback information for system monitoring), or by completely blocking the data transmission between the controller and the plant (in terms of, e.g., denial-of-service attacks). An attack can be either brute force, e.g., via hardware destruction or signal jamming, or covert (or stealthy), i.e., the attacking process is hidden from the controller or any other monitoring mechanism. We adopt the control system setup introduced in the Ramadge-Wonham supervisory control paradigm [3,12], which is depicted in Figure 1.1. In this paradigm, the plant generates observable outputs, received by the supervisor via an observation channel, and each control command specified as a set of allowable events is generated by the supervisor and fed to the plant via a command channel. The plant will nondeterministically pick one event from the control command and execute it. Unlike attacks in time-driven systems, attacks under consideration in a DES aim to change the order of events in specific system runs. There are two different streams of research on cyberattacks and resilient control. The first stream is to treat each attack as a fault that alters event orders in the system by either removing existing events or inserting fictitious events. In this case, research focuses firstly on how to decide the existence of an attack in the system based on a finite number of observations, similar to verifying diagnosability in fault diagnosis, and secondly on how to ensure sufficient control abilities to stop the propagation of the attack effect, e.g., by shutting down the entire system. Partial observation and existence of uncontrollable events complicate the synthesis process. The second stream is to develop a specific "smart" attack model that ensures certain intuitive properties such as covertness and guaranteed (strong or weak) damage infliction. Under such a smart attack model, the research focuses on analyzing how the attack may affect the closed-loop behavior, deciding whether the system is vulnerable to such an attack, and finally computing a supervisor that is resilient to the concerned attack. In this monograph, we will provide a detailed account of existing state-of-the-art modeling and resiliency results associated with smart attacks and point out challenges for future exploration.

In the following sections, we will provide some real cyberattack cases and illustrate how they could be considered in a DES framework. This will provide motivations for technical developments introduced in this monograph and also provide future research topics that the community may consider. After that, we provide a brief overview of existing DES cybersecurity research and some mathematical preliminaries on DES supervisory control theory, which will be used in the remainder of this monograph.

1.2 MOTIVATION EXAMPLES OF CYBERATTACKS

1.2.1 Stuxnet – The First Known Cyber Weapon

Stuxnet is a malicious computer worm first uncovered in 2010 and thought to have been in development since at least 2005. Stuxnet targets supervisory control and data acquisition (SCADA) systems and is believed to be responsible for causing substantial damage to the nuclear program of Iran. There are lots of stories and reports about this attack, which have been well disseminated in the media and academic communities. Here, we are interested in a high-level overview of its attack mechanism.

According to a report by Kim Zetter [5], Stuxnet attack targeted at the following SCADA architecture depicted in Figure 1.2. In a normal operational condition, Siemens' WinCC/PCS7 SCADA control software [75] (Step 7) issued relevant control commands, including information about operational frequencies of centrifuges, to Programmable Logic Controller (PLC), via a key communication library of WinCC called s7otbxdx.dll. The PLC also sent the system's operational conditions back to Step 7 via s7otbxdx.dll. Normally, centrifuges operate at a frequency well above 1,000 Hz. Any drastic change of operational frequencies might damage centrifuges, which was a known fact to experts.

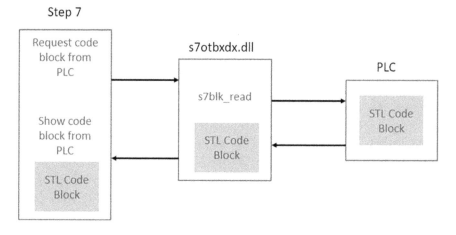

Figure 1.2 The control architecture targeted by Stuxnet attack.

A group of attackers managed to install Stuxnet code in the system. According to researcher Ralph Langner [6], once installed on a Windows system Stuxnet infected project files belonging to Step 7, and subverted the key communication library s7otbxdx.dll, by firstly inserting a malicious wrapper code between Step 7 and s7otbxdx.dll, and then renaming s7otbxdx.dll to s7otbxsx.dll, and passing the original name s7otbxdx.dll to the inserted malicious wrapper code. To successfully achieve this wrapping goal, attackers utilized a security vulnerability published by Siemens only one year before the attack, which however had not caused any public notice. This malicious code was able to intercept communications between the WinCC software running under Windows and the target Siemens PLC devices, when the two were connected via a data cable. Basically, the malicious code could change the operational frequency issued by Step 7 before passing to the PLC, possibly via the original but renamed communication library. To make the entire attack moves stealthy, the frequency changes were only done from time to time to avoid being detected. It was reported that when the malicious code caused centrifuges to operate at a much lowered frequency, a false fault alarm was sent to the system to ensure that such a low-frequency operation was due to some temporary sensor fault; thus, no emergency actions such as system shutdown would be taken by the system operators. Each feedback information from the

PLC about the system's operational conditions was also intercepted by the malicious code and modified before being passed to Step 7, making Step 7 believe that nothing abnormal happened in the system. The actual details are very complicated. However, a simplified high-level illustration of the attack scheme is shown in Figure 1.3.

It was believed that periodic changes of operational frequencies of centrifuges eventually caused irreversible damage to centrifuges. The whole attack process took a long period to complete, making each attack move unnoticed by the system monitor. This is one typical example of a smart attack, which will be cast in a DES framework and addressed in this monograph. If we consider the PLC as a plant to be controlled, then Step 7 becomes a supervisor. The original communication library s7otbxdx.dll essentially creates communication channels between the plant and supervisor. The Stuxnet attack basically attacks both the information feedback channel from the plant to the supervisor and the control command channel from the supervisor to the plant, which is depicted in Figure 1.4. Later in this monograph, we will dub this type of smart attacks as *sensor-actuator attacks*, as

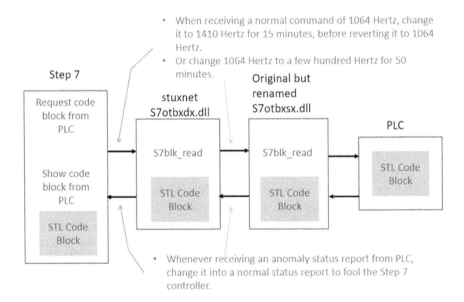

Figure 1.3 Illustration of Stuxnet attack mechanism.

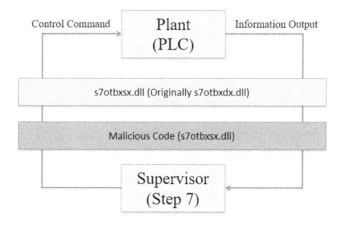

Figure 1.4 A DES view of Stuxnet attack mechanism.

it attacks both the information channel and the command channel. From an attacker's viewpoint, one fundamental question is how to ensure a successful cyberattack. In the Stuxnet attack, we can see that attackers had two pieces of knowledge. Firstly, they had a clear attack goal, namely to adjust operational frequencies of centrifuges to damage centrifuges. Secondly, they knew how to achieve their goal by exploiting functional vulnerabilities of the original Siemens control system to deploy malicious code to hijack the information and command channels and, most importantly, to operate attack moves in a stealthy manner. These two features, i.e., guarantee of damage infliction and attack stealthiness (or covertness), will be used in this monograph to characterize so-called smart attacks. On the other hand, from a defender's viewpoint, one fundamental question is how to design system functions that deprive any potential attacker from attaining sufficient system resources for a successful attack, especially a stealthy attack. For example, in the Stuxnet attack case, if the Siemens control system vulnerability were fully aware of earlier, it would be much more difficult, if still possible, for the attackers to deploy their attack code. Basically, how to identify system vulnerabilities or critical assets and how to protect them are interesting and potential important topics for research, which will be addressed in this monograph.

1.2.2 SQL Injection Attack

An SQL injection attack is a technique that attackers use to gain unauthorized access to a web application database by adding a string of malicious code to a database query. It is considered as one of the most common web attack mechanisms used by attackers to steal sensitive data from organizations, alter data and access database servers with operating system privileges, and use these permissions to access other sensitive systems. In a report dated back to 2015 by Alastair Stevenson [7], A hacker group, known online as Team GhostShell, claims it successfully hacked over 300 websites and has posted over 13,000 users' personal details online. The actually number of victims could be much bigger. In 2014, security researchers publicized that they were able to breach the website of Tesla using SQL injection, gain administrative privileges, and steal user data. In 2018, a SQL injection vulnerability was found in Cisco Prime License Manager. The vulnerability allowed attackers to gain shell access to systems on which the license manager was deployed. Cisco has patched the vulnerability. Fortnite is an online game with over 350 million users. In 2019, a SQL injection vulnerability was discovered, which could let attackers access user accounts. The vulnerability was patched. Although SQL injection attacks have been discovered for more than a quarter of century, it is still included in the Open Worldwide Application Security Project (OWASP) Top 10 list of security vulnerabilities.

There are many different types of SQL injection attacks, among which the Union-based SQL injection attack is the most popular type, which uses the UNION statement that represents the combination of two select statements to retrieve data from the database. We use a simple example to illustrate one such attack. Figure 1.5 illustrates one database, which consists of information of different products. The last column denotes whether a concerned row is publicly accessible: value 1 indicates "yes", and value 0 indicates "no". Assume that each user is assigned with a specific access authorization grade, which is associated with a set of predetermined accessible product categories. An example of an SQL query command is shown below:

SELECT * FROM product **where** Category='Sports' **AND** released=1

which states that this user is allowed to inquire information about all products in the Sports category, which is accessible to this user

Products

Category	Name	Price	Stock	Released
Sports	XXX	XXX	XX	1
	XXX	XXX	XX	0
	XXX	XXX	XX	1
	...	...	...	...
Living	XXX	XXX	XX	0
	XXX	XXX	XX	0
	XXX	XXX	XX	1
	...	...	...	...

1 ———► Allowed to be retrieved
0 ———► Not allowed to be retrieved

Figure 1.5 A simple database.

Figure 1.6 A normal query command and three injection attacks.

(denoted by "released=1"). This query command is susceptible to SQL injection attacks. There are at least three different injections by an attacker that could allow unauthorized information access, which are depicted in Figure 1.6. The first attack replaces the argument 'Category='Sports'' with a new argument 'Category='Sports' **OR** True –', which will trick the SQL database to bypass the last condition check of 'Released=1', namely allowing the attacker to access product information in the Sports category, which is originally not accessible to the attacker. The second attack replaces the argument 'Category='Sports' ' with a new argument 'Category='Sports' **OR** True', which allows the attacker to access the information of all products. The last attack replaces the argument 'Category='Sports' ' with a new argument 'True', which leads to the same attack effect as that of the second attack. Although the above three injection attacks can be easily avoided by using the latest techniques such

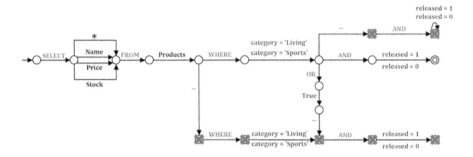

Figure 1.7 A DES model of possible injection attacks.

as restricting certain parameters and keywords, one fundamental question has not been properly addressed, that is, how to effectively identify existing loopholes in a database, which might permit injection attacks. To answer this question, one idea is to provide a formal model of database inquiry process, upon which any query that may violate formal requirements may be revealed. A DES framework could be one option for such a formal model. For example, Figure 1.7 depicts one transitional model, which describes different attack sequences that could be applied to a legal query sequence. In this formal model, the backbone of the transition structure is the list of all possible sequences of keywords highlighted in blue. Others in black are arguments of each relevant keyword, which could be potentially altered by an injection attack. Each string from the initial state to a final state denotes one information query. There are a fixed number of sequences of keywords, with possibly an indefinite number of arguments. Intuitively, an attacker aims to use an injection attack on one query of a specific sequence of keywords to derive another sequence of keywords that allows the attacker to access some sensitive information. Upon this understanding, this model indicates that, in principle, it is possible to enumerate different possibilities of imposing an injection attack, which preserves an order of a standard query keywords, although keyword skipping is allowed. With this model, it might be possible to develop a systematic procedure to identify relevant injection vulnerabilities, which will help database designers find ways to eliminate such vulnerabilities.

1.3 OVERVIEW OF DES CYBERSECURITY RESEARCH

Cybersecurity is a very broad subject. So far, the DES community mainly focuses on problems related to two cybersecurity topics, that is, *information confidentiality*, which is cast as system opacity under eavesdropping, and *functional integrity*, which is captured as event integrity under cyberattacks. In this section, we aim to provide a brief chronicle account of major idea conceptions, hoping that this could provide readers with motivations for technical treatments in subsequent chapters. The actual detailed literature review, however, will be presented in each subsequent chapter.

As mentioned previously, in a generic sense, cybersecurity is about the practice of protecting systems against digital attacks. In this type of problems, there are always two players: an attacker and a defender. We study such problems only aiming to make defenders smart, even though frequently we look at a system from an attacker's viewpoint. This thinking method is certainly not new. More than two thousand years ago, one famous Chinese strategist, Sun Tse, shown in Figure 1.8, said that *"if you know the enemy and know yourself, you need not fear the result of a hundred battles"*. Intuitively, a defender needs to answer several questions, when analyzing system cybersecurity vulnerability and designing a defense approach. Firstly, what system components can be attacked, how can they be attacked, and why are they attacked? Secondly, are there any observable symptoms to

知己知彼，百战不殆!

－孙子

If you know the enemy
and know yourself, you
need not fear the result
of a hundred battles.

－ Sun Tzu

孙子 (Sun Tzu, 544 – 496 BC)

Figure 1.8 A famous quote from Sun Tse. [The picture is taken from highlander.fandom.com/wiki/Sun_Tzu.]

manifest the existence of an attack? Thirdly, are there any preventive means to deter an attacker? The first two questions are essentially related to attack modeling, which is closely related to existing works on anomaly detection such as fault diagnosis. Therefore, it is not surprising to see early cybersecurity-related works cast in a framework similar to fault diagnosis, which heavily relies on state estimation.

The earliest influential works on fault diagnosis in a DES framework can be dated back to 1994–1995 [44,45], where the key concept of *diagnosability* in the DES framework was introduced. Since then, this topic has become one of the most published topics in the DES community and is still active nowadays. In such frameworks, each fault, considered as an undesirable functional deviation, is modeled by an unobservable event, whose occurrence will take a system to an undesirable state, either permanently [45] or temporarily [46]. The key solution strategies for fault diagnosis mainly rely on subset construction under partial observation [10] to identify sets of states that cannot be distinguished from observable behaviors – a system becomes diagnosable if after each (unobservable) fault occurrence, its presence can be unambiguously confirmed by a state estimator (or observer) within a finite number of event occurrences. When fault tolerance is under consideration, all faults are assumed to be feasible in the system, making the solution methods follow a worst-case strategy, commonly seen in robust control. A good survey article on this subject can be found in Refs. [4,47].

In contrast to fault diagnosis, where system functional deviations are under investigation, opacity is an information-flow property used in confidentiality and security applications. Intuitively, a dynamic system is opaque if an external observer with possibly prior knowledge about the system model cannot decide whether certain secret information about the system, such as an initial state or the current state, has been confirmed. The earliest influential works on this topic can be traced back to 2005–2008 [21–24]. This line of research has emerged as one of the most active research topics in the DES community, along with the rising concerns of data confidentiality and personal privacy [141–167]. A good summary of opacity research can be found in Refs. [4,25].

There were few works before 2016 to mention cyberattacks from a defender's viewpoint, e.g., a game-theoretical supervisory control framework was reported in Ref. [118], discrete event simulation of cyberattacks was reported in Refs. [119–121], Petri net models were adopted for detecting cyberattacks on supervisory control and data acquisition (SCADA) systems or computer systems. In about 2016–2018, researchers in the DES community started to be more active in addressing cyberattacks, which aim to deliberately drive a target system toward an undesirable state. Some influential works can be found in Refs. [51,53,55,56,79,80]. There is a clear bifurcation of two different types of technical treatments on this topic. The works presented in Refs. [51,53] treat each attack instance as a set of undesirable event changes that bear large similarity to fault occurrence on sensor events. An attacker has no intention to hide each attack move, just like each fault event occurrence in a system. In contrast, in Refs. [55,56,58,59], an attacker is considered as an intelligent foe, who, with prior knowledge about a target system and controller, can craft a stealthy (or covert) attack strategy that, if existing, can hide each attack move until some state is reached, where damage is irreversible. Such stealthy attacks are called smart attacks. Only after a smart attack strategy is understood, a defense strategy can be designed, which aims to prevent any understood smart attack. Following this line of thinking, there is always a dual problem to be analyzed and solved, namely a best attack strategy and a best defense strategy against the best attack strategy. Figure 1.9 depicts an intuitive architecture of smart attacks. An attacker can either attack the observation channel and replace true observations with "fake" ones, thus, affecting the input of the supervisor, or attack the command channel and replace each true

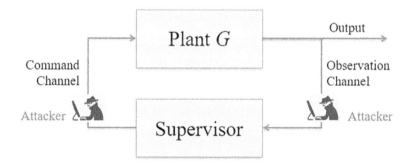

Figure 1.9 Intuitive architecture of smart cyberattack.

control command issued by the supervisor with a "fake" one, thus, affecting the output of the supervisor. In many cases, the attacker may be able to attack both the observation channel and command channel.

The earliest smart attacks on observation channels, dubbed as *smart sensor attacks*, appeared in 2017–2018 [55,56,79]. The basic idea is intuitive, that is, each event (or function) that is susceptible to cyberattacks can be replaced by another event or even a string of events, including an empty string representing event erasure. By doing this, an attacker aims to influence the input of a supervisor and trick it to issue inappropriate control commands that could lead the plant to an undesirable state. By using proper modeling techniques, e.g., event relabeling in Ref. [79–82] and an I/O transducer model in Ref. [55,56], an attack synthesis problem can be transformed into a form similar to supervisor synthesis [3]. Ultimately, we want to know whether there exists a supervisor, which is resilient to all possible smart sensor attacks. This question has been answered in Ref. [57], which confirms that the existence of a supervisor resilient to all smart sensor attacks is decidable. This result is different from those considering the worst-case scenario [60] with all attacks not necessarily smart in the sense that each supervisor that is robust to all attacks must be robust to all smart attacks, but the opposite may not be true. This means that a supervisor robust to smart attacks has a higher chance to exist than that of a supervisor robust to all attacks.

In contrast to smart sensor attacks, so far, there are few works on smart attacks of command channels, dubbed as *smart actuator attacks*, possibly due to the fact that an attacker has few attack options, i.e., either enabling or disabling some events to cause damage. For example, to prevent the plant from reaching some special states, or to lead the plant to go through a specific legal path towards a state, where an illegal event may be actuated, an attacker may disable events to limit the firing choices for the plant, which is called a *disabling attack* (or *disablement attack*). On the other hand, to move the plant out of its legal behavior set, the attacker will enable events at some states of the plant originally disabled by the supervisor. This type of attack is called *enabling attacks* (or *enablement attacks*). The earliest works on smart actuator attacks appeared in 2019–2020. In Ref. [62], the authors introduce an enablement attack, which smartly chooses a state to enable an event, originally disabled by the supervisor at that state, to lead the plant to reach a damage state irreversibly, and ensure that, even when an actuator attack move is not successful due to inaccurate state estimation, the supervisor will not be aware of the existence of the actuator attack. The latter property is called attack covertness. In Ref. [70], the authors present a systematic transformation procedure to convert a smart actuator attack synthesis problem into a standard supervisor synthesis problem. From a defense viewpoint, in Ref. [71], the authors present a novel supervisor obfuscation strategy to "fool" an actuator attacker from achieving an informative state estimate that might permit a smart actuator attack. The culmination of this line of research is achieved in Ref. [72], where the authors prove that the existence of an obfuscated (or fortified) supervisor robust to all smart actuator attacks is decidable.

Apart from early works on worst-case scenarios in supervisory control against sensor-actuator attacks, e.g., [51,53], in 2019, the authors in Ref. [64] presented an approach for synthesizing robust supervisors against smart sensor-actuator attacks, where an attacker tries to hide attack moves until a state is reached where damage is unavoidable. In this framework, an attacker can partially observe the input of a supervisor and fully observe the supervisor's output control commands. The authors present a novel algorithm, which transforms the concerned robust supervisor synthesis problem into a problem of solving quantified Boolean formulas (QBF), which are extensions of Boolean formulas where each variable can be quantified either universally or existentially. The quantified Boolean formula is true if and only if there is an n-bounded resilient supervisor against all smart sensor-actuator attacks; in particular, if the formula is true, such an n-bounded supervisor can be extracted from the assignment on the existentially quantified Boolean variables that witnesses the validity of the formula. SAT solvers can be used to attain assignments satisfying those QBFs [174–176]. The proposed transformation only works when the number of states of each concerned robust supervisor is uniformly bounded with a known value. However, the article does not discuss how to solve the QBF problem efficiently, and how to address properties beyond safety. The smart sensor-actuator attack synthesis problem can also be formulated and solved in a standard supervisor synthesis framework, as introduced in, e.g., [63,67,68].

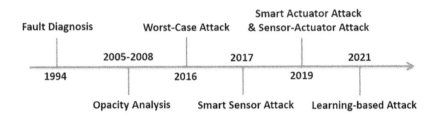

Figure 1.10 Timeline of major new frameworks about DES cybersecurity.

All previous works assume that an attacker has perfect knowledge about the plant and supervisor models, which may not be feasible in reality. Thus, starting in 2021, more and more interests are channeled into model learning part, where an attacker needs to decide, based on learned plant or supervisor's behavior, whether it is possible to carry out a covert attack. One such framework is introduced in Refs. [65,69,84,116]. A defender, on the other hand, needs to know which part of the system information is critical for a successful smart attack, thus, requires special protections. In Ref. [66], the authors present a method to identify key system assets required by a specific smart attack strategy to carry out a convert sensor attack. This method relies on an automaton-based model reduction approach, whose idea was originally developed for supervisor reduction that manifests key control actions in a given supervisor [135].

As a closing remark of this section, we use the following timeline shown in Figure 1.10, which is derived based on the existing literature, to illustrate how ideas of cybersecurity in the DES framework evolves over time, which we hope could shed light on future research directions. The timeline is not meant for providing a comprehensive overview of all relevant works up to the date, but rather for sketching some major ideas that result in a good number of follow-up activities in the DES community. Detailed literature reviews and historical accounts will be provided in each relevant chapter.

1.4 PRELIMINARIES ON SUPERVISORY CONTROL THEORY

In this section, we introduce basic concepts and notations that will be used in the remainder of this monograph to facilitate discussions of resilient control in DES. We will start with the concepts of regular languages and finite-state automata, and relevant language operations such as natural projection and synchronous product. After that, we provide a detailed account of Ramadge-Wonham (RW) supervisory control theory. We first introduce the closed-loop control architecture, the concepts of controllability and observability, and relevant assumptions about information generated by the plant and available for the supervisor. Then we present the supervisor existence conditions relying on the concepts of controllability and observability. Finally, we present the supervisor synthesis problem and some state-of-the-art synthesis frameworks. This section only aims to provide a concise overview of the RW framework and introduce standard notations which will be used consistently throughout this monograph. For a comprehensive introduction of the RW framework, we refer readers to Ref. [3]. For more advanced topics on languages and finite-state automata, we refer readers to Ref. [10,114].

1.4.1   Languages and Finite-State Automata

Let $\mathbb{N}$ be the set of natural numbers and $\mathbb{R}^+$ the set of all non-negative reals. Let Σ be a finite set of symbols. Each symbol denotes an *event* (or *action*) that can occur in a given DES. The occurrence of each event in Σ is assumed to be instantaneous, unless stated otherwise. Each finite sequence of events from Σ forms a finite *string*, including a special string ϵ, which denotes the empty string, whose length is considered as 0. String $s = \sigma_1 \sigma_2 \ldots \sigma_n$ can be *concatenated* with another string $t = \hat{\sigma}_1 \hat{\sigma}_2 \ldots \hat{\sigma}_m$, to form the string

$$st := \sigma_1 \sigma_2 \ldots \sigma_n \hat{\sigma}_1 \hat{\sigma}_2 \ldots \hat{\sigma}_m,$$

which captures the sequence of events in s followed by the sequence of events in t. We use Σ^* to denote the set of all finite strings, and for any $s \in \Sigma^*$ we have $s\epsilon = \epsilon s = s$. Formally, Σ^* is the free monoid over Σ, whose unit element is ϵ and the binary operation involved is concatenation. Given two strings $s, t \in \Sigma^*$, we say s is a *prefix substring* of t, denoted as $s \leq t$, if there exists $u \in \Sigma^*$ such that $su = t$. We use $|s|$ to denote the length of s; by convention, $|\epsilon| = 0$. We use $s^\uparrow$ to denote the last symbol of s; by convention, $\epsilon^\uparrow = \epsilon$. We use $\sigma \in s$ to denote that event σ appears at least once in s.

Any subset of Σ^*, say $L \subseteq \Sigma^*$, is a *language*. The *prefix closure* of L, denoted as $\overline{L}$, is defined as the collection of strings, each of which is a prefix substring of some string in L, that is, $\overline{L} := \{s \in \Sigma^* | (\exists t \in L)s \leq t\}$. If $L = \overline{L}$, then L is called *prefix closed*. Let

$$En_L : \overline{L} \rightarrow 2^{\Sigma} : s \mapsto En_L(s) := \{\sigma \in \Sigma | s\sigma \in \overline{L}\}$$

be a mapping that maps each string $s \in \overline{L}$ to the set of events allowed after s in $\overline{L}$. We call $En_L(s)$ the *enabled event set* after s in $\overline{L}$. For each $s \in \Sigma^*$, we use $L/s := \{t \in \Sigma^* | st \in L\}$ to denote the *suffix string set* of s in L. Given two languages L_1 and L_2, one can talk about the union of the two languages $L_1 \cup L_2$ or the intersection of the two languages $L_1 \cap L_2$ in terms of the usual set operations:

For notational simplicity, we will use "∧" to denote the logical conjunction "AND", and "∨" for logical disjunction "OR". In addition, we use $L_1 L_2 := \{st \in \Sigma^* | s \in L_1 \wedge t \in L_2\}$ to denote the concatenation of two languages. We use $|A|$ to denote the size (i.e., the cardinality or number of elements) of an arbitrary set A.

We also use standard *regular expression* notations to describe a set of strings (subset of Σ^*) that follow a particular pattern. More specifically, we make use of the following operators:

1. The superscript ^{n} (where n is a positive integer) is used to denote n repetitions of its argument. For example, given a string s, s^3 denotes the singleton set $\{sss\}$ or sometimes, abusing notation, the string sss itself. Similarly, $ab^n c$ denotes the singleton set $\{abb..bc\}$ (or string $abb..bc$) where b appears n times.

2. Given a string s, s^* denotes the set of strings that involve arbitrary (but finite) repetitions of s, including no repetition, i.e., $s^* = \{\epsilon, s, ss, sss, \ldots\}$. Similarly, $ab^* c$ denotes the set of strings that involve an a, followed by zero, one or more occurrences of b, followed by c, i.e., $ab^* c = \{ac, abc, abbc, abbbc, \ldots\}$.

3. The $+$ operator is used to denote unions of two sets of strings. For example, $a^* + bc^* d$ denotes the set of strings of the form $aa\ldots a$ (where a appears zero, one or more times) or b followed by zero, one or more occurrences of c, followed by d. In other words, $a^* + bc^* d = \{\epsilon, a, aa, aaa, \ldots, bd, bcd, bccd, \ldots\}$.

The above operations can be combined. For example, $(a+b)^*c(d+e)^*$ denotes the following set of strings (ordered according to their length):

$$\{c, ac, bc, cd, ce, acd, ace, bcd, bce, aac, bbc, abc, bac, cdd, cee, cde, ced, \ldots\} \ .$$

Let $\Sigma' \subseteq \Sigma$. A mapping $P : \Sigma^* \to \Sigma'^*$ is called the *natural projection* with respect to (Σ, Σ'), if

1. $P(\epsilon) = \epsilon$,

2. $(\forall \sigma \in \Sigma) \, P(\sigma) := \begin{cases} \sigma & \text{if } \sigma \in \Sigma', \\ \epsilon & \text{otherwise,} \end{cases}$

3. $(\forall s\sigma \in \Sigma^*) \, P(s\sigma) = P(s)P(\sigma)$.

Given a language $L \subseteq \Sigma^*$, $P(L) := \{P(s) \in \Sigma'^* | s \in L\}$. The inverse image mapping of P is defined as:

$$P^{-1} : 2^{\Sigma'^*} \to 2^{\Sigma^*} : L \mapsto P^{-1}(L) := \{s \in \Sigma^* | P(s) \in L\}.$$

Given $L_1 \subseteq \Sigma_1^*$ and $L_2 \subseteq \Sigma_2^*$, the *synchronous product* of L_1 and L_2 is defined as $L_1 \| L_2 := P_1^{-1}(L_1) \cap P_2^{-1}(L_2)$, where $P_1 : (\Sigma_1 \cup \Sigma_2)^* \to \Sigma_1^*$ and $P_2 : (\Sigma_1 \cup \Sigma_2)^* \to \Sigma_2^*$ are natural projections. Clearly, $\|$ is commutative and associative.

Definition 1.1 A *deterministic finite-state automaton* (DFSA or simply FSA) is captured by $\mathbf{G} = (X, \Sigma, \xi, x_0, X_m)$, where X is a finite set of states, $x_0 \in X$ an initial state, $X_m \subseteq X$ a set of marker (or final) states, and Σ a finite alphabet, $\xi : X \times \Sigma \to X$ a (partial) state transition function. For each $x \in X$ and $\sigma \in \Sigma$, we use $\xi(x, \sigma)!$ to denote that there exists an outgoing transition at state x, labeled by event σ. □

For simplicity of analysis, we can extend the domain of ξ from $X \times \Sigma$ to $X \times \Sigma^*$ in the following manner:

1. $(\forall x \in X)\xi(x, \epsilon) := x$;

2. $(\forall x \in X)(\forall s \in \Sigma^*)(\forall \sigma \in \Sigma) \, \xi(x, s\sigma) := \xi(\xi(x, s), \sigma)$.

Let

$$En_{\mathbf{G}} : X \to 2^\Sigma : x \mapsto En_{\mathbf{G}}(x) := \{\sigma \in \Sigma | \xi(x, \sigma)!$$

be a mapping that maps each state $x \in X$ to the set of events allowed at x in **G**. We call $En_{\mathbf{G}}(x)$ the *enabled event set* at x in **G**. **G** is called *reachable* if

$$(\forall x \in X)(\exists s \in \Sigma^*)\xi(x_0, s) = x,$$

namely, each state can be reached from the initial state; and *coreachable* if

$$(\forall x \in X)(\exists s \in \Sigma^*)\xi(x, s) \in X_m,$$

namely, from each state there is a directed path towards one marker state. **G** is called *trimmed* if it is both reachable and coreachable.

A *sub-automaton* of **G** is an automaton $\mathbf{G}_{\mathrm{sub}} = (X_{\mathrm{sub}}, \Sigma, \xi_{\mathrm{sub}}, x_0, X_{m,\mathrm{sub}})$, not necessarily trimmed, such that $X_{\mathrm{sub}} \subseteq X$, $X_{m,\mathrm{sub}} \subseteq X_m$ and

$$(\forall x, x' \in X)(\forall \sigma \in \Sigma)\,\xi_{\mathrm{sub}}(x, \sigma) = x' \Rightarrow \xi(x, \sigma) = x',$$

that is, each transition of $\mathbf{G}_{\mathrm{sub}}$ must be a transition in **G**. However, the opposite may not be true.

The language *generated* by FSA **G** (or the *closed behaviour* of **G**) captures all allowable sequences of events and is defined as

$$L(\mathbf{G}) := \{s \in \Sigma^* | \xi(x_0, s)!\}.$$

The language *recognized* by **G** (or the *marked behaviour* of **G**) is defined as

$$L_m(\mathbf{G}) := \{s \in L(\mathbf{G}) | \xi(x_0, s) \in X_m\}.$$

Later, we will interpret each string $s \in L(\mathbf{G})$ as a task, either completed or uncompleted, and each string $t \in L_m(\mathbf{G})$ will denote only a completed task.

If we let $L(\mathbf{G}, x)$ denote the set of all traces that originate from state x of **G** (i.e., $L(\mathbf{G}, x) := \{s \in \Sigma^* | \xi(x, s)!\}$), then we have $L(\mathbf{G}) = L(\mathbf{G}, x_0)$.

In contrast to a DFSA, occasionally, in this book, we also use an automaton, whose initial state is not unique and transition mapping is also not deterministic in the sense that there may be more than one target state for each transition, in order to represent a non-deterministic outcomes. To this end, we introduce the concept of *nondeterministic finite-state automaton*.

Definition 1.2 A *nondeterministic finite-state automaton* (NFSA) is captured by $\mathbf{G} = (X, \Sigma, \xi, X_0, X_m)$, where X is a finite set of states, $X_0 \subseteq X$ a set of initial states, $X_m \subseteq X$ a set of marker (or final) states, and Σ a finite alphabet, $\xi : X \times \Sigma^* \rightarrow 2^X$ a (total) state transition function, where for all $x \in X$, we have $\xi(x, \epsilon) := \{x\}$ and for all $s \in \Sigma^*$ and $\sigma \in \Sigma$, we have $\xi(x, s\sigma) = \cup_{x' \in \xi(x,s)} \xi(x', \sigma)$. □

For an NFSA $\mathbf{G}$, its *closed behavior* is $L(\mathbf{G}) := \{s \in \Sigma^* | (\exists x_0 \in X_0) \xi(x_0, s) \neq \emptyset\}$, and its *marked behavior* is $L_m(\mathbf{G}) := \{s \in \Sigma^* | (\exists x_0 \in X_0) \xi(x_0, s) \cap X_m \neq \emptyset\}$. Similarly, we write $En_{\mathbf{G}}(x) := \{\text{sigma} \in \Sigma | \xi(x, \sigma) \neq \emptyset\}$ to denote the enabled event set at state x in an FSA $\mathbf{G}$, and use $L(\mathbf{G}, x) := \{s \in \Sigma^* | \xi(x, s) \neq \emptyset\}$ to denote the set of all traces that originate from state x of $\mathbf{G}$. In the remainder of this monograph, if we do not explicitly state that an FSA is an NFSA, by default, it is deterministic.

Given two FSAs $\mathbf{G}_i = (X_i, \Sigma_i, \xi_i, x_{i,0}, X_{i,m})$ $(i = 1, 2)$, their *parallel composition* is denoted as $\mathbf{G}_1 \times \mathbf{G}_2 := (X_1 \times X_2, \Sigma_1 \cup \Sigma_2, \xi_1 \times \xi_2, (x_{1,0}, x_{2,0}), X_{1,m} \times X_{2,m})$, where the (partial) transition function $\xi_1 \times \xi_2$ is defined as follows, for all $(x_1, x_2) \in X_1 \times X_2$ and $\sigma \in \Sigma = \Sigma_1 \cup \Sigma_2$:

$$\xi_1 \times \xi_2(x_1, x_2, \sigma) := \begin{cases} (\xi_1(x_1, \sigma), \xi_2(x_2, \sigma)) & \sigma \in \Sigma_1 \cap \Sigma_2 \wedge \xi_1(x_1, \sigma) \\ & ! \wedge \xi_2(x_2, \sigma)!, \\ (\xi_1(x_1, \sigma), x_2) & \sigma \in \Sigma_1 \setminus \Sigma_2 \wedge \xi_1(x_1, \sigma)!, \\ (x_1, \xi_2(x_2, \sigma)) & \sigma \in \Sigma_2 \setminus \Sigma_1 \wedge \xi_2(x_2, \sigma)!, \\ \text{undefined} & \text{otherwise.} \end{cases}$$

Definition 1.3 Given two FSAs $\mathbf{G}_i = (X_i, \Sigma, \xi_i, x_{i,0}, X_{i,m})$ $(i = 1, 2)$, we say $\mathbf{G}_1$ is *DES-isomorphic* to $\mathbf{G}_2$ if there exists a bijection $\theta : X_1 \rightarrow X_2$ such that the following hold:

1. $\theta(x_{1,0}) = x_{2,0}$,

2. $\theta(X_{1,m}) = X_{2,m}$,

3. $(\forall x, x' \in X_1)(\forall \sigma \in \Sigma) \xi_1(x, \sigma) = x' \iff \xi_2(\theta(x), \sigma) = \theta(x')$. □

We can check that automaton parallel composition is commutative and associative under DES-isomorphism. In addition, it has been shown in Ref. [3] that $L(\mathbf{G}_1 \times \mathbf{G}_2) = L(\mathbf{G}_1)||L(\mathbf{G}_2)$ and $L_m(\mathbf{G}_1 \times \mathbf{G}_2) = L_m(\mathbf{G}_1)||L_m(\mathbf{G}_2)$. If we consider two languages $L(\mathbf{G})$ and

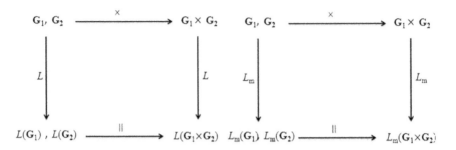

Figure 1.11 Relationship between automaton parallel composition and language synchronous product

$L_m(\mathbf{G})$ as the result of applying two mappings L and L_m on $\mathbf{G}$ that map an automaton $\mathbf{G}$ to two subsets in Σ^*, respectively, then the following commutative diagram in Figure 1.11 clearly displays the relationship between automaton parallel composition and the corresponding language synchronous product.

In a special case, when $\Sigma_1 = \Sigma_2$, the parallel composition of $\mathbf{G}_1$ and $\mathbf{G}_2$ is called *meet*, denoted as $\mathbf{G}_1 \wedge \mathbf{G}_2$, where $L(\mathbf{G}_1 \wedge \mathbf{G}_2) = L(\mathbf{G}_1) \cap L(\mathbf{G}_2)$ and $L_m(\mathbf{G}_1 \wedge \mathbf{G}_2) = L_m(\mathbf{G}_1) \cap L_m(\mathbf{G}_2)$.

A weighted FSA is a 2-tuple $(\mathbf{G} = (X, \Sigma, \xi, x_0, X_m), f)$, where $\mathbf{G}$ is an FSA and $f : X \times \Sigma \rightarrow \mathbb{R}^+ \cup \{\infty\}$ is the (partial) weight function. Given two finite-state weighted automata $(\mathbf{G}_1 = (X_1, \Sigma_1, \xi_1, x_{1,0}, X_{1,m}), f_1)$ and $(\mathbf{G}_2 = (X_2, \Sigma_2, \xi_2, x_{2,0}, X_{2,m}), f_2)$, the weighted parallel composition of $(\mathbf{G}_1, f_1)$ and $(\mathbf{G}_2, f_2)$, denoted as $(\mathbf{G}_1, f_1) \times (\mathbf{G}_2, f_2)$, is a finite-state weighted automaton $(\mathbf{G} = \mathbf{G}_1 \times \mathbf{G}_2, f)$, where $f : X_1 \times X_2 \times (\Sigma_1 \cup \Sigma_2) \rightarrow \mathbb{R}^+ \cup \{\infty\}$ is defined as follows: for any $x_1 \in X_1$, $x_2 \in X_2$ and $\sigma \in \Sigma$,

$$
f((x_1, x_2), \sigma) := \begin{cases} g(f_1(x_1, \sigma), f_2(x_2, \sigma)) & \text{if } \sigma \in En_{G_1}(q_1) \cap En_{G_2}(q_2), \\ f_1(x_1, \sigma) & \text{if } \sigma \in En_{G_1}(q_1) \backslash \Sigma_2, \\ f_2(x_2, \sigma) & \text{if } \sigma \in En_{G_2}(q_2) \backslash \Sigma_1, \\ \text{undefined} & \text{otherwise.} \end{cases}
$$

where $g : (\mathbb{R}^+ \cup \{\infty\}) \times (\mathbb{R}^+ \cup \{\infty\}) \rightarrow (\mathbb{R}^+ \cup \{\infty\})$ is a function to specify the weight of a transition, whose definition is dependent on the type of optimization objective and would be specified later.

1.4.2 Supervisory Control

Next, we introduce the basic concepts of the Ramadge-Wonham supervisory control paradigm [12]. A plant is modeled as an FSA $\mathbf{G} = (X, \Sigma, \delta, x_0, X_m)$, which generates event outputs that may be externally observed. The plant alphabet Σ is partitioned into *controllable* and *uncontrollable* alphabets, represented by Σ_c and Σ_{uc}, respectively. Each controllable event $\sigma \in \Sigma_c$ denotes one plant action (or function) that can be disabled externally, typically by a controller, whereas each uncontrollable event $\sigma' \in \Sigma_{uc}$ denotes an action (or function) whose occurrence cannot be stopped by the controller. Some examples of controllable actions include turning on or off a machine in manufacturing, opening or closing a valve in access control, and dispatching or retrieving AGVs in robotic operations. Some examples of uncontrollable actions include component failures, completion of a chemical reaction, sensor output values, or cyber attacks, which are beyond the reach of the controller. To capture observability of the plant output, the alphabet Σ is also partitioned into observable and unobservable alphabets, represented by Σ_o and Σ_{uo}, respectively. Each observable event is typically associated with an action (or function) whose execution can be monitored by the controller via suitable sensors, whereas an unobservable event denotes an action (or function) whose execution cannot be detected externally by the controller.

Let $P_o : \Sigma^* \to \Sigma_o^*$ be the natural projection. A supervisor is modeled by a mapping

$$V : P_o(L(G)) \to \Gamma := \{\gamma \subseteq \Sigma | \Sigma_{uc} \subseteq \gamma\},$$

where Γ is the set of all *control patterns* (or *control commands*), and each control pattern $\gamma \in \Gamma$ must contain all uncontrollable events, i.e., $\Sigma_{uc} \subseteq \gamma$. In the Ramadge-Wonham paradigm, the supervisor sends a control pattern to the plant $\mathbf{G}$, instead of a single event typically seen in the systems and control literature. This is mainly due to the existence of uncontrollable events, which does not allow the supervisor to generate a unique control input to the plant $\mathbf{G}$. By adopting this nondeterministic execution mechanism, the plant G is expected to choose one event from the control pattern and execute it. The details of this nondeterministic choice are not explicitly explained in the original Ramadge-Wonham paradigm, but could play a key role

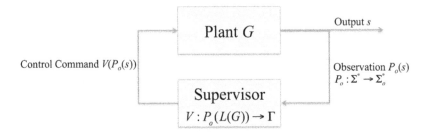

Figure 1.12 The Ramadge-Wonham supervisory control architecture.

in the networked control frameworks with imperfect communication channels [177], and cyber security analysis and control, which will be discussed in subsequent chapters.

The standard Ramadge-Wonham supervisory control architecture is depicted in Figure 1.12, where event executions in the plant **G** are assumed to be instantaneous and asynchronous, i.e., at any time instant there can be no more than one event being executed. Although these assumptions have been relaxed in works on time-weighted automata and product systems that allow non-zero durations for event occurrences and concurrent event occurrences, respectively, in this monograph, we keep these assumptions to make relevant analyses and synthesis simple and easily comprehensible.

If we carefully look at the definition of the supervisory control mapping V, we can see that the definition imposes two constraints on the supervisor. That is, first of all, the supervisor cannot disable any uncontrollable events, which is reflected in the property that $\Sigma_{uc} \subseteq \gamma$ for each control pattern $\gamma \in \Gamma$, and secondly, if two strings $s, s' \in L(\mathbf{G})$ are observably identical, i.e., $P_o(s) = P_o(s')$, then the resulting control patterns must be identical, which is reflected in the domain of V that is defined over $P_o(L(\mathbf{G}))$. Under the influence of V, the closed-loop system is denoted as $V/\mathbf{G}$. The closed behaviour of $V/\mathbf{G}$ is defined as follows:

1. $\epsilon \in L(V/\mathbf{G})$,

2. $(\forall s \in L(V/\mathbf{G}))(\forall \sigma \in \Sigma)[s\sigma \in L(\mathbf{G}) \wedge \sigma \in V(P_o(s))] \Rightarrow s\sigma \in L(V/\mathbf{G})$,

3. All strings in $L(V/\mathbf{G})$ are generated in Steps (1)–(2).

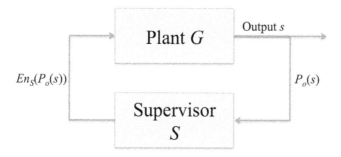

Figure 1.13 Automaton realization of V.

The marked behaviour of $V/\mathbf{G}$ is defined as follows:

$$L_m(V/\mathbf{G}) = L(V/\mathbf{G}) \cap L_m(\mathbf{G}).$$

In the case that $L(V/\mathbf{G})$ is regular (i.e., it can be generated by a finite state automaton), there exists an FSA $\mathbf{S} = (Z, \Sigma, \eta, z_0, Z_m)$ such that

$$L(V/\mathbf{G}) = L(\mathbf{S} \wedge \mathbf{G}) \text{ and } L_m(V/\mathbf{G}) = L_m(\mathbf{S} \wedge \mathbf{G}).$$

Figure 1.13 depicts the realization of V by automaton $\mathbf{S}$, where the output control pattern of $\mathbf{S}$ for each observation input $P_o(s) \in P_o(L(\mathbf{G}))$ is simply the collection of all outgoing transitions after $P_o(s)$ in $\mathbf{S}$, i.e., $En_{\mathbf{S}}(P_o(s)) := \{\sigma \in \Sigma | P_o(s)\sigma \in L(\mathbf{S})\}$.

There are two fundamental questions in the Ramadge-Wonham paradigm, which are listed below:

Problem 1.1 *What language $K \subseteq L_m(\mathbf{G})$ admits a supervisor V such that $K = L_m(V/\mathbf{G})$?*

Problem 1.2 *How can one synthesize a supervisor V such that $L_m(V/\mathbf{G}) \subseteq E \subseteq L_m(\mathbf{G})$, where E is a requirement language, and the closed-loop system is nonblocking (to ensure that every incomplete task may be completed later), i.e., $L(V/\mathbf{G}) = \overline{L_m(V/\mathbf{G})}$?*

To answer the first question, two fundamental concepts are introduced, i.e., controllability and observability.

Definition 1.4 (Controllability) *A language $K \subseteq L_m(\mathbf{G})$ is controllable with respect to $\mathbf{G}$ and Σ_{uc}, if $\overline{K}\Sigma_{uc} \cap L(\mathbf{G}) \subseteq \overline{K}$.* ☐

Definition 1.5 (Observability) [11] A language $K \subseteq L(\mathbf{G})$ is *observable* with respect to $\mathbf{G}$ and P_o, if

$$(\forall s, s' \in \overline{K})(\forall \sigma \in \Sigma)\,[s\sigma \in \overline{K} \wedge s'\sigma \in L(\mathbf{G}) \wedge P_o(s) = P_o(s')] \Rightarrow s'\sigma \in \overline{K}.$$

A language $K \subseteq L(\mathbf{G})$ is (prefix) *normal* with respect to $\mathbf{G}$ and P_o, if

$$P_o^{-1}(P_o(\overline{K})) \cap L(\mathbf{G}) = \overline{K}.$$

A language $K \subseteq C \subseteq L(\mathbf{G})$ is *relatively observable* [125] with respect to $\overline{C}$, $\mathbf{G}$ and P_o, or simply $\overline{C}$-*observable*, if for all $s \in \overline{K}$, $s' \in \overline{C}$ and $\sigma \in \Sigma$,

$$[s\sigma \in \overline{K} \wedge s'\sigma \in L(\mathbf{G}) \wedge P_o(s) = P_o(s')] \Rightarrow s'\sigma \in \overline{K}.$$

$\square$

It is known that observability is not closed under the set union, unlike (prefix) normality and $\overline{C}$-observability. It has been shown that (prefix) normality implies observability, and observability together with the condition that $\Sigma_c \subseteq \Sigma_o$ implies (prefix) normality. Because $K \subseteq C$, we can see that $\overline{C}$-observability implies observability. On the other hand, when K is (prefix) normal with respect to $\mathbf{G}$ and P_o, K is also $\overline{C}$-observable, namely (prefix) normality implies $\overline{C}$-observability. With the concepts of controllability and observability, a sufficient and necessary condition to ensure the existence of a supervisory control mapping for a given language $K \subseteq L_m(\mathbf{G})$ is given in the following theorem.

Theorem 1.1 A language $K \subseteq L_m(\mathbf{G})$ is realizable by a supervisory control mapping V, i.e., $K = L_m(V/\mathbf{G})$, if and only if K is controllable with respect to $\mathbf{G}$ and Σ_{uc}, and observable with respect to $\mathbf{G}$ and P_o, and $L_m(\mathbf{G})$-closed, i.e., $\overline{K} \cap L_m(\mathbf{G}) = K$. $\square$

Intuitively, controllability of K ensures the existence of a supervisor V that does not disable any uncontrollable event, and observability of K ensures that V can be defined over $P_o(L(\mathbf{G}))$. The last condition of being $L_m(\mathbf{G})$-closed is to ensure that any string $s \in K$ can be identified (via only the marking information of the plant) when it occurs. Since the supervisor V does not carry any marking information, to recognize a string in K, we can only rely on the marking of the plant $\mathbf{G}$, i.e., we need to ensure that, under the influence of V, a string $s \in K$ holds if and only if $s \in L(V/\mathbf{G})$ and $s \in L_m(\mathbf{G})$.

To answer the second question, we need to find a controllable, observable, and nonblocking sublanguage of E. A solution is typically not unique. This may cause practical issues, as sometimes trivial solutions may be generated. To avoid this unpleasant situation, it has been shown that, controllable and observable languages form a partially ordered set (poset) with the partial order induced by the set inclusion. Thus, typically a maximal controllable and observable sublanguage within a given requirement language E is sought in synthesis. When observability is strengthened as relative observability or normality, the poset becomes an upper semilattice and a unique supremal element exists, which is sought in most supervisor synthesis literature. Tools are available to synthesize such supremal controllable and normal (or relatively observable) sublanguages, see, e.g., SuSYNA developed at Nanyang Technological University (https://personal.ntu.edu.sg/rsu/Downloads.htm), TCT [122] (https://www.control.utoronto.ca/~wonham/Research.html) developed at the University of Toronto, and Supremica [123] (https://supremica.org/) developed at Chalmers University of Technology .

This section is not meant to provide a thorough overview of supervisory control theory, which would fit in a separate monograph. More advanced supervisory control theory, e.g., decentralized control, modular control, distributed control, hierarchical control, symbolic synthesis, etc., can be found in Refs. [2,3].

I

Modeling and Synthesis of Smart Attacks

CHAPTER 2

Smart Sensor Attacks

We start with sensor attacks, which are commonly seen in our daily life and conceptually simple. Such simplicity will make it relatively easy for us to introduce a formal modeling framework and relevant design techniques. We will follow a natural order of thinking typically used by a rational person to investigate a new phenomenon and answer the following questions: what is a sensor attack; when can we say a sensor attack is smart; how to design a smart sensor attack; and finally, how to defend a system against all smart sensor attacks. A sensor attack in this chapter will be modeled as a function, which maps each intercepted plant observable output to a "faked" observable output that eventually affects the output of a given supervisor. We will illustrate that, by "smartly" changing the supervisor's observable input, a sensor attack can leverage on existing supervisory control function to inflict damage to the plant, without being detected by the supervisor. That is, we consider an attack to be *smart* if it is kept covert (or stealthy) until irreversible damage is inflicted on a target system. We will explain how to decide whether a given closed-loop system permits a smart sensor attack. Upon such knowledge, we will introduce one method to design a supervisor that is robust to all possible smart sensor attacks. This chapter serves as one major building block for subsequent technical development.

2.1 INTRODUCTION

A cyber-physical system (CPS) is a mechanism controlled or monitored by computer-based algorithms. Examples of CPS include smart grid,

DOI: 10.1201/9781003333883-3

autonomous automobile systems, medical monitoring, process control systems, distributed robotics, and automatic pilot avionics, etc. The connection between the cyber part and the physical part heavily relies on sensor and communication networks, which raise a major security concern. Different types of cyber attacks can tamper the data collection processes and interfere safety critical decision making processes, which may cause irreparable damage to a physical system under control and to people who depend on those systems [30,31].

There has been a growing number of publications addressing the cybersecurity issues from both the computer science community, which focuses on the computer computation-related issues, and the systems and control community, which focuses on issues related to the system dynamics affected by cyber attacks. Recently, more and more efforts have been made in classifying different types of malicious attacks, assuming that the attackers are sufficiently intelligent [19,20,32,33, 55,56,58,59,85], instead of merely just generating random failures, which is well studied in the fields of reliability and fault tolerant control. Typically, an intelligent attacker is required to possess relevant system knowledge, and abilities for resource disclosure and resource disruption in order to carry out a successful attack, which is covert to a system user until the attacker's goal of causing damage to the system is achieved. So *covertness* and *damage infliction* are two major characteristics of a successful attack. By analyzing different intelligent cyber attacks, proper countermeasures may be developed to prevent a target system from being harmed by a specific type of attacks.

In this chapter, we introduce a special type of data deception attacks in the discrete-event system framework, where an attacker can intercept sensor measurements (or observations) modeled by observable events and alter them arbitrarily but with an upper bound imposed on the length of each altered observation sequence. By sending those altered observation sequences to a given supervisor, whose function is known to the attacker in advance, the attacker can deliberately and covertly guide the system to move into some undesirable states without making any change to the supervisory control function. The key challenge is how to "fool" the supervisor to believe that the system is operating normally while using the supervisor's own control function to carry out an attack that leads the system to move into a bad state. To this end, we first propose a novel concept of *attackability* and the concept of *smart sensor attack* (SSA), which can be modeled as a DFA, possessing the properties of covertness and damage infliction under partial observations. Then we show that the supremal (or least restrictive) SSA exists and is computable via a specific synthesis algorithm, as long as both the plant model $\mathbf{G}$ and the given supervisor S are finitely representable. Upon this novel synthesis algorithm, we show that a nonempty synthesized supervisor will be "robust" to any SSA, in the sense that such an attack will either reveal itself to the supervisor owing to abnormal event executions (so that contingent actions can be taken by the supervisor) or will not be able to take the system to a bad state (i.e., no damage will be inflicted).

Our construction of an SSA model is inspired by recent works on opacity analysis and enforcement [26,34,35,40,73], which aim to analyze and/or enhance (via observable event insertions) the capability of a system to prevent a potential attacker from correctly determining the actual state of the system. A comprehensive survey on this subject can be found in Refs. [4,36]. There are some works on cyberattack detection and prevention in the discrete-event community [27–29], mainly from an adaptive fault tolerant control point of view, which heavily rely on real-time fault diagnosis to identify the existence of an attack and then take necessary supervisory control actions. In Ref. [37], the authors present a supervisory control approach for a dynamic cybersecurity problem that captures progressive attacks to a computer network, which aims to compute an optimal policy in a game theoretical setup. In those works, the intelligence of an attacker is not explicitly modeled, and an attack is treated as a fault or an (unintelligent) opponent. In contrast, the method introduced in this chapter does not rely on real-time attack detection, but on prior knowledge of attack models, which assume that an attacker is intelligent to deliver attacks covertly and effectively, as captured by the concept of attackability. Our goal is to build eventually attack-robustness features into a supervisor to ensure that its control functionality will not be affected by any SSA unnoticeably. It is this robust control nature manifested in the proposed method that distinguishes it from other existing DES-based cyberattack detection and prevention approaches, which fall in the category of adaptive control. Some features of SSA-robust supervisor synthesis bear a slight conceptual similarity to the problem of supervisory control with intermittent sensor failures [41,42], where an attack can be considered as sporadic changes of sensor data. However, the imposing of attack intelligence makes the problem formulation and solution strategy different.

The remainder of the chapter is organized as follows. In Section 2.2, we formulate an SSA synthesis problem, where we show that the supremal SSA exists. In Section 2.3, a specific synthesis algorithm is presented, which computes the supremal SSA. After that, we present an algorithm to synthesize an SSA-robust supervisor in Section 2.4. A simple yet realistic example runs through the entire chapter to illustrate all relevant concepts and algorithms. Conclusions are drawn in Section 2.5.

2.2 A SMART SENSOR ATTACK PROBLEM

In this section, we introduce the concept of SSA and show that the supremal SSA exists, if there exists at least one SSA.

2.2.1 A Non-Deterministic Sensor Attack Model

We assume that *an attacker can intercept each observable event generated by the plant* **G**, *and replace it by a sequence of observable events from* Σ_o in order to "fool" the given supervisor S, whose function is known to the attacker. Considering that in practice any event occurrence takes a non-negligible amount of time, it is impossible for an attacker to insert an arbitrarily long observable sequence to replace a received observable event. For this reason, we assume that there exists a known natural number $n \in \mathbb{N}$ such that the length of any observable sequence that the attacker can insert is no more than n. Let $\Delta_n := \{s \in \Sigma_o^* | |s| \le n\}$ be the set of all such bounded observable sequences, where $|s|$ denotes the length of s, and by convention, $|\epsilon| = 0$.

Definition 2.1 Given a plant **G**, a *non-deterministic sensor attack* of **G** with respect to (Σ_o, Δ_n) is a mapping $A : P_o(L(\mathbf{G})) \to 2^{\Delta_n^* \cap P_o(L(\mathbf{G}))}$, where

1. $A(\epsilon) = \epsilon$;

2. $(\forall s \in P_o(L(G)))(\forall \sigma \in \Sigma_o)s\sigma \in P_o(L(G)) \Rightarrow A(s\sigma) = A(s)W$
   where $W \subseteq \Delta_n$. □

Basically, a sensor attack will not generate any observable behavior, if no observation from the plant G is received; each observation $\sigma \in \Sigma_o$ will be replaced by a "fake" observable string from Δ_n. To restrict possibilities of "fake" strings, the definition requires the sensor attack A to map one observable string of G to another observable string of G. This restriction is quite mild, as any observable behaviors outside G will be immediately detected by a supervisor. By the definition of Δ_n, we can see that it is possible for a sensor attack to either hide the true observable from the plant by setting $W = \{\epsilon\}$ or simply relay the true observation without making any change by setting $W = \{\sigma\}$. Thus, the definition is sufficiently generic to capture different attack scenarios. Please be reminded that W might be empty. In this case, for some string $s \in P_o(L(G))$, we allow $A(s) = \emptyset$, namely the sensor attack A does not consider such observable strings.

To describe the impact of a sensor attack on a given supervisor S of G, recall that the supervisor $S : P_o(L(G)) \rightarrow \Gamma$ aims to achieve a specific (prefix) language $K \subseteq L(G)$, namely

$$(\forall s \in L(G))S(P_o(s)) := \begin{cases} \gamma \in \Gamma & \text{if } s \in K, \\ \Sigma_{uc} & \text{otherwise.} \end{cases}$$

That is, the supervisor S will only allow all uncontrollable events if a received observation is not part of the desired sublanguage K of the plant G. Basically, the appearance of such undefined observable behaviors will alert the supervisor S that some anomaly occurs in the plant, which may trigger relevant recovery actions, namely S has a basic anomaly detection capability.

The composition of a sensor attack model A and a supervisor S forms a *non-deterministic compromised supervisor*

$$S \circ A : P_o(L(G)) \rightarrow 2^\Gamma : t \mapsto S \circ A(t) := \cup_{u \in A(t)}\{S(u)\}.$$

The closed behavior of the plant G under the supervision of the non-deterministic compromised supervisor $S \circ A$ is defined as follows:

1. $\epsilon \in L(S \circ A/\mathbf{G})$,

2. $(\forall s \in L(S \circ A/\mathbf{G}))(\forall \sigma \in \Sigma)[s\sigma \in L(\mathbf{G}) \wedge (\exists \gamma \in S \circ A(P_o(s)))\sigma \in \gamma] \Rightarrow s\sigma \in L(S \circ A/\mathbf{G})$,

3. All strings in $L(S \circ A/\mathbf{G})$ are generated in Steps (1)–(2).

The marked behavior of $S \circ A/\mathbf{G}$ is defined as follows:

$$L_m(S \circ A/\mathbf{G}) = L(S \circ A/\mathbf{G}) \cap L_m(\mathbf{G}).$$

Proposition 2.1 Given a plant $\mathbf{G}$ and a supervisor S, let A be a sensor attack. Then $L(S \circ A/\mathbf{G})$ is controllable with respect to $\mathbf{G}$ and Σ_{uc} and observable with respect to $\mathbf{G}$ and P_o.

Proof

1. *We first show the controllability of $L(S \circ A/\mathbf{G})$ with respect to $\mathbf{G}$ and Σ_{uc}. Let $s \in L(S \circ A/\mathbf{G})$ and $\sigma \in \Sigma_{uc}$. Assume that $s\sigma \in L(\mathbf{G})$. Since $s \in L(S \circ A/\mathbf{G})$, by the definition of $S \circ A$, for each $\gamma \in S \circ A(P_o(s))$, we have $\Sigma_{uc} \subseteq \gamma$. Thus, $\sigma \in \gamma$. Since $s\sigma \in L(\mathbf{G})$ and $s \in L(S \circ A/\mathbf{G})$, by the definition of $L(S \circ A/\mathbf{G})$, we have $s\sigma \in L(S \circ A/\mathbf{G})$.*

2. *Next, we show the observability of $L(S \circ A/\mathbf{G})$ with respect to $\mathbf{G}$ and P_o. Let $s, s' \in L(S \circ A/\mathbf{G})$ and $P_o(s) = P_o(s')$. For each $\sigma \in \Sigma$, if $s\sigma \in L(S \circ A/\mathbf{G})$ and $s'\sigma \in L(\mathbf{G})$, we need to show that $s'\sigma \in L(S \circ A/\mathbf{G})$. Since $s\sigma \in L(S \circ A/\mathbf{G})$, by the definition of $L(S \circ A/\mathbf{G})$, we know that there must exist $\gamma \in S \circ A(P_o(s))$ such that $\sigma \in \gamma$. Since $P_o(s) = P_o(s')$, we know that $\gamma \in S \circ A(P_o(s)) = S \circ A(P_o(s'))$. Since $s'\sigma \in L(\mathbf{G})$ and $s' \in L(S \circ A/\mathbf{G})$, by the definition of $L(S \circ A/\mathbf{G})$, we know that $s'\sigma \in L(S \circ A/\mathbf{G})$.* ■

Proposition 2.1 confirms that the previously defined non-deterministic compromised supervisor $S \circ A$ behaves indeed as a supervisor that complies with the requirements of controllability and observability. However, it is worth to point out that this result is valid if the supervisor S always generates a control command, even though its input may not be in $P_o(L(\mathbf{G}))$.

Figure 2.1 depicts the closed-loop supervisory control architecture with a sensor attack between the output of plant $\mathbf{G}$ and the input of supervisor S.

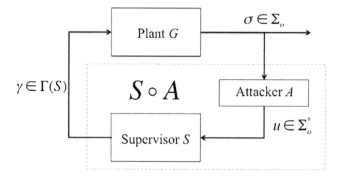

Figure 2.1 The block diagram of a plant under sensor attack.

2.2.2 An Automaton Realization of a Sensor Attack

Previously, we have introduced a non-deterministic sensor attack as a mapping. However, it is interesting to know whether this mapping can be represented by a specific computation model. To answer this question, we model a non-deterministic sensor attack as a finite state automaton $\mathbf{A} = (Y, \Sigma_o^\epsilon \times \Delta_n, \eta, y_0, Y_m)$, where $\Sigma_o^\epsilon := \Sigma_o \cup \{\epsilon\}$, Y is the state set, Σ the input alphabet, Δ_n the output alphabets, y_0 the initial state, Y_m the marker state set, which is specifically set as $Y_m = Y$, and $\eta : Y \times \Sigma_o^\epsilon \times \Delta_n \to Y$ the (partial) transition map, where

$$(\forall y, y' \in Y)\eta(y, \epsilon, \nu) = y' \iff y = y' \wedge \nu = \epsilon,$$

which matches our previous setting that the sensor attack will only make a move after receiving an observable event. The marking information of a sensor attack is not important; thus, we simply set $Y = Y_m$, i.e., every state is a marker state. We still keep the marker state set for the sake of facilitating subsequent composition with a plant $\mathbf{G}$, which contains marking information. Let $\psi : (\Sigma_o^\epsilon \times \Delta_n)^* \to (\Sigma_o^\epsilon)^*$ and $\theta : (\Sigma_o^\epsilon \times \Delta_n)^* \to \Delta_n^*$ be the *input* and *output* mappings, respectively, where for each $\mu = (\sigma_1, u_1)(\sigma_2, u_2) \ldots (\sigma_l, u_l) \in (\Sigma_o^\epsilon \times \Delta_n)^*$, $\psi(\mu) = \sigma_1 \sigma_2 \ldots \sigma_l$ and $\theta(\mu) = u_1 u_2 \ldots u_l$.

The automaton $\mathbf{A}$ introduced above is essentially a transducer, which maps each observable event $\sigma \in \Sigma_o$ to a fake string $\nu \in \Delta_n$. $\mathbf{A}$ is deterministic. However, it allows the same input observable event σ to be associated with multiple fake strings at a state, where each input-output association denotes one attack move. Due to this multiple attack options for each input observation, $\mathbf{A}$ can capture a non-deterministic sensor attack. Given a plant model $\mathbf{G}$, we define the following mapping $A : \psi(L(\mathbf{A})) \rightarrow 2^{\theta(L(\mathbf{A}))}$, where

$$(\forall s \in \psi(L(\mathbf{A})))A(s) := \{\theta(\nu) \in \Delta_n^* | \nu \in \psi^{-1}(s) \cap L(\mathbf{A})\}.$$

Lemma 2.1 Let the mapping A be constructed above from $\mathbf{A}$ and $\mathbf{G}$. If $P_o(L(\mathbf{G})) = \psi(L(\mathbf{A}))$ and $\theta(L(\mathbf{A})) \subseteq P_o(L(\mathbf{G}))$, then A is a non-deterministic sensor attack of $\mathbf{G}$.

Proof *Assume that $P_o(L(\mathbf{G})) = \psi(L(\mathbf{A}))$ and $\theta(L(\mathbf{A})) \subseteq P_o(L(\mathbf{G}))$. By the definition of A induced from $\mathbf{A}$, we can check that $A : P_o(L(\mathbf{G})) \rightarrow 2^{\Delta_n^* \cap P_o(L(\mathbf{G}))}$. The lemma follows.* ■

Lemma 2.1 indicates that $\mathbf{A}$ essentially an automaton realization of one sensor attack A. Next, we will show that the composition of a sensor attack A and a supervisor S, i.e., $S \circ A$, can be realized by automaton operations. Let $\mathbf{S} = (Z, \Sigma, \delta, z_0, Z_m)$ be an automaton realization of the supervisor S, where

$$(\forall s \in L(\mathbf{G}))\, S(P_o(s)) = En_{\mathbf{S}}(\delta(z_0, P_o(s))).$$

Let $\mathbf{S} \times \mathbf{A} = (Z \times Y \cup \{d\}, \Sigma \times \Delta_n, \zeta, (z_0, y_0), Z_m \times Y_m)$ be the composition of $\mathbf{S}$ and $\mathbf{A}$, where d is a dump state, and for each $w \in Z \times Y \cup \{d\}$ and $(\sigma, \nu) \in \Sigma \times \Delta_n$,

$$\zeta(w, \sigma, \nu) := \begin{cases} (z', y') & \text{if } w = (z, y) \wedge \eta(y, P_o(\sigma), \nu) = y' \wedge \delta(z, \nu) = z', \\ d & \text{if } w = (z, y) \wedge \eta(y, P_o(\sigma), \nu) = y' \wedge \delta(z, \sigma)! \wedge \\ & \neg \delta(z, \nu)! \vee w = d \wedge \sigma \in \Sigma_{uc}, \\ \text{undefined} & \text{otherwise.} \end{cases}$$

In the definition of ζ each transition going to the dump state d in $\mathbf{S} \times \mathbf{A}$ may potentially reveal the attack, which, for an intelligent attack, should be avoided. We have the following result.

Lemma 2.2 Let $\mathbf{S}$ be an automaton realization of a supervisory control mapping S and $\mathbf{A}$ an automaton realization of a sensor attack A. Then for every string $s \in P_o(L(\mathbf{G}))$, we have

$$(\forall s \in P_o(L(\mathbf{G})))S \circ A(s) = \{En_{\mathbf{S}}(\delta(z_0, \theta(\nu)))| \nu \in L(\mathbf{S} \times \mathbf{A}) \wedge \psi(\nu) = s\}.$$

Proof *For each $s \in P_o(L(\mathbf{G}))$, we have*

$$
\begin{aligned}
S \circ A(s) &= \{S(u) \in \Gamma | u \in A(s)\} \text{ by the definition of } S \circ A \\
&= \{En_{\mathbf{S}}(\delta(z_0, u)) | u \in A(s)\} \text{ since } \mathbf{S} \text{ is a realization of } S \\
&= \{En_{\mathbf{S}}(\delta(z_0, \psi(\nu))) | \nu \in \psi^{-1}(u) \wedge \nu \in L(\mathbf{S} \times \mathbf{A})\} \\
&\qquad \text{by the definition of } \mathbf{S} \times \mathbf{A}
\end{aligned}
$$

Thus, the lemma follows. ■

Lemma 2.2 shows that the composition of automata $\mathbf{S} \times \mathbf{A}$ is an automaton realization of the compromised supervisor $S \circ A$. Next, we show how to represent the closed-loop system $S \circ A/\mathbf{G}$. Let

$$\mathbf{G} \times (\mathbf{S} \times \mathbf{A}) := (X \times (Z \times Y \cup \{d\}), \Sigma \times \Delta_n, \kappa, (x_0, z_0, y_0), X_m \times Z_m \times Y_m),$$

where for each $(x, w) \in X \times (Z \times Y \cup \{d\})$ and each $(\sigma, \nu) \in \Sigma \times \Delta_n$,

$$
\kappa(x, w, \sigma, \nu) := \begin{cases} (x', w') & \text{if } \xi(x, \sigma) = x' \wedge w' = \zeta(w, \sigma, \nu), \\ \text{undefined} & \text{otherwise.} \end{cases}
$$

Note that it is possible that $\psi(L_m(\mathbf{G} \times (\mathbf{S} \times \mathbf{A}))) \not\subseteq L_m(\mathbf{S})$, namely the sensor attack may change the closed-loop behavior by altering the received observable sequences fed to the supervisor S.

Lemma 2.3 Given a plant $\mathbf{G}$, let S and A be the supervisory control mapping and a sensor attack, whose automaton realizations are $\mathbf{S}$ and $\mathbf{A}$, respectively. Then $L(S \circ A/\mathbf{G}) = \psi(L(\mathbf{G} \times (\mathbf{S} \times \mathbf{A})))$.

Proof *We use proof by induction. Base Step: Clearly, $\epsilon \in L(S \circ A/\mathbf{G}) \cap \psi(L(\mathbf{G} \times (\mathbf{S} \times \mathbf{A})))$. Hypothesis Step: Assume that for all strings s, as long as $|s| \leq n$, the statement holds. Induction Step: for each $s \in L(S \circ A/\mathbf{G})$ with $|s| = n + 1$. There must exist $s' \in \Sigma^*$ and $\sigma \in \Sigma$ such that $s = s'\sigma$ and $|s'| = n$. Clearly, $s' \in L(S \circ A/\mathbf{G}) \cap \psi(L(\mathbf{G} \times (\mathbf{S} \times \mathbf{A})))$.*

$$
\begin{aligned}
& s'\sigma \in L(S \circ A/\mathbf{G}) \\
\Longleftrightarrow \quad & s' \in L(S \circ A/\mathbf{G}) \wedge \sigma \in \gamma \in S \circ A(P_o(s')) \wedge s'\sigma \in L(\mathbf{G}) \\
\Longleftrightarrow \quad & (\exists \nu \in L(\mathbf{G} \times (\mathbf{S} \times \mathbf{A}))\psi(\nu) = s' \wedge \sigma \in En_{\mathbf{S}}(\delta(z_0, \psi(\nu)) \wedge s'\sigma \in L(\mathbf{G}) \\
\Longleftrightarrow \quad & (\exists (x, w), (x', w') \in X \times (Z \times Y \cup \{d\}))(x, w) = \kappa(x_0, z_0, y_0, \nu) \wedge \\
& \qquad \xi(x, \sigma) = x' \wedge (\exists \nu' \in \Delta_n)\zeta(w, \sigma, \nu') = w' \\
\Longleftrightarrow \quad & \nu(\sigma, \nu') \in L(\mathbf{G} \times (\mathbf{S} \times \mathbf{A})) \\
\Longleftrightarrow \quad & \psi(\nu(\sigma, \nu')) = s'\sigma \in \psi(L(\mathbf{G} \times (\mathbf{S} \times \mathbf{A})))
\end{aligned}
$$

The lemma follows. ■

Lemma 2.3 indicates that the closed-loop behavior $S \circ A/\mathbf{G}$ can be represented by automaton composition $\mathbf{G} \times (\mathbf{S} \times \mathbf{A})$, if both S and A can be represented by $\mathbf{S}$ and $\mathbf{A}$.

Example 2.1 *To illustrate the aforementioned concepts, let us go through a simple single-tank example depicted in Figure 2.2, which consists of a water supply whose supply rate is q_i, a tank, and a control valve at the bottom of the tank controlling the outgoing flow rate q_o, whose value depends on the valve opening and the water level h. We assume that the valve can only be fully open or fully closed. The water level h can be measured, whose value can trigger some predefined events, denoting the water levels:* low $(h = L)$, high $(h = H)$, *and* extremely high $(h = EH)$. *We construct a simple discrete-event model of the system depicted in Figure 2.3, where the alphabet Σ contains all events shown in the figure. All events are observable, i.e., $\Sigma_o = \Sigma$. Only the actions of opening the valve $(q_o = 1)$ and closing the valve $(q_o = 0)$ are controllable, and all water level events are uncontrollable. In the model,*

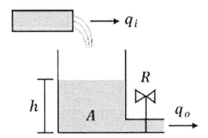

Figure 2.2 A single tank system.

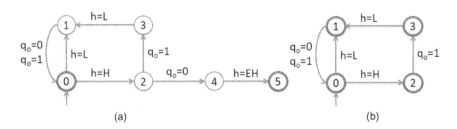

Figure 2.3 Models of the plant $\mathbf{G}$ (a) and the supervisor S (b) (or the automation realization $\mathbf{S}$).

we use a shaded double-edge oval to denote a marker state, i.e., state
0 and state 5 in Figure 2.3. Assume that we do not want the water
level to be extremely high, i.e., the event h = EH should not occur.
A supervisor S, derivable by using the standard Ramadge-Wonham
supervisor synthesis technique, is also depicted in Figure 2.3. It is clear
that the supervisor S opens the valve when the water level is high, i.e.,
it disables the event $q_o = 0$ at state 2 when the event h = H occurs.
Our intuition tells us that if an attack always change events h = H and
h = EH to the event h = L, then the supervisor will not prevent the
water level from reaching the extreme high level, i.e., the event h = EH
will happen. For this reason, we conjecture an attack model A shown in
Figure 2.4, where water levels will be altered to h = L from originally
received observations, whereas all other events will remain unchanged.
In the picture, we use the notation a/b to denote that the concerned
event is $(\sigma, u) = (a, b) \in \Sigma \times \Delta_n$, where a is an event actually received
from the plant and b is the "fake" observation created by the attack A,
after event a is intercepted, which will be passed to the supervisor S.
The sequential composition S ∘ A indicates that, no matter which water
level is reached, the attack A always sends h = L to the supervisor S,
which tricks it to believe that it is safe to allow the valve to be either
closed or opened. The impact of A on the closed-loop system $(\boldsymbol{G}, S)$

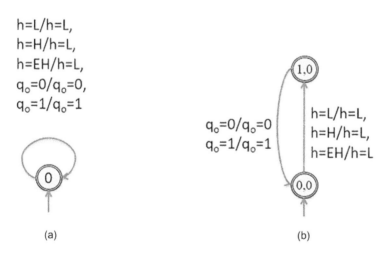

(a)   (b)

Figure 2.4 Automaton models of an attack A (a) and the sequential composition $S \circ A$ (b).

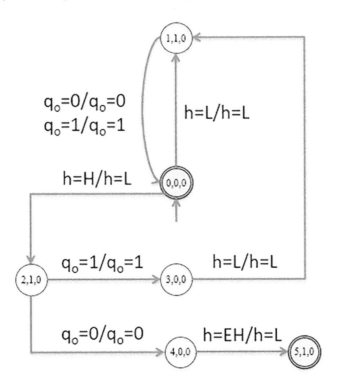

Figure 2.5 Automaton model of the closed-loop system $S \circ A/\mathbf{G}$.

is depicted in Figure 2.5, which indicates that, under the influence of attack A, the closed-loop system can produce an illegal behaviour, where the water level can be extremely high, i.e., the event $h = EH$ occurs.

Proposition 2.2 Given two sensor attacks A_1 and A_2 of a plant $\mathbf{G}$ with respect to Δ_n, if for all $s \in P_o(L(\mathbf{G}))$, we have $A_1(s) \subseteq A_2(s)$, then for any supervisor S of G, we have $S \circ A_1(s) \subseteq S \circ A_2(s)$.

Proof *For all $s \in P_o(L(\mathbf{G}))$,*

$$S \circ A_1(s) = \cup_{u \in A_1(s)}\{S(u)\}$$
$$\subseteq \cup_{u \in A_2(s)}\{S(u)\}$$
$$= S \circ A_2(s)$$

The proposition follows. ■

Given two sensor attacks A_1 and A_2 of a plant $\mathbf{G}$ with respect to Δ_n, let $A_1 \cup A_2$ denote the join of two mappings, i.e., for all $s \in P_o(L(\mathbf{G}))$, $A_1 \cup A_2(s) := A_1(s) \cup A_2(s)$.

Proposition 2.3 Given a finite set of sensor attacks $\{A_i | i \in I\}$ of a plant $\mathbf{G}$ with respect to Δ_n, where I is a (possibly infinite) index set, for any supervisor S of $\mathbf{G}$, we have that, for each $s \in P_o(L(\mathbf{G}))$, $S \circ (\cup_{i \in I} A_i)(s) = \cup_{i \in I} S \circ A_i(s)$.

Proof *For all $s \in P_o(L(\mathbf{G}))$,*

$$\begin{aligned} S \circ (\cup_{i \in I} A_i)(s) &= \cup_{u \in (\cup_{i \in I} A_i(s))} \{S(u)\} \\ &= \cup_{i \in I} \cup_{u \in A_i(s)} \{S(u)\} \\ &= \cup_{i \in I} S \circ A_i(s) \end{aligned}$$

The proposition follows. ■

Proposition 2.4 Given two sensor attacks A_1 and A_2 of a plant $\mathbf{G}$ with respect to Δ_n, for any supervisor S of $\mathbf{G}$, we have $L(S \circ (A_1 \cup A_2)/G) = L(S \circ A_1/G) \cup L(S \circ A_2/G)$.

Proof *We use proof of induction. Base Step: clearly, $\epsilon \in L(S \circ (A_1 \cup A_2)/G) \cap (L(S \circ A_1/G) \cup L(S \circ A_2/G))$. Hypothesis Step: assume that for all strings $s \in \Sigma^*$ with $|s| \leq n$, we have $s \in L(S \circ (A_1 \cup A_2)/G)$ if and only if $s \in L(S \circ A_1/G) \cup L(S \circ A_2/G)$. We now show the Induction Step. Let $s \in \Sigma^*$ with $|s| = n + 1$. Clearly, there exist $s' \in \Sigma^*$ with $|s'| = n$ and $\sigma \in \Sigma$ such that $s = s'\sigma$.*

$$\begin{aligned} &s'\sigma \in L(S \circ (A_1 \cup A_2)/G) \\ \iff\ &s' \in L(S \circ (A_1 \cup A_2)/G) \land \sigma \in \gamma \in S \circ (A_1 \cup A_2)(s') \land s'\sigma \in L(\mathbf{G}) \\ \iff\ &s' \in L(S \circ A_1/G) \cup L(S \circ A_2/G)) \land \sigma \in \gamma \in \cup_{u \in A_1(s') \cup A_2(s')} \{S(u)\} \\ &\qquad\qquad\qquad\qquad \land s'\sigma \in L(\mathbf{G}) \\ \iff\ &s' \in [L(S \circ A_1/G) \land \sigma \in \gamma \in S \circ A_1(s') \land s'\sigma \in L(\mathbf{G})] \lor \\ &\qquad [s' \in L(S \circ A_2/G) \land \sigma \in \gamma \in S \circ A_2(s') \land s'\sigma \in L(\mathbf{G})] \\ \iff\ &s'\sigma \in L(S \circ A_1/G) \lor s'\sigma \in L(S \circ A_2/G) \\ \iff\ &s'\sigma \in L(S \circ A_1/G) \cup L(S \circ A_2/G) \end{aligned}$$

The proposition follows. ■

So far we have introduced a simple sensor attack model and explained how this attack affects the closed-loop system. But we have not described what kind of sensor attacks can be considered intelligent. Next, we will introduce the concept of smart sensor attack (SSA).

2.2.3 A Smart Sensor Attack Model

Definition 2.2 A given closed loop system $(\mathbf{G}, S)$ is *attackable* if there exists a non-empty sensor attack A such that the following properties hold:

1. **Covertness**: Event alteration by A must be covert to S, i.e.,

$$A(P_o(L(\mathbf{G}))) \subseteq P_o(L(S/\mathbf{G})), \tag{2.1}$$

   namely the supervisor will not see any unexpected observations from A.

2. **Damage infliction**: Let $L_{\mathrm{dam}} \subseteq L(\mathbf{G})$ be a damage language. Either one of the following properties hold:

   - Strong Damage Infliction (SDI)

   $$L(S \circ A/\mathbf{G}) = \overline{L(S \circ A/\mathbf{G}) \cap L_{\mathrm{dam}}}, \tag{2.2}$$

      namely A will cause $\mathbf{G}$ to generate forbidden behaviors eventually.

   - Weak Damage Infliction (WDI)

   $$L(S \circ A/\mathbf{G}) \cap L_{\mathrm{dam}} \neq \emptyset, \tag{2.3}$$

      namely A will sometimes cause $\mathbf{G}$ to generate forbidden behaviors.

A is called a *Smart Sensor Attack* (SSA) of $(\mathbf{G}, S)$ with respect to L_{dam}. □

Theorem 2.1 Given a plant $\mathbf{G}$ and a supervisor S, let $\{A_i | i \in I\}$ be a (possibly infinite) collection of smart sensor attacks with respect to $(\mathbf{G}, S)$ and a damage language $L_{\mathrm{dam}} \subseteq L(\mathbf{G})$. Then $A := \cup_{i \in I} A_i$ satisfies properties (1) and (2).

Proof *Assume that each A_i ($i \in I$) satisfies properties of covertness and strong or weak damage infliction. We will show that the join of all smart sensor attacks $A := \cup_{i \in I} A_i$ also satisfies those properties.*

To show the validity of the covertness property, we have

$$A(P_o(L(\mathbf{G}))) = (\cup_{i \in I} A_i)(P_o(L(\mathbf{G})))$$
$$= \cup_{i \in I} A_i(P_o(L(\mathbf{G})))$$
$$\subseteq \cup_{i \in I} P_o(L(S/\mathbf{G}))$$
$$= P_o(L(S/\mathbf{G}))$$

Next, to show the validity of the strong damage infliction property, we have

$$L(S \circ A/\mathbf{G}) = L(S \circ (\cup_{i \in I} A_i)/\mathbf{G})$$
$$= \cup_{i \in I} L(S \circ A_i/\mathbf{G})$$
$$= \cup_{i \in I} \overline{L(S \circ A_i/\mathbf{G}) \cap L_{dam}}$$
$$= \overline{\cup_{i \in I} L(S \circ A_i/\mathbf{G}) \cap L_{dam}}$$
$$= \overline{L(S \circ (\cup_{i \in I} A_i)/\mathbf{G}) \cap L_{dam}}$$
$$= \overline{L(S \circ A/\mathbf{G}) \cap L_{dam}}$$

To show the validity of the weak damage infliction property, we have

$$L(S \circ A/\mathbf{G}) \cap L_{dam} = L(S \circ (\cup_{i \in I} A_i)/\mathbf{G}) \cap L_{dam}$$
$$= (\cup_{i \in I} L(S \circ A_i/\mathbf{G})) \cap L_{dam}$$
$$\neq \emptyset$$

This completes the proof of the theorem. ■

We introduce a binary relation $\preceq$ over the set of all smart sensor attacks of $(\mathbf{G}, S)$ with respect to L_{dam}, denoted as $\mathcal{A}(\mathbf{G}, S, L_{\text{dam}})$, where for any $A_1, A_2 \in \mathcal{A}(\mathbf{G}, S, L_{\text{dam}})$, $A_1 \preceq A_2$ iff for all $s \in P_o(L(\mathbf{G}))$, $A_1(s) \subseteq A_2(s)$. Let $A_{\text{sup}} = \cup_{A \in \mathcal{A}(\mathbf{G},S,L_{\text{dam}})} A$. It is clear that $A \preceq A_{\text{sup}}$ for all $A \in \mathcal{A}(\mathbf{G}, S, L_{\text{dam}})$. By Theorem 2.1, we know that A_{sup} is also a smart sensor attack, namely $A_{\text{sup}} \in \mathcal{A}(\mathbf{G}, S, L_{\text{dam}})$. We call A_{sup} the *supremal smart sensor attack* of the closed-loop system $(\mathbf{G}, S, L_{\text{dam}})$.

Although the supremal smart sensor attack exists theoretically, it is unknown whether it is computable, even though each individual smart sensor attack is assumed computable, that is, it can be represented by a finite-state transducer, as indicated by Lemma 2.1. In the next section, we discuss how to compute a smart sensor attack, and answer the question whether the supremal smart sensor attack can be computed.

2.3 SYNTHESIS OF A SMART SENSOR ATTACK

Recall that a smart sensor attack A maps each observable output of the plant $\mathbf{G}$ to an observable input of the supervisor S. The impact of A on the supervisor S is essentially the extension of the domain of S from $P_o(L(\mathbf{G}))$ to $A(P_o(L(\mathbf{G})))$. To determine the existence of A, we need to first encode the impact of all possible sensor attacks on the behavior of the supervisor S. To this end, let $\Upsilon = \{\varsigma_1, \ldots, \varsigma_{|\Delta_n|}\}$ be a new alphabet and $\mathcal{I} : \Upsilon \to \Delta_n$ a bijection, i.e., each $\varsigma \in \Upsilon$ represents a unique string in Δ_n. As usual, we extend the domain of $\mathcal{I}$ from Υ to Υ^* as follows:

- $\mathcal{I}(\epsilon) = \epsilon$;

- $(\forall s \in \Upsilon^+)(\forall u \in \Upsilon)\mathcal{I}(su) = \mathcal{I}(s)\mathcal{I}(u)$.

Let $S_a : \Upsilon^* \to \Gamma$ be a mapping, where

$$(\forall u \in \Upsilon^*)S_a(u) := \begin{cases} S(\mathcal{I}(u)) & \text{if } \mathcal{I}(u) \in P_o(L(\mathbf{G})), \\ \text{undefined} & \text{otherwise.} \end{cases}$$

Recall that $\Sigma_o \subseteq \Delta_n$. Thus, S_a represents a control function that maps each (possibly fake) observable string to a specific control pattern that could be generated by the original supervisor S, if the observable string looks like being generated by the plant $\mathbf{G}$. Let $h_I : (\Sigma \times \Upsilon)^* \to \Sigma^*$ and $h_o : (\Sigma \times \Upsilon)^* \to \Upsilon^*$ be the *input* and *output* mappings, respectively, where $h_I(\epsilon) = h_o(\epsilon) = \epsilon$ and for each $\mu = (\sigma_1, u_1)(\sigma_2, u_2)\ldots(\sigma_l, u_l) \in (\Sigma \times \Upsilon)^*$, $h_I(\mu) = \sigma_1\sigma_2\ldots\sigma_l$ and $h_o(\mu) = u_1u_2\ldots u_l$.

Considering that in reality some observable events from the plant $\mathbf{G}$ cannot be changed by an attack, let $\Sigma_{o,p} \subseteq \Sigma_o$ denote such a set of *protected* observable events. Let

$$\Lambda := (\Sigma_o \setminus \Sigma_{o,p}) \times \Upsilon \cup \{(\sigma, \mathcal{I}^{-1}(\sigma)) \in \Sigma \times \Upsilon | \sigma \in \Sigma_{o,p}\} \cup \Sigma_{uo} \times \{\mathcal{I}^{-1}(\epsilon)\},$$

which denotes that, (1) each observable but unprotected event can be arbitrarily changed, as captured by $(\Sigma_o \setminus \Sigma_{o,p}) \times \Upsilon$; (2) each protected observable event cannot be changed, as captured by $\{(\sigma, \mathcal{I}^{-1}(\sigma)) \in \Sigma \times \Upsilon | \sigma \in \Sigma_{o,p}\}$; (3) each unobservable event cannot cause any observable "fake" string, as captured by $\Sigma_{uo} \times \{\mathcal{I}^{-1}(\epsilon)\}$. Basically, Λ denotes all possible attack moves that may be taken by a smart sensor attack.

The closed and marked behavior of the closed-loop system $(\mathbf{G}, S_a)$ are denoted as $L(S_a/\mathbf{G}) \subseteq \Lambda^*$ and $L_m(S_a/\mathbf{G}) \subseteq \Lambda^*$, respectively, where

1. $\epsilon \in L(S_a/\mathbf{G})$;

2. $(\forall \mu \in L(S_a/\mathbf{G}))(\forall(\sigma, u) \in \Lambda)h_I(\mu)\sigma \in L(\mathbf{G}) \wedge \sigma \in S_a(h_o(\mu)) \wedge \mathcal{I}(h_o(\mu)u) \in P_o(L(S/\mathbf{G})) \Rightarrow \mu(\sigma, u) \in L(S_a/\mathbf{G})$;

3. All strings in $L(S_a/\mathbf{G})$ are generated in the previous two steps;

4. $L_m(S_a/\mathbf{G}) := L(S_a/\mathbf{G}) \cap L_m(\mathbf{G})$.

Condition 2 of the definition of the closed behavior $L(S_a/\mathbf{G})$ of the closed-loop system states that a string of compound events $\mu(\sigma, u) \in L(S_a/\mathbf{G})$ if and only if (i) $\mu \in L(S_a/\mathbf{G})$; (2) it is possible in the plant $\mathbf{G}$, i.e., $h_o(\mu)\sigma \in L(\mathbf{G})$; (3) σ is allowed by the previous supervisory control command, i.e., $\sigma \in S_a(h_o(\mu))$; (4) the new "fake" string u is acceptable by the supervisor, i.e., $h_o(\mu)u \in P_o(L(\mathbf{G}))$. Later, we will show that the closed behavior of the closed-loop system contains all possible sequences of attack moves that are covert to the supervisor.

A sensor attack A aims to make a change to a received observation, which is equivalent to saying that some compound event $(\sigma, u) \in \Lambda$ will happen, but some others will not. For those not happening, we can think of them being disabled by the sensor attack A - in this case, A functions like a supervisor on the closed-loop system $(\mathbf{G}, S_a)$. To model such a control mechanism, we first identify compound events that can be stopped by an attack A from happening, which is equivalent to the concept of those compound events being controllable, introduced below.

Definition 2.3 All events in $\Lambda_c := (\Sigma_o \setminus \Sigma_{o,p}) \times \Upsilon \subseteq \Lambda$ are *controllable*, and all other events in $\Lambda_{uc} := \Lambda \setminus \Lambda_c$ are *uncontrollable*. □

Thus, a compound event (σ, u) is controllable if σ, denoting the plant output, must be observable and not protected. In contrast, (σ, u) is uncontrollable if either σ is unobservable or σ is a protected observable event - in this case, the resulting "fake" string u is simply the same as the plant output σ, namely $u = \mathcal{I}^{-1}(\sigma)$, that is, no change is allowed.

Definition 2.4 Given a damage set $L_{\text{dam}} \subseteq L(\mathbf{G})$, a non-empty prefix-closed sublanguage $D \subseteq L(S_a/\mathbf{G})$ is a *smart attack language* of the closed-loop system $(\mathbf{G}, S_a)$ with respect to L_{dam}, if the following properties hold:

1. **Controllability**: $D\Lambda_{uc} \cap L(S_a/\mathbf{G}) \subseteq D$;

2. **Observability**: for all $t \in D$, $t' \in L(S_a/\mathbf{G})$, and for all $\sigma, \hat{\sigma} \in \Sigma$ and $u \in \Upsilon$,

$$P_o(h_I(t)\sigma) = P_o(h_I(t')\sigma') \wedge t(\sigma, u) \in D \wedge$$
$$h_I(t')\hat{\sigma} \in h_I(L(S_a/\mathbf{G})) \Rightarrow t'(\hat{\sigma}, u) \in D.$$

3. **Damage infliction**:

   (a) **Strong Damage Infliction (SDI)**: $D = \overline{D \cap h_I^{-1}(L_{\text{dam}})}$;

   (b) **Weak Damage Infliction (WDI)**: $D \cap h_I^{-1}(L_{\text{dam}}) \neq \emptyset$;

4. **Integrity of control command**:

$$(\forall \mu \in D)(\forall \sigma \in S_a(\mu))h_I(\mu)\sigma \in L(\mathbf{G}) \Rightarrow (\exists(\sigma, u) \in \Lambda)\mu(\sigma, u) \in D.$$

The smart attack language D is *supremal* if for all other existing smart attack languages $D' \subseteq L(S_a/\mathbf{G})$, we have $D' \subseteq D$. □.

   If we interpret a smart attack language as an outcome of a specific smart sensor attack on a closed-loop system, the first controllability property states that the attack cannot make any change in response to an unobservable or a protected observable output of the plant. The second property requires the attack to inflict either strong or weak damage to the plant. The last property states that the attack cannot stop the plant from executing any event allowed by the supervisor, that is, the attack can only intervene the input, not output, of the supervisor. It is interesting to point out that the definition does not require any explicit observability property, even although the plant contains unobservable behaviors. However, the property of Integrity of

Control Command ensures implicitly the observability property that guarantees the existence of a smart sensor attack decoded from the smart attack language, which will be shown shortly.

Proposition 2.5 Let $\mathcal{D}(G, S_a, L_{dam})$ be the collection of all smart attack languages of (G, S_a) with respect to $L_{dam} \subseteq L(G)$. If $\mathcal{D}(G, S_a, L_{dam}) \neq \emptyset$, then the supremal smart attack language exists.

Proof *Assume that* $\mathcal{D}(G, S_a, L_{dam}) \neq \emptyset$. *Let* $D_{sup} := \cup_{D \in \mathcal{D}(G, S_a, L_{dam})} D$. *Then we have*

1. *Controllability:*

$$D_{sup}\Lambda_{uc} \cap L(S_a/G) = (\cup_{D \in \mathcal{D}(G, S_a, L_{dam})}D)\Lambda_{uc} \cap L(S_a/G)$$
$$= \cup_{D \in \mathcal{D}(G, S_a, L_{dam})}(D\Lambda_{uc} \cap L(S_a/G)$$
$$\subseteq \cup_{D \in \mathcal{D}(G, S_a, L_{dam})}D$$
$$= D_{sup}$$

2. *Observability: for all* $t \in D_{sup}$, $t' \in L(S_a/G)$, *and for all* $\sigma, \hat{\sigma} \in \Sigma$ *and* $u \in \Upsilon$, *if* $P_o(h_I(t)\sigma) = P_o(h_I(t')\hat{\sigma})$, $t(\sigma, u) \in D$ *and* $h_I(t')\hat{\sigma} \in L(G)$, *then since there exists* $D \in \mathcal{D}(G, S_a, L_{dam})$ *such that* $t \in D$, *and by observability of* D, *we have* $t'(\hat{\sigma}, u) \in D \subseteq D_{sup}$. *Thus,* D_{sup} *is observable.*

(3.1) *Strong damage infliction:*

$$\overline{D_{sup} \cap h_I^{-1}(L_{dam})} = \overline{(\cup_{D \in \mathcal{D}(G, S_a, L_{dam})}D) \cap h_I^{-1}(L_{dam})}$$
$$= \cup_{D \in \mathcal{D}(G, S_a, L_{dam})}\overline{D \cap h_I^{-1}(L_{dam})}$$
$$= \cup_{D \in \mathcal{D}(G, S_a, L_{dam})}D$$
$$= D$$

(3.2) *Weak damage infliction:*

$$D_{sup} \cap h_I^{-1}(L_{dam}) = (\cup_{D \in \mathcal{D}(G, S_a, L_{dam})}D) \cap h_I^{-1}(L_{dam})$$
$$= \cup_{D \in \mathcal{D}(G, S_a, L_{dam})}D \cap h_I^{-1}(L_{dam})$$
$$\neq \emptyset$$

4. *Integrity of control command: For all $\mu \in D_{sup}$, there exists at least one smart attack language D such that $\mu \in D$. Because D is a smart attack language, we know that for all $\sigma \in S_a(\mu)$, if $h_I(\mu)\sigma \in L(\mathbf{G})$, then there exists $(\sigma, u) \in \Lambda$ such that $\mu(\sigma, u) \in D$. Because $D \subseteq D_{sup}$, we have $\mu(\sigma, u) \in D_{sup}$.*

This means that $D_{sup} \in \mathcal{D}(\mathbf{G}, S_a, L_{dam})$. Clearly, for all $D \in \mathcal{D}(\mathbf{G}, S_a, L_{dam})$, we have $D \subseteq D_{sup}$. Thus, D_{sup} is the supremal smart attack language. ■

Theorem 2.2 Given a plant model $\mathbf{G}$ and a supervisor S, let S_a be constructed above. Let $L_{dam} := L(\mathbf{G}) \setminus L(S/\mathbf{G})$. Given a smart attack language $D \in \mathcal{D}(\mathbf{G}, S_a, L_{dam})$, let $A : P_o(L(\mathbf{G})) \to \Delta_n^*$ be a mapping, where

$$(\forall s \in P_o(L(\mathbf{G})))A(s) := \{u \in \Delta_n^* | (\exists \mu \in D)\mathcal{I}(h_o(\mu))$$
$$= u \wedge P_o(h_I(\mu)) = s\}.$$

or equivalently, $A(s) := \mathcal{I}(h_o(h_I^{-1}(P_o^{-1}(s)) \cap D))$. Then A is a smart sensor attack of $(\mathbf{G}, S)$ with respect to L_{dam} such that $L(S \circ A/\mathbf{G}) = h_I(D)$.

Proof

1. *First, we show the covertness of A. Since $D \subseteq L(S_a/\mathbf{G})$, and by the definition of $L(S_a/\mathbf{G})$, we have $\mathcal{I}(h_o(L(S_a/\mathbf{G}))) \subseteq P_o(L(S/\mathbf{G}))$. Thus,*

$$(\forall s \in P_o(L(\mathbf{G})))A(s) = \mathcal{I}(h_o(h_I^{-1}(P_o^{-1}(s)) \cap D))$$
$$\subseteq \mathcal{I}(h_o(L(S_a/\mathbf{G})))$$
$$\subseteq P_o(L(S/\mathbf{G}))$$

Thus, $A(P_o(L(\mathbf{G}))) \subseteq P_o(L(S/\mathbf{G}))$.

2. *Next, we show damage infliction of A. We first show that $L(S \circ A/\mathbf{G}) = h_I(D)$ by using proof of induction. Base Case: Clearly, $\epsilon \in L(S \circ A/\mathbf{G})$ and $\epsilon \in D$, thus, $\epsilon \in h_I(D)$. Hypothesis: for all $s \in \Sigma^*$ with $|s| \leq n$, we have $s \in L(S \circ A/\mathbf{G})$ if and only if $s \in h_I(D)$. Induction: we need to show that, for all $s \in \Sigma^*$ with $|s| = n+1$, we have $s \in L(S \circ A/\mathbf{G})$ if and only if $s \in h_I(D)$.*

(2.a) *Assume that $s \in L(S \circ A/G)$. Clearly, there exists $s' \in L(S \circ A/G)$ and $\sigma \in \Sigma$ such that $s = s'\sigma$. Since $|s| = n+1$, we have $|s'| = n$. Thus, by Hypothesis, we have $s' \in h_I(D)$, which means there exists $\mu' \in D$ such that $h_I(\mu') = s'$. Since $s'\sigma \in L(S \circ A/G)$, we know that there exists $(\sigma, u) \in \Lambda$ such that $\sigma \in \gamma \in S(A(P_o(s')))$ and there exists another $\hat{\mu}(\hat{\sigma}, u) \in D$ such that $P_o(h_I(\mu)\hat{\sigma}) = P_o(s) = P_o(h_I(\mu')\sigma)$. Clearly, $h_I(\mu')\sigma \in L(G)$. Because D is observable, we know that $\mu'(\sigma, u) \in D$, which means $s = s'\sigma \in h_I(D)$. Thus, $L(S \circ A/G) \subseteq h_I(D)$.*

(2.b) *Assume that $s \in h_I(D)$. Then there must exist $s' \in h_I(D)$ and $\sigma \in \Sigma$ such that $s = s'\sigma$, where $|s'| = n$. By Hypothesis, we have $s' \in L(S \circ A/G)$. Since $s'\sigma \in h_I(D) \subseteq L(G)$, we know that there exists $\mu' \in D$ and $(\sigma, u) \in \Upsilon$ such that $\mu'(\sigma, u) \in D$, $h_I(\mu') = s'$, $\sigma \in S_a(h_o(\mu'))$ and $\mathcal{I}(h_o(\mu')u) \in L(S/G)$. Since $h_I(\mu') = s'$, we have $\mathcal{I}(h_o(\mu')) \in A(P_o(s'))$. Thus, $\sigma \in S \circ A(P_o(s'))$. Together with $s' \in L(S \circ A/G)$ and $s'\sigma \in L(G)$, we have $s = s'\sigma \in L(S \circ A/G)$. Thus, $h_I(D) \subseteq L(S \circ A/G)$, which completes the induction step.*

Since $L(S \circ A/G) = h_I(D)$, we can show that, if D satisfies SDI, then

$$L(S \circ A/G) = h_I(D)$$
$$= h_I(\overline{D \cap h_I^{-1}(L_{dam})})$$
$$= \overline{h_I(D \cap h_I^{-1}(L_{dam}))}$$
$$= \overline{h_I(D) \cap L_{dam}}$$
$$= \overline{L(S \circ A/G) \cap L_{dam}}$$

and if D satisfies WDI, then

$$L(S \circ A/G) \cap L_{dam} = h_I(D) \cap L_{dam}$$
$$= h_I(h_I^{-1}(h_I(D) \cap L_{dam}))$$
$$\supseteq h_I(D \cap h_I^{-1}(L_{dam}))$$
$$\neq \emptyset$$

> *Till now, A satisfies either SDI or WDI, depending on whether D satisifies SDI or WDI. This completes the proof.*

■

Theorem 2.3 Given a plant model **G**, a supervisor S and a damage language $L_{\mathrm{dam}} \subseteq L(\mathbf{G})$, let A be a smart sensor attack of $(\mathbf{G}, S)$ with respect to L_{dam}. Then there exists a smart attack language $D \in \mathcal{D}(\mathbf{G}, S_a, L_{\mathrm{dam}})$ such that $L(S \circ A/\mathbf{G}) = h_I(D)$.

Proof *We use the construction method to explicitly derive one specific smart attack language $D \in \mathcal{D}(\mathbf{G}, S_a, L_{\mathrm{dam}})$.*

1. $\epsilon \in D$;

2. $(\epsilon, A(\epsilon)) \in D$;

3. $(\forall \mu \in D)(\forall \sigma \in \Sigma)h_I(D)\sigma \in L(S \circ A/\mathbf{G}) \Rightarrow \{\mu(\sigma, u)|u \in A(P_o(h_I(\mu)\sigma))/A(P_o(h_I(\mu)))\} \subseteq D$;

4. *All strings in D are generated in Steps 1–3.*

By the construction of D, it is clear that $L(S \circ A/\mathbf{G}) = h_I(D)$. Next, we need to show that $D \in \mathcal{D}(\mathbf{G}, S_a, L_{\mathrm{dam}})$.

1. *We first show the Controllability property. Recall that $\Lambda_{uc} = \{(\sigma, \mathcal{I}^{-1}(\sigma)) \in \Sigma \times \Upsilon | \sigma \in \Sigma_{o,p}\} \cup \Sigma_{uo} \times \{\mathcal{I}^{-1}(\epsilon)\}$. For each $\mu \in D$, let $(\sigma, u) \in \Lambda_{uc}$. Assume that $\mu(\sigma, u) \in L(S_a/\mathbf{G})$. We need to show that $\mu(\sigma, u) \in D$. We consider two cases.*

   Case 1: $\sigma \in \Sigma_{uo}$. By the definition of Λ_{uc}, we know that $u = \epsilon$. Since $\mu \in D$, we know that $h_I(\mu) \in h_I(D) = L(S \circ A/\mathbf{G})$. Since $P_o(h_I(\mu)\sigma) = P_o(h_I(\mu))$, we know that $h_I(\mu)\sigma \in L(S \circ A/\mathbf{G})$. In addition, $\epsilon \in A(P_o(h_I(\mu)\sigma))/A(P_o(h_I(\mu)))$. Thus, by the definition of D, we know that $\mu(\sigma, u) \in D$.

   Case 2: $\sigma \in \Sigma_{o,p}$. In this case, $u = \sigma$. Since $\mu(\sigma, u) \in L(S_a/\mathbf{G})$, by the definition of $L(S_a/\mathbf{G})$, we know that $h_I(\mu)\sigma \in L(S \circ A/\mathbf{G})$. In addition, because $\sigma \in \Sigma_{o,p}$, we have $\sigma \in A(P_o(h_I(\mu)\sigma))/A(P_o(h_I(\mu)))$. Thus, $\mu(\sigma, \sigma) \in D$.

   By Case 1 and Case 2, we know that $D\Lambda_{uc} \cap L(S_a/\mathbf{G}) \subseteq D$.

2. *Next, we show that D is observable. We use induction. For all $t \in D$, $t' \in L(S_a/\boldsymbol{G})$ and for all $\sigma, \sigma' \in \Sigma$ and $u \in \Upsilon$, assume that $P_o(h_I(t)\sigma) = P_o(h_I(t')\sigma')$, $t(\sigma, u) \in D$ and $h_I(t')\sigma' \in h_I(L(S_a/\boldsymbol{G}))$. If $|P_o(h_I(t')\sigma')| = 0$, then it is clear that $t'(\sigma', u) = t'(\sigma', h_o^{-1}(\epsilon)) \in D$ because $A(P_o(h_I(t')\sigma')) = \epsilon$. Assume that when $|P_o(h_I(t')\sigma')| = k$, we have $t'(\sigma', u) \in D$. We need to show that when $|P_o(h_I(t')\sigma')| = k+1$, we also have $t'(\sigma', u) \in D$. We consider two cases.*

   Case 1: $\sigma' \in \Sigma_o$. In this case, by the hypothesis, we know that $t' \in D$ because $t(\sigma, u) \in D$ and $P_o(h_I(t')) \leq P_o(h_I(t)\sigma)$ and $|P_o(h_I(t'))| = k$. Because $t(\sigma, u) \in D$, by the definition of $L(S_a/\boldsymbol{G})$, we know that $u = h_o^{-1}(A(h_I(t)\sigma))$. Because $h_I(t')\sigma' \in L(\boldsymbol{G})$, we know that $u = h_o^{-1}(A(h_I(t')\sigma'))$. Since $P_o(h_I(t)\sigma) = P_o(h_I(t')\sigma')$ and $h_I(t)\sigma \in h_I(D) \subseteq L(S \circ A/\boldsymbol{G})$, we know that $\sigma' \in S(A(P_o(h_I(t'))))$. Thus, $t'(\sigma', u) \in D$.

   Case 2: $\sigma' \in \Sigma_{uo}$. Thus, there exists $\hat{t}' \leq t'$ and $\sigma_1 \ldots \sigma_l \sigma' \in \Sigma_{uo}^*$ such that $h_I(\hat{t}') \in \Sigma^* \Sigma_o$ and $h_I(t') = h_I(\hat{t}')\sigma_1 \ldots \sigma_l \sigma'$. Based on Case 1, we know $\hat{t}' \in D$. Because $h_I(t')\sigma' \in h_I(L(S_a/\boldsymbol{G}))$, we know that there exists $\gamma \in S(A(P_o(h_I(\hat{t}'))))$ such that $\sigma_1 \ldots \sigma_l \sigma' \in \gamma^*$. Based on the definition of D, we know that $t'(\sigma', h_o^{-1}(\epsilon)) = \hat{t}'(\sigma_1, h_o^{-1}(\epsilon)) \ldots (\sigma_l, h_o^{-1}(\epsilon))(\sigma', h_o^{-1}(\epsilon)) \in D$, which completes the induction.

3. *Next, we show that the damage infliction property holds.*

   (3.1) For the SDI property, it is always true that $\overline{D \cap h_I^{-1}(D)} \subseteq D$. To show the other direction of set inclusion, since $L(S \circ A/\boldsymbol{G}) = h_I(D)$, if $L(S \circ A/\boldsymbol{G})$ satisfies SDI, namely

$$L(S \circ A/\boldsymbol{G}) = \overline{L(S \circ A/\boldsymbol{G}) \cap L_{dam}},$$

   then $h_I(D) = \overline{h_I(D) \cap L_{dam}}$. Thus, for each $\mu \in D$, we know that there exists $s \in h_I(D) \cap L_{dam}$ such that $h_I(\mu) \leq s$. Clearly, there exists $\mu' \in D$ with $h_I(\mu') = s$ and $\mu \leq \mu'$. Since $s \in L(S \circ A/\boldsymbol{G})L_{dam}$, we can show that there exists $\mu'' \in L(S_a/\boldsymbol{G})$ such that $h_I(\mu'') = s$ and $h_o(\mu'') = h_o(\mu')$, which means $\mu'' = \mu$. Thus, $\mu \in h_I^{-1}(L_{dam})$, which means $\mu \in \overline{D \cap h_I^{-1}(L_{dam})}$. Thus, $D = \overline{D \cap h_I^{-1}(L_{dam})}$.

(3.2) For the WDI property, if $L(S \circ A/G)$ satisfies WDI, then

$$L(S \circ A/G) \cap L_{dam} \neq \emptyset,$$

which means $h_I(D) \cap L_{dam} \neq \emptyset$. Thus, there exists $\mu \in D$ such that $h_I(\mu) \in L_{dam}$. Since $h_I(\mu) \in L(S \circ A/G) \cap L_{dam}$, we know that $\mu \in h_I^{-1}(L_{dam})$. Thus, $\mu \in D \cap h_I^{-1}(L_{dam})$, namely $D \cap h_I^{-1}(L_{dam}) \neq \emptyset$.

4. To show the Integrity of Control Command property, let $\mu \in D$. For each $\sigma \in S_a(\mu) = S(\mathcal{I}(h_o(\mu))) = S \circ A(P_o(h_I(\mu)))$, by the definition of D, we know that $\mu(\sigma, u) \in D$, where $u = A(P_o(h_I(\mu)\sigma))/A(P_o(h_I(\mu)))$. Thus, the Integrity of Control Command holds. ■

Corollary 2.1 Given a plant model $\mathbf{G}$, a supervisor S and a damage language $L_{\text{dam}} \subseteq L(\mathbf{G})$, the supremal smart attack language $D_{\text{sup}} \in \mathcal{D}(\mathbf{G}, S_a, L_{\text{dam}})$ induces the supremal smart sensor attack $A_{\text{sup}} \in \mathcal{A}(\mathbf{G}, S, L_{\text{dam}})$.

Proof *Theorem 2.2 indicates that each synthesized smart attack language $D \in \mathcal{D}(\mathbf{G}, S_a, L_{dam})$ induces a smart sensor attack A. In particular, the supremal attack language D_{sup} also induces a smart sensor attack A'. Clearly, $A' \preceq A_{sup}$. On the other hand, by Theorem 2.3 we know that there exists a smart attack language D' such that $h_I(D') = L(S \circ A_{sup}/G)$, namely D' induces A_{sup}. Thus, $L(S \circ A_{sup}/G) = h_I(D') \subseteq h_I(D_{sup}) = L(S \circ A'/G)$, which means $A_{sup} \preceq A'$. This means $A' = A_{sup}$, which completes the proof.* ■

Corollary 2.1 indicates that the supremal smart sensor attack A_{sup} may be computable, if the mapping S_a can be constructed via finite-state automaton, as the subsequent computation of the supremal attack language D_{sup} can be achieved by using standard automaton operations.

To construct S_a, let $\mathbf{S} = (Z, \Sigma, \delta, z_0, Z_m)$ be a realization of the supervisor S. We create the following automaton $\mathbf{S}_a := (Z, \Sigma_{uo} \cup \Upsilon, \delta_a, z_0, Z_m)$, where $\delta_a : Z \times (\Sigma_{uo} \cup \Upsilon) \to \Gamma$ be a partial transition mapping, where

$$(\forall z \in Z)(\forall \sigma \in \Sigma_{uo} \cup \Upsilon)\delta_a(z,\sigma) := \begin{cases} \delta(z,\sigma) & \text{if } \sigma \in \Sigma_{uo} \wedge \delta(z,\sigma)! \\ \delta(z,\mathcal{I}(\sigma)) & \text{if } \sigma \in \Upsilon \wedge \delta(z,\mathcal{I}(\sigma)) \\ \text{undefined} & \text{otherwise.} \end{cases}$$

Essentially, $\mathbf{S}_a$ records all unobservable events defined at each state of $\mathbf{S}$, but adds new transitions labeled by events in Υ that represent possible attack moves. For each $z \in Z$, let

$$En_{\mathbf{S}_a}(z) := \{\sigma \in \Sigma | \sigma \in \Sigma_{uo} \wedge \delta_a(z,\sigma)! \vee \sigma \in \Sigma_o \wedge (\exists u \in \Upsilon)\sigma \leq \mathcal{I}(u) \wedge \delta_a(z,u)!\}$$

Next, we define the composition of $\mathbf{G}$ and $\mathbf{S}_a$. Let

$$\mathbf{G} \times \mathbf{S}_a = (X \times Z, \Lambda, \varpi, (x_0, z_0), X_m \times Z_m)$$

be an automaton, where $\varpi : X \times Z \times (\Sigma_{uo} \cup \Lambda) \to X \times Z$ is the partial transition mapping defined as follows: for all $(x, z) \in X \times Z$ and for $(\sigma, u) \in \Lambda$,

$$\varpi(x, z, \sigma, u) := \begin{cases} (\xi(x,\sigma), \delta_a(z,u)) & \text{if } \xi(x,\sigma)! \wedge \delta_a(z,u)! \wedge \sigma \in En_{\mathbf{S}_a}(z), \\ \text{undefined} & \text{otherwise.} \end{cases}$$

Proposition 2.6 Given a closed-loop system $(\mathbf{G}, S)$, let S_a be derived from S. Let $\mathbf{S}$ be a realization of S and $\mathbf{S}_a$ be derived from $\mathbf{S}$. Then $L(S_a/\mathbf{G}) = L(\mathbf{G} \times \mathbf{S}_a)$.

Proof *Clearly,* $\epsilon \in L(S_a/\mathbf{G}) \cap L(\mathbf{G} \times \mathbf{S}_a)$. *Assume that for all* $\mu \in \Lambda^*$ *with* $|\mu| \leq n$, $\mu \in L(S_a/\mathbf{G})$ *if and only if* $\mu \in L(\mathbf{G} \times \mathbf{S}_a)$. *We need to show that for each* $\mu \in \Lambda^*$ *with* $|\mu| = n+1$, $\mu \in L(S_a/\mathbf{G})$ *if and only if* $\mu \in L(\mathbf{G} \times \mathbf{S}_a)$.

$$\mu \in L(S_a/\mathbf{G}) \wedge |\mu| = n+1$$
$$\Longleftrightarrow (\exists\mu' \in \Lambda^*)(\exists(\sigma,u) \in \Lambda)\mu = \mu'(\sigma,u) \wedge |\mu'| = n$$
$$\Longleftrightarrow \mu' \in L(S_a/\mathbf{G}) \wedge h_I(\mu')\sigma \in L(\mathbf{G}) \wedge \sigma \in S_a(h_o(\mu')) \wedge$$
$$\quad \mathcal{I}(h_o(\mu')u) \in P_o(L(S/\mathbf{G})) \text{by the definition of } L(S_a/\mathbf{G})$$
$$\Longleftrightarrow \mu' \in L(\mathbf{G} \times \mathbf{S}_a) \wedge h_I(\mu')\sigma \in L(\mathbf{G}) \wedge \sigma \in S_a(h_o(\mu')) \wedge$$
$$\quad \mathcal{I}(h_o(\mu')u) \in P_o(L(S/\mathbf{G})) \text{by the hypothesis, as } |\mu'| \leq n$$
$$\Longleftrightarrow (\exists(x,z) \in X \times Z)\varpi(x_0, z_0, \mu') \wedge \xi(x,\sigma)! \wedge \sigma \in En_{\mathbf{S}_a}(z) \wedge \delta_a(z,u)!$$
$$\Longleftrightarrow \varpi(x, z, \sigma, u)!$$
$$\Longleftrightarrow \mu'(\sigma, u) = \mu \in L(\mathbf{G} \times \mathbf{S}_a)$$

The proposition follows. ■

Proposition 2.6 shows that, as long as both the plant $\mathbf{G}$ and the supervisor $\mathbf{S}$ are finitely represented, it is possible to encode all attack moves in $\mathbf{G} \times \mathbf{S}_a$, where $\mathbf{S}_a$ is derived from $\mathbf{S}$. Let $\mathbf{E} = (W, \Sigma, \kappa, w_0, W_m)$ be a realization of $L_{\text{dam}} \subseteq L(\mathbf{G})$. Let $\mathbf{G}_h = (X_h, \Sigma_o, \xi_h, x_{0,h}, X_{m,h})$ be an observer of $\mathbf{G}$, where

- $X_h = 2^X$ and $X_{m,h} := \{x_h \in X_h | x_h \cap X_m \neq \varnothing\}$;

- $x_{0,h} := \{x \in X | (\exists t \in \Sigma_{uo}^*) \xi(x_0, t) = x\}$;

- for all $x_h \in X_h$ and for all $\sigma \in \Sigma_o$

$$\xi_h(x_h, \sigma) := \{x \in X | (\exists x' \in x_h)(\exists u \in \Sigma_{uo}^*) \xi(x', \sigma u) = x\}.$$

Let $\mathbf{G} \times \mathbf{S}_a \times \mathbf{E} \times \mathbf{G}_h = (Q = X \times Z \times (W \cup \{d\}) \times X_h, \Lambda, \iota, q_0 = (x_0, z_0, w_0, x_h), Q_m = X_m \times Z_m \times W_m \times X_{m,h})$ be a new automaton, where for all $(x, z, w, x_h) \in Q$ and for all $(\sigma, u) \in \Lambda$,

$$\iota(q, \sigma, u) := \begin{cases} (\varpi(x, z, \sigma, u), \kappa(w, \sigma), \xi_h(x_h, P_o(\sigma))) & \text{if } \varpi(x, z, \sigma, u)! \wedge \kappa(w, \sigma)!, \\ (\varpi(x, z, \sigma, u), d, \xi_h(x_h, P_o(\sigma))) & \text{if } \varpi(x, z, \sigma, u)! \wedge \\ & (\neg\kappa(w, \sigma)! \vee w = d), \\ \text{undefine} & \text{otherwise.} \end{cases}$$

Next, we propose an algorithm to compute the supremal attack language.

2.3.1 Procedure for Supremal Attack Language

1. Given $\mathbf{G}, \mathbf{S}_a, \mathbf{E},$ and $\mathbf{G}_h$, compute $\mathbf{G} \times \mathbf{S}_a \times \mathbf{E} \times \mathbf{G}_h$ as above.

2. Find the largest sub-automaton $\mathbf{D} = (Q_{\mathbf{D}}, \Lambda, \iota_{\mathbf{D}}, q_0, Q_{m,\mathbf{D}})$ of $\mathbf{G} \times \mathbf{S}_a \times \mathbf{E} \times \mathbf{G}_h$, where $Q_{\mathbf{D}} \subseteq Q$, $Q_{m,\mathbf{D}} \subseteq Q_m$ and $\iota_{\mathbf{D}}$ is the restriction of ι on $Q_{\mathbf{D}}$, such that the following hold:

(a) Controllability: $(\forall q \in Q_{\mathbf{D}})(\forall \nu \in \Lambda_{uc})\iota(q, \nu)! \Rightarrow \iota_{\mathbf{D}}(q, \nu)!$

(b) Observability: for all $q = (x, z, w, x_h) \in Q_{\mathbf{D}}$ and for all $(\sigma, u) \in \Lambda$,

$$\iota_{\mathbf{D}}(q, \sigma, u)! \Rightarrow (\forall x' \in x_h)[\xi(x', \sigma)! \Rightarrow (\exists q' \\ = (x', z, w', x_h) \in Q)\iota_{\mathbf{D}}(q, \sigma, u)!]$$

(c) Damage Infliction:

    i. SDI: $(\forall q \in Q_{\mathbf{D}})(\exists \mu \in \Lambda^*)\iota_{\mathbf{D}}(q, \mu) \in Q_{m,\mathbf{D}}$

    ii. WDI: $(\exists q \in Q_{\mathbf{D}})(\exists \mu \in \Lambda^*)\iota_{\mathbf{D}}(q, \mu) \in Q_{m,\mathbf{D}}$

3. Integrity of Control Command:

$$(\forall q = (x, z, w, x_h) \in Q_{\mathbf{D}})(\forall \sigma \in En_{\mathbf{S}_a}(z))\xi(x, \sigma)!$$
$$\Rightarrow (\exists(\sigma, u) \in \Lambda)\iota_{\mathbf{D}}(q, \sigma, u)!.$$

Proposition 2.7 Given a plant $\mathbf{G}$, a supervisor S realized by $\mathbf{S}$ and a damage language L_{dam} represented by $\mathbf{E}$, let $\mathbf{D}$ be computed by PSAL. If $\mathbf{D}$ is nonempty, then $L(\mathbf{D})$ is the supremal attack language of $\mathcal{D}(\mathbf{G}, S, L_{\mathrm{dam}})$, and its induced smart sensor attack is supremal in $\mathcal{A}(\mathbf{G}, S, L_{\mathrm{dam}})$.

Proof *By PSAL, it is clear that $L(\mathbf{D})$ satisfies three properties in Def. 2.4. Thus, $L(\mathbf{D})$ is a smart attack language. Since $\mathbf{D}$ is the largest sub-automaton that satisfies three properties, we know that $L(\mathbf{D})$ is the supremal attack language. By Corollary 2.1, $L(\mathbf{D})$ induces the supremal sensor attack $A_{sup} \in \mathcal{A}(\mathbf{G}, S, L_{dam})$.* ∎

Proposition 2.7 finally establishes the fact that, as long as both the supervisor S and a damage language L_{dam} are finitely representable by automata, the supremal smart sensor attack $A_{\mathrm{sup}} \in \mathcal{A}(\mathbf{G}, S, L_{\mathrm{dam}})$ is always computable, whenever it exists. This also shows that existence of the supremal smart sensor attack is decidable.

The computational complexity of Procedure PSAL can be roughly estimated as follows. The number of states $|Q|$ is upper bounded by $|X||Z||W||X_h|$. Thus, the complexity of constructing $\mathbf{G} \times \mathbf{S} \times \mathbf{E} \times \mathbf{G}_h$ is $O(|X|^2|Z|^2|W|^2|\Sigma||\Delta_n|2^{2|X|}) = O(|X|^2|Z|^2|W|^2|\Sigma|\frac{|\Sigma|^{n+1}-1}{|\Sigma|-1}2^{2|X|}) = O(|X|^2|Z|^2|W|^2|\Sigma|^{n+1}2^{2|X|})$. Since the complexities of checking Controllability, SDI/WDI (which is one type of liveliness), and Integrity of Control Command are all linear to the total number of transitions in $\mathbf{D}$, which is $O(|X|^2|Z|^2|W|^2|\Sigma||\Delta_n|2^{2|X|}) = O(|X|^2|Z|^2|W|^2|\Sigma|^{n+1}2^{2|X|})$, the complexity of computing the supremal attack language $L(\mathbf{D})$ is $O(|X|^2|Z|^2|W|^2|\Sigma|^{n+1}2^{2|X|})$, which is exponential in time. Based on the definition of a smart sensor attack induced from a smart attack language, shown in Theorem 2.2, the complexity of deriving the supremal sensor attack A_{sup} is linear in time with respect to the number of transitions in **D**. Thus, the final complexity of deriving A_{sup} is $O(|X|^2|Z|^2|W|^2|\Sigma|^{n+1}2^{2|X|})$.

Example 2.2 *As an illustration, we apply Procedure PSAL to the plant **G** and the supervisor S shown in Figure 2.3. Assume that $\Sigma_{o,p} = \{q_0 = 0, q_0 = 1\}$. Since $\Delta_n = \Sigma_o^{\epsilon}$, let $\Lambda = \{\alpha_1, \cdots, \alpha_5, \alpha_6\}$, where $\mathcal{I}(\alpha_1) = \epsilon$, $\mathcal{I}(\alpha_2) = \text{"}h = L\text{"}$, $\mathcal{I}(\alpha_3) = \text{"}h = H\text{"}$, $\mathcal{I}(\alpha_4) = \text{"}h = EH\text{"}$, $\mathcal{I}(\alpha_5) = \text{"}q_0\text{"}$, $\mathcal{I}(\alpha_6) = \text{"}q_1\text{"}$. The automaton realizations $\mathbf{S}_a$ and $\mathbf{E}$ are depicted in Figure 2.6. Because all events are observable, $\mathbf{G}_h = \mathbf{G}$. Thus, the finite-state automaton $\mathbf{D} = \mathbf{G} \times \mathbf{S}_a \times \mathbf{E} \times \mathbf{G}_h$ is isomorphic to $\mathbf{G} \times \mathbf{S}_a \times \mathbf{E}$, which is depicted in Figure 2.7. We can check that*

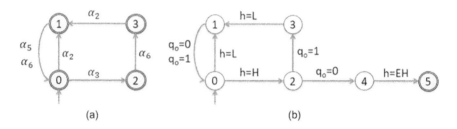

(a)   (b)

Figure 2.6   The finite-state automata $\mathbf{S}_a$ (a) and damage language $\mathbf{E}$ (b).

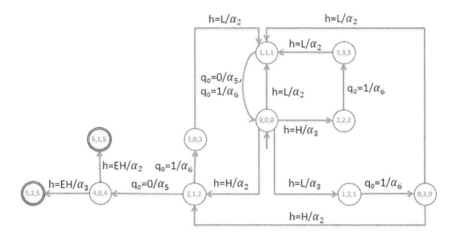

Figure 2.7   The finite-state automaton $\mathbf{D} = \mathbf{G} \times \mathbf{S}_a \times \mathbf{E} \times \mathbf{G}_h$.

$L(\boldsymbol{D})$ *is controllable with respect to* $L(S_a/\boldsymbol{G})$ *and* Λ_{uc}. *In addition, it is strong-damage-infliction, thus, also weak-damage-infliction. Finally, it satisfies integrity of control command. Thus,* $L(\boldsymbol{D})$ *is a smart attack language. Clearly,* $\boldsymbol{D}$ *is the largest sub-automaton of* $\boldsymbol{G} \times S_a \times E \times \boldsymbol{G}_h$. *By Proposition 2.7,* $L(\boldsymbol{D})$ *is the supremal one with respect to* $(\boldsymbol{G}, S_a, L_{dam})$, *which induces the smart sensor attack* A_{sup}.

2.4 SYNTHESIS OF AN SSA-ROBUST SUPERVISOR

Previously, we have discussed how to design a smart sensor attack (SSA) model to interrupt a given system's operations from an attacker's point of view. In this section we present a synthesis approach to design a supervisor S, which is "robust" to any SSA in the sense that either the attack is not covert or incurs no damage to the system. More precisely, we introduce the following concept of *robustness*.

Definition 2.5 Given a closed-loop system $(\boldsymbol{G}, S)$ and a damage language $L_{\mathrm{dam}} \subseteq L(\boldsymbol{G})$, S is *SSA-robust* with respect to L_{dam} if $\mathcal{A}(\boldsymbol{G}, S, L_{\mathrm{dam}}) = \emptyset$. □

Example 2.3 *In general, given two SSA-robust supervisors* S_1 *and* S_2, *their union need not be SSA-robust. A simple example is shown in Figure 2.8, where* $\Sigma = \{a, b, c, d\}$, $\Sigma_o = \Sigma$, $\Sigma_{uc} = \emptyset$, *and* $\Sigma_{o,p} = \{c, d\}$. *We can check that both* S_1 *and* S_2 *are SSA-robust with respect to* $\Sigma_{o,p}$ *because there is no sensor attack satisfying the covertness property and*

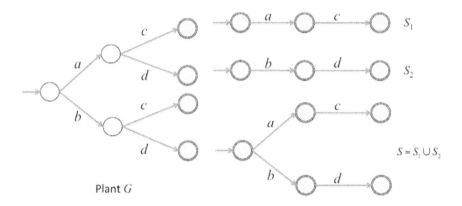

Plant G

Figure 2.8 Non-closure of ABSRA-robustness under union.

damage infliction property simultaneously. But $S = S_1 \cup S_2$ is not SSA-robust because an SSA can replace a with b, and replace b with a. This example shows that the supremal SSA-robust supervisor does not exist.

With the concept of SSA-robustness, we introduce the following problem.

Problem 2.1 Given a plant $\mathbf{G}$ and a requirement $E \subseteq \Sigma^*$, synthesize an SSA-robust supervisor S. □

Let $\mathcal{CN}(\mathbf{G}, E)$ be the collection of all controllable and normal sublanguage of $L(\mathbf{G}) \cap E$ [17]. Each controllable and normal sublanguage induces a supervisor. Let $\hat{K} = \sup\mathcal{CN}(\mathbf{G}, E)$, which always exists and computable. Our goal is to design a supervisor S induced from one controllable and normal sublanguage in $\mathcal{CN}(\mathbf{G}, E)$ such that Procedure PSAL returns an empty SSA. To this end, we present the following procedure:

Procedure for SSA-Robust Supervisor (SSA-RS)

1. Input: a plant $\mathbf{G}$ and a requirement $E \subseteq \Sigma^*$.

2. Compute $\hat{K} := \sup\mathcal{CN}(\mathbf{G}, E)$. If $\hat{K} = \emptyset$, then set $K = \emptyset$ and go to Step (5). Otherwise, continue.

3. Compute $D_{\sup} \in \mathcal{D}(\mathbf{G}, \hat{K}, L_{\mathrm{dam}})$ by using Procedure PSAL.

4. Compute $K := \sup\mathcal{CN}(\mathbf{G}, \hat{K} \setminus \mathcal{I}(h_o(D_{\sup}))\Sigma^*)$.

5. Output: the supervisor S induced from K. □

Theorem 2.4 Given a plant $\mathbf{G}$ and a requirement $E \subseteq \Sigma^*$, let S be computed in SSA-RS. If S is nonempty, then S is SSA-robust with respect to $\Sigma_{o,p}$.

Proof *To show that S, induced from K, is SSA-robust, assume that it is not true. Then Procedure PSAL returns a non-empty smart attack language $D \in \mathcal{D}(\mathbf{G}, S, L_{dam})$. On the other hand, we know that $K \subseteq \hat{K} \setminus \mathcal{I}(h_o(D_{sup}))\Sigma^*$, which means $D \notin \mathcal{D}(\mathbf{G}, S, L_{dam})$. This leads to a contradiction. Thus, S must be SSA-robust.* ■

By Theorem 2.4 we know that, if SSA-RS returns a nonempty supervisor S, then S must be SSA-robust. However, when SSA-RS returns an empty supervisor S, it does not necessarily mean that there is no SSA-robust supervisor. In other words, SSA-RS may not guarantee to find an SSA-robust supervisor. The reason is that, at Step 4 of SSA-RS, the entire set $\mathcal{I}(h_o(D_{\text{sup}}))$ is removed from $\hat{K}$. Indeed, this will guarantee to remove each string that may be used by an SSA, namely it will certainly prevent the existence of an SSA. But to prevent an SSA, it is not necessary to remove every string that may be used by an SSA, as long as the covertness property does not hold. Thus, Step 4 in SSA-RS only provides a sufficient way of preventing an SSA, but may not be necessary.

We would like to point out that when Procedure PSAL returns an empty D_{sup}, and by Proposition 2.7 we conclude that there is no SSA for the closed-loop system $(\mathbf{G}, S)$, it does not mean that a sensor attack will not be carried out by an attacker. But such an attack will either not be able to inflict any damage to the system or reveal itself to the supervisor before it achieves its attack goal owing to abnormal system executions, which can be formulated as an abnormality detection problem similar to fault diagnosis [45] and proper contingent actions such as system shutdown can be taken by the supervisor, which is nevertheless outside the scope of this chapter.

To determine the complexity of Procedure SSA-RS, let $|E|$ denote the number of states of a canonical recognizer of E. We know the complexity of Step (2) is $O(2^{2|X||E|}|\Sigma|^2)$, where the state size of $\hat{K}$ is $|\hat{K}| \leq 2^{|X||E|}|\Sigma|$. Then the complexity of Step (3) is the same as that of Procedure PSAL, where the state size of D_{sup} is $|D_{\text{sup}}| \leq |X|^2|\hat{K}|2^{|X|}$. The state size of $\hat{K}\backslash\mathcal{I}(h_o(D_{\text{sup}}))\Sigma^*$ in Step (4) is $|\hat{K}|^2|X|^22^{|X|}$. The final complexity of computing S is $O(|\hat{K}|^4|X|^42^{2|X|}) = O(2^{4|X||E|}|\Sigma|^4|X|^4|\Sigma|^{n+1}2^{2|X|}) = O(2^{4|X||E|}|X|^4|\Sigma|^{n+5})$, which is exponential in $|X||E|$, given Σ and n.

Example 2.4 *As an illustration of Procedure SSA-RS, we revisit the plant $\mathbf{G}$ depicted in Figure 2.3 with the same requirement that the water level should not be extremely high, i.e., the event $h = EH$ should never occur. Then we can see that the supremal controllable and normal sublanguage $\hat{K}$ is the same as the supervisor S shown in Figure 2.3. Assume that $\Sigma_{o,p} = \{q_o = 0, q_o = 1\}$. After applying Procedure PSAL,* *the resulting supremal attack language D_{sup} is depicted in Figure 2.7. A nondeterministic automaton representation of $\mathcal{I}(h_o(D_{sup}))$ is depicted in the left picture of Figure 2.9, and the corresponding automaton representation of $\mathcal{I}(h_o(D_{sup}))$ is depicted in the right picture of Figure 2.9. The language $\hat{K} \setminus \mathcal{I}(h_o(D_{sup}))\Sigma^*$ is depicted in Figure 2.10. The sublanguage $K = supCN(G, \hat{K} \setminus \mathcal{I}(h_o(D_{sup}))\Sigma^*)$ is depicted in Figure 2.11, which indicates that the event $q_o = 0$ cannot occur after an odd number of sensor reading $h = L$. Let us check whether this*

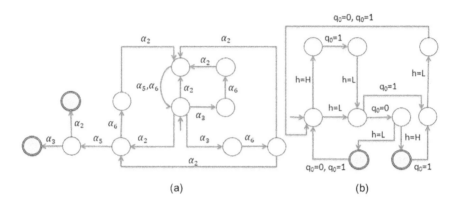

(a)   (b)

Figure 2.9 A nondeterministic automaton for $h_o(D_{sup})$ (a) and an automaton for $\mathcal{I}(h_o(D_{sup}))$ (b).

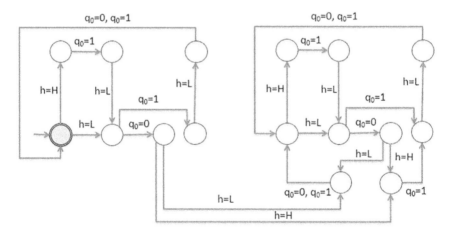

Figure 2.10 $\hat{K} \setminus \mathcal{I}(h_o(D_{sup}))\Sigma^*$.

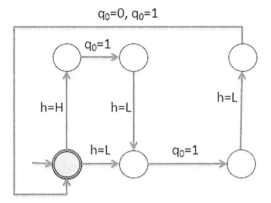

Figure 2.11 Sublanguage $K = \sup\mathcal{CN}(\mathbf{G}, \hat{K} \setminus \mathcal{I}(h_o(D_{\sup}))\Sigma^*)$.

makes sense. When the first $h = L$ is received by the supervisor S, it may be actually $h = H$ but simply changed by an SSA. Thus, to play safe, the supervisor S cannot close the valve, namely $q_o = 0$ cannot be allowed. Then after $q_o = 1$ takes place, namely the valve is opened, the supervisor S is certain that the water level must be low, namely $h = L$. Thus, the second received sensor reading $h = L$ must be true. In this case, the supervisor S allows the valve to be either closed or open, namely both $q_0 = 0$ and $q_0 = 1$ are allowed. In case $q_0 = 0$ takes place, then the next received sensor reading $h = L$ is suspicious and may possibly be attacked by the SSA, thus, after the reception of the third copy of $h = L$, only $q_0 = 1$ is allowed, until the reception of the fourth copy of $h = L$ is received, which assures the supervisor S to allow both $q_0 = 0$ and $q_0 = 1$. The same process repeats.

Recall that an SSA affects a target system $(\mathbf{G}, S)$ by altering the sequence of observable events, which tricks S to issue commands improperly. By protecting observable events from being altered unnoticeably can in principle effectively deter an SSA. An observable event in this framework denotes a specific set of strongly associated measurements. For example, in the aforementioned single-tank system, the event $h = H$ may either be associated with one simple water level measurement or possibly several sensor measurements such as the actual water level, and the corresponding pressure on the bottom of the tank - the more sensor measurements associated with the event, the harder for an attacker to alter the event without being detected. When applying suitable encryption techniques, it is even more complicated for an attacker to complete the job. Thus, it is indeed technically feasible to prevent observable events from being altered either by adopting new secure information transmission technologies or by introducing more sensors to significantly increase the complication of altering the corresponding observable event without being detected. Nevertheless, there is always a financial consideration. An attractive solution to a potential industrial user is to identify only critical observable events, which, when being protected from external alterations, will lead to a supervisor robust to any SSA. Thus, we have another interesting problem, which is stated below.

Problem 2.2 Given a plant G and a requirement E, compute a protected observable alphabet $\Sigma_{o,p} \subseteq \Sigma_o$ of the minimum size such that a nonempty SSA-robust supervisor S exists. ☐

It is clear that Problem 2.2 is solvable in the sense that it is decidable whether there exists such a $\Sigma_{o,p}$ with the minimum size because we can simply apply Procedure SSA-RS on each subset of Σ_o to compute the corresponding supervisor S. Since there is a finite number of such subsets, this brutal-force method will terminate and provide a protected observable alphabet of the minimum size together with the corresponding supervisor, if it exists. The complexity of this brute-force procedure is simply $2^{|\Sigma_o|}$ times of the complexity of Procedure SSA-RS, which is exponential in time with respect to $|G||E|$.

Example 2.5 *We now use that simple single-tank system to illustrate how to determine a minimum protected observable alphabet, which allows the existence of an SSA-robust supervisor. Let $\Sigma_{o,p} = \{q_0{=}0, q_0{=}1, h = H\}$. The model $\hat{K}$ and E are still the same as the supervisor S and requirement E shown in Figure 2.3 and Figure 2.6, respectively. The models of S_a and $G \times S_a \times E \times G_h$, which is isomorphic to $G \times S_a \times E$, are shown in Figure 2.12, where the transition labeled with $(h = H, h = L)$ does not exist, due to the fact that $h = H$ is protected, namely $(h = H, h = L) \notin \Lambda$. Since $G \times S_a \times E \times G_h$ does not contain a marker state, namely, no damage state can be reached, when we run Procedure PSAL, it is clear that there does not exist a*

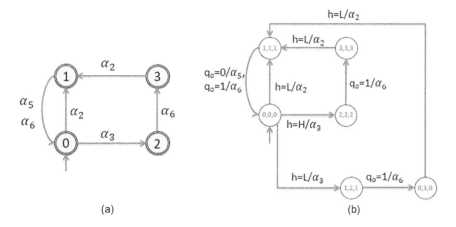

Figure 2.12 Models of $\mathbf{S}_a$ (a) and $\mathbf{G} \times \mathbf{S}_a \times \mathbf{E} \times \mathbf{G}_h$ (b).

subautomaton $\mathbf{D}$ that satisfies the damage infliction property. Thus, PSAL will return an empty solution $\mathbf{D}$, which, by Proposition 2.7, implies that there is no SSA. Thus, Procedure SSA-RS will return S induced from $\hat{K} = \sup\mathcal{CN}(\mathbf{G}, E)$.

In contrast, if we set $h = L$ to be protected instead of $h = H$, the resulting $\mathbf{G} \times \mathbf{S}_a \times \mathbf{E}$ is depicted in Figure 2.13. In this case, there exists an SSA. We can check that the minimum size of any other protected

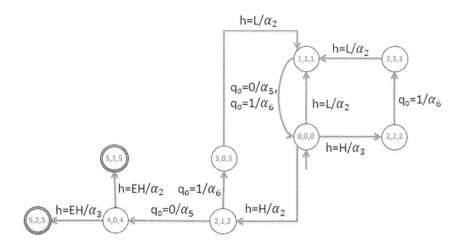

Figure 2.13 Model of $\mathbf{G} \times \mathbf{S}_a \times \mathbf{E} \times \mathbf{G}_h$ with $h = L \in \Sigma_{o,p}$.

observable alphabet containing events $q_o=0$ and $q_o=1$ that renders an SSA-robust supervisor for this example is 3, and the only sensor reading to be protected is $h = H$.

2.5 CONCLUSIONS

So far, we have first introduced the concept of attackability and the concept of smart sensor attack (SSA), upon which we have shown that the supremal SSA exists and computable by Procedure PSAL, as long as the plant model **G** and the supervisor S are finitely representable, i.e., their languages are regular. After that, we have formulated the problem of synthesizing an SSA-robust supervisor, and provided a concrete algorithm of Procedure SSA-RS to solve it. We have also shown that it is possible to find a minimum protected observable sub-alphabet, which may render an SSA-robust supervisor.

It has been shown that the complexity of Procedure SSA-RS is exponential in time, making the SSA-robust supervisor synthesis problem NP-hard, as it is more complex than synthesizing the supremal controllable and normal supervisor, which is NP-hard [48]. How to synthesize an SSA-robust supervisor, not necessarily the supremal one, with a tractable computational complexity will be an interesting topic for future research. For example, if the natural projection P_o happens to be a natural observer [16], then the time complexity of Procedure 2 will be polynomial with respect to $|G||E|$ (and a fixed Σ and n), whose degree may yet still be high for real applications.

CHAPTER 3

Smart Sensor-Actuator Attacks

After introducing sensor attacks previously in Chapter 2, considered as the simplest attacks, we would like to consider an even more challenging scenario for a defender. That is, an attacker is not only able to alter the input of a supervisor via sensor attacks but also to alter the output of the supervisor, i.e., control commands fed to the plant. The latter is called *actuator attack*. An interesting observation is that adding a sensor attack and an actuator attack together is not just $1+1=2$, but rather $1+1>2$, that is, a sensor-actuator attack can induce damage that could never be achieved by simply running a sensor attack and an actuator attack simultaneously and independently. To show this interesting phenomenon, we will first formally introduce the concept of *smart sensor-actuator attack* (SSAA) and show how to analyze the impact of an SSAA on a closed-loop system. After that, we provide a specific method to decide whether a given system permits an SSAA. As a slight extension, we address an attack cost issue by introducing the concept of weighted SSAA. However, to avoid introducing any extra complication due to partial observation, we only consider a full-observation case, when focusing on the attack cost. We hope that the idea could encourage readers to explore more sophisticated scenarios such as minimal-cost SSAA under partial observation. Theoretically speaking, the sensor-actuator attack model introduced in this chapter provides a general attack model, which consumes smart sensor attacks or smart actuator attacks as a special case. By disabling either changes

DOI: 10.1201/9781003333883-4

of control commands or changes of observation events, the model can be used to study smart sensor attacks or actuator attacks, respectively.

3.1 INTRODUCTION

Previously, we have introduced smart sensor attacks, where the key conceptual innovation is to introduce the concept of *smartness* in an attack. Basically, an attack must possess two characteristics: covertness and damage infliction, before it can be considered smart. In case that an attacker is capable of changing each intercepted control command, while still enjoying the sensor attack capability, the resulting attack is called *sensor-actuator attack* (SAA). However, to avoid creating a too powerful attacker, possessing too much knowledge about a target system, we assume that the observation capability of the attacker is lower than the supervisor, that is, the attacker may not be able to see all observations seen by the supervisor, which could better match the reality. Nevertheless, the attacker can compensate the partial loss of observation with the new capability of using intercepted control commands. This essentially creates a more sophisticated observation capability of the attacker. Upon this new scenario setup, following a similar technical treatment, we formulate the concept of *smart sensor-actuator attack* (SSAA), which imposes covertness and damage infliction on SSAA. An SSAA requires a co-design of sensor attack and actuator attack so that, jointly, a damage state can be reached before being detected by the supervisor. Similar to SSA, with a mild assumption we show that the existence of a least restrictive (or supremal) SSAA in a given system is decidable and, this supremal SSAA is computable, if existing. An interesting observation, derived from a small example, is that, in some cases, the covertness can be ensured by an SSA, and damage infliction can be achieved via smart actuator attack - lack of either one will render an unsuccessful SSAA.

To extend the SSAA framework further, considering that any attack move incurs some cost, we consider an SSAA model equipped with an additive cost function that associates each event with a cost. Upon this extra feature, we formulate a weighted SSAA problem that aims to find a least restrictive SSAA that incurs the minimum cost, where the cost of a language is defined as the highest additive cost of string in this language. Basically, besides solving an SSAA problem, we also simultaneously solve a minimum-cost optimal attack synthesis problem. It turns out that the least restrictive (or supremal) minimum-weighted SSAA exists. However, computing it effectively is still a challenge. In this chapter, to avoid any potential complication introduced by partial observation, we assume that all events are observable when dealing with the minimum-cost issue. Readers, who are interested in the partial-observation case, are referred to Ref. [68] for a more comprehensive treatment on this topic. It is worth pointing out that there exists another method introduced in Refs.[63,70,83], which transforms the original optimal attack synthesis problem to an optimal supervisor synthesis problem in order to leverage on existing optimal supervisor synthesis results shown in, e.g., [88–92].

This chapter is organized as follows. In Section 3.2, a language-based sensor-actuator attack framework is introduced to provide an insight into the problem to readers. In Section 3.3, an FSA-based modeling framework is introduced in order to address computation issues, followed by a procedure for the synthesis of supremal smart lean sensor-actuator attacks in Section 3.4. A synthesis procedure for supremal minimum-weighted SSAA is introduced in Section 3.5. Conclusions are drawn in Section 3.6.

3.2 A LANGUAGE FRAMEWORK

In this section, we introduce component models in the supervisory control architecture under sensor-actuator attack, which is shown in Figure 3.1. It consists of two attacks in the control loop, that is, a sensor attack A_s sitting between the plant output and the supervisor input, and an actuator attack A_c sitting between the supervisor output and the plant input. A_s aims to change the input signal of the supervisor and A_c aims for the output signal of the supervisor, i.e., each control command to the plant. This architecture indicates that both A_s and A_c have the same capability of intercepting the plant observable outputs. In reality, this may not always be the case, and an attacker can certainly make observable plant outputs to be sent to A_s and A_c in different ways. In this chapter, we focus on a simple setup to avoid any unnecessary complication when introducing the key attack synthesis ideas. Next, we will first present a language-based framework, followed by a weighted automaton-based realization framework. By doing this,

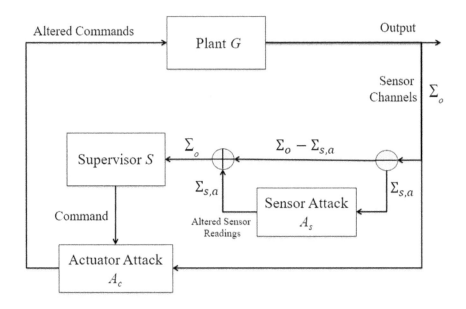

Figure 3.1 Control architecture under sensor-actuator attack.

we hope readers to grasp the essential ideas from the language-based descriptions and then to understand how computation could be carried out via weighted automata.

3.2.1 The Concept of Sensor-Actuator Attack

Given a plant $\mathbf{G}$, let $S : L(\mathbf{G}) \to \Gamma$ be a supervisor, as introduced in Chapters 1 and 2. Assume that $\Sigma_{s,a} \subseteq \Sigma_o$ denotes all observable events that can be changed by an attack, that is, $\Sigma_{s,a} = \Sigma_o \setminus \Sigma_{o,p}$, where $\Sigma_{o,p}$ denotes protected observable events introduced in Chapter 2. Let $\Sigma_{s,a}^\epsilon := \Sigma_{s,a} \cup \{\epsilon\}$. Let $\Sigma_{c,a} \subseteq \Sigma_c$ denote the set of controllable events, whose occurrences can be disabled or enabled by an attack. A *sensor-actuator* attack A consists of two sub-attacks: (1) A sensor attack $A_s : P_o(L(\mathbf{G})) \to 2^{\Sigma_o^*}$, where

- $A_s(\epsilon) = \{\epsilon\}$;

- $(\forall t \in P_o(L(\mathbf{G})))(\forall \sigma \in \Sigma_o) t\sigma \in P_o(L(\mathbf{G})) \Rightarrow A_s(t\sigma) = A_s(t)W$, where $W \subseteq \Sigma_{s,a}^\epsilon$, if $\sigma \in \Sigma_{s,a}$; and $W = \{\sigma\}$, otherwise.

That is, a sensor attack A_s may replace an attackable observable event $\sigma \in \Sigma_{s,a}$ with any event in $\Sigma_{s,a}^\epsilon$, which includes the silent event ϵ, denoting an information blockage by A_s. (2) An actuator attack A_c : $P_o(L(\mathbf{G})) \times \Gamma \to 2^\Gamma$, where for all $t \in P_o(L(\mathbf{G}))$ and for all $\gamma \in \Gamma$,

$$A_c(t, \gamma) \subseteq \{\gamma' \in \Gamma | (\exists W \subseteq \Sigma_{c,a})\gamma' = (\gamma \setminus \Sigma_{c,a}) \cup W\}.$$

That is, an actuator attack A_c may replace each attackable controllable event in a control pattern $\gamma \in \Gamma$ with a subset of attackable controllable events $W \subseteq \Sigma_{c,a}$, and leave other events in γ intact. The definition indicates that A_c can "block" transmission of any control pattern sent by any supervisor S from reaching the plant. It is also possible for A_c to send $\emptyset$ as a control pattern, when $\Sigma_{c,a} = \Sigma$, namely all events are disabled.

The effect of a sensor-actuator attack $A = (A_s, A_c)$ on a given supervisor $S : P_o(L(\mathbf{G})) \to \Gamma$ can be captured by the following (non-deterministic) mapping $S \circ A : P_o(L(\mathbf{G})) \to 2^\Gamma$, where

$$(\forall t \in P_o(L(\mathbf{G})))S \circ A(t) := \{\gamma \in \Gamma | (\exists u \in A_s(t))\gamma \in A_c(t, S(u))\}.$$

If we extend the definition of S to

$$S : 2^{P_o(L(\mathbf{G}))} \to 2^\Gamma : W \mapsto S(W) := \{S(t) \in \Gamma | t \in W\},$$

with $S(\emptyset) := \emptyset$, and the definition of A_c to

$$A_c : P_o(L(\mathbf{G})) \times 2^\Gamma \to 2^\Gamma : (t, U) \mapsto A_c(t, U) := \cup_{\gamma \in U} A_c(t, \gamma),$$

with $A_c(t, \emptyset) := \emptyset$ for all $t \in P_o(L(\mathbf{G}))$, then $S \circ A(t) = A_c(t, S(A_s(t)))$. That is, the sensor attack A_s may non-deterministically replace each intercepted plant observable output $t \in P_o(L(\mathbf{G}))$ into another string $u \in A_s(t)$, which then triggers the supervisor S to generate a control command $S(u)$. The control command $S(u)$ is non-deterministically replaced with another control command by the actuator attack A_c. The above non-determinism is due to non-determinism in the sensor attack A_s and actuator attack A_c. We call $S \circ A$ a *compromised* supervisory control with respect to (S, A). In case that there is no sensor attack, that is, $A_s(t) = \{t\}$ for all $t \in P_o(L(\mathbf{G}))$, the compromised supervisor $S \circ A$ only captured the impact of actuator attack on S. Similarly, when there is no actuator attack, that is, $A_c(t, \gamma) = \{\gamma\}$ for all $t \in P_o(L(\mathbf{G}))$

and $\gamma \in \Gamma$, the compromised supervisor $S \circ A$ only captures the impact of sensor attack.

The closed and marked behaviors of the closed-loop compromised system $S \circ A/\mathbf{G}$, that is, $L(S \circ A/\mathbf{G})$ and $L_m(S \circ A/\mathbf{G})$, are defined as follows:

1. $\epsilon \in L(S \circ A/\mathbf{G})$;

2. For all $t \in L(S \circ A/\mathbf{G})$ and $\sigma \in \Sigma$,

$$t\sigma \in L(\mathbf{G}) \wedge (\exists \gamma \in S \circ A(P_o(t)))\sigma \in \gamma \Rightarrow t\sigma \in L(S \circ A/\mathbf{G}),$$

3. All strings in $L(S \circ A/\mathbf{G})$ are generated in Steps (1) and (2),

4. $L_m(L(S \circ A/\mathbf{G})) = L(S \circ A/\mathbf{G}) \cap L_m(\mathbf{G})$.

Example 3.1 *We use an example to illustrate the concepts introduced above. Figure 3.2 depicts the plant $\mathbf{G}$ and the supervisor S, where $\Sigma = \Sigma_o = \Sigma_c = \{a, b, c, d\}$. One sensor-actuator attack $A = (A_s, A_c)$ is depicted in Figure 3.3, where the sensor attack A_s replaces the observable event a with event b and keeps others intact, while the actuator attack A_c replaces the control command $\{d\}$ with command $\{c\}$, regardless of what observable output of the plant is received. Please be reminded that both sensor and actuator attacks are defined over states, meaning that the same event appearing at different states may*

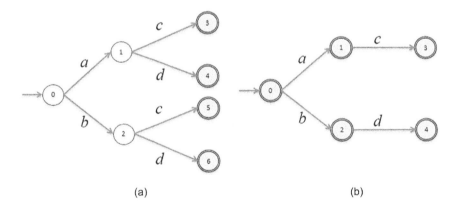

(a) (b)

Figure 3.2 The plant $\mathbf{G}$ (a) and supervisor S (b).

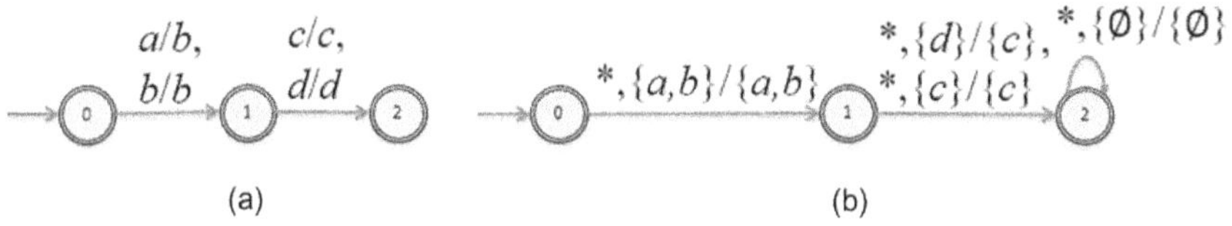

a/b,   c/c,
b/b   d/d

*,{d}/{c},   *,{∅}/{∅}
*,{a,b}/{a,b}   *,{c}/{c}

(a)   (b)

Figure 3.3 Sensor attack A_s (a) and actuator attack A_c (b).

*result in different attack moves. The final closed-loop compromised system model is depicted in Figure 3.4, which is derived in the following way: Here, we use automata to model each component, aiming to illustrate that the previously introduced concepts are indeed computable, even though the formal definition of the computation framework will be introduced later. Initially, the plant **G** is at the initial state 0. The observable output is ϵ, resulting in the output of A_s to be ϵ, namely the sensor attack model stays at the initial state 0. The supervisor S is at the initial state 0 and will not make a state change, due to the lack of observable input from A_s. However, S produces an initial control command $S(\epsilon) = \{a, b\}$, which triggers the actuator attack A_c to make a move to state 1 after receiving the control command $\{a, b\}$ from S. From a state transition point of view, the closed-loop system moves from the initial state 0000, where the first entry refers to the plant state, the second entry for the sensor attack state, the third entry for the supervisor state and the last entry for the actuator state, to state 0001, after firing the compound event $(\epsilon, \{a, b\})/(\epsilon, \{a, b\})$, where the first tuple $(\epsilon, \{a, b\})$ denotes the output of the plant **G** is currently ϵ and the resulting control command from S is $\{a, b\}$, and the second tuple $(\epsilon, \{a, b\})$ refers that the output of the sensor attack is ϵ and the output of the actuator attack is $\{a, b\}$. After the (compromised) control command $\{a, b\}$ is received by **G**, either event a or event b may (non-deterministically) occur. If a occurs, then **G** moves to state 1. Since a*

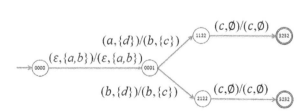

Figure 3.4 The closed-loop compromised system $S \circ A/\mathbf{G}$.

*is observable, A_s changes it to b and moves to state 1. The supervisor receives b from A_s and moves to state 2, after that, generates the control command $\{d\}$. The actuator attack A_c receives the command $\{d\}$ from S, changes to $\{c\}$ and forward it to the plant **G**, and after that, moves to state 2. Thus, the closed-loop system makes a state transition from 0001 to 1122, via the compound event $(a, \{d\})/(b, \{c\})$. After the control command $\{c\}$ is received by **G**, it changes its state to 3. The sensor attack A_s receives event c and relies on it to S, and moves to state 2. The supervisor S receives event c, moves to state 3, and generates the control command $\emptyset$. The actuator attack A_c receives the command $\emptyset$ and relays it to the plant **G** and keeps the current state 2. Thus, the closed-loop system makes a state transition from 1122 to 3232, via the compound event $(c, \emptyset)/(c, \emptyset)$. Other transitions in $S \circ A/$**G** are constructed in a similar manner. We can clearly see that, under the sensor-actuator attack A, the illegal behavior bc appears, which is not allowed by S in the original unattacked system.*

3.2.2 The Concept of Smart Sensor-Actuator Attack

Although a sensor-actuator attack A can be arbitrary, it is always desirable for an attack to be covert to the supervisor until irreversible damage is about to occur. To capture this idea, we follow the same spirit shown in Chapter 2 and introduce the concept of smart sensor-actuator attack.

Definition 3.1 A given closed loop system $(\mathbf{G}, S)$ is *attackable* if there exists a non-empty sensor-actuator attack $A = (A_s, A_c)$ such that the following properties hold:

1. **Covertness**: Attack moves by A must be covert to S, i.e.,

$$A_s(P_o(L(\mathbf{G}))) \subseteq P_o(L(S/\mathbf{G})), \tag{3.1}$$

   namely the supervisor will not see any unexpected observations from A.

2. **Damage infliction**: Let $L_{\mathrm{dam}} \subseteq L(\mathbf{G})$ be a damage language. Either one of the following properties hold:

   • Strong Damage Infliction (SDI)

$$L(S \circ A/\mathbf{G}) = \overline{L(S \circ A/\mathbf{G}) \cap L_{\mathrm{dam}}}, \tag{3.2}$$

namely A will cause $\mathbf{G}$ to generate forbidden behaviors eventually.

- Weak Damage Infliction (WDI)

$$L(S \circ A/\mathbf{G}) \cap L_{\text{dam}} \neq \emptyset, \tag{3.3}$$

namely A will sometimes cause $\mathbf{G}$ to generate forbidden behaviors.

A is a *Smart Sensor-Actuator Attack* of $(\mathbf{G}, S)$ with respect to L_{dam}. □

Given two sensor attacks $A_{s,1}$ and $A_{s,2}$ of a plant $\mathbf{G}$ with respect to $\Sigma_{s,a}$, let $A_{s,1} \cup A_{s,2}$ denote the join of two mappings, i.e., for all $t \in P_o(L(\mathbf{G}))$, $A_{s,1} \cup A_{s,2}(t) := A_{s,1}(t) \cup A_{s,2}(t)$. Similarly, given two actuator attacks $A_{c,1}$ and $A_{c,2}$ of a plant $\mathbf{G}$ with respect to $\Sigma_{c,a}$, let $A_{c,1} \cup A_{c,2}$ denote the join of two mappings, i.e., for all $t \in P_o(L(\mathbf{G}))$ and $\gamma \in \Gamma$, $A_{c,1} \cup A_{c,2}(t, \gamma) := A_{c,1}(t, \gamma) \cup A_{c,2}(t, \gamma)$. Given two sensor-actuator attacks $A_1 = (A_{s,1}, A_{c,1})$ and $A_2 = (A_{s,2}, A_{c,2})$, let $A_1 \uplus A_2 = (A_s, A_c)$ be the join of A_1 and A_2, where for all $t \in P_o(L(\mathbf{G}))$ and for all supervisor S of $\mathbf{G}$, $S \circ (A_1 \uplus A_2)(t) := (S \circ A_1(t)) \cup (S \circ A_2(t))$, $A_s(t) \subseteq A_{s,1} \cup A_{s,2}(t)$ and $A_c(t, \gamma) \subseteq A_{c,1} \cup A_{c,2}(t, \gamma)$ for all $\gamma \in \Gamma$. Basically, when $A_1 \uplus A_2$ is applied, at each stage of attack, only one sensor-actuator is applied, and it is not allowed to combine the sensor attack of one sensor-actuator attack and the actuator attack of the other sensor-actuator attack.

Proposition 3.1 Given a set of sensor-actuator attacks $\{A_i = (A_{s,i}, A_{c,i}) | i \in I\}$ of a plant $\mathbf{G}$, where I is a (possibly infinite) index set, for any supervisor S of $\mathbf{G}$ and for each $t \in P_o(L(\mathbf{G}))$, $S \circ (\uplus_{i \in I} A_i)(t) = \cup_{i \in I} S \circ A_i(t)$.

Proof *We use induction. Clearly, it holds for I with $|I| = 1$ and $|I| = 2$. Assume that it also holds for I with $|I| \leq n$. We now consider I with $|I| = n + 1$. For all $t \in P_o(L(\mathbf{G}))$,*

$$\begin{aligned}
S \circ (\uplus_{i \in I} A_i)(t) &= S \circ ((\uplus_{i \in I \setminus \{j\}} A_i) \uplus A_j)(t) \\
&= S \circ (\uplus_{i \in I \setminus \{j\}} A_i)(t) \cup S \circ A_j(t) \\
&= \cup_{i \in I \setminus \{j\}} S \circ A_i(t) \cup S \circ A_j(t) \\
&= \cup_{i \in I} S \circ A_i(t)
\end{aligned}$$

The proposition follows. ■

Definition 3.2 A sensor-actuator attack A of a plant $\mathbf{G}$ and a supervisor S is called *lean* with respect to $(\mathbf{G}, S)$ if for all $t \in L(\mathbf{G})$, $S \circ A(P_o(t)) \neq \emptyset$ implies that $t \in L(S \circ A/\mathbf{G})$. □

A lean sensor-actuator attack A essentially stops all control commands triggered by any string t outside the compromised behavior $L(S \circ A/\mathbf{G})$. In reality, any string outside $L(S \circ A/\mathbf{G})$ will not trigger the supervisor S to issue a control command. Thus, it is natural that $S \circ A(P_o(t)) = \emptyset$. Thus, the concept of lean sensor-actuator attack does not impose any practical constraint on the framework, which however has some theoretical needs shown below.

Proposition 3.2 Given a (possibly infinite) set of lean sensor-actuator attacks $\{A_i | i \in I\}$ of a plant $\mathbf{G}$, for any supervisor S of $\mathbf{G}$, we have $L(S \circ (\uplus_{i \in I} A_i)/\mathbf{G}) = \cup_{i \in I} L(S \circ A_i/\mathbf{G})$.

Proof *We use proof of induction. Base Step: clearly, $\epsilon \in L(S \circ (\uplus_{i \in I} A_i)/\mathbf{G})$. Hypothesis Step: assume that for all strings $t \in \Sigma^*$ with $|t| \leq n$, we have $t \in L(S \circ (\uplus_{i \in I} A_i)/\mathbf{G})$ if and only if $t \in \cup_{i \in I} L(S \circ A_i/\mathbf{G})$. We now show the Induction Step. Let $t \in \Sigma^*$ with $|t| = n + 1$. Clearly, there exist $t' \in \Sigma^*$ with $|t'| = n$ and $\sigma \in \Sigma$ such that $t = t'\sigma$.*

$$t'\sigma \in L(S \circ (\uplus_{i \in I} A_1)/\mathbf{G})$$
$$\Longleftrightarrow t' \in L(S \circ (\uplus_{i \in I} A_i)/\mathbf{G}) \land \sigma \in \gamma \in S \circ (\uplus_{i \in I} A_i)(t') \land t'\sigma \in L(\mathbf{G})$$
$$\Longleftrightarrow t' \in \cup_{i \in I} L(S \circ A_i/\mathbf{G}) \land \sigma \in \gamma \in \cup_{i \in I} S \circ A_i(P_o(t')) \land t'\sigma \in L(\mathbf{G})$$
$$\Longleftrightarrow t' \in \vee_{i \in I}[L(S \circ A_i/\mathbf{G}) \land \sigma \in \gamma \in S \circ A_1(P_o(t')) \land t'\sigma \in L(\mathbf{G})]$$
$$\Longleftrightarrow t'\sigma \in \vee_{i \in I} L(S \circ A_i/\mathbf{G})$$
$$\Longleftrightarrow t'\sigma \in \cup_{i \in I} L(S \circ A_i/\mathbf{G})$$

The proposition follows. ■

Theorem 3.1 Given a plant $\mathbf{G}$ and a supervisor S, let $\{A_i | i \in I\}$ be a (possibly infinite) collection of smart and lean sensor-actuator attacks with respect to $(\mathbf{G}, S)$ and a damage language $L_{\text{dam}} \subseteq L(\mathbf{G})$. Then $A := \uplus_{i \in I} A_i$ satisfies properties (1) and (2).

Proof *Assume that each A_i $(i \in I)$ satisfies properties of covertness and strong or weak damage infliction. We will show that the join of* all smart lean sensor-actuator attacks $A := \uplus_{i \in I} A_i = (A_s, A_c)$ also satisfies those properties.

To show the validity of the covertness property, we have

$$\begin{aligned}
A_s(P_o(L(\mathbf{G}))) &\subseteq (\cup_{i \in I} A_{s,i})(P_o(L(\mathbf{G}))) \\
&= \cup_{i \in I} A_{s,i}(P_o(L(\mathbf{G}))) \\
&\subseteq \cup_{i \in I} P_o(L(S/\mathbf{G})) \\
&= P_o(L(S/\mathbf{G}))
\end{aligned}$$

Next, to show the validity of the strong damage infliction property, we have

$$\begin{aligned}
L(S \circ A/\mathbf{G}) &= L(S \circ (\uplus_{i \in I} A_i)/\mathbf{G}) \\
&= \cup_{i \in I} L(S \circ A_i/\mathbf{G}) \\
&= \cup_{i \in I} \overline{L(S \circ A_i/\mathbf{G}) \cap L_{dam}} \\
&= \overline{\cup_{i \in I} L(S \circ A_i/\mathbf{G}) \cap L_{dam}} \\
&= \overline{L(S \circ (\uplus_{i \in I} A_i)/\mathbf{G}) \cap L_{dam}} \\
&= \overline{L(S \circ A/\mathbf{G}) \cap L_{dam}}
\end{aligned}$$

To show the validity of the weak damage infliction property, we have

$$\begin{aligned}
L(S \circ A/\mathbf{G}) \cap L_{dam} &= L(S \circ (\uplus_{i \in I} A_i)/\mathbf{G}) \cap L_{dam} \\
&= (\cup_{i \in I} L(S \circ A_i/\mathbf{G})) \cap L_{dam} \\
&\neq \emptyset
\end{aligned}$$

This completes the proof of the theorem. ■

We introduce a binary relation $\preceq$ over the set of all smart lean sensor-actuator attacks of $(\mathbf{G}, S)$ with respect to L_{dam}, denoted as $\mathcal{A}(\mathbf{G}, S, L_{\text{dam}})$, where for any $A_1, A_2 \in \mathcal{A}(\mathbf{G}, S, L_{\text{dam}})$,

$$A_1 \preceq A_2 \iff L(S \circ A_1/\mathbf{G}) \subseteq L(S \circ A_2/\mathbf{G}).$$

Let $A_{\text{sup}} = \uplus_{A \in \mathcal{A}(\mathbf{G}, S, L_{\text{dam}})} A$. It is clear that $A \preceq A_{\text{sup}}$ for all $A \in \mathcal{A}(\mathbf{G}, S, L_{\text{dam}})$. By Theorem 3.1, we know that A_{sup} is also a smart lean sensor-actuator attack, namely $A_{\text{sup}} \in \mathcal{A}(\mathbf{G}, S, L_{\text{dam}})$. We call A_{sup} the supremal smart lean sensor-actuator attack of the closed-loop system $(\mathbf{G}, S, L_{\text{dam}})$.

3.2.3   Weighted Sensor-Actuator Attack

To consider additive costs, such as energy consumption and financial expenses, associated with a sensor-actuator attack, we can introduce weights to the attack model A or the plant $\mathbf{G}$. To simplify the subsequent analysis, we choose to associate weights to the plant $\mathbf{G}$ so that the costs are invariant with respect to possible different attacks. However, the framework can be extended to scenarios, where each attack may have a different cost scheme – in this case, we simply update the plant weight setting accordingly.

Given a weighted plant $(\mathbf{G}, f)$, where $f : X \times \Sigma \to \mathbb{R}^+ \cup \{\infty\}$, we replace f with an induced function $h_f : L(\mathbf{G}) \to \mathbb{R}^+ \cup \{\infty\}$ to facilitate a language-based analysis, where

- $h_f(\epsilon) := 0$;

- $(\forall s \in L(\mathbf{G}))(\forall \sigma \in \Sigma)h_f(s\sigma) := h_f(s) + f(\xi(x_0, s), \sigma)$.

Basically, $h_f(s)$ for $s \in L(\mathbf{G})$ denotes the total cost incurred by firing s in $\mathbf{G}$.

Given a smart sensor-actuator attack A with respect to $(\mathbf{G}, S, L_{\text{dam}})$, the resulting attack cost is determined by

$$\Theta(L(S \circ A/\mathbf{G})) := \max_{t \in L(S \circ A/\mathbf{G})} h_f(t).$$

Let $\mathcal{WA}(\mathbf{G}, S, L_{\text{dam}}) := \{A \in \mathcal{A}(\mathbf{G}, S, L_{\text{dam}}) | \Theta(L(S \circ A/\mathbf{G})) < \infty\}$ be the collection of all finitely weighted smart sensor-actuator attacks with respect to $(\mathbf{G}, S, L_{\text{dam}})$.

Proposition 3.3 There exists $A_* \in \mathcal{WA}(\mathbf{G}, S, L_{\text{dam}})$ such that the following properties hold:

1. $(\forall A \in \mathcal{WA}(\mathbf{G}, S, L_{\text{dam}}))\Theta(L(S \circ A_*/\mathbf{G})) \leq \Theta(L(S \circ A/\mathbf{G}))$,

2. $(\forall A \in \mathcal{WA}(\mathbf{G}, S, L_{\text{dam}}))\Theta(L(S \circ A_*/\mathbf{G})) = \Theta(L(S \circ A/\mathbf{G})) \Rightarrow A \preceq A_*$.

Proof *We can order all elements in $\mathcal{WA}(\mathbf{G}, S, L_{dam})$ based on their weights. Clearly, the resulting partial order is a total order. Thus, the set of minimum weighted sensor-actuator attacks, denoted* *as $\mathcal{MWA}(G, S, L_{dam})$ is nonempty, as long as $\mathcal{WA}(G, S, L_{dam})$ is nonempty. Let*

$$A_* := \biguplus_{A \in \mathcal{MWA}(G,S,L_{dam})} A.$$

By the proof of Theorem 3.1, we know that $A_* \in \mathcal{A}(G, S, L_{dam})$. In addition,

$$
\begin{aligned}
\Theta(L(S \circ A_*/G)) &= \Theta(\cup_{A \in \mathcal{MWA}(G,S,L_{dam})} L(S \circ A/G)) \\
&= \max_{t \in \cup_{A \in \mathcal{MWA}(G,S,L_{dam})} L(S \circ A/G)} h_f(t) \\
&= \max_{A \in \mathcal{MWA}(G,S,L_{dam})} \max_{t \in L(S \circ A/G)} h_f(t) \\
&= \max_{t \in L(S \circ A/G)} h_f(t) \ \forall A \in \mathcal{MWA}(G, S, L_{dam})
\end{aligned}
$$

This means that A_* has the minimum cost, thus, $A_* \in \mathcal{MWA}(G, S, L_{dam})$. Clearly, for all $A \in \mathcal{MWA}(G, S, L_{dam})$, we have $A \preceq A_*$, which completes the proof. ■

We call A_* in Proposition 3.3 the *supremal minimum weighted smart sensor-actuator attack* of (G, S, L_{dam}), denoted as $\sup\mathcal{MWA}$ (G, S, L_{dam}).

Problem 3.1 *Given a closed-loop weighted system (G, S) and a damage language $L_{dam} \subseteq L(G)$, decide whether $\mathcal{WA}(G, S, L_{dam}) \neq \emptyset$. In case yes, compute $\sup\mathcal{MWA}(G, S, L_{dam})$.*

To solve Problem 3.1, we introduce a weighted finite-state automaton framework, which provides a glimpse on how computation may be carried out to derive a solution to the problem.

3.3 AN FSA-BASED MODELING FRAMEWORK

The plant is modeled by a weighted FSA $(G = (X, \Sigma, \xi, x_0, X_m), f)$, which is introduced previously. We assume that the supervisor S is described by an FSA $S = (Z, \Sigma, \delta, z_0, Z_m)$, where for each $t \in L(G)$, we have

1. $En_S(\delta(z_0, t)) = S(P_o(t))$,

2. $(\forall t, t' \in L(G)) P_o(t) = P_o(t') \Rightarrow \delta(z_0, t) = \delta(z_0, t')$.

Basically, each control pattern in $S(P_o(L(G)))$ is called an *effective control pattern* of S (or $\mathbf{S}$) with respect to G.

Example 3.2 *Consider the plant **G** and supervisor **S** shown in Figure 3.5, where $\Sigma = \Sigma_o = \{a, b, c, d, e\}$. $\Sigma_c = \{a, c, d, e\}$. State 8 in **G** is a damage state, namely $L_{dam} = L_m(\mathbf{G})$. It can be checked that **G** would not reach the damage state under the control of **S**. In addition, according to the structure of **S**, the set of all "effective" control patterns is $\Gamma = \{\{b\}, \{b, d\}, \{b, e\}, \{a, b, c\}\}$.*

After the supervisor **S** sends out a control command (or pattern), the command will pass through a command channel before reaching the plant **G**. It is possible that an actuator attack A_c can intercept the command and change its attackable content, namely enabling or disabling those events in $\Sigma_{c,a}$, and then send the compromised command to the plant **G**. Next, we describe how to capture such an actuator attack in automata.

Let $\mathbf{A}_c = (W, \Sigma_o^\epsilon \times \Gamma \times \Gamma, \iota, w_0, W_m = Q)$ be a transducer, where for all $w \in W$ and for all $(\sigma, \gamma, \gamma') \in \Sigma_o^\epsilon \times \Gamma \times \Gamma$,

$$\iota(w, \sigma, \gamma, \gamma')! \Rightarrow \gamma' \in \{(\gamma \setminus \Sigma_{c,a}) \cup W | W \subseteq \Sigma_{c,a}\},$$

namely the actuator attack $\mathbf{A}_c$ change a control command γ into γ' by enabling or disabling attackable events in $\Sigma_{c,a}$ at state q. This model allows multiple attack moves for each received control command, namely at each state q there can be more than one γ' to be associated with a received γ. This is a non-deterministic actuator attack model, allowing us to discuss the issue of the least restrictive actuator attack. However, if we restrict each control command γ to be associated with a unique attack move γ', we can use the same model to describe a deterministic actuator attack.

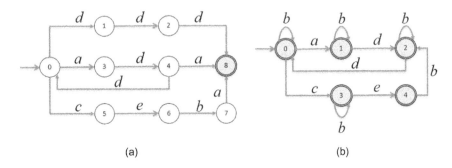

(a) (b)

Figure 3.5 Plant **G** (a) and supervisor **S** (b).

As for a sensor attack, we follow the same model as described in Chapter 2, where $\mathbf{A}_s = (Y, \Sigma_o^\epsilon \times \Sigma_o^\epsilon, \eta, y_0, Y_m = Y)$ with the partial transition mapping $\eta : Y \times \Sigma_o^\epsilon \times \Sigma_o^\epsilon \to Y$,

1. $(\forall y \in Y)(\forall (\epsilon, \sigma) \in \Sigma_o^\epsilon \times \Sigma_o^\epsilon) \eta(y, \epsilon, \sigma)! \Rightarrow \sigma = \epsilon$,

2. $(\forall y \in Y)(\forall (\sigma, \sigma') \in \Sigma_o^\epsilon \times \Sigma_o^\epsilon) \eta(y, \sigma, \sigma')! \wedge \sigma \neq \sigma' \Rightarrow \sigma \in \Sigma_{s,a} \wedge \sigma' \in \Sigma_{s,a}^\epsilon$.

The sensor attack model $\mathbf{A}_s$ describes that the attack will make a move only after receiving an observable output from the plant $\mathbf{G}$ (specified by Property (1)), and the attack can change an observable output σ only when σ is attackable, namely $\sigma \in \Sigma_{s,a}$, and the resulting event is either another observable event $\sigma' \in \Sigma_{s,a}$ or a silent event ϵ.

The impact of a sensor-actuator attack $A = (\mathbf{A}_s, \mathbf{A}_c)$ on a closed-loop system $(\mathbf{G}, \mathbf{S})$ is captured by the composition $\mathbf{G} \times \mathbf{S} \times \mathbf{A}_s \times \mathbf{A}_c = (Q, \Sigma \times \Sigma_o^\epsilon \times \Gamma, \kappa, q_0, Q_m)$, where

1. $Q = X \times Y \times Z \times W$, $Q_m = X_m \times Y_m \times Z_m \times W_m$, $q_0 = (x_0, y_0, z_0, w_0)$,

2. For all $q = (x, y, z, w), q' = (x', y', z', w') \in Q$ and $(\sigma, \sigma', \gamma) \in \Sigma \times \Sigma_o^\epsilon \times \Gamma$,

$$
\kappa(q, \sigma, \sigma', \gamma) = \begin{cases} (x', y', z', w') & \text{if } \sigma \in \gamma \wedge \xi(x, \sigma) = x' \wedge \\ & \eta(y, P_o(\sigma), \sigma') = y' \wedge \delta(z, \sigma') = z' \wedge \\ & \iota(w, P_o(\sigma), En_{\mathbf{S}}(z), \gamma) = w' \\ \text{undefined} & \text{otherwise.} \end{cases}
$$

Basically, in the tuple $(\sigma, \sigma', \gamma)$ at the state $q = (x, y, z, w)$, the first event σ denotes the output of the plant $\mathbf{G}$, which must be (non-deterministically) chosen from the "fake" control command γ generated by the actuator attack $\mathbf{A}_c$. This fake control command γ is triggered by the plant observable output $P_o(\sigma)$ and the true control command $En_{\mathbf{S}}(z)$ generated by the supervisor $\mathbf{S}$. The supervisor $\mathbf{S}$ will update its state after taking the "fake" observable event σ' generated by the sensor attack $\mathbf{A}_s$ upon the reception of the true observable output $P_o(\sigma)$ by $\mathbf{A}_s$ from the plant $\mathbf{G}$.

Example 3.3 *To illustrate the aforementioned concepts, we continue Example 3.2, where $\Sigma_{s,a} = \{a, d\}$ and $\Sigma_{c,a} = \{a, d\}$. One sensor-actuator attack model is depicted in Figure 3.6. In this model, the*

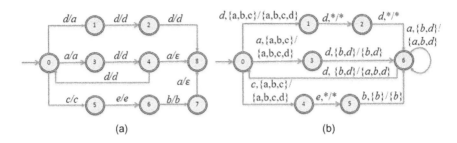

Figure 3.6 Sensor attack $\mathbf{A}_s$ (a) and actuator attack $\mathbf{A}_c$ (b).

actuator attack $\mathbf{A}_c$ changes the initial control command $S(\epsilon) = En_S(0) = \{a, b, c\}$ into a "fake" control command $\{a, b, c, d\}$, and later at state 3 and state 5 it changes the control command $\{b, d\}$ into a "fake" control command $\{a, b, d\}$. For all other control commands, $\mathbf{A}_c$ does not make any change. The sensor attack $\mathbf{A}_s$ makes three attack moves, namely at state 0, if event d is received, it will change it into event a; and at states 4 and 7, if event a is received, it will change it into a silent event ϵ. For any other received observable event, $\mathbf{A}_s$ does not make any change. The outcome of the composition $\mathbf{G} \times \mathbf{S} \times \mathbf{A}_s \times \mathbf{A}_c$ is depicted in Figure 3.7. We can check that the sensor-actuator attack successfully makes the damage state 8 in the plant $\mathbf{G}$ become accessible. It is interesting to see that, without using the actuator attack $\mathbf{A}_c$, it is impossible for any sensor attack alone to achieve the attack goal. On the other hand, without using the sensor attack $\mathbf{A}_s$, any actuator attack will not achieve the attack goal without being detected by the supervisor.

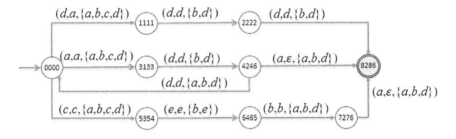

Figure 3.7 Composition $\mathbf{G} \times \mathbf{S} \times \mathbf{A}_s \times \mathbf{A}_c$.

3.4   SUPREMAL SMART LEAN SENSOR-ACTUATOR ATTACK

By Theorem 3.1, we know that the supremal smart lean sensor-actuator attack of a closed-loop system $(\mathbf{G}, \mathbf{S})$ with respect to a damage language L_{dam} exists, as long as there exists at least one smart lean sensor-actuator attack. In this section, we describe how to decide the existence of a smart lean sensor-actuator attack, upon which, to compute the supremal one, in case it exists.

Given a plant $\mathbf{G}$ and a damage language $L_{\mathrm{dam}} \subseteq L(\mathbf{G})$, it is always possible to adjust the marker states of $\mathbf{G}$ so that $L_m(\mathbf{G}) = L_{\mathrm{dam}}$. In this chapter, to simplify our discussion, we assume that the marked behavior of the plant $\mathbf{G}$ is the damage language. In practical applications, if there are other specifications, we can always apply the standard Ramadge-Wonham supervisor synthesis method to compute the supremal nonblocking controllable and normal sublanguage (or maximally nonblocking controllable and observable sublanguage) and treat the prefix closure of this resulting sublanguage as the closed behavior of the plant. After that, we can impose the marked behavior of this newly derived plant as the damage language. In this way, the synthesis framework that we are going to develop in this section will be applicable to a general problem setup, where other behavioral requirements, other than the damage language, can be handled.

Given a closed-loop system $(\mathbf{G}, \mathbf{S})$, let $\mathbf{A}_s^0 = (Y, \Sigma_o^\epsilon \times \Sigma_o^\epsilon, \eta^0, y_0, Y_m = Y)$ be a singleton-state FSA of a sensor attack, namely $Y = \{y_0\}$, where

$$\eta^0(y_0, \sigma, \sigma') = y_0 \iff [\sigma \neq \sigma' \Rightarrow \sigma \in \Sigma_{s,a} \wedge \sigma' \in \Sigma_{s,a}^\epsilon],$$

namely all possible sensor attack moves are allowed by $\mathbf{A}_s^0$. Similarly, let $\mathbf{A}_c^0 = (W, \Sigma_o^\epsilon \times \Gamma \times \Gamma, \iota^0, w_0, W_m = Q)$ be a singleton-state FSA of an actuator attack, where

$$\iota^0(w_0, \sigma, \gamma, \gamma') = w_0 \iff \gamma' \in \{(\gamma \setminus \Sigma_{c,a}) \cup W | W \subseteq \Sigma_{c,a}\},$$

namely all possible actuator attack moves are allowed by $\mathbf{A}_c^0$.

We compute the composition of $\mathbf{G}_a := \mathbf{G} \times \mathbf{S} \times \mathbf{A}_s^0 \times \mathbf{A}_c^0 = (Q, \Sigma \times \Sigma_o^\epsilon \times \Gamma, \kappa^0, q_0, Q_m)$. For notation simplicity, let $\Omega = \Sigma \times \Sigma_o^\epsilon \times \Gamma$. When we talk about a specific control command γ, we use $\Omega(\gamma)$ to denote $\Sigma \times \Sigma_o^\epsilon \times \{\gamma\}$. Occasionally, we write $\Omega(\sigma, \gamma)$ to denote $\{\sigma\} \times \Sigma_o^\epsilon \times \{\gamma\}$. Because all attack moves can be enabled or disabled by the attack, we consider compound events in $\Omega_c := \{(\sigma, \sigma', \gamma) \in \Sigma \times \Sigma_o^\epsilon \times \Gamma | \sigma \in \Sigma_{s,a} \wedge \sigma' \in \Sigma_{s,a}^\epsilon \vee \Sigma_{c,a} \neq \varnothing\}$ as being *controllable*, or more precisely, *disableable*, namely their occurrences can be disabled. In other words, a compound event $(\sigma, \sigma', \gamma)$ is controllable if either σ is an attackable observable event and the resulting fake observable event σ' is in $\Sigma_{s,a}^\epsilon$ or there is at least one attackable controllable event - in the former case, by changing event σ', we can disable the original compound event $(\sigma, \sigma', \gamma)$; and in the latter case, by changing control command γ via adding or removing some event(s) in $\Sigma_{c,a}$, we can disable the compound event. Similarly, we consider compound events in $\Omega_o := \Sigma_o \times \Sigma_o^\epsilon \times \Gamma$ to be *observable*. Let

$$\Psi_1 : \Omega^* \to \Sigma^* : t = (\sigma_1, \sigma_1', \gamma_1) \dots (\sigma_n, \sigma_n', \gamma_n) \mapsto \Psi_1(t) = \sigma_1 \dots \sigma_n,$$

with $\Psi_1(\epsilon) := \epsilon$, and

$$\Psi_2 : \Omega^* \to (\Sigma_o^\epsilon)^* : t = (\sigma_1, \sigma_1', \gamma_1) \dots (\sigma_n, \sigma_n', \gamma_n) \mapsto \Psi_2(t) = \sigma_1' \dots \sigma_n',$$

with $\Psi_2(\epsilon) := \epsilon$, and

$$\Psi_3 : \Omega^* \to \Gamma^* : t = (\sigma_1, \sigma_1', \gamma_1) \dots (\sigma_n, \sigma_n', \gamma_n) \mapsto \Psi_3(t) = \gamma_n,$$

with $\Psi_3(\epsilon) := \epsilon$. The domains of Ψ_i $(i = 1, 2, 3)$ can be extended to 2^{Ω^*} in a usual manner, namely

$$(\forall L \subseteq \Omega^*) \Psi_i(L) := \cup_{\mu \in L} \Psi_i(\mu).$$

Definition 3.3 Let $\mathbf{G}_a := \mathbf{G} \times \mathbf{S} \times \mathbf{A}_s^0 \times \mathbf{A}_c^0$. A prefix-closed sub-language $L_a \subseteq L(\mathbf{G}_a)$ is *(strong or weak) attack feasible* if the following hold:

1. L_a is controllable with respect to $L(\mathbf{G}_a)$ and $\Omega_{uc} = \Omega \backslash \Omega_c$, namely

$$L_a \Omega_{uc} \cap L(\mathbf{G}_a) \subseteq L_a.$$

2. L_a is observable with respect to $L(\mathbf{G}_a)$ and $P_o \circ \Psi_1$, namely for all $t \in L_a$, $t' \in L(\mathbf{G}_a)$, and for all $\sigma, \hat{\sigma} \in \Sigma^\epsilon$ and $(\sigma', \gamma) \in \Sigma_o^\epsilon \times \Gamma$,

$$P_o(\Psi_1(t)\sigma) = P_o(\Psi_1(t')\sigma') \wedge t(\sigma, \sigma', \gamma) \in L_a \wedge$$
$$\Psi_1(t')\hat{\sigma} \in \Psi_1(L(\mathbf{G}_a)) \Rightarrow t'(\hat{\sigma}, \sigma', \gamma) \in L_a.$$

3. (strong attack) $\overline{L_a \cap \Psi_1^{-1}(L_m(\mathbf{G}))} = L_a$,
   (weak attack) $L_a \cap \Psi_1^{-1}(L_m(\mathbf{G})) \neq \varnothing$.

4. L_a is control-integrity preserved, that is, for all $t \in L_a$ and $u \in \Omega$,

$$tu \in L_a \Rightarrow \Psi_1(En_{L_a}(t) \cap \Omega(\Psi_3(u))) = En_{\mathbf{G}}(\xi(x_0, \Psi_1(t))) \cap \Psi_3(u).$$

$\square$

That is, a sub-language L_a is attack feasible if, firstly, it does not block any feasible "uncontrollable" compound event, which permits neither a sensor attack nor an actuator attack; secondly, for any strings $t, t' \in L_a$ observably identical, i.e., $P_o(\Psi_1(t)) = P_o(\Psi_1(t'))$, any attack move feasible for t, i.e., $tu \in L_a$, must also be feasible for t', i.e., $t'u \in L_a$. Thirdly, it induces either a strong attack or a weak one; and lastly, any "fake" control command γ generated by an actuator attack, i.e., $\gamma = \Psi_3(u)$ for some $u \in En_{L_a}(t)$ and $t \in L_a$, will behave like a real control command, that is, any event σ allowed by the plant $\mathbf{G}$ and γ, i.e., $\sigma \in En_{\mathbf{G}}(\xi(x_0, \Psi(t))) \cap \gamma$, should not be blocked by L_a, i.e., there must exist $u' \in En_{L_a}(t))$ such that $\sigma = \Psi_1(u')^{\uparrow}$. For notation simplicity, for each $\gamma \in \Gamma$, let $L_a(\gamma) := L_a \cap \Omega^* \Omega(\gamma)$, namely all strings in L_a with γ being the last "fake" control command.

Theorem 3.2 Given a closed-loop system $(\mathbf{G}, S)$, where S is realized by $\mathbf{S}$, let $L_a \subseteq L(\mathbf{G}_a)$ be nonempty and (strong or weak) attack feasible. Let $A_s : P_o(L(\mathbf{G})) \to 2^{\Sigma_o^*}$, where for all $t \in P_o(L(\mathbf{G}))$,

$$A_s(t) := \begin{cases} \Psi_2(\Psi_1^{-1}(P_o^{-1}(\{t\})) \cap L_a) & \text{if } \Psi_1^{-1}(P_o^{-1}(\{t\})) \cap L_a \neq \emptyset, \\ \emptyset & \text{otherwise.} \end{cases}$$

and let $A_c : P_o(L(\mathbf{G})) \times \Gamma \to 2^{\Gamma}$, where for all $(t, \gamma) \in P_o(L(\mathbf{G})) \times \Gamma$,

$$A_c(t, \gamma) := \begin{cases} \Psi_3(\Psi_1^{-1}(P_o^{-1}(\{t\}))) \Omega \cap L_a) & \text{if } \Psi_1^{-1}(P_o^{-1}(\{t\})) \cap L_a \neq \emptyset \wedge \\ & \quad \gamma \in S(A_s(t)), \\ \emptyset & \text{otherwise.} \end{cases}$$

Then $A = (A_s, A_c)$ is a smart sensor-actuator attack of $(\mathbf{G}, \mathbf{S})$ with respect to $L_{\text{dam}} = L_m(\mathbf{G})$ such that $L(S \circ A/\mathbf{G}) = \Psi_1(L_a)$.

Proof *Because both A_s and A_c cannot change events outside attackable alphabets, L_a must be controllable with respect to $L(\mathbf{G}_a)$ and Ω_{uc}.*

(1) To show that A is covert, we first show that $\Psi_2(L_a) \subseteq P_o(L(S/\mathbf{G}))$ by induction, where S is realized by $\mathbf{S}$. Since $L_a \neq \emptyset$, we know that $\epsilon \in \Psi_2(L_a) \cap P_o(L(S/\mathbf{G}))$. Assume that for all string $t \in L_a$, as long as $|t| \leq n$ for some $n \in \mathbb{N}$, we have $\Psi_2(t) \subseteq P_o(L(S/\mathbf{G}))$. We now show that the set inclusion also holds for each string $t \in L_a$ with $|t| = n+1$.

Since $|t| = n+1$, we know that $t = t'(\sigma, \sigma', \gamma)$, where $|t'| = n$ and $t' \in L_a$. Thus, there exists $q = (x, y, z, w), q' = (x', y', z', w') \in Q$ such that $\kappa(q_0, t') = q$ and $\kappa(q, \sigma, \sigma', \gamma) = q'$, namely $\sigma \in \gamma$ and

$$\xi(x, \sigma) = x' \wedge \eta(y, P_o(\sigma), \sigma') = y' \wedge \delta(z, \sigma') = z' \wedge \iota(w, P_o(\sigma), En_\mathbf{S}(z), \gamma) = w'.$$

By the assumption, we know that $\Psi_2(t') \subseteq P_o(L(S/\mathbf{G})) = P_o(L(\mathbf{S}) \cap L(\mathbf{G}))$ and by the definition of L_a, in particular, the property of observability, we know that $\delta(z_0, \Psi_2(t')) = z$. Thus, we know that $\Psi_2(t) = \Psi_2(t'(\sigma, \sigma', \gamma)) = \Psi_2(t')\sigma' \in P_o(L(\mathbf{S}) \cap L(\mathbf{G})) = P_o(L(S/\mathbf{G}))$, which completes the induction.

By the definition of A_s, for $t \in P_o(L(\mathbf{G}))$, if $\Psi_1^{-1}(P_o^{-1}(\{t\})) \cap L_a \neq \emptyset$, then

$$A_s(t) = \Psi_2(\Psi_1^{-1}(P_o^{-1}(\{t\})) \cap L_a) \subseteq \Psi_2(L_a) \subseteq P_o(L(S/\mathbf{G})).$$

In case that $\Psi_1^{-1}(P_o^{-1}(\{t\})) \cap L_a = \emptyset$, we have $A_s(t) = \emptyset$. Thus, we have $A_s(P_o(L(\mathbf{G}))) \subseteq P_o(L(S/\mathbf{G}))$.

(2) To show that the derived attack A is damage inflicting, we first need to show that $L(S \circ A/\mathbf{G}) = \Psi_1(L_a)$. To this end, we first show that $L(S \circ A/\mathbf{G}) \subseteq \Psi_1(L_a)$ by induction. Since $L_a \neq \emptyset$, clearly, $\epsilon \in L(S \circ A/\mathbf{G}) \cap \Psi_1(L_a)$. We assume that for each string $t \in L(S \circ A/\mathbf{G})$ with $|t| \leq n$ ($n \in \mathbb{N}$), we have $t \in \Psi_1(L_a)$. Next, we need to show that for each string $t \in L(S \circ A/\mathbf{G})$ with $|t| = n+1$, we have $t \in \Psi_1(L_a)$. Since $|t| = n+1$, there must exist $t' \in \Sigma^*$ and $\sigma \in \Sigma$ such that $t = t'\sigma$ with $|t'| = n$. Clearly, $t' \in L(S \circ A/\mathbf{G})$. By the assumption, $t' \in \Psi_1(L_a)$. Since $t'\sigma \in L(S \circ A/\mathbf{G})$, by the definition of $L(S \circ A/\mathbf{G})$, we know that

$$t'\sigma \in L(\mathbf{G}) \wedge (\exists \gamma \in A_c(P_o(t'), S(A_s(P_o(t')))))\sigma \in \gamma.$$

Clearly, $A_c(P_o(t'), \gamma) \neq \emptyset$. Thus, by the definition of A_c, we know that $\Psi_1^{-1}(t')\Omega \cap L_a \neq \emptyset$, which also means that $\Psi_1^{-1}(t') \cap L_a \neq \emptyset$. Thus, there exists $\mu \in \Psi_1^{-1}(t')$ such that $\mu(\hat{\sigma}, \hat{\sigma}', \gamma) \in L_a$, where $\Psi_2(\mu) \in A_s(P_o(t'))$. By the last property of attack feasibility of L_a, we have

$$\mu(\hat{\sigma}, \hat{\sigma}', \gamma) \in L_a \Rightarrow \Psi_1(En_{L_a}(\mu)) \cap \gamma = En_\mathbf{G}(\xi(x_0, \Psi_1(\mu))) \cap \gamma.$$

Since $\sigma \in \gamma$ and $t'\sigma \in En_G(\xi(x_0, \Psi_1(\mu)))$, we know that $\sigma \in \Psi_1(En_{L_a}(\mu) \cap \Omega(\gamma))$, namely there exists $(\sigma, \sigma', \gamma) \in \Omega$ such that $\mu(\sigma, \sigma', \gamma) \in L_a$. Thus, $\Psi_1(\mu(\sigma, \sigma', \gamma) = \Psi_1(\mu)\Psi_1(\sigma, \sigma', \gamma) = t'\sigma = t \in \Psi_1(L_a)$, which completes the induction step.

Next, we show that $L(S \circ A/G) \supseteq \Psi_1(L_a)$ by induction. Again, since $L_a \neq \emptyset$, we know that $\epsilon \in L(S \circ A/G) \cap \Psi_1(L_a)$. We assume that for each string $t \in \Psi_1(L_a)$ with $|t| \leq n$ $(n \in \mathbb{N})$, we have $t \in L(S \circ A/G)$. Next, we need to show that for each string $t \in \Psi_1(L_a)$ with $|t| = n+1$, we have $t \in L(S \circ A/G)$. Since $|t| = n+1$, there must exist $t' \in \Sigma^*$ and $\sigma \in \Sigma$ such that $t = t'\sigma$ with $|t'| = n$. Clearly, $t' \in \Psi_1(L_a)$. By the assumption, $t' \in L(S \circ A/G)$. Since $t \in \Psi_1(L_a)$, by the definition of L_a, we know that there exists $\mu \in L_a$ such that $\Psi_1(\mu) = t$, namely, there exists $\mu' \in \Omega^*$ and $(\sigma, \sigma', \gamma) \in \Omega$ such that $\mu = \mu'(\sigma, \sigma', \gamma)$ and $\Psi_1(\mu') = t'$. Since $\mu \in \Psi_1^{-1}(t) \cap L_a \neq \emptyset$, we have $\Psi_2(\mu')\sigma' = \Psi_2(\mu) \in A_s(P_o(t))$. In addition, since $\mu'(\sigma, \sigma', gamma) \in \Psi_1^{-1}(t) \cap L_a \neq \emptyset$, we have $\Psi_3(\sigma, \sigma', \gamma) = \gamma \in A_c(P_o(t), S(A_s(P_o(t'))))$. By the definition of L_a, we know that $\sigma \in \gamma$. Since $t' \in L(S \circ A/G)$, and $t'\sigma = t \in L(G)$ and $\sigma \in \gamma$, we know that $t = t'\sigma \in L(S \circ A/G)$, which completes the induction step, and also establishes the result that $L(S \circ A/G) = \Psi_1(L_a)$.

Since $L(S \circ A/G) = \Psi_1(L_a)$, and L_a satisfies the (strong or weak) attack property, we know that either

$$
\begin{aligned}
L(S \circ A/G) &= \Psi_1(L_a) \\
&= \Psi_1(\overline{L_a \cap \Psi_1^{-1}(L_m(G))}) \text{ if } L_a \text{ satisfies strong attack property} \\
&\subseteq \overline{\Psi_1(L_a) \cap L_m(G)} \\
&= \overline{L(S \circ A/G) \cap L_m(G)} \\
&\subseteq L(S \circ A/G)
\end{aligned}
$$

namely $\overline{L(S \circ A/G) \cap L_m(G)} = L(S \circ A/G)$ (strong damage infliction), or

$$
\begin{aligned}
L(S \circ A/G) \cap L_{\mathrm{dam}} &= \Psi_1(L_a) \cap L_m(G) \\
&\supseteq \Psi_1(L_a \cap \Psi_1^{-1}(L_m(G))) \\
&\neq \emptyset \text{ if } L_a \text{ satisfies the weak attack property}
\end{aligned}
$$

which means $L(S \circ A/G) \cap L_{\mathrm{dam}} \neq \emptyset$. This completes the proof. ■

Theorem 3.2 indicates that each attack feasible language L_a induces a smart sensor-actuator attack.

Similar to Theorem 2.3 in Chapter 2, we also have the following result, indicating that any (strong or weak) smart sensor-actuator attack also induces a (strong or weak) attack feasible language. Let $\mathcal{LSSA}(\mathbf{G}, S)$ denote the set of all smart (strong or weak) attack feasible sub-languages of $L(\mathbf{G}_a)$.

Theorem 3.3 Given a plant model $\mathbf{G}$, a supervisor S and a damage language $L_{\text{dam}} \subseteq L(\mathbf{G})$, let A be a smart sensor-actuator attack of $(\mathbf{G}, S)$ with respect to L_{dam}. Then there exists a smart attack feasible language $L_a \in \mathcal{LSSA}(\mathbf{G}, S)$ such that $L(S \circ A/\mathbf{G}) = \Psi_1(L_a)$.

Proof *We follow a similar procedure as shown in the proof of Theorem 2.3 in Chapter 2 to verify all properties of a smart attack feasible language.* ∎

Proposition 3.4 Let $\mathbf{G}_a$ be constructed as above with respect to a given closed-loop system $(\mathbf{G}, S)$, where S is realized by an FSA $\mathbf{S}$ and $L_{\text{dam}} = L_m(\mathbf{G})$. Then for any (possibly infinite) collection of (strong or weak) attack feasible sub-language $\{L_{a,i} \subseteq L(\mathbf{G}_a) | i \in I\}$, the sub-language $L_* := \cup_{i \in I} L_{a,i}$ is also (strong or weak) attack feasible.

Proof *We check each required property one by one.*

(1) To show that L_* is controllable with respect to $L(\mathbf{G}_a)$ and Ω_{uc}, we have

$$L_* \Omega_{uc} \cap L(\mathbf{G}_a) = \cup_{i \in I} L_{a,i} \Omega_{uc} \cap L(\mathbf{G}_a) \subseteq \cup_{i \in I} L_a = L_*.$$

(2) To show that L_* is observable with respect to $L(\mathbf{G}_a)$ and $P_o \circ \Psi_1$, for all $t \in L_*$, $t' \in L(\mathbf{G}_a)$, and for all $\sigma, \hat{\sigma} \in \Sigma^{\epsilon}$ and $(\sigma', \gamma) \in \Sigma_o^{\epsilon} \times \Gamma$, if $P_o(\Psi_1(t)\sigma) = P_o(\Psi_1(t')\sigma')$, $t(\sigma, \sigma', \gamma) \in L_*$ and $\Psi_1(t')\hat{\sigma} \in \Psi_1(L(\mathbf{G}_a))$, then since there exists $i \in I$ such that $t \in L_{a,i}$, and by observability of $L_{a,i}$, we have $t'(\hat{\sigma}, \sigma', \gamma) \in L_{a,i} \subseteq L_*$. Thus, L_* is observable.

(3.1) (strong attack) $\overline{L_* \cap \Psi_1^{-1}(L_m(\mathbf{G}))} = \overline{\cup_{i \in I} L_{a,i} \cap \Psi_1^{-1}(L_m(\mathbf{G}))} = \cup_{i \in I} L_{a,i} = L_*$,

(3.2) (weak attack) $L_* \cap \Psi_1^{-1}(L_m(\mathbf{G})) = \cup_{i \in I} L_{a,i} \cap \Psi_1^{-1}(L_m(\mathbf{G})) \neq \emptyset$.

For all $t \in L_*$ and $u \in \Omega$, if $tu \in L_*$, then

$$
\begin{aligned}
\Psi_1(En_{L_*}(t)) \cap \Psi_3(u) &= \Psi_1(En_{\cup_{i \in I} L_{a,i}}(t)) \cap \Psi_3(u) \\
&= \cup_{i \in I} \Psi_1(En_{L_{a,i}}(t)) \cap \Psi_3(u) \\
&= \cup_{i \in I} En_{\boldsymbol{G}}(\xi(x_0, \Psi_1(t))) \cap \Psi_3(u) \\
&= En_{\boldsymbol{G}}(\xi(x_0, \Psi_1(t))) \cap \Psi_3(u)
\end{aligned}
$$

Thus, the proposition follows. ■

By Proposition 3.4, we know that the set $\mathcal{LSSA}(\boldsymbol{G}, S)$ containing all (strong or weak) attack feasible sub-languages contain a unique supremal element with respect to the partial order of language set inclusion, which is called the *supremal (strong or weak) attack feasible language* with respect to $(\boldsymbol{G}, S)$, denoted as $\sup\mathcal{LSSA}(\boldsymbol{G}, S)$.

Theorem 3.4 Given a closed-loop system $(\boldsymbol{G}, S)$ with S being realized by an FSA $\boldsymbol{S}$, let $L_{\mathrm{dam}} = L_m(\boldsymbol{G})$. Then the supremal (strong or weak) smart sensor-actuator attack is computable from the supremal attack feasible sub-language of $L(\boldsymbol{G}_a)$ that is derivable in the complexity of $O(|X|^2|Z|^2|\Sigma|^2 2^{|\Sigma|+2|X|})$.

Proof *We first construct $\boldsymbol{G}_a = \boldsymbol{G} \times \boldsymbol{S} \times \boldsymbol{A}_s^0 \times \boldsymbol{A}_c^0$, where $\boldsymbol{A}_s^0$ and $\boldsymbol{A}_c^0$ are single-state transducers. Definition 3.3 essentially provides a synthesis algorithm, where we compute the largest sub-automaton of $\boldsymbol{G}_a$, whose corresponding sub-language L_* satisfies all three properties. By Theorem 3.2, we know that L_* is a smart sensor-actuator attack. Because L_* is induced from the largest sub-automaton, satisfying all properties in Definition 3.3, together with Theorem 3.5, the supremality follows. The overall time complexity of computing L_* can be roughly estimated as $O(|X|^2|Y|^2|Z|^2|W|^2|\Omega|2^{2|X|}) = O(|X|^2|Z|^2|\Sigma|^2|\Gamma|2^{2|X|}) = O(|X|^2|Z|^2|\Sigma|^2 2^{|\Sigma|+2|X|})$, where the exponential term $2^{|X|}$ is due to the need of verifying observability property, requiring a subset construction over $\boldsymbol{G}$.* ■

We will use an example to illustrate the entire construction process.

Example 3.4 *We revisit Example 3.2 with $\Sigma = \Sigma_o = \{a, b, c, d, e\}$, $\Sigma_c = \{a, c, d, e\}$, $\Sigma_{s,a} = \Sigma_{c,a} = \{a, d\}$, and $L_{dam} = L(\boldsymbol{G})$. The models of $\boldsymbol{A}_s^0$ and $\boldsymbol{A}_c^0$ are depicted in Figure 3.8, where, to simplify the actuator attack model $\boldsymbol{A}_c$, only control patterns used in the supervisor*

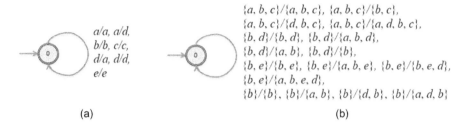

Figure 3.8 FSA models of $\mathbf{A}_s$ (a) and $\mathbf{A}_c$ (b).

S are considered as inputs of $\mathbf{A}_c$. The composition model $\mathbf{G}_a = \mathbf{G} \times \mathbf{S} \times \mathbf{A}_s \times \mathbf{A}_c$ is depicted in Figure 3.9. Because $\Sigma_{c,a} \neq \emptyset$, basically $\Omega_c = \Omega$, namely all compound events in $\mathbf{G}_a$ are controllable. Thus, the controllability property in Definition 3.3 automatically holds, so does the observability property, due to the fact that all events are observable. By carefully checking the transition structure of $\mathbf{G}_a$ in Figure 3.9, $L(\mathbf{G}_a)$ satisfies both property 3 and property 4 in Definition 3.3. By Theorem 3.4, we know that $\sup \mathcal{LSSA}(\mathbf{G}, \mathbf{S}) = L(\mathbf{G}_a)$.

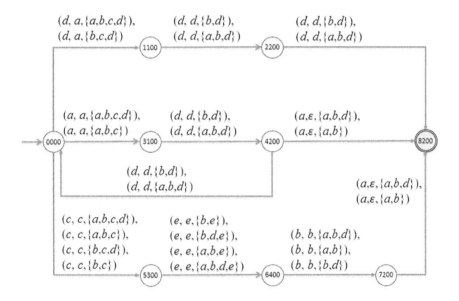

Figure 3.9 FSA models of $\mathbf{G}_a = \mathbf{G} \times \mathbf{S} \times \mathbf{A}_s \times \mathbf{A}_c$.

3.5 SUPREMAL MINIMUM-WEIGHTED SMART SENSOR-ACTUATOR ATTACK

Finally, we are ready to address the issue of attack costs and solve Problem 3.1. As previously described, we introduce a weighted automaton $(\mathbf{G}, f)$ with $f : X \times \Sigma \to \mathbb{R}^+ \cup \{\infty\}$ to capture any costs associated with each attack move, namely each transition in the plant carries a non-negative cost. To simplify our discussion on cost, we assume that all events are observable. Recall that we introduce a language-based version of the cost function: $h_f : L(\mathcal{G}) \to \mathbb{R}^+ \cup \{\infty\}$, where

1. $h_f(\epsilon) = 0$;

2. $(\forall s \in L(\mathbf{G}))(\forall \sigma \in \Sigma)s\sigma \in L(\mathcal{G}) \Rightarrow h_f(s\sigma) = h_f(s) + f(\xi(x_0, s), \sigma)$.

We call such a costing scheme *additive*.

Assumption 3.1 *Only additive costs are considered.* □

For each sub-language $L_a \subseteq L(\mathbf{G}_a)$, let $h_f(L_a) := \max_{t \in L_a} h_f(t)$. That is, the cost of L_a is denoted as the largest single-string cost.

Definition 3.4 Given a closed-loop system $(\mathbf{G}, S)$ with S being realized by an FSA $\mathbf{S}$ and $L_{\text{dam}} = L_m(\mathbf{G})$, let $\mathcal{FWSLSSA}(\mathbf{G}, S) := \{L_a \in \mathcal{LSSA}(\mathbf{G}, S) | h_f(L_a) < \infty\}$ be the collection of all *finitely weighted strong attack feasible sub-languages* of $L(\mathbf{G}_a)$. A sub-language $L_{a,\text{sup}} \in \mathcal{FWSLSSA}(\mathbf{G}, S)$ is *supremal minimum-weighted strong attack feasible* if the following properties hold:

1. $(\forall L_a \in \mathcal{FWSLSSA}(\mathbf{G}, S))h_f(L_{a,\text{sup}}) \leq h_f(L_a)$,

2. $(\forall L_a \in \mathcal{FWSLSSA}(\mathbf{G}, S))h_f(L_{a,\text{sup}}) = h_f(L_a) \Rightarrow L_a \subseteq L_{a,\text{sup}}$.

We denote $L_{a,\text{sup}}$ as $\sup \mathcal{FWSLSSA}(\mathbf{G}, S)$.

Proposition 3.5 If $\mathcal{FWSLSSA}(\mathbf{G}, S) \neq \emptyset$, then the supremal minimum-weighted strong attack feasible sub-language $L_{a,\text{sup}}$ always exists.

Proof *Assume that* $\mathcal{FWSLSSA}(\mathbf{G}, S) \neq \emptyset$. *Since a partial order on language weights is a total order, the set of all minimum-weighted* *strong attack feasible sub-languages* $\mathcal{MWSLSSA}(G, S) := \{L_a \in \mathcal{FWSLSSA}(G, S) | (\forall L'_a \in \mathcal{FWSLSSA}(G, S)) h_f(L_a) \leq h_f(L'_a)\}$ *is non-empty. Let* $L_{a,sup} := \cup_{L_a \in \mathcal{MWSLSSA}(G,S)} L_a$. *Clearly, for all* $L'_a \in \mathcal{FWSLSSA}(G, S)$, $h_f(L_{a,sup}) = \max_{L_a \in \mathcal{MWSLSSA}(G,S)} h_f(L_a) \leq h_f(L'_a)$. *In addition, by Proposition 3.4, we know that* $L_{a,sup} \in \mathcal{FWSLSSA}(G, S)$. *Thus, we have* $L_{a,sup} \in \mathcal{MWSLSSA}(G, S)$. *Clearly, for all* $L_a \in \mathcal{MWSLSSA}(G, S)$, *we have* $L_a \subseteq L_{a,sup}$. *The proposition follows.* ∎

To compute $L_{a,\text{sup}}$, we propose the following algorithm:

Algorithm 3.1 *Computing* $L_{a,\text{sup}}$ *for Supremal Minimum-Weighted Strong Attack Feasible Sub-language*

1. *Input: plant* (G, f) *and supervisor* S.

2. *Initialization: Compute* $G_a = G \times S \times A_s^0 \times A_c^0 = (Q, \Omega, \kappa, q_o, Q_m)$. *The weight function* $f_a : Q \times \Omega \to \mathbb{R}^+ \cup \{\infty\}$ *is defined as follows:*

   $(\forall q = (x, z, y, w) \in Q)(\forall u = (\sigma, \sigma', \gamma) \in \Omega) f_a(q, u) := f(x, \sigma)$.

   Let $\nu_0 : Q \to \mathbb{R} \cup \{\infty\}$, *where* $\nu_0(q) = 0$, $q \in Q_m$; $\nu_0(q') = \infty$, $q' \notin Q_m$.

3. *Iteration on step* $k = 1, \ldots$:

   (a) *For all* $q \in Q_m$, $\nu_k(q) := 0$.

   (b) *For all* $q \notin Q_m$ *and for all* $\gamma \in \Gamma$,

      i. $v_{q,uc}(\gamma) := \max_{u \in \Omega_{uc} \cap \Omega(\gamma): \kappa(q,u)=q'} [\nu_{k-1}(q') + f_a(q, u)]$;

      ii. $v_{q,c}(\gamma) := \max_{\sigma \in \gamma} \min_{u \in \Omega_c \cap \Omega(\sigma,\gamma): \kappa(q,u)=q'} [\nu_{k-1}(q') + f_a(q, u)]$;

      iii. $\nu_k(q) := \min_{\gamma \in \Gamma} \max\{v_{q,uc}(\gamma), v_{q,c}(\gamma)\}$.

   (c) *If for all* $q \in Q$, $\nu_k(q) = \nu_{k-1}(q)$, *then break the iteration at* k. *Otherwise, continue with* $k + 1$.

4. *Construct a sub-automaton* $G_{a,sup} = (Q, \Omega, \kappa_{sup}, q_0, Q_m)$, *where for all* $q, q' \in Q$ *and for all* $u \in \Omega$, $\kappa_{sup}(q, u) := q'$ *if and only if* $\nu_k(q) < \infty$, $\kappa(q, u) = q'$ *and for all* $\sigma \in \Psi_1(En_{G_a}(q) \cap \Omega(\Psi_3(u)))$,

   $(\exists u' \in En_{G_a}(q) \cap \Omega(\sigma, \Psi_3(u))) \nu_k(q) \geq \nu_k(q') + f_a(q, u')$.

5. *Output:* $L_{a,\text{sup}} := L(G_{a,\text{sup}})$.

Proposition 3.6 Algorithm 3.1 terminates in a finite number of iterations.

Proof *For each $q \in Q$, if $q \in Q_m$, then its state label $\nu_k(q) = 0$ for all k. If $q \notin Q_m$, then we can see that its state label is monotonically non-increasing, namely $\nu_{k-1}(q) \geq \nu_k(q)$. Each value reduction is no smaller than $\min_{q \in Q, u \in \Omega : \kappa(q,u)! \wedge f_a(q,u) > 0} f_a(q,u)$. Since at each step k, at least one state label becomes finite and is reduced, and there are finite states, we know that within a finite number of steps, all state labels will be unchanged, namely the algorithm will terminate.* ■

Theorem 3.5 Let $L_{a,\sup}$ be the output of Algorithm 3.1. If $L_{a,\sup} \neq \emptyset$, then $L_{a,\sup} = \sup\mathcal{FWSLSSA}(\mathbf{G}, S)$. Otherwise, $\mathcal{FWSLSSA}(\mathbf{G}, S) = \emptyset$.

Proof *The state label updating rule and the final sub-automaton construction method guarantee that (1) each state is coreachable to the marker state set Q_m, i.e., the strong attack property holds; (2) all uncontrollable transitions at each selected state are allowed, i.e., the controllability property holds; (3) at each state q, whenever a control command γ is allowed, each feasible event σ must be associated with at least one compound transition, i.e., the last property in Definition 3.3 holds. Thus, $L_{a,\sup} \in \mathcal{FWSLSSA}(\mathbf{G}, S)$. Clearly, its cost is minimum, namely $L_{a,\sup} \in \mathcal{MWSLSSA}(\mathbf{G}, S)$. Finally, $L_{a,\sup}$ is the largest sub-automaton of $L(\mathbf{G}_a$, whose cost is minimum. Thus, we have $L_{a,\sup} = \sup\mathcal{FWSLSSA}(\mathbf{G}, S)$.* ■

The concept of minimum-weighted weak attack feasible sub-languages is quite different from that of strong attack feasible sub-languages. The deviation comes from the fact that, in a weak attack feasible sub-language, there may be some strings which will never be extended to some marker states, namely some sequences of attack moves may never render damage to the plant. From an application point of view, such unnecessary attack moves should be as few as possible. Due to this consideration, we present the following definition.

Definition 3.5 Given a closed-loop system $(\mathbf{G}, S)$ with S being realized by an FSA $\mathbf{S}$ and $L_{\mathrm{dam}} = L_m(\mathbf{G})$, let $\mathcal{FWWLSSA}(\mathbf{G}, S) := \{L_a \in \mathcal{LSSA}(\mathbf{G}, S) | h_f(L_a) < \infty\}$ be the collection of all *finitely weighted weak attack feasible sub-languages* of $L(\mathbf{G}_a)$. A sub-language

$L_{a,\text{sup}} \in \mathcal{FWWLSSA}(\mathbf{G}, S)$ is *supremal minimum-weighted weak attack feasible* if the following properties hold:

1. $L_{a,\text{sup}} \subseteq \overline{L_m(\mathbf{G}_a)}\Omega$,

2. $(\forall L_a \in \mathcal{FWWLSSA}(\mathbf{G}, S))h_f(L_{a,\text{sup}} \cap \overline{L(\mathbf{G}_a)}) \leq h_f(L_a \cap \overline{L(\mathbf{G}_a)})$,

3. $(\forall L_a \in \mathcal{FWWLSSA}(\mathbf{G}, S))h_f(L_{a,\text{sup}} \cap \overline{L(\mathbf{G}_a)}) = h_f(L_a \cap \overline{L(\mathbf{G}_a)}) \Rightarrow L_a \subseteq L_{a,\text{sup}}$.

We denote $L_{a,\text{sup}}$ as $\sup\mathcal{FWWLSSA}(\mathbf{G}, S)$.

Essentially, the supremal minimum-weighted weak attack feasible sub-language has the minimum weight over nonblocking behaviors. The cost of those blocking behaviors will not be considered. However, to minimum the blocking moves, only one-step deviations from non-blocking behaviors are allowed, under the consideration that, once the plant reaches a blocking state, there is no point to continue attack moves, as no damage will be inflicted subsequently. We can easily show the following result.

Proposition 3.7 If $\mathcal{FWWLSSA}(\mathbf{G}, S) \neq \emptyset$, then the supremal minimum-weighted weak attack feasible sub-language $L_{a,\text{sup}}$ always exists.

Proof *Similar to the proof of Proposition 3.5.* ◼

Algorithm 3.2 *Computing $L_{a,\text{sup}}$ for Supremal Minimum-Weighted Weak Attack Feasible Sub-language*

1. *Input: plant $(\mathbf{G}, f)$ and supervisor S.*

2. *Initialization: Compute $\mathbf{G}_a = \mathbf{G} \times \mathbf{S} \times \mathbf{A}_s^0 \times \mathbf{A}_c^0 = (Q, \Omega, \kappa, q_o, Q_m)$. The weight function $f_a : Q \times \Omega \to \mathbb{R}^+ \cup \{\infty\}$ is defined as follows:*

$$(\forall q = (x, z, y, w) \in Q)(\forall u = (\sigma, \sigma', \gamma) \in \Omega)f_a(q, u) := f(x, \sigma).$$

Let $\nu_0 : Q \to \mathbb{R} \cup \{\infty\}$, where $\nu_0(q) = 0$, if $q \in Q_m$ or $q \in Q_{block} := \{q' \in Q | (\forall \mu \in \Omega^*)\kappa(q, \mu) \notin Q_m\}$; $\nu_0(q') = \infty$, $q' \notin Q_m \cup Q_{block}$.

3. *Iteration on step $k = 1, \ldots$:*

    (a) For all $q \in Q_m \cup Q_{block}$, $\nu_k(q) := 0$.

    (b) For all $q \in Q \setminus (Q_m \cup Q_{bloack})$ and for all $\gamma \in \Gamma$,

        i. $v_{q,uc}(\gamma) := \max_{u \in \Omega_{uc} \cap \Omega(\gamma):\kappa(q,u)=q'}[\nu_{k-1}(q') + f_a(q, u)]$;

        ii. $v_{q,c}(\gamma) := \max_{\sigma \in \gamma} \min_{u \in \Omega_c \cap \Omega(\sigma,\gamma):\kappa(q,u)=q'}[\nu_{k-1}(q') + f_a(q, u)]$;

        iii. $\nu_k(q) := \min_{\gamma \in \Gamma} \max\{v_{q,uc}(\gamma), v_{q,c}(\gamma)\}$.

    (c) If for all $q \in Q$, $\nu_k(q) = \nu_{k-1}(q)$, then break the iteration at k. Otherwise, continue with $k + 1$.

4. *Construct a sub-automaton $\boldsymbol{G}_{a,sup} = (Q, \Omega, \kappa_{sup}, q_0, Q_m)$, where for all $q, q' \in Q$ and for all $u \in \Omega$, $\kappa_{sup}(q, u) := q'$ if and only if $\nu_k(q) < \infty$, $\kappa(q, u) = q'$, $q \notin Q_{block}$, and for all $\sigma \in \Psi_1(En_{\boldsymbol{G}_a}(q) \cap \Omega(\Psi_3(u)))$,*

$$(\exists u' \in En_{\boldsymbol{G}_a}(q) \cap \Omega(\sigma, \Psi_3(u)))\nu_k(q) \geq \nu_k(q') + f_a(q, u').$$

5. *Output: $L_{a,sup} := L(\boldsymbol{G}_{a,sup})$.*

Proposition 3.8 Algorithm 3.1 terminates in a finite number of iterations.

Proof *Similar to the proof of Proposition 3.6.* ■

Theorem 3.6 Let $L_{a,\text{sup}}$ be the output of Algorithm 3.1. If $L_{a,\text{sup}} \neq \emptyset$, then $L_{a,\text{sup}} = \sup \mathcal{FWSLSSA}(\mathbf{G}, S)$. Otherwise, $\mathcal{FWSLSSA}(\mathbf{G}, S) = \emptyset$.

Proof *Similar to the proof of Theorem 3.5.* ■

Example 3.5 *We revisit Example 3.4 and add transition weights to the plant model $\boldsymbol{G}$, which is depicted in Figure 3.10. After computing $(\boldsymbol{G}_a, f_a)$, the outcome of the initialization at $k = 0$ is depicted in Figure 3.11, where all states, except for the marker state "8200", are assigned with value "∞". After the iteration process starts, we track the changes of state labels. When $k = 1$, the labels of three states: "2200", "4200" and "7200", are changed, which are depicted in Figure 3.12. At state "4200", it turns out that, for the control command $\{a, b\}$, the resulting value is $f_a(4200, a, \epsilon, \{a, b\}) + \nu_1(8200) = 4 + 0 = 4$. If we*

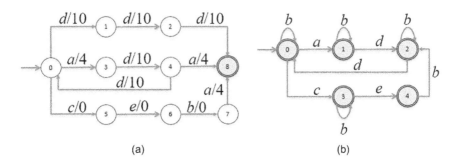

Figure 3.10 FSA models of (G, f) (a) and S (b).

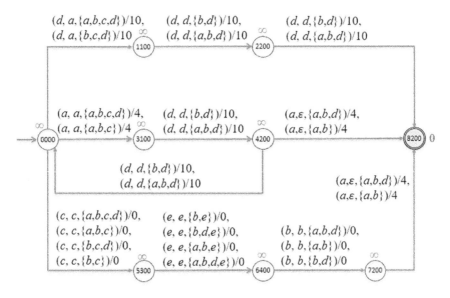

Figure 3.11 FSA model of (G_a, f_a) with state labels at $k = 0$.

choose the control command $\{a, b, d\}$, then there are two transitions allowed: $\kappa(4200, a, \epsilon, \{a, b, d\}) = 8200$ and $\kappa(4200, d, d, \{a, b, d\}) = 0000$, and the resulting value is: $\min\{4 + 0, \max\{4 + 0, 10 + \infty\}\} = \min\{4, \infty\} = 4$. We continue this process with $k = 2$, and the outcome is depicted in Figure 3.13. The outcome of $k = 3$ is depicted in Figure 3.14, and finally the outcome of $k = 4$ is depicted in Figure 3.15. We can check that the algorithm will terminate at $k = 5$, as the resulting state labels will be the same as those in the case of $k = 4$. To construct $L_{a,sup}$, we start with the initial state "0000", whose state

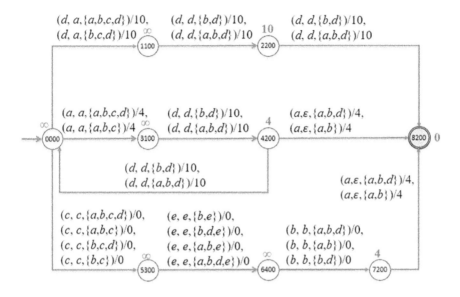

Figure 3.12 FSA model of $(\mathbf{G}_a, f_a)$ with state labels at $k = 1$.

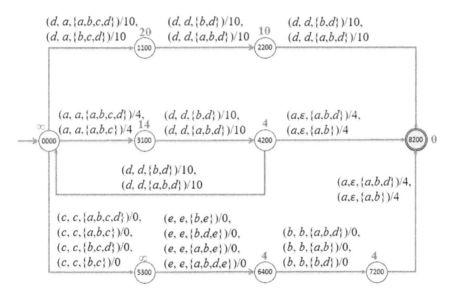

Figure 3.13 FSA model of $(\mathbf{G}_a, f_a)$ with state labels at $k = 2$.

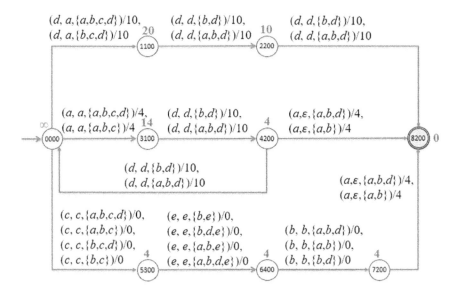

Figure 3.14 FSA model of $(\mathbf{G}_a, f_a)$ with state labels at $k = 3$.

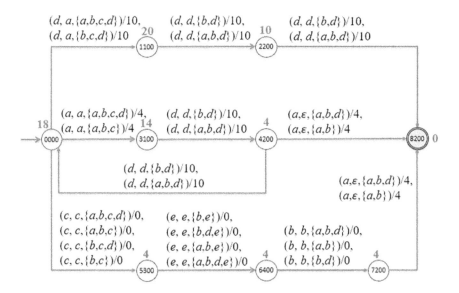

Figure 3.15 FSA model of $(\mathbf{G}_a, f_a)$ with state labels at $k = 4$.

label is 18. Since the cost over the transitions $\kappa(0000, d, d, \{a, b, c, d\})+$
$\nu_5(1111) = \kappa(0000, d, d, \{b, c, d\}) + \nu_5(1111) = 10 + 20 = 30 > 18,$
both transitions are not taken in $L_{a,sup}$. *However, with this choice,*
the control commands $\{a, b, c, d\}$ *and* $\{a, c, d\}$ *cannot be taken at*
state "0000". Thus, any compound transitions involving these control
commands at state "0000" must be disabled. Similarly, at state "4200",
the state label is 4, which is lower than the cost of the transition
$\kappa(4200, d, d, \{b, d\}) + \nu_5(0000) = \kappa(4200, d, d, \{a, b, d\}) + \nu_5(0000) =$
$18 + 10 = 28.$ *Thus, both transitions will not be selected in* $L_{a,sup}$.
But this means any control command containing event "d" must be
removed, thus, the transition $\kappa(4200, a, \epsilon, \{a, b, d\})$ *cannot be selected.*
The above selection process is depicted in Figure 3.16, and a clean
copy of the final supremal minimum-weighted strong attack feasible
sub-language $L_{a,sup}$ *is depicted in Figure 3.17.*

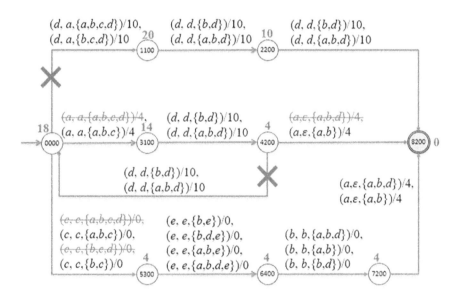

Figure 3.16 FSA model of $L_{a,\text{sup}}$ with transition disablement.

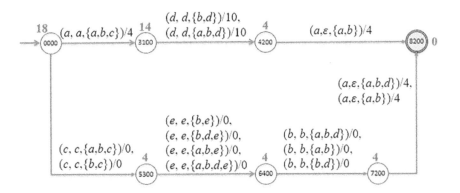

Figure 3.17 Final FSA model of $L_{a,\text{sup}}$.

3.6 CONCLUSIONS

In this chapter, we have first introduced the concept of smart sensor-actuator attack, which essentially consists of two correlated sub-attacks: a sensor attack and an actuator attack. Both sub-attacks need to collaborate with each other in order to achieve covertness and damage infliction. It has been shown that the supremal smart sensor-actuator attack may exist for each closed-loop system $(\mathbf{G}, S)$ and can be computed whenever it does exist. A simple example shows that a sensor-actuator attack is not a simple combination of a smart sensor attack and a smart actuator attack, but rather a coherent solution that ensures a successful attack not achievable by any single attack. Similar to Chapter 2, it has been shown that the supremal smart sensor-actuator attack is embedded in an attack feasible language that can be derived in exponential time from the plant model $\mathbf{G}$ and a supervisor model $\mathbf{S}$, assuming that the damage language L_{dam} is encoded by the marked behavior of $\mathbf{G}$. The exponential time complexity is mainly due to the need to impose an observability property to ensure the existence of an attack that relies on new observations before making an attack move.

After introducing the concept of supremal smart sensor-actuator attack, we have associated additive transition weights to transitions of the plant $\mathbf{G}$ to capture the needs of quantifying the cost of attacks and introduced the concept of minimum-weighted smart sensor-actuator. To avoid any extra complication introduced by partial observation, when we address the cost issue, we assume that all events are observable. It turns out that the concept of supremal minimum-weighted strong smart sensor-actuator attack can be easily defined, and a concrete polynomial-time algorithm is proposed to compute an attack language that contains such a supremal attack model. In contrast to strong attack, the concept of minimum-weighted weak smart sensor-actuator attack is not so straightforward. The main conceptual hurdle is how to treat behaviors that are deemed not reaching any damage state. In this chapter, we have introduced a concept that focuses only on the cost of successful attack behaviors, while minimizing the number of blocking behaviors. With this concept, a specific algorithm is proposed to compute the supremal minimum-weighted weak smart sensor-actuator attack. Similar to the strong attack case, the complexity of deriving an attack feasible language containing the supremal minimum-weighted weak smart sensor-actuator attack is exponential in time.

In this chapter, we only consider the simplest scenario, where both the sensor attack and actuator attack have the same observation capability, which can certainly be relaxed in the future.

CHAPTER 4

Smart Attacks with Unknown Supervisor

In this chapter, we consider the problem of synthesizing an SSAA under the assumption that the model of the supervisor is unknown to an attacker. However, the plant model is known to the attacker in advance. By recording sequences of the plant output and supervisory commands, the attacker aims to construct a transition structure that matches all previously received system observations, upon which the attacker is capable of deciding whether it is covert to carry out an attack to ensure strong or weak damage. By leveraging on the existing smart attack synthesis strategy introduced in Chapter 3, the focus of this chapter is on learning a target supervisor's behavior.

4.1 SYNCHRONIZED ATTACK

We adopt the same closed-loop control architecture under sensor-actuator attack shown in Chapter 3, where the existence of an SSAA $A = (A_s, A_c)$ against a closed-loop system $(\mathbf{G}, S)$ with $L_{\text{dam}} = L_m(\mathbf{G})$ is decidable and the supremal (strong or weak) SSAA can be synthesized, if existing. The validity of that framework relies on an assumption that the models of both plant $\mathbf{G}$ and supervisor S are known in advance to an attacker. In reality, an attacker may not always know the details of a specific supervisor. For this reason, it is interesting to know whether it is possible to use knowledge derived from

DOI: 10.1201/9781003333883-5

intercepted output information to construct a smart sensor-actuator attack.

Due to the lack of prior knowledge of the supervisor S, an attacker needs to construct a surrogate model of S based on the plant and supervisor outputs. We assume that the system $(\mathbf{G}, S)$ runs repetitively, for example, each day it runs within a certain period of time, whose starting time might not be necessarily known in advance to the attacker in the most general case. We index each run by a unique natural number and let I be the index set. Let $\alpha : (\Sigma_o^\epsilon \times \Gamma)^* \to (\Sigma_o^\epsilon)^*$ be a mapping, where $\alpha(\epsilon) := \epsilon$ and for all $s \in (\Sigma_o^\epsilon \times \Gamma)^*$ and $(\sigma, \gamma) \in \Sigma_o^\epsilon \times \Gamma$, $\alpha(s(\sigma, \gamma)) = \alpha(s)\sigma$. Similarly, let $\beta : (\Sigma_o^\epsilon \times \Gamma)^* \to \Gamma^*$ be a mapping, where $\beta(\epsilon) := \epsilon$ and for all $s \in (\Sigma_o^\epsilon \times \Gamma)^*$ and $(\sigma, \gamma) \in \Sigma_o^\epsilon \times \Gamma$, $\beta(s(\sigma, \gamma)) = \beta(s)\gamma$. Both α and β are extended to the domain of $2^{(\Sigma_o^\epsilon \times \Gamma)^*}$ in a conventional way, that is, for each $L \subseteq (\Sigma_o^\epsilon \times \Gamma)^*$, $\alpha(L) := \{\alpha(s)|s \in L\}$ and $\beta(L) := \{\beta(s)|s \in L\}$. Recall that for each string $s \in (\Sigma_o^\epsilon \times \Gamma)^*$, we use $s^\uparrow$ to denote the last element of s. As a convention, $\epsilon^\uparrow := \epsilon$.

In this section, we consider the simplest situation, where the attacker starts data collection at the moment the system starts to run, i.e., the starting times of an attack and the system are perfectly synchronized. During each run $i \in I$, the attacker collects a set of observation sequences $O_i = \{w \in (\Sigma_o^\epsilon \times \Gamma)^* | \alpha(w) \in P_o(L(S/\mathbf{G})) \wedge S(\alpha(w)) = \beta(w)^\uparrow\}$. Up to a specific run $k \in I$, the set of collected system outputs is $O(k) := \cup_{i=1}^k O_i$, where, due to the assumption of perfect starting time synchronization, we have $\alpha(O(k)) \subseteq P_o(L(S/\mathbf{G}))$, and for each $w \in O(k)$, $S(\alpha(w)) = \beta(w)^\uparrow$. In addition, all strings $w \in O(k)$ share the first event (ϵ, γ_0), where $\gamma_0 = En_S(\epsilon)$, because S is a deterministic supervisor and always sends the first control command γ_0 at the initial state.

For each string $(\sigma_1, \gamma_1) \dots (\sigma_n, \gamma_n) \in O(k)$, where $n \in \mathbb{N}$, we create a surrogate $\hat{S}_k$ of S with respect to $O(k)$ as follows. Let $\Phi : O(k) \to 2^{\Sigma^*}$ be a mapping, where

1. $\Phi(\epsilon, \gamma_0) := (\Sigma_{uo} \cap \gamma_0)^*(\gamma_0 \cap \Sigma_o)$;

2. For all $s \in O(k)$ and $(\sigma, \gamma) \in \Sigma_o^\epsilon \times \Gamma$, if $s(\sigma, \gamma) \in O(k)$, then

$$\Phi(s(\sigma, \gamma)) :=$$
$$\begin{cases} (\Phi(s) \cap \Sigma^*\{\sigma\} \cap P_o^{-1}(\alpha(s)\sigma))[(\Sigma_{uo} \cap \gamma)^*(\gamma \cap \Sigma_o)] & \text{if } \sigma \in \Sigma_o, \\ \Phi(s) & \text{otherwise.} \end{cases}$$

The definition of Φ indicates that $\Phi(O(k))$ is prefix-closed. Next, we introduce a mapping $\hat{S}_k : P_o(\Phi(O(k))) \to \Gamma$, where

$$(\forall s \in P_o(\Phi(O(k)))) \hat{S}_k(s) := En_{\Phi(O(k))}(s).$$

Theorem 4.1 Given a closed-loop system $(\mathbf{G}, S)$, let $O(k)$ and $\hat{S}_k$ be introduced above. Then for all $s \in \Phi(O(k))$, if $\{s\}\Sigma \cap \Phi(O(k)) \neq \varnothing$, then $S(P_o(s)) = \hat{S}_k(P_o(s))$.

Proof *We use induction. When $s = \epsilon$, we know that the plant has no observable output and the supervisor S generates the first control command $S(\epsilon) = \gamma_0$. By the definition of $O(k)$, we know that $(\epsilon, \gamma_0) \in O(k)$, and $(\Sigma_{uo}\cap\gamma_0)^*(\gamma_0\cap\Sigma_o) \subseteq \Phi(O(k))$, upon which we have $\hat{S}_k(\epsilon) = En_{\Phi(O(k))}(\epsilon) = \gamma_0 = S(\epsilon)$. Thus, the base case holds. Assume that for all $s \in \Phi(O(k))$, if $\{s\}\Sigma \cap \Phi(O(k)) \neq \varnothing$ and $|s| \leq n$, then $S(P_o(s)) = \hat{S}_k(P_o(s))$. We need to show that, for each $s \in \Phi(O(k))$ with $\{s\}\Sigma \cap \Phi(O(k)) \neq \varnothing$ and $|s| = n+1$, we have $S(P_o(s)) = \hat{S}_k(P_o(s))$. Clearly, there exists $s' \in \Phi(O(k))$ and $\sigma \in \Sigma$ such that $s = s'\sigma$. Since $|s'| = n$ and $\{s'\}\Sigma \cap \Phi(O(k)) \neq \varnothing$, by the assumption we have $S(P_o(s')) = \hat{S}_k(P_o(s'))$. Because $\sigma \in En_{\Phi(O(k))}(s) = \hat{S}_k(P_o(s'))$, we know that $\sigma \in S(P_o(s'))$. We have two cases to consider.*

> *Case 1: $\sigma \in \Sigma_{uo}$. Then we know that the plant $\mathbf{G}$ generates ϵ as the output, and the supervisor maintains the same control output as s', namely $S(P_o(s)) = S(P_o(s'\sigma)) = S(P_o(s'))$. On the other hand, $\hat{S}_k(P_o(s)) = En_{\Phi(O(k))}(P_o(s'\sigma)) = En_{\Phi(O(k))}(P_o(s')) = \hat{S}_k(P_o(s')) = S(P_o(s')) = S(P_o(s))$.*

> *Case 2: $\sigma \in \Sigma_o$. In this case, the plant$\mathbf{G}$ generates σ as the observable output, which triggers the supervisor S to generate a new control command $S(P_o(s'\sigma)) = S(P_o(s')\sigma) = \gamma$. On the other hand, let $\mu \in O(k)$ that is associated with s' and $\mu(\sigma, \gamma) \in O(k)$. Then we know that $(\Phi(\mu) \cap \Sigma^*\{\sigma\} \cap P_o^{-1}(s'))[(\Sigma_{uo} \cap \gamma)^*(\gamma \cap \Sigma_o)] \subseteq \Phi(O(k))$. This means that $En_{\Phi(O(k))}(P_o(s)) = En_{\Phi(O(k))}(P_o(s')\sigma) = \hat{S}_k(P_o(s)) = \gamma = S(P_o(s))$, which completes the induction.* ■

Theorem 4.1 indicates that $\hat{S}_k$ is a surrogate of S for all live strings in $\Phi(O(k))$. That is, as long as a string s can be extended in $\Phi(O(k))$, the induced control command $\hat{S}_k(P_o(s))$ is the same as $S(P_o(s))$ generated by S.

Corollary 4.1 Given a closed-loop system $(\mathbf{G}, S)$, let $O(k)$ and $\hat{S}_k$ be introduced above. Then $L(\hat{S}_k/\mathbf{G}) \subseteq L(S/\mathbf{G})$.

Proof *We use induction. Clearly, $\epsilon \in L(\hat{S}_k/\mathbf{G}) \cap L(S/\mathbf{G})$. Assume that for all $s \in L(\hat{S}_k/\mathbf{G})$, if $|s| \leq n$, then $s \in L(S/\mathbf{G})$. Let $s \in\in L(\hat{S}_k/\mathbf{G})$ with $|s| = n + 1$. Then there exist $s' \in L(\hat{S}_k/\mathbf{G})$ and $\sigma \in \Sigma$ such that $s = s'\sigma$. Clearly, $s'\sigma \in L(\mathbf{G})$. Since s' is live, by Theorem 4.1, we know that $\hat{S}_k(P_o(s')) = S(P_o(s'))$. Clearly, $\sigma \in \hat{S}_k(P_o(s'))$. Thus, we know that $\sigma \in S(P_o(s'))$, which means $s'\sigma = s \in L(S/\mathbf{G})$, which completes the induction part. Thus, $L(\hat{S}_k/\mathbf{G}) \subseteq L(S/\mathbf{G})$.* ∎

Since $L(\hat{S}_k/\mathbf{G}) \subseteq L(S/\mathbf{G})$, there may still exist a smart strong sensor-actuator attack of $(\mathbf{G}, S)$, even when there does not exist one for $(\mathbf{G}, \hat{S}_k)$. However, the following result indicates that the existence of a smart strong (or weak) sensor-actuator attack for $(\mathbf{G}, \hat{S}_k)$ suggests the existence of a smart strong (or weak) sensor-actuator attack for $(\mathbf{G}, S)$.

Theorem 4.2 Given a closed-loop system $(\mathbf{G}, S)$, let $O(k)$ and $\hat{S}_k$ be introduced above. Then each smart strong (or weak) sensor-actuator attack $A_k = (A_{s,k}, A_{c,k})$ of $(\mathbf{G}, \hat{S}_k)$ with respect to $L_{\text{dam}} = L_m(\mathbf{G})$ must also be a smart strong (or weak) sensor-actuator attack of $(\mathbf{G}, S)$ with respect to L_{dam}, as long as $A_{s,k}(s) = \emptyset$ for all $s \in P_o(L(\mathbf{G})) \setminus P_o(L(\hat{S}_k/\mathbf{G}))$.

Proof *By Corollary 4.1, we know that $L(\hat{S}_k/\mathbf{G}) \subseteq L(S/\mathbf{G})$. In addition, since $A_{s,k}(s) = \emptyset$ for all $s \in P_o(L(\mathbf{G})) \setminus P_o(L(\hat{S}_k/\mathbf{G}))$, we know that $L(\hat{S}_k \circ A_k/\mathbf{G}) = L(S \circ A_k/\mathbf{G})$. Since A_k is a smart strong (or weak) sensor-actuator attack of $(\mathbf{G}, \hat{S}_k)$, we know that*

$$A_{s,k}(P_o(L(\mathbf{G}))) \subseteq L(\hat{S}_k/\mathbf{G}) \subseteq L(S/\mathbf{G}),$$

namely the covertness property holds. In addition, since

$$L(S \circ A_k/\mathbf{G}) \cap L_{dam} = L(\hat{S}_k \circ A_k/\mathbf{G}) \cap L_{dam} \supseteq \emptyset,$$

and

$$L(S \circ A_k/\mathbf{G}) = L(\hat{S}_k \circ A_k/\mathbf{G}) = \overline{L(\hat{S}_k \circ A_k/\mathbf{G}) \cap L_{dam}} = \overline{L(S \circ A_k/\mathbf{G}) \cap L_{dam}},$$

we know A_k inflicts strong (or weak) damage. Thus, the theorem follows. ∎

Example 4.1 *We use a closed-loop system* (G, S) *depicted in Figure 4.1 to explain the aforementioned construction procedure. Here,* $\Sigma = \Sigma_o = \{a, b, c, d, e\}$, *and* $\Sigma_c = \{a, c, d, e\}$. *Assume that an attacker closely monitors multiple runs of the system, and the intercepted sequences of compound events are displayed in Figure 4.1. For example, initially there is no plant output and the supervisor* S *generates the first control command, which is* $\{a, b, c\}$, *and the resulting compound event is* $(\epsilon, \{a, b, c\})$. *After event* a *takes place in the plant* G, *the supervisor* S *generates the second control command* $\{b, d\}$, *and the resulting compound event is* $(a, \{b, d\})$. *Other compound events are generated similarly. Let* $O(3) = O_1 \cup O_2 \cup O_3$. *After applying the mapping* Φ, *the outcome* $\Phi(O(3))$ *is depicted in Figure 4.2. We can check that* $\hat{S}_3(\epsilon) = En_{\Phi(O(k))}(\epsilon) = \{a, b, c\} = S(\epsilon)$. *Similarly,* $\hat{S}_3(a) = En_{\Phi(O(k))}(a) = \{b, d\} = S(a)$. *We can easily check that Theorem 4.1 holds for this example.*

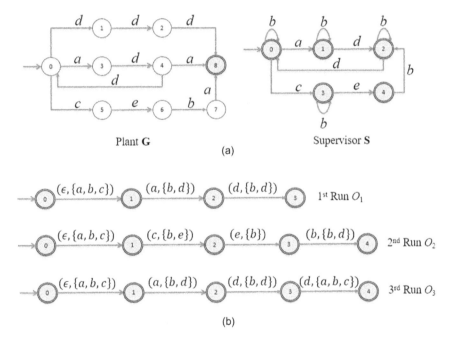

Figure 4.1 A closed-loop system (G, S) (a) and three runs O_1, O_2 and O_3 (b).

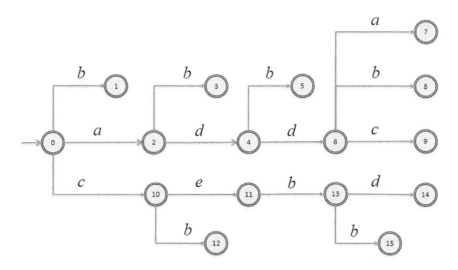

Figure 4.2 An FSA model of $\Phi(O(3))$.

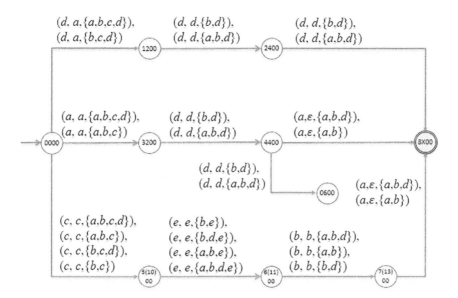

Figure 4.3 The Supremal weak sensor-actuator attack A_3 of $(\mathbf{G}, \hat{S}_3)$.

Next, we synthesize the supremal smart weak sensor-actuator attack A_3 associated with $(\mathbf{G}, \hat{S}_3)$, where $L_{dam} = L_m(\mathbf{G})$. The outcome is depicted in Figure 4.3, where the letter "X" in the state label "8X00" *denotes either 4 or 13, depending on the incoming state. It is clear that the sensor-actuator attack A_3 is actually strong. By Theorem 4.2, A_3 is also a smart strong sensor-actuator attack of (G, S), however, not necessarily supremal.*

4.2 NONSYNCHRONIZED ATTACK

Previously, we have discussed how to design a smart (strong or weak) sensor-actuator attack, when an attacker can observe the system output from the initial time. However, in real situations it is difficult for an attacker to start the observation process perfectly synchronized with the start of the closed-loop system. In this case, for each received observation sequence in each run, there could be more than one system trajectory that can generate the observation sequence, which imposes a challenge for ensuring covertness in an SSAA. In this section, we will address this challenge and propose a new model learning strategy for an attacker.

Following the same spirit of Section 4.1, let $O_i = \{w \in (\Sigma_o^\epsilon \times \Gamma)^*\}$ be the collection of system observations received by an attacker. Due to the asynchrony of the starting times of the closed-loop system and attacker's observer, it may not be true that $\alpha(w) \in P_o(L(S/G))$ and $S(\alpha(w)) = \beta(w)^\uparrow$. Instead, there exists one string $s \in P_o(L(S/G))$ such that $s = s'\alpha(w)$ for some $s' \in P_o(L(S/G))$ and $S(s) = \beta(w)^\uparrow$. Up to a specific run $k \in I$, the set of collected (partial) system outputs is $O(k) := \cup_{i=1}^k O_i$. Since in general $\alpha(O(k)) \not\subseteq P_o(L(S/G))$, we need to design a method to "guess" relevant control sequences generated by S. For each string $w \in O(k)$, let $h(w) := \{w' \in (\Sigma_o^\epsilon \times \Gamma)^* | (\exists w_1, w_2 \in (\Sigma_o^\epsilon \times \Gamma)^*)w = w_1 w' w_2\}$, namely $h(w)$ contains all segments of w. Let $O(k)_{\max} := \{w \in O(k) | (\forall w' \in O(k))w \notin h(w')\}$ such that $O(k) \subseteq \cup_{w \in O(k)_{\max}} h(w)$. Basically, $O(k)_{\max}$ is the smallest cover of $O(k)$ in the sense that $O(k)_{\max}$ contains a minimum set of incompatible strings from $O(k)$, whose segment union covers $O(k)$.

Example 4.2 *We use a small example depicted in Figure 4.4 to explain the concept of $O(k)_{\max}$. In this example, the set $O(k) = \{s_1, s_2, s_3\}$, where*

- $s_1 = (a, \{a, b\})(c, \{b, c\})(a, \{a, b, d\})$,

- $s_2 = (a, \{a, b\})(d, \{b, c, d\})(d, \{b, d\})(a, \{a, b, d\})$,

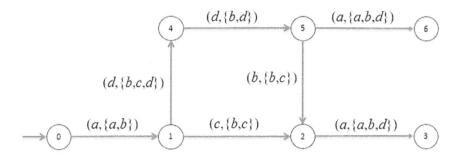

Figure 4.4 Example of $O(k)_{\max}$.

- $s_3 = (a, \{a, b\})(d, \{b, c, d\})(d, \{b, d\})(b, \{b, c\})(a, \{a, b, d\})$.

We can check that $O(k)_{\max} = \{s_1, s_2, s_3\}$, that is, the set of all longest incompatible strings in $O(k)$.

In the previous section, when the system and a smart attacker start actions simultaneously, the attacker knows that the plant **G** starts at the initial state x_0 and so does the supervisor S. Thus, the attacker can precisely track expected behaviors of the closed-loop system $(\mathbf{G}, S)$. Upon such knowledge, the attacker can decide whether a smart attack exists based on collected information in $O(k)$, which has been explained in the previous section. However, if the system and attacker do not start actions at the same time, the attacker does not know the precise state of the plant **G**, before the first observation is received. To apply the previously developed attack synthesis method, the attacker needs to consider ambiguity of the current plant state estimate based on collected information in $O(k)$.

We adopt the same closed-loop control architecture under sensor-actuator attack shown in Chapter 3, as explained in Section 4.1. With collected information set $O(k)$, we aim to decide the existence of a smart sensor-actuator attack $A = (A_s, A_c)$ against a closed-loop system $(\mathbf{G}, S)$, where $L_{\text{dam}} = L_m(\mathbf{G})$, and show that the supremal (strong or weak) smart sensor-actuator attack exists and synthesizable, if there exists at least one smart sensor-actuator attack. Because the attacker does not know the precise state of the plant **G** before the first observation is collected, in the worst-case situation, the plant **G** could be at any state. To capture this understanding, we create a new nondeterministic plant model $\mathbf{G}_{\text{ext}} = (X \cup \{x_{0,\text{ext}}\}, \Sigma^\epsilon, \xi_{\text{ext}}, x_{0,\text{ext}}, X_m)$, where

1. $x_{0,\text{ext}}$ is a new dummy initial state,

2. $\xi_{\text{ext}} : (X \cup \{x_{0,\text{ext}}\}) \times \Sigma^\epsilon \to 2^X$ is a nondeterministic transition mapping, where

   - $(\forall x, x' \in X)(\forall \sigma \in \Sigma)\, \xi(x, \sigma) = x' \Rightarrow \xi_{\text{ext}}(x, \sigma) = \{x'\}$,
   - $\xi_{\text{ext}}(x_{0,\text{ext}}, \epsilon) = X$.

The only difference between $\mathbf{G}$ and $\mathbf{G}_{\text{ext}}$ is that $\mathbf{G}_{\text{ext}}$ starts from a new initial state $x_{0,\text{ext}}$ and has a nondeterministic silent transition labeled by ϵ from $x_{0,\text{ext}}$ to every other state $x \in X$.

Next, we try to recover a language from $O(k)_{\max}$, upon which we could derive a surrogate of the supervisor S. Let $\Phi_a : \overline{O(k)_{\max}} \to 2^{\Sigma^*}$ be a mapping, where

$$\gamma_\epsilon := \bigcup_{w \in \overline{O(k)_{\max}} \cap (\Sigma_o^\epsilon \times \Gamma)} \beta(w)$$

and

1. $\Phi_a(\epsilon, \gamma_\epsilon) := (\Sigma_{uo} \cap \gamma_\epsilon)^* (\gamma_\epsilon \cap \Sigma_o)$;

2. For all $s \in \overline{O(k)_{\max}}$ and $\sigma \in \Sigma_o^\epsilon$, let

$$\gamma_{s,\sigma} = \bigcup_{w \in \Sigma_o^\epsilon \cap \Gamma:\, \alpha(w) = \sigma \wedge sw \in \overline{O(k)_{\max}}} \beta(w).$$

If $\gamma_{s,\sigma} \neq \emptyset$, then

$$
\Phi_a(s(\sigma, \gamma_{s,\sigma})) :=
\begin{cases}
(\Phi_a(s) \cap \Sigma^*\{\sigma\} \cap P_o^{-1}(\alpha(s)\sigma)) \\
\quad [(\Sigma_{uo} \cap \gamma_{s,\sigma})^* (\gamma_{s,\sigma} \cap \Sigma_o)] & \text{if } \sigma \in \Sigma_o, \\
\Phi_a(s) & \text{otherwise.}
\end{cases}
$$

The motivation behind construction of Φ_a is briefly explained as follows. The set $O(k)_{\max}$ contains at most k incompatible finite sub-languages from $(\Sigma_o^\epsilon \times \Gamma)^*$, each of which can be represented as a tree-like finite-state automaton. Each sub-language, say O_i, is associated with a specific starting time, when the closed-loop system $(\mathbf{G}, S)$ is at a specific state tuple, say (x_i, y_i). For each received sequence of compound events $s \in \overline{O(k)}_{\max}$, after a new observable event $\sigma \in \Sigma_o^\epsilon$ is received, the resulting control patterns in different runs may be different, that is, $\Gamma(s, \sigma) = \{\gamma_i \in \Gamma | s(\sigma, \gamma_i) \in O_i\}$ is typically not a singleton, unlike the synchronous case described in the previous section. In reality, at any time instant, there is only one control pattern being active in $(\mathbf{G}, S)$, which however is unknown to an attacker. Any guess of the control pattern that is not a subset of the true control pattern will expose the existence of an attack. Thus, the covert way to guess this control pattern, from an attacker's viewpoint, is to identify a control pattern contained in all possible control patterns associated with that time instant. A natural idea is to take an intersection over all control patterns in $\Gamma(s, \sigma)$. However, there is one potential risk of covertness violation, that is, $\Gamma(s, \sigma)$ may not include all feasible control patterns generated by S after $\alpha(s)\sigma$ is intercepted, and blindly applying a control pattern derived from $\gamma(s, \sigma)$ may expose the existence of an attack to the unknown supervisor S. Unfortunately, it is impossible to know exactly which control patterns may not be included in $\gamma(s, \sigma)$. To make the problem solvable, one straightforward way is to require that there exist some $s \in \overline{O(k)}_{\max}$ and $\nu \in \Sigma_o^\epsilon \times \Gamma$ such that the estimate of the state of $\mathbf{G}$

$$\Delta(s, \nu) := \{x \in X | (\exists x' \in X)(\exists t \in P_o^{-1}(\alpha(s\nu)) \cap \Sigma^* \Sigma_o) \xi(x', t) = x\}$$

is a singleton. In other words, after observing the string $\alpha(s\nu)$, there exists a unique state reachable by $\alpha(s\nu)$ from any other state in $\mathbf{G}$. This special state can be treated as a new initial state for subsequent event executions. There could be more than one such special state associated with different (s, ν) pairs. Before such special states are reached, the attacker will not make any change to intercepted observable events and control commands. This idea is reflected in the construction of γ_ϵ and $\gamma_{s,\sigma}$ in Step (2) of the definition of Φ_a above. Attacks may take place after a special state is reached, due to the fact that all subsequent control patterns generated by the unknown S can be known and "confined" by the attacker via proper attack moves.

Example 4.3 *We revisit the closed-loop system $(\mathbf{G}, S)$ depicted in Figure 4.1 to explain the concepts introduced above. In this example, assume that $O_1 = \overline{\{(a, \{b, d\})(d, \{b, d\})\}}$, $O_2 = \overline{\{(a, \{b, d\})(d, \{b, d\})(d, \{a, b, c\})\}}$ and $O_3 = \overline{\{(e, \{b\})(b, \{b, d\})\}}$. The resulting $O(3)$ equals $O_1 \cup O_2 \cup_O 3$.*

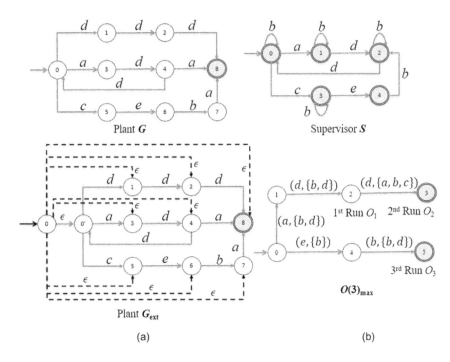

Figure 4.5 Models of plant $\mathbf{G}_{\text{ext}}$ (a) and $O(k)_{\max}$ (b).

The final $O(3)_{max} = \{(a, \{b, d\})(d, \{b, d\})(d, \{a, b, c\}), (e, \{b\})(b, \{b, d\})\}$ is depicted in Figure 4.5. It is clear that O_1 and O_2 are received when the closed-loop system and attacker start simultaneously. However, O_3 is received when the attacker starts after the closed-loop system generates the observable event c. After applying Φ_a on $\overline{O(3)_{max}}$, the outcome is depicted in Figure 4.6. We now apply the mapping Δ on $O(3)_{max}$ to estimate relevant of states in the plant $\mathbf{G}$. Initially, the plant $\mathbf{G}$ could be in any state in X. Thus, the initial state is labeled with X. After event a is received, we can check that $\mathbf{G}$ must uniquely enter state 3, which is labeled in Figure 4.6, namely $\Delta(\epsilon, (a, \{b, d\})) = \{3\}$. Similarly, after event d is received after a, $\mathbf{G}$ enters state 4, namely $\Delta((a, \{b, d\}), (d, \{b, d\})) = \{4\}$.

As a comparison, assume that $O_1 = \overline{\{(d, \{b, d\})\}}$ and $O_2 = \overline{\{((d, \{b, d\})(d, \{a, b, c\}))\}}$, namely the attacker starts after the plant generates event a. The new $O(3)_{max}$ and resulting $\Phi_a(\overline{O(3)_{max}})$ are depicted in Figure 4.7. In this new $O(3)_{max}$, after event $(d, \{b, d\})$ is received, the state estimate is $\Delta(\epsilon, (d, \{b, d\})) = \{0, 1, 2, 4, 8\}$.

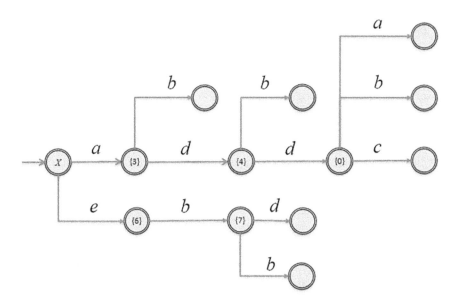

Figure 4.6 Model of $\Phi_a(\overline{O(3)_{\max}})$.

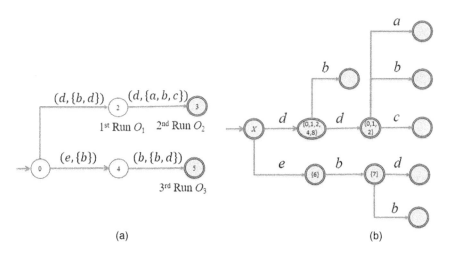

Figure 4.7 Models of updated $O(3)_{\max}$ (a) and $\Phi_a(\overline{O(3)_{\max}})$ (b).

After another event $(d, \{a, b, c\})$ is received, the state estimate is $\Delta((d, \{b, d\}), (d, \{a, b, c\})) = \{0, 1, 2\}$.

Next, we introduce a mapping $\hat{S}_k : P_o(\Phi_a(\overline{O(k)_{\max}})) \to \Gamma$, where

$$(\forall s \in P_o(\Phi_a(\overline{O(k)_{\max}})))\hat{S}_k(s) := En_{\Phi_a(\overline{O(k)_{\max}})}(s),$$

which will serve a surrogate of the unknown supervisor S.

Theorem 4.3 Given a closed-loop system $(\mathbf{G}, S)$, let $O(k)_{\max}$ and $\hat{S}_k$ be introduced above. Then for all $s \in \Phi_a(O(k)_{\max})$, if for all $\nu \in \Phi_a^{-1}(s)$, we have $|\Delta(\nu, \epsilon)| = 1$, then for each $s' \in \Sigma^*$ with $ss' \in \Phi_a(\overline{O(k)_{\max}})$ and $\{ss'\}\Sigma \cap \Phi_a(\overline{O(k)_{\max}}) \neq \emptyset$, we have $S(P_o(ss')) = \hat{S}_k(P_o(ss'))$.

Proof *For each $s \in \Phi_a(\overline{O(k)_{max}})$, if for all $\nu \in \Phi_a^{-1}(s)$, we have $|\Delta(\nu, \epsilon)| = 1$, then we set the state in $\Delta(\nu, \epsilon)$, say $x_s \in X$, as the initial state of the plant. After that, we apply the same proof idea in Theorem 4.1. We use induction. When $s' = \epsilon$, we know that the plant has no observable output at x_s and the supervisor S generates the first control command $S(s) = \gamma_0$. By the definition of $O(k)_{max}$, we know that $(\nu, \gamma_0) \in \overline{O(k)_{max}}$, and $\{s\}(\Sigma_{uo} \cap \gamma_0)^*(\gamma_0 \cap \Sigma_o) \subseteq \Phi_a(\overline{O(k)_{max}})$, upon which we have $\hat{S}_k(s) = En_{\Phi_a(\overline{O(k)_{max}})}(s) = \gamma_0 = S(s)$. Thus, the base case holds. Assume that for all $s' \in \Sigma^*$ with $ss' \in \Phi_a(\overline{O(k)_{max}})$, if $\{ss'\}\Sigma \cap \Phi_a(\overline{O(k)_{max}}) \neq \emptyset$ and $|s'| \leq n$, then $S(P_o(ss')) = \hat{S}_k(P_o(ss'))$. We need to show that, for each $s' \in \Phi_a(\overline{O(k)_{max}})$ with $\{ss'\}\Sigma \cap \Phi_a(\overline{O(k)_{max}}) \neq \emptyset$ and $|s'| = n + 1$, we have $S(P_o(ss')) = \hat{S}_k(P_o(ss'))$. Clearly, there exists $s'' \in \Phi_a(\overline{O(k)_{max}})$ and $\sigma \in \Sigma$ such that $s' = s''\sigma$. Since $|s''| = n$ and $\{ss''\}\Sigma \cap \Phi_a(\overline{O(k)_{max}}) \neq \emptyset$, by the assumption we have $S(P_o(ss'')) = \hat{S}_k(P_o(ss''))$. Because $\sigma \in En_{\Phi_a(\overline{O(k)_{max}})}(ss'') = \hat{S}_k(P_o(ss''))$, we know that $\sigma \in S(P_o(ss''))$. We have two cases to consider.*

Case 1: $\sigma \in \Sigma_{uo}$. Then we know that the plant $\mathbf{G}$ generates ϵ as the output, and the supervisor maintains the same control output as ss'', namely $S(P_o(ss'')) = S(P_o(ss''\sigma)) = S(P_o(ss'))$. On the other hand, $\hat{S}_k(P_o(ss')) = En_{\Phi_a(\overline{O(k)_{max}})}(P_o(ss''\sigma)) = En_{\Phi_a(\overline{O(k)_{max}})}(P_o(ss'')) = \hat{S}_k(P_o(ss'')) = S(P_o(ss'')) = S(P_o(ss'))$.

Case 2: $\sigma \in \Sigma_o$. In this case, the plant $\mathbf{G}$ generates σ as the observable output, which triggers the supervisor S to *generate a new control command* $S(P_o(ss''\sigma)) = S(P_o(ss''))\sigma =$ *γ. On the other hand, let μ' be associated with ss'' and $\mu(\sigma, \gamma) \in \overline{O(k)_{max}}$. Then we know that $(\Phi_a(\mu) \cap \Sigma^*\{\sigma\} \cap P_o^{-1}(ss''\sigma))[(\Sigma_{uo} \cap \gamma)^*(\gamma \cap \Sigma_o)] \subseteq \Phi_a(\overline{O(k)_{max}})$. This means that $En_{\Phi_a(\overline{O(k)_{max}})}(P_o(ss''\sigma)) = En_{\Phi_a(\overline{O(k)_{max}})}(P_o(ss''))\sigma = \hat{S}_k(P_o(ss')) = \gamma = S(P_o(ss'))$, which completes the induction.* ■

Theorem 4.3 indicates that $\hat{S}_k$ can be a surrogate of S for all live strings in $\Phi_a(\overline{O(k)_{\max}})$, as long as such live strings contain one prefix substring, upon which the state estimate of the plant **G** is a singleton. For each $s \in \Sigma^*$, let $L(\hat{S}_k/\mathbf{G}, s) := L(\hat{S}_k/\mathbf{G}) \cap \{s\}\Sigma^*$ and $L(S/\mathbf{G}, s) := L(S/\mathbf{G}) \cap \{s\}\Sigma^*$, namely suffix languages after s in $L(\hat{S}_k/\mathbf{G})$ and $L(S/\mathbf{G})$, respectively.

Corollary 4.2 Given a closed-loop system $(\mathbf{G}, S)$, let $O(k)_{\max}$ and $\hat{S}_k$ be introduced above. Then for each $s \in \Phi_a(\overline{O(k)_{\max}}) \cap L(\hat{S}_k/\mathbf{G})$, if for all $\nu \in \Phi_a^{-1}(s)$, we have $|\Delta(\nu, \epsilon)| = 1$, then $L(\hat{S}_k/\mathbf{G}, s) \subseteq L(S/\mathbf{G}, s)$.

Proof *For each $s \in \Phi_a(\overline{O(k)_{\max}})$, if for all $\nu \in \Phi_a^{-1}(s)$, we have $|\Delta(\nu, \epsilon)| = 1$, then we set the state in $\Delta(\mu, \epsilon)$, say x_s, as the initial state of the plant. We use induction. Clearly, $\epsilon \in L(\hat{S}_k/\mathbf{G}, s) \cap L(S/\mathbf{G}, s)$. Assume that for all $s' \in L(\hat{S}_k/\mathbf{G}, s)$, if $|s'| \leq n$, then $s' \in L(S/\mathbf{G}, s)$. Let $s' \in\in L(\hat{S}_k/\mathbf{G}, s)$ with $|s'| = n + 1$. Then there exist $s'' \in L(\hat{S}_k/\mathbf{G}, s)$ and $\sigma \in \Sigma$ such that $s' = s''\sigma$. Clearly, $s''\sigma \in L(\mathbf{G}, s)$. Since s'' is live, by Theorem 4.3, we know that $\hat{S}_k(P_o(ss'')) = S(P_o(ss''))$. Clearly, $\sigma \in \hat{S}_k(P_o(ss''))$. Thus, we know that $\sigma \in S(P_o(ss''))$, which means $s''\sigma = s' \in L(S/\mathbf{G}, s)$, which completes the induction part. Thus, $L(\hat{S}_k/\mathbf{G}, s) \subseteq L(S/\mathbf{G}, s)$.* ■

From Corollary 4.2, we know that only after some string s, whose resulting estimate of the plant state is singleton, we have $L(\hat{S}_k/\mathbf{G}, s) \subseteq L(S/\mathbf{G}, s)$. We now use $\hat{S}_k$ to synthesize a smart sensor-actuator attack. Because $\hat{S}_k$ becomes a proper surrogate of S only after some special s, we need to revise our synthesis procedure previously introduced in Chapter 3. Let $\mathbf{S}_k$ be an automaton realization of $\mathbf{S}_k = (\hat{Z}, \Sigma, \hat{\delta}, \hat{z}_0, \hat{Z}_m = \hat{Z})$. Because $O(k)_{\max}$ is finite, $\hat{\mathbf{S}}_k$ can be designed as a tree structure, namely, each state, other than the initial state, can have only one incoming transition. That is,

$$(\forall z \in \hat{Z} \setminus \{\hat{z}_0\}) |\{(z', \sigma) \in \hat{Z} \times \Sigma | \hat{\delta}(z', \sigma) = z\}| = 1.$$

Let $\Theta : \hat{Z} \to \{0, 1\}$, where for all $z \in \hat{Z}$, $\Theta(z) = 1$ if and only if

$$(\forall s \in L(\hat{\mathbf{S}}_k))\hat{\delta}(\hat{z}_0, s) = z$$
$$\Rightarrow |\{x \in X | (\exists t \in P_o^{-1}(P_o(s)) \cap \Sigma^* \Sigma_o) \xi(x_0, t) = x\}| \leq 1.$$

That is, $\Theta(z) = 1$ if and only if the estimate of states in $\mathbf{G}$ based on the observation generated by $s \in L(\hat{S}_k)$ that reaches z contains no more than one state. We say that z *induces an unambiguous state estimate in* $\mathbf{G}$, or z is *control unambiguous with respect to* $\mathbf{G}$, because any subsequent control patterns can be determined without any ambiguity.

Let $\mathbf{S}_k := \mathbf{G}_{\text{ext}} \times \hat{\mathbf{S}}_k = (X \times \hat{Z} \cup \hat{Z}, \Sigma^\epsilon, \xi \times \hat{\delta}, (x_0, \hat{z}_0), X_m \times \hat{Z}_m)$ be the synchronous product of the plant $\mathbf{G}$ and surrogate supervisor $\hat{\mathbf{S}}_k$, whose (partial) transition mapping $\xi \times \hat{\delta}$ is defined as follows: for all $w \in X \times \hat{Z} \cup \hat{Z}$ and for all $\sigma \in \Sigma^\epsilon$,

$$\xi \times \hat{\delta}(w, \sigma) = \begin{cases} (\xi(x, \sigma), \hat{\delta}(z, \sigma)) & \text{if } w = (x, z) \wedge \xi(x, \sigma)! \wedge \hat{\delta}(z, \sigma)!, \\ \hat{\delta}(z, \sigma) & \text{if } w = z \wedge \hat{\delta}(z, \sigma)! \vee \\ & \quad w = (x, z) \wedge \neg\xi(x, \sigma)! \wedge \hat{\delta}(z, \sigma)!, \\ \text{undefined} & \text{otherwise.} \end{cases}$$

Because $\hat{\mathbf{S}}_k$ is a tree structure, the product $\mathbf{G} \times \hat{\mathbf{S}}_k$ is also a tree structure. Let

$$\Xi := \{(x, z) \in X \times \hat{Z} | (\exists s \in \Sigma^* \Sigma_o) \xi \times \hat{\delta}(x_0, \hat{z}_0, s) = (x, z) \wedge \Theta(z) = 1\},$$

namely Ξ contains all states in the product, whose corresponding states in $\hat{S}_k$ are control unambiguous. For each $(x, z) \in \Xi$, let $\mathbf{S}_k(x, z)$ be a reachable sub-automaton of $\mathbf{S}_k$ by setting (x, z) as the initial state. We now treat $\mathbf{S}_k(x, z)$ as a new surrogate supervisor of the new plant $\mathbf{G}(x)$, which is derived by replacing the initial state x_0 with x.

Theorem 4.4 Given a closed-loop system $(\mathbf{G}, S)$, let Ξ be introduced above. For each $(x, z) \in \Xi$, let $\mathbf{S}_k(x, z)$ be introduced above. Assume that S is state consistent with respect to $\mathbf{G}$, that is, for all $t, t' \in L(S/\mathbf{G})$, if $\xi(x_0, t) = \xi(x_0, t')$ then $S(P_o(t)) = S(P_o(t'))$. Then for any string $s \in L(S/\mathbf{G})$, if there exists a suffix string $s' \in \Sigma^*$ of s, namely $s = ts'$ for some $t \in \Sigma^*$, such that $\hat{\delta}(\hat{z}_0, P_o(s)) = z$ and $\xi(x_0, s) = x$, then $En_{\hat{S}_k}(z) = S(P_o(s))$.

Proof *By the definition of $\hat{\boldsymbol{S}}_k$, which is derived from $\hat{S}_k$ that is derived from $O(k)_{\max}$, we know that, for the string s' mentioned above, there must exist a string $\mu \in \overline{O(k)_{\max}}$ such that $\alpha(\mu) = P_o(s')$ and $\gamma :=$ $\beta(\mu)^\uparrow \in \Gamma$ is a control pattern associated with the reception of the last observable event in $P_o(s')$, i.e., $P_o(s')^\uparrow$. This γ' is generated by an unknown supervisor S. On the other hand, when $P_o(s')$ is received by $\hat{\boldsymbol{S}}_k$, there must be a state in the plant $\boldsymbol{G}$ reached by a string $s \in L(S/\boldsymbol{G}) \cap \Sigma^*\Sigma_o$ - we only consider a state reached by an observable event in the plant. Since $\Theta(z) = 1$, we know that, when z is reached in $\hat{\boldsymbol{S}}_k$, there is no more than one state reached in $\boldsymbol{G}$. Because $s \in L(S/\boldsymbol{G})$ and s' is a suffix of s such that $P_o(s')$ reaches z in $\hat{\boldsymbol{S}}_k$, we know that the state $\xi(x_0, s) = x$ must be in the state estimate set induced by z. Because this induced set contains no more than one state, x must be the one. The corresponding control pattern is $S(P_o(s))$. Because S is state consistent with respect to $\boldsymbol{G}$, we know that $En_{hat{S}_k}(z) = S(P_o(s))$.* ∎

Theorem 4.4 indicates that, if S is state consistent with respect to $\boldsymbol{G}$, then whenever a tuple (x, z) is reached in $\boldsymbol{G}_k$, where $\Theta(z) = 1$, we can uniquely determine the current control pattern in the closed-loop system, which is $En_{\hat{S}_k}(z)$. At this moment, an attacker essentially synchronizes an attack model with the closed-loop system, and the attack synthesis and deployment strategy described in the previous section can be applied straightforwardly. Upon this idea, a simple attack synthesis procedure is presented below.

Algorithm 4.1 *Synthesis Procedure for Non-Synchronized Attack*

1. *Input: $\boldsymbol{G}$ with $\Sigma_{s,a}$ and $\Sigma_{c,a}$, and $O(k)_{\max}$;*

2. *Generate $\boldsymbol{G}_{\text{ext}}$ and $\hat{\boldsymbol{S}}_k$;*

3. *Calculate $\boldsymbol{S}_k = \boldsymbol{G}_{\text{ext}} \times \hat{\boldsymbol{S}}_k$;*

4. *Calculate the set Ξ from $\boldsymbol{S}_k$;*

5. *For each $(x, z) \in \Xi$, generate $\boldsymbol{S}_k(x, z)$ and synthesize a smart sensor-actuator attack $A(z)$ with respect to $(\boldsymbol{G}(x), \boldsymbol{S}_k(x, z))$.*

6. *Output: $\mathcal{A}(k) := \{A(z) | (\exists(x, z) \in \Xi) A(z) \text{ is nonempty}\}$.*

We can easily see that $A(z)$ in Step 5 is well defined, because if there are two states $(x, z), (x', z) \in \Xi$ such that $\Theta(z) = 1$, we must have $x = x'$. In case that $\mathcal{A}(k) \neq \emptyset$, the following attack deployment strategy will be implemented:

4.2.1 Deployment of Non-Synchronized Attack

- Start $\hat{\mathbf{S}}_k$ and track the observable output of $\mathbf{G}$;

- For each received observable event, update the state z in $\hat{\mathbf{S}}_k$;

    - If $\Theta(z) = 0$, then no attack is applied to the input and output of S;

    - If $\Theta(z) = 1$, activate $A(z)$ on the input and output of S.

Under this attack deployment strategy, we write $S \circ \mathcal{A}_k$ to denote the compromised supervisor.

Unlike the synchronized case, where an attack can be deployed at the initial time when the system starts, in a non-synchronized case, an attack has to wait until some control unambiguous state z is reached, which however may or may not happen in a specific run. Thus, for a non-synchronized case, a strong attack typically does not exist. However, a weak attack may still be feasible.

Theorem 4.5 Given a closed-loop system $(\mathbf{G}, S)$, let $O(k)_{\max}$, $\hat{\mathbf{S}}_k$ and Ξ be introduced above. Then under the Deployment Procedure of Non-synchronized Attack, each non-empty smart weak sensor-actuator attack $A(z) \in \mathcal{A}_k$ of $(\mathbf{G}(x), \mathbf{S}_k(x, z))$ with respect to $L_{\text{dam}} = L_m(\mathbf{G})$ and $(x, z) \in \Xi$ also induces a smart weak sensor-actuator attack of $(\mathbf{G}, S)$ with respect to L_{dam}.

Proof *If $\mathcal{A}(k) \neq \emptyset$, there must exist a smart weak attack $A(z)$ associated with $\mathbf{G}(x)$ for some $(x, z) \in \Xi$ under $\mathbf{S}_k(x, z)$. By Theorem 4.4, $\mathbf{S}_k(x, z)$ is a surrogate of S after z. This means there exists a string $s \in L(S \circ A(z) / \mathbf{G}(x))$ that leads to a damage state. On the other hand, there must exist another string $s' \in L(S/\mathbf{G})$ such that s' can reach (x, z). Thus, the string $s's$ must be in $L(S \circ \mathcal{A}(k)/\mathbf{G})$ such that a damage state will be reached. Thus, the theorem follows.* ■

Example 4.4 *We revisit the closed-loop system $(\mathbf{G}, S)$ depicted in Figure 4.5, where $\Sigma = \Sigma_o = \Sigma_{s,a} = \{a, b, c, d, e\}$, $\Sigma_c = \{a, c, d, e\}$*

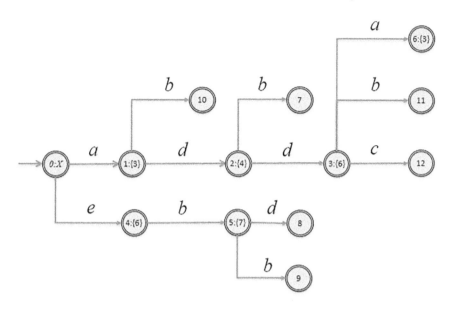

Figure 4.8 The model of $\hat{\mathbf{S}}_k$.

and $\Sigma_{c,a} = \{a\}$. We now follow the Synthesis Procedure for Non-synchronized Attack. The extended model $\mathbf{G}_{ext}$ is depicted in Figure 4.5, and $\hat{\mathbf{S}}_k$ is depicted in Figure 4.8, where $\Theta^{-1}(1) = \{1, 2, 3, 4, 5, 6\}$. Next, we compute $\mathbf{S}_k = \mathbf{G}_{ext} \times \hat{\mathbf{S}}_k$, which is depicted in Figure 4.9. We can check that $\Xi = \{(3, 1), (4, 2), (0', 3), (3, 6), (6, 4), (7, 5)\}$. Next, we pick each element (x, z) in Ξ and synthesize a smart attack with respect to $(\mathbf{G}(x), \mathbf{S}_k(x, z))$. For example, let $(x, z) = (3, 1)$. Then $(\mathbf{G}(x), \mathbf{S}_k(x, z))$ is depicted in Figure 4.10. By applying the attack synthesis procedure introduced in Section 5.1, the resulting smart attack model $\mathbf{A}(1)$ is depicted in Figure 4.11. Based on the closed-loop model $\mathbf{G}(3) \times \mathbf{S}(3, 1) \times \mathbf{A}(1)$, it is clear that there exists a weak attack. By Theorem 4.5, we know that the original system $(\mathbf{G}, \mathbf{S})$ permits smart weak sensor-actuator attacks.

The work in this section on non-synchronized attacks is a rather superficial treatment. It takes a quite restrictive view on how knowledge obtained from observations, i.e., $O(k)$, is represented. The choice of $O(k)_{max}$ cannot guarantee that all useful information will be kept in the model. Instead, it only provides a coarse view of what could be control information. It is likely that, by using a different way of constructing

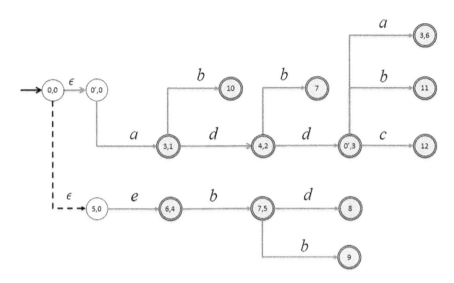

Figure 4.9 The model of $\mathbf{S}_k = \mathbf{G}_{\mathrm{ext}} \times \hat{\mathbf{S}}_k$.

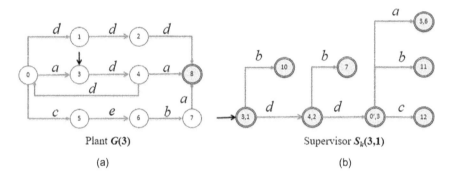

Figure 4.10 The models of plant $\mathbf{G}(3)$ (a) and supervisor $\mathbf{S}_k(3,1)$ (b).

$O(k)_{\mathrm{max}}$, the chance of finding a smart attack might be higher. The study, however, does reveal some fundamental difference between synchronized attacks and non-synchronized attacks. That is, for a synchronized attack, an attacker is certain that, as long as a previously obtained observation sequence appears, the resulting control pattern can be uniquely determined. In contrast, in a non-synchronized attack, only based on obtained observation sequence, it is not necessarily possible to uniquely determine the resulting control pattern, making the satisfaction of covertness requirement a daunting challenge. In this

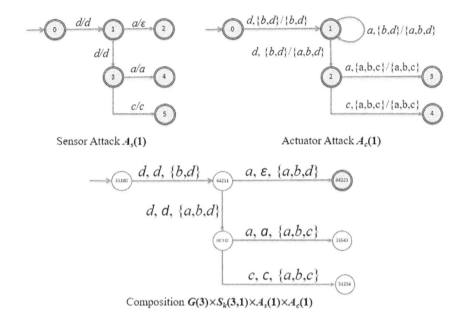

Figure 4.11 The models of smart attack $\mathbf{A}(1) = (\mathbf{A}_s(1), \mathbf{A}_c(1))$ and the closed-loop system $\mathbf{G}(3) \times \mathbf{S}(3,1) \times \mathbf{A}(1)$.

section, we present one simple way of overcoming this challenge by putting an observer in front of an attack model. Only when the observer can uniquely determine the current system state, it will be safe for the attacker to initiate an attack. It will be interesting to know whether this insertion of an observer in the attack loop is necessary.

4.3 CONCLUSIONS

Following Chapter 3, where an SSAA is synthesized with perfect knowledge about the plant $\mathbf{G}$ and supervisor S, in this chapter we have discussed the synthesis of SSAA with an unknown supervisor, whose control logic can only be inferred from observed input and output of the supervisor. An attacker continuously collects observable data from a target closed-loop system $(\mathbf{G}, S)$, and makes a decision whether the collected data are sufficient to synthesize a smart attack model. There are two different situations that need to be considered. When an attack is perfectly synchronized with the plant execution, namely it starts to collect observable data when the plant is at the initial state, the synthesis can be reduced to the case with perfect knowledge of the supervisor model. The only difference is that the chance of finding a non-empty smart attack might be lower than the case with perfect knowledge. However, when an attack is not perfectly synchronized with the plant execution, it is challenging to ensure attack covertness, due to the uncertainty of the exact plant state at each attacking point. To address this challenge, a new framework consisting of a state observer and a smart sensor-actuator attack is proposed. Basically, an attacker uses a state observer to decide whether a unique state in the plant has been reached, upon which the attacker can be certain whether a specific observed control pattern is indeed the right control pattern in the system. Only at this point, the problem can be converted into the previously studied attack synthesis under perfect knowledge. There could be more than one such unique state, making the attack strategy a switching one, where, depending on which unique state is reached, a specific follow-up smart attack is activated. However, there is a chance in a specific run that none of the unique states is reached. In this case, no smart attack will be activated. In this sense, a strong attack typically does not exist for a non-synchronized attack situation. I would like to point out that the information processing for non-synchronized case is rather primitive, only serving to shed light on how such a type of problems could be approached. It is still open exactly what more information can be extracted from collected observable data and whether a state observer is necessary. Hopefully, such questions could be answered in the future.

II

Modeling and Synthesis of Resilient Supervisors

CHAPTER 5

Resilient Supervisory Control against Smart Sensor Attacks

After gaining knowledge about several smart attack strategies in the previous chapters, we are now ready to explore the feasibility of designing resilient supervisors against previously introduced smart attacks. In this chapter, we focus on resilient control against smart sensor attacks (SSA). One fundamental question is whether there exists a resilient supervisor against a certain type of smart attack on a given plant while satisfying certain requirements. To answer this question, we investigate the decidability issue of the existence of a resilient supervisor. We first present a sufficient and necessary condition that ensures the existence of an SSA, which reveals a novel demand-supply relationship between an attacker and a controlled plant, represented as a set of risky pairs. Each risky pair consists of a damage string desired by the attacker and an observable sequence feasible in the supervisor such that the latter induces a sequence of control patterns, which allows the damage string to happen. It turns out that each risky pair can induce a smart weak sensor attack. When the plant, supervisor and damage language are regular, it is possible to identify and remove all such risky pairs from the plant behavior, via a genuine encoding scheme. Based on this insight about the existence of an SSA, we establish our key result that the existence of a nonblocking supervisor resilient to all SSAs is decidable.

5.1 INTRODUCTION

As mentioned previously there are two different streams of research on cyberattacks and resilient control. The first stream refers to a set of worst-case methods that treat attacks as undesirable (either intentional or unintentional) uncontrollable and mostly unobservable disturbances to a given closed-loop system. Existing works include, e.g., a game theoretical approach [37], fault-tolerance-based approaches such as [52] and [74] on sensor attacks, [29] on actuator attacks, and [50,51,53] on sensor+actuator attacks, and transducer-based modeling and synthesis approaches such as [54,99]. In the worst-case methods, system vulnerability is typically modeled by concepts similar to diagnosability described in, e.g., [45], and system resilience bears similarity to fault tolerant control described in, e.g., [27,41], that concerns whether there is a supervisor that can perform satisfactorily under the worst case attack scenarios. The second stream refers to a set of intelligent-foe methods, aiming to develop a specific smart attack model that ensures certain intuitive properties such as covertness and guaranteed (strong or weak) damage infliction. Existing works include, e.g., [55,56,58,59,61,75] on SSAs, [62,70,71] on smart actuator attacks, and [63,64,76] on smart sensor+actuator attacks. With such smart attack models, existing research works address the impact of a specific attack on the closed-loop behavior, the vulnerability of a system to such an attack, and finally the resilience of a supervisor to a concerned attack.

After examining those existing works on smart cyberattacks, it is clear that most works focus on how to derive a proper smart attack model. Various synthesis algorithms have been proposed under relevant assumptions. Nevertheless, the existence of a supervisor that is resilient to *ALL* possible smart cyberattacks is still open for research. In Refs. [77,78] the authors present synthesis methods for resilient control against a specific sensor attack model described by a finite-state automaton in different scenarios. Thus, the synthesized supervisor is not designed to be resilient to all possible SSAs. In case of a worst-case sensor attack scenario, no smartness in terms of, e.g., covertness, is considered by the authors. There are a few heuristic synthesis approaches proposed in the literature, e.g., [56] proposes one algorithm against smart sensor attacks, [64] proposes one algorithm that generates a resilient supervisor whose state set is bounded by a known value, and [71] presents an algorithm to synthesize a supervisor, which is control equivalent to an original supervisor and resilient to smart actuator attacks. But none of those existing algorithms can guarantee to find one resilient supervisor, if it exists. That is, when those algorithms terminate and return an empty solution, it does not necessarily mean that there is no solution.

Before any attempt of overcoming a complexity challenge in order to derive a resilient solution, it is critical to answer a computability question first, that is, how to decide whether a solution exists. To address this important decidability issue, in this chapter, we focus only on sensor attacks, but hoping that our derived result may shed light on research of other types of attacks. We follow a sensor attack model introduced in Chapter 2, which associates each observed sequence from the plant $\mathbf{G}$ with an altered observable sequence that becomes the input of a given supervisor. It turns out that the existence of a smart weak sensor attack, which is not necessarily regular (i.e., representable by a finite-state automaton), is solely determined by the existence of at least one risky pair that consists of a damage string desired by the attacker and an observable sequence feasible in the supervisor such that the latter induces a sequence of control patterns, which allows the concerned damage string to happen. Because any strong sensor attack is also a weak attack, the existence of such a risky pair becomes the sufficient and necessary condition for the existence of a smart sensor attack. In Ref. [55] and its journal version [56], by imposing language normality to the closed-loop behavior, it is shown that the supremal SSA language can be synthesized, whenever it exists, upon which a specific SSA model can be derived. In Ref. [58] and its journal version [59], the language normality is dropped, and it is shown that an SSA model (not necessarily supremal) can be synthesized via a special insertion-deletion attack structure, whenever it exists. However, none of these works reveals the aforementioned demand-supply relationship reflected in risky pairs that capture the nature of sensor attacks. Due to this insightful concept of risky pairs, it is possible to show that the existence of a nonblocking controllable and observable supervisor that is resilient to all regular SSAs is decidable. To this end, we develop a genuine encoding mechanism that reveals all possible sequences of control patterns required by a regular sensor attack and all sequences of control patterns feasible in the plant, allowing us to remove the set of all risky pairs from the plant behavior. After that, we introduce a language-based concept of *nonblocking resilient supervisor candidate* and its automaton-counterpart *control feasible sub-automaton* that does not contain any risky pair, upon which we are able to decide the existence of a resilient supervisor. The proposed decision process renders a concrete synthesis procedure that guarantees to compute a nonblocking supervisor resilient to SSAs, whenever it exists.

The remainder of this chapter is organized as follows. In Section 5.2, we present a motivation example. Then in Section 5.3, we review a specific smart sensor attack model, where the concept of *attackability* is introduced. Then we present a sufficient and necessary condition to ensure a smart sensor attack in Section 5.4, where the key concept of risky pairs is introduced. After that, we present a sufficient and necessary condition for the existence of a nonblocking supervisor that is resilient to SSAs in Section 5.5, and show that this sufficient and necessary condition is verifiable in Section 5.6, which finally establishes the decidability result for the existence of a resilient supervisor. Conclusions are drawn in Section 5.7.

5.2 MOTIVATION – ATTACK OF NAVIGATOR

Imagine that Bob would like to ride his autonomous car from his home to his office. There is a GPS navigator installed inside his car. The navigator first generates a shortest path based on traffic conditions, then guides the vehicle to make required turns at planned junctions. However, Bob's friend Peter plans to play a prank on Bob by tricking the navigator to lead Bob's car to another location via GPS spoofing, shown in Figure 5.1. Peter has the city road map and also knows Bob's home address and office address. In addition, he has a navigator of the same model as the one installed in Bob's car. Thus, by running his

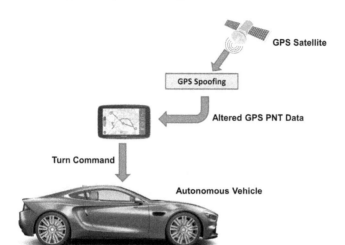

Figure 5.1   An example of attack of navigator.

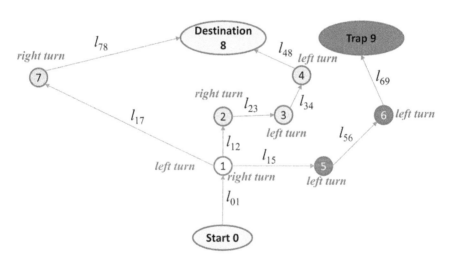

Figure 5.2   Road network setup.

own navigator over the same origin-destination pair, Peter will know Bob's route plan. Figure 5.2 depicts the system setup, where Bob's home is at "start 0" node, his office is at "Destination 8" node, and the prank location is at "Trap 9" node. Each symbol "l_{ij}" denotes the length of the road segment between node i and node j. In addition, the position of each node in the map is publicly known. By simply running the navigator of the same model, Peter knows that Bob's car will choose the shortest path "$0 \rightarrow 1 \rightarrow 2 \rightarrow 3 \rightarrow 4 \rightarrow 8$", which leads to the following navigation commands: (1) *right turn* (at node 2), followed by (2) *left turn* (at node 3), followed by (3) *left turn* (at node 4). To trick the navigator to issue the same sequence of commands but at incorrect junctions, say, *right turn* at node 1, followed by *left turn* at node 5, and followed by *left turn* at node 6, Peter only needs to buy a GPS spoofing device available in the market that can send fake GPS position signals to Bob's navigator. Peter can easily determine the spoofed GPS position signal by using the actual GPS signal, which could be obtained by an extra GPS signal transceiver secretly installed underneath Bob's car. With this trick, Peter can make Bob's navigator believe that node 2 is reached, when the actual node reached is node 1. With a similar GPS position spoofing scheme, Peter can misguide Bob's car to reach node 9, instead of node 8, without being detected. Such GPS spoofing is one specific example of a *smart sensor attack*, whose formal definition will be given in the next section. Intuitively, it contains the following basic characteristics: by knowing sufficient information in advance, an attacker can trick a victim to issue the correct order of commands but at incorrect states (or locations), which leads to an unwanted consequence.

If Bob somehow knows that Peter will use GPS spoofing to play a trick on his car, he can simply choose the path "$0 \rightarrow 1 \rightarrow 7 \rightarrow 8$". In this case, even though Peter knows this new path, he cannot spoof the GPS signals to trick Bob's car to node 9 without being detected, as the new path generates a new sequence of navigation commands: (1) *left turn* (at node 1), then (2) *right turn* (at node 7), which, no matter how Peter changes GPS position signals, cannot bring Bob to node 9. Such a path plan is a specific example of a *resilient supervisor* against SSAs, whose definition will be given later in this chapter. Intuitively, a resilient supervisor will ensure that, for **any** sensor attack, either it can be detected before inflicting damage, or it will not lead to any damage.

One big question is, for an arbitrary network, how to decide whether a resilient path plan (or navigation supervisor) exists. In this chapter, we will investigate this decidability problem against SSAs. The computational efficiency, i.e., the complexity issue, however, will not be addressed here.

5.3   SMART SENSOR ATTACK

We recall some basic concepts introduced in Chapter 2 about sensor attacks. We assume that an attacker can observe each observable event generated by the plant $\mathbf{G}$, and replace the observable event with a sequence of observable events from Σ_o^*, including the empty string ϵ, in order to "fool" the given supervisor S, known to the attacker. Considering that in practice any event occurrence takes a non-negligible amount of time, it is impossible for an attacker to insert an arbitrarily long observable sequence to replace a received observable event. Thus, we assume that there exists a known number $n \in \mathbb{N}$ such that the length of any "reasonable" observable sequence that the attacker can insert is no more than n. Let $\Delta_n \subseteq \{s \in \Sigma_o^* \| s | \leq n\}$ be the set of all n-bounded observable sequences possibly inserted by an attacker. Unlike the non-deterministic sensor attack concept, in this chapter we focus on deterministic attacks. In contrast to a nondeterministic sensor attack model introduced in Chapter 2, a *deterministic* sensor attack is a (partial) mapping $A : P_o(L(\mathbf{G})) \to \Delta_n^*$, where

- $A(\epsilon) = \epsilon$,

- $(\forall s \in P_o(L(\mathbf{G})))(\forall \sigma \in \Sigma_o)\, s\sigma \in P_o(L(\mathbf{G})) \Rightarrow A(s\sigma) = A(s)W$,
  where $W \subseteq \Delta_n$.   □

The first condition states that, before any observation is obtained, the attack cannot generate any non-empty output, because, otherwise, such a fake observation sequence may reveal the existence of an attack, if the plant has not started yet, whose starting time is unknown to the attacker. The second condition states that each received observation $\sigma \in \Sigma_o$ will trigger a string W in Δ_n, which may or may not be the same as the ground truth event σ.

An attack model A is *regular* if there exists a finite-state transducer $\mathbf{A} = (Y, \Sigma_o^\epsilon \times \Delta_n, \eta, I, O, y_0, Y_m)$, where $Y_m = Y$, $\eta : Y \times \Sigma_o^\epsilon \times \Delta_n \to Y$ is the (partial) transition mapping such that if $\eta(y, \sigma, u)!$ and $\sigma = \epsilon$ then $u = \epsilon$, i.e., if there is no observation input, then there should be no observation output. The functions $I : (\Sigma_o^\epsilon \times \Delta_n)^* \to \Sigma_o^*$ and $O : (\Sigma_o^\epsilon \times \Delta_n)^* \to \Delta_n^*$ are the *input* and *output* mappings, respectively, such that for each $\mu = (a_1, b_1)(a_2, b_2) \ldots (a_l, b_l) \in (\Sigma_o^\epsilon \times \Delta_n)^*$, $I(\mu) = a_1 a_2 \ldots a_l$

and $O(\mu) = b_1 b_2 \ldots b_l$. We require that, for each $\mu \in L(\mathbf{A})$, we have $A(I(\mu)) = O(\mu)$ and $I(L(\mathbf{A})) \subseteq P_o(L(\mathbf{G}))$. Since A is a function, we know that for all $\mu, \mu' \in L(\mathbf{A})$, if $I(\mu) = I(\mu')$, then $O(\mu) = A(I(\mu)) = A(I(\mu')) = O(\mu')$, that is, the same input should result in the same output.

Although a deterministic attack model A introduced in this chapter is more restrictive than a nondeterministic attack model introduced in Chapter 2 and also in Ref. [55,56], adopting such a model does not affect the generality of our subsequent results on decidability of existence of a smart sensor attack and attack resilient supervisor. This is due to the fact that there exists a nondeterministic attack if and only if there exists a deterministic one. To see this fact, it is clear that each deterministic model is a nondeterministic model. Thus, we only need to show that from each nondeterministic model we can derive at least one deterministic model. We will use a simple example to illustrate the construction procedure. Recall the nondeterministic attack model A in Chapter 2, as shown in Figure 5.3, which is a transducer. We first start from damage states (i.e., marker states), and perform co-reachability search to find all states in the nondeterministic model that satisfy the following two conditions: (1) each state is reachable from the initial state, (2) at each state, each observable event is associated with only one transition (denoting an attack move). After that, we perform reachability search upon those states derived from the first step and add new necessary states in so that the following condition holds: at each state, each observable event is associated with only one transition (denoting an attack move) if and only if it is associated with at least one transition in the original nondeterministic model. This construction will result in a deterministic smart sensor attack model, shown in Figure 5.3. In this example, we can see that there can be several deterministic attack models derivable from the nondeterministic model.

Assumption 5.1 *Only regular attacks are considered.*

Because A is deterministic, the combination of the attack A and the supervisor S forms a new supervisor $S \circ A : P_o(L(\mathbf{G})) \to \Gamma$, where

$$(\forall s \in P_o(L(\mathbf{G})))A(s)! \Rightarrow S \circ A(s) = S(A(s)).$$

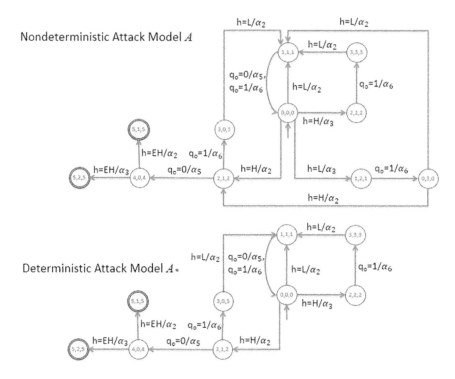

Figure 5.3 Derive a deterministic attack from a nondeterministic attack.

We call $S \circ A$ a *compromised supervisor under A*. The closed and marked behaviors, $L(S \circ A/\mathbf{G})$ and $L_m(S \circ A/\mathbf{G})$, of the closed-loop system $S \circ A/\mathbf{G}$ are defined accordingly, as shown in Chapter 1. We call $L(S \circ A/\mathbf{G})$ an *attacked language* of $S/\mathbf{G}$ under A. The closed-loop system is depicted in Figure 5.4.

Definition 5.1 Given a closed-loop system $(\mathbf{G}, S)$, let $L_{\mathrm{dam}} \subseteq L(\mathbf{G}) \setminus L(S/\mathbf{G})$ be a damage language. $(\mathbf{G}, S)$ is said *attackable* with respect to L_{dam}, if there exists an attack A, called a *smart sensor attack* of $(\mathbf{G}, S)$, such that the following hold:

1. **Covertness**: Moves of A are covert to the supervisor S, i.e.,

$$A(P_o(L(\mathbf{G}))) \subseteq L(S/\mathbf{G}). \tag{5.1}$$

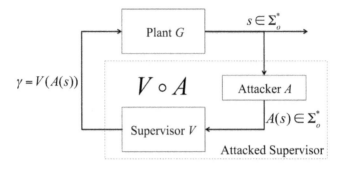

Figure 5.4 The block diagram of a plant under attack.

2. **Damage infliction**: A causes "damage" to **G**, i.e.,

- Strong attack: Any string may lead to damage:

$$L(S \circ A/\mathbf{G}) = \overline{L(S \circ A/\mathbf{G}) \cap L_{\text{dam}}}; \qquad (5.2)$$

- Weak attack: Some string may lead to damage:

$$L(S \circ A/\mathbf{G}) \cap L_{\text{dam}} \neq \varnothing. \qquad (5.3)$$

If $(\mathbf{G}, S)$ is not attackable with respect to L_{dam}, then S is said *resilient* to smart attacks with respect to L_{dam}. □

The concept of attackability in Definition 6.2 is slightly different from Definition 2.2 in Chapter 2, where the latter involves a nondeterministic sensor attack A.

Remark 5.1 *In Chapter 2 and also [56], a special subset of observable events called* protected events *is introduced, which is denoted by $\Sigma_{o,p} \subseteq \Sigma_o$, representing observable events in the plant that cannot be changed by any sensor attack. This feature makes the modeling framework more general. However, it diminishes the chance of having a smart sensor attack, due to the challenge of ensuring the covertness property, when the system trajectory $s \in L(S \circ A/\mathbf{G})$ is outside the legal language $L(S/\mathbf{G})$ and there are a few protected system output events that will inevitably reveal the attack. Due to this complication, we lack a simple sufficient and necessary condition to characterize the existence of a smart sensor attack, making the subsequent study of the existence of a* *supervisor resilient to such SSAs infeasible. To overcome this challenge, we could restrict the damage language L_{dam} to be $L(G) \setminus L(S/G)$, i.e., any string outside $L(S/G)$ is a damage string. This will allow an attacker not to make any event change, after the system trajectory is outside $L(S/G)$, as damage has been inflicted. Then all results presented in this paper will still be valid. So a user of this theory has two options for the system setup, that is, either $\Sigma_{o,p} = \varnothing$ and $L_{dam} \subseteq L(G) \setminus L(S/G)$, as adopted in this chapter, or $\Sigma_{o,p} \neq \varnothing$ and $L_{dam} = L(G) \setminus L(S/G)$.*

Let $\mathcal{A}(\mathbf{G}, S, L_{\text{dam}})$ be the collection of all attacked languages caused by SSAs. Clearly, $(\mathcal{A}(\mathbf{G}, S, L_{\text{dam}}), \subseteq)$ is a partially ordered set. Unlike the non-deterministic case described in Chapter 2, the supremal deterministic attack model may not always exist, due to the fact that the set union of multiple smart attack languages may not be achieved by one single deterministic sensor attack. However, it is possible to compute a maximal smart sensor attack. In the example depicted in Figure 5.3, the illustrated deterministic smart attack model results in a maximal attacked language. We can see in that example that there is no supremal attacked language induced by a deterministic smart weak attack.

5.4   A SUFFICIENT AND NECESSARY CONDITION FOR ATTACK EXISTENCE

Example 5.1 *Let us start with a small example, which is depicted in Figure 5.5. Assume that the attacker A wants to achieve a string $abc \in L_{\text{dam}}$, which leads to a damage state. Assume that event a is contained in control pattern γ_1, event b is in control pattern γ_2, and event c in control pattern γ_3. After event a fires, the attacker wants the control pattern γ_2 to be issued. Since event a does not lead to control pattern γ_2, but event d does, the attacker A will replace event a with d to trick the supervisor S to generate γ_2. Assume that b is fired afterward. The attacker wants γ_3 to be issued. Since event b does not lead to γ_3, instead, event e does, the attacker A replaces event b with event e to trick the supervisor S to issue γ_3, if event c happens afterward, the attacker achieves his/her goal without being detected by the supervisor. The attacker could continue this trick as long as it is possible. So essentially, by faking some observable string, the attacker*

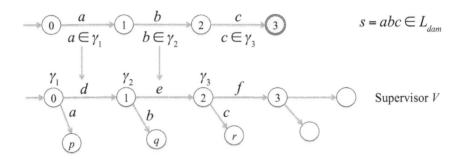

Figure 5.5   A smart sensor attack.

hopes to trick the supervisor to issue a sequence of control patterns, which contain some damaging strings, without being detected by the supervisor.

We now generalize this attack idea. For notation simplicity, given a string $t = \nu_1 \ldots \nu_n \in \Sigma^*$ with $n \in \mathbb{N}$, for each $i \in \{1, \ldots, n\}$, we use t^i to denote the prefix substring $\nu_1 \ldots \nu_i$. By convention, $t^0 := \epsilon$.

Theorem 5.1 Given a plant $\mathbf{G}$, a supervisor S and a damage language $L_{\text{dam}} \subseteq L(\mathbf{G}) \setminus L(S/\mathbf{G})$, there is a smart weak sensor attack A, if and only if the following condition holds: there exists $s = u_1\sigma_1 \ldots u_r\sigma_r u_{r+1} \in L_{\text{dam}}$, with $r \in \mathbb{N}$, $u_1, \ldots, u_{r+1} \in \Sigma_{uo}^*$ and $\sigma_1, \ldots, \sigma_r \in \Sigma_o$, and $t = \nu_1 \ldots \nu_r \in P_o(L(S/\mathbf{G}))$ with $\nu_1, \ldots, \nu_r \in \Delta_n$ such that (1) $u_1, \sigma_1 \in S(t^0)^*$; (2) for each $i \in \{2, \ldots, r\}$, $u_i, \sigma_i \in S(t^{i-1})^*$; (3) $u_{r+1} \in S(t)^*$.

Proof

1. *We first show the IF part. Assume that there exist $s = u_1\sigma_1 \ldots u_r\sigma_r u_{r+1} \in L_{\text{dam}}$, with $r \in \mathbb{N}$, $u_1, \ldots, u_{r+1} \in \Sigma_{uo}^*$ and $\sigma_1, \ldots, \sigma_r \in \Sigma_o$, and $t = \nu_1 \ldots \nu_r \in P_o(L(S/\mathbf{G}))$ with $\nu_1, \ldots, \nu_r \in \Delta_n$ such that (1) $u_1, \sigma_1 \in S(t^0)^*$; (2) for each $i \in \{2, \ldots, r\}$, $u_i, \sigma_i \in S(t^{i-1})^*$; (3) $u_{r+1} \in S(t)^*$. We now explicitly design an attack model A as follows. For each $\hat{t} \in P_o(L(\mathbf{G}))$, let $B(\hat{t}, t) := \nu_1 \ldots \nu_i t'$, where $s = u_1\sigma_1 \ldots u_i\sigma_i t'$ and $\{P_o(t')\} \cap \{\sigma_{i+1} \ldots \sigma_r\} = \emptyset$.*

(a) $A(\epsilon) := \epsilon$;

(b) for each $\hat{t} \in P_o(L(G))$, where $A(\hat{t})$ has been defined, for each $\sigma \in \Sigma_o$ with $\hat{t}\sigma \in P_o(L(G))$,

$$A(\hat{t}\sigma) := \begin{cases} A(\hat{t})\nu_i & \text{if } \hat{t}\sigma = \sigma_1 \ldots \sigma_i, \; i \in \{1,\ldots,r\}; \\ A(\hat{t})\sigma & \text{if } B(\hat{t},t)\sigma \in P_o(L(S/G)) \setminus \overline{\{\sigma_1 \ldots \sigma_r\}}; \\ A(\hat{t}) & \text{otherwise.} \end{cases}$$

Clearly, A is well defined. We now show that $A(P_o(L(G))) \subseteq L(S/G)$, i.e., A is covert, by using induction on the length of strings in $P_o(L(G))$. Clearly, $\epsilon \in P_o(L(G))$, and $A(\epsilon) = \epsilon \in L(S/G)$. Assume that for all strings $\hat{t} \in P_o(L(G))$ with $|\hat{t}| \leq n$, where $n \in \mathbb{N}$, we have $A(\hat{t}) \in L(S/G)$. We need to show that for each $\sigma \in \Sigma_o$ with $\hat{t}\sigma \in P_o(L(G))$, we have $A(\hat{t}\sigma) \in L(S/\mathit{textbf}G)$. If $\hat{t}\sigma = \sigma_1 \ldots \sigma_{n+1}$, where $n + 1 \leq r$, then we have $A(\hat{t}\sigma) = \nu_1 \ldots \nu_{n+1} \in \overline{\{t\}} \subseteq P_o(L(S/G))$. If $B(\hat{t},t)\sigma \in L(S/G) \setminus \overline{\{\sigma_1 \ldots \sigma_r\}}$, then $A(\hat{t}\sigma) = A(\hat{t})\sigma = B(\hat{t},t)\sigma \in P_o(L(S/G))$. Otherwise, since $A(\hat{t}\sigma) = A(\hat{t}) \in P_o(L(S/G))$, the induction step holds, which means A is covert.

Since A results in weak damage due to the existence of $\hat{s}$, by Definition 6.2, A is a smart weak sensor attack.

2. Next, we show the ONLY IF part. Assume that there exists a smart weak sensor attack A. By Definition 5.1, we know that $A(P_o(L(G))) \subseteq L(S/G)$ and $L(S \circ A/G) \cap L_{dam} \neq \varnothing$. Thus, there exists $s = u_1\sigma_1 \ldots u_r\sigma_r u_{r+1} \in L(S \circ A/G) \cap L_{dam}$ with $r \in \mathbb{N}$, $u_1,\ldots,u_{r+1} \in \Sigma_{uo}^*$ and $\sigma_1,\ldots,\sigma_r \in \Sigma_o$, such that $A(P_o(u_1)) = \epsilon$, $A(P_o(u_1)\sigma_1) = \nu_1 \in \Delta_n$; $A(P_o(u_1)\sigma_1 \ldots P_o(u_j)) = A(P_o(u_1)\sigma_1 \ldots P_o(u_{j-1})\sigma_{j-1})$ and $A(P_o(u_1)\sigma_1 \ldots P_o(u_j)\sigma_j) = \nu_1 \ldots \nu_j$ with $\nu_j \in \Delta_n$ for all $j \in \{2,\ldots,r\}$; and finally,

$$A(P_o(s)) = A(P_o(u_1)\sigma_1 \ldots P_o(u_r)\sigma_r).$$

Let $t = \nu_1 \ldots \nu_r$. Since $s \in L(S \circ A/G)$, by the definition of $L(S \circ A/G)$, we know that (1) $u_1, \sigma_1 \in S(t^0)^*$; (2) for each $i \in \{2,\ldots,r\}$, $u_i, \sigma_i \in S(t^{i-1})^*$;

3. $u_{r+1} \in S(t)^*$. Thus, the theorem follows. ∎

As an illustration, in the example depicted in Figure 5.5, we can see that $r = 3$, $\sigma_1 = a$, $\sigma_2 = b$, $\sigma_3 = c$, $\nu_1 = d$, $\nu_2 = e$, $u_1 = u_2 = u_3 = u_4 = \epsilon$.

The strings s and t in Theorem 5.1 form a risky pair $(s, t) \in L_{\mathrm{dam}} \times \Delta_n^*$ such that, by mapping $P_o(s)$ to t, the attacker can rely on the existing supervisor S to inflict a weak attack on the plant $\mathbf{G}$, without being detected by the supervisor. Since the existence of a risky pair is sufficient and necessary for the existence of a smart weak sensor attack, we will use this fact to determine the existence of a resilient supervisor.

5.5 SUPERVISOR RESILIENT TO SMART SENSOR ATTACKS

In this section, we explore whether there exists a sufficient and necessary condition to ensure the existence of a supervisor that is resilient to all regular SSAs, i.e., the closed-loop system is not attackable by any regular smart sensor attack. In Section 5.4, we have shown that there is a sufficient and necessary condition for the existence of a smart weak sensor attack shown in Theorem 5.1. Since each strong attack is also a weak attack, if we can effectively eliminate those risky pairs described in Theorem 5.1, we shall be able to prevent the existence of any smart sensor attack. Since, given a plant $\mathbf{G}$ and a requirement $Spec$, we can always synthesize a controllable and observable sublanguage of $L_m(\mathbf{G}) \cap L_m(\mathrm{Spec})$, without loss of generality, we assume that the plant $\mathbf{G}$ satisfies all given requirements. Thus, we will only focus on the following problem.

Problem 5.1 *Given a plant $\mathbf{G}$ and a damage language $L_{\mathrm{dam}} \subseteq L(\mathbf{G})$, synthesize a supervisor S such that $(\mathbf{G}, S)$ is not attackable by any regular smart sensor attack with respect to L_{dam}.* □

To solve this problem, we first intend to find a proper way of encoding all risky pairs. Recall that, given a string $s \in \Sigma^*$, we use $s^\uparrow$ to denote the last event of s. If $s = \epsilon$, by convention, $s^\uparrow := \epsilon$. In addition, we use s_o to denote the longest prefix substring of s, whose last event is observable, i.e., $s_o \in \overline{\{s\}} \cap (\Sigma_{uo}^* \Sigma_o)^* \cap P_o^{-1}(P_o(\{s\}))$. Thus, if $s \in \Sigma_{uo}^*$, then we can derive that $s_o = \epsilon$.

Let $\iota : \Sigma^* \to 2^{(\Sigma \times \Gamma)^*}$ be a partial mapping, where

- $\iota(\epsilon) := \{\epsilon\}$;

- $(\forall s \in \Sigma^*)(\forall \sigma \in \Sigma)\, \iota(s\sigma) := \iota(s)\{(\sigma, \gamma) | \sigma \in \gamma\}$.

In Example 5.1, we have $(a, \gamma_1)(b, \gamma_2)(c, \gamma_3) \in \iota(abc)$. What the map ι does is to map each string $s \in \Sigma^*$ to a set of sequences of control patterns such that each derived control pattern sequence, say $\gamma_1 \ldots \gamma_r \in \Gamma^*$, contains the string s in the sense that $s \in \gamma_1 \ldots \gamma_r \subseteq \Sigma^*$. By applying the map ι to the damage language L_{dam}, the result $\iota(L_{\text{dam}}) := \bigcup_{s \in L_{\text{dam}}} \iota(s)$ presents all possible sequences of control patterns, each of which contains at least one string in L_{dam} - in other words, each string in $\iota(L_{\text{dam}})$ may potentially result in damage.

Example 5.2 *To further illustrate how this function works, we introduce another simple example depicted in Figure 5.6, where $\Sigma = \{a, b, c, d, v\}$, $\Sigma_c = \{a, b, d\}$ and $\Sigma_o = \{a, b, c, d\}$. To simplify our illustration, in this example we assume that $\Delta_n = \Sigma_o^\epsilon$, i.e., $n = 1$. The damage language $L_{dam} = \{ad\}$, which is shown by a dashed line leading to state 3. Figure 5.7 depicts the outcome of $\iota(L_{dam})$.*

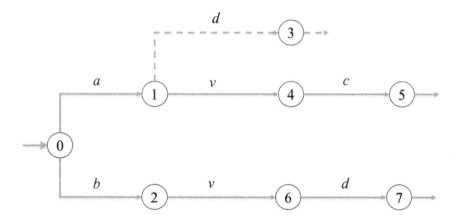

Figure 5.6 A small plant **G**.

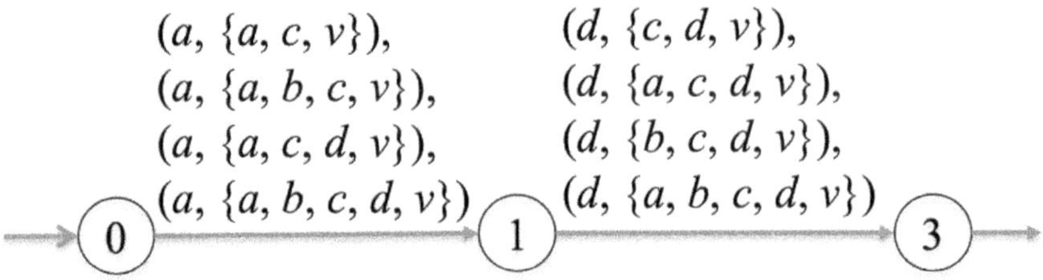

$$(a, \{a, c, v\}), \qquad (d, \{c, d, v\}),$$
$$(a, \{a, b, c, v\}), \qquad (d, \{a, c, d, v\}),$$
$$(a, \{a, c, d, v\}), \qquad (d, \{b, c, d, v\}),$$
$$(a, \{a, b, c, d, v\}) \qquad (d, \{a, b, c, d, v\})$$

Figure 5.7 The model of $\iota(L_{\mathrm{dam}})$.

A smart sensor attack replaces each intercepted observable event $\sigma \in \Sigma_o$ with a string in Δ_n, unless σ is silent, i.e., $\sigma = \epsilon$. To capture the impact of such changes on the control pattern sequences, we introduce a mapping $\psi : (\Sigma \times \Gamma)^* \to 2^{((\Sigma \cup \Delta_n) \times \Gamma)^*}$, where

- $\psi(\epsilon) := \{\epsilon\}$;

- For each $\mu \in (\Sigma \times \Gamma)^*$ and $(\sigma, \gamma) \in \Sigma \times \Gamma$, we have

$$\psi(\mu(\sigma, \gamma)) := \begin{cases} \psi(\mu)\{(\sigma, \gamma)\} & \text{if } \sigma \in \Sigma_{uo}, \\ \psi(\mu)(\Delta_n \times \{\gamma\}) & \text{otherwise.} \end{cases}$$

We extend the domain of ψ to languages in the usual way, i.e., for all $L \subseteq (\Sigma \times \Gamma)^*$, $\psi(L) := \bigcup_{s \in L} \psi(s)$.

To explicitly describe how a smart attack may utilize possible sequences of control patterns, we introduce one more mapping

$$\nu : ((\Sigma \cup \Delta_n) \times \Gamma)^* \to 2^{(\Sigma_o^\epsilon \times \Gamma)^*},$$

where

- $\nu(\epsilon) := \{\epsilon\}$;

- For all $(\sigma, \gamma) \in (\Sigma \cup \{\epsilon\}) \times \Gamma$,

$$\nu(\sigma, \gamma) = \begin{cases} (\sigma, \gamma) & \text{if } \sigma \in \Sigma_o \wedge \sigma \in \gamma; \\ (\epsilon, \gamma) & \text{if } \sigma \in \Sigma_{uo} \wedge \sigma \in \gamma \vee \sigma = \epsilon; \\ \varnothing & \text{otherwise.} \end{cases}$$

- For all $s = \sigma_1 \ldots \sigma_r \in \Delta_n$, $|P_o(s)| = r \geq 2$, and $\gamma \in \Gamma$,

$$\nu(s, \gamma) := \{(\sigma_1, \gamma_1) \ldots (\sigma_r, \gamma) | \sigma_r \in \gamma \wedge$$
$$(\forall i \in \{1, \ldots, r-1\})\sigma_i \in \gamma_i \in \Gamma\}.$$

- $(\forall \mu(s, \gamma) \in ((\Sigma \cup \Delta_n) \times \Gamma)^+) \, \nu(\mu(s, \gamma)) = \nu(\mu)\nu(s, \gamma).$

Example 5.3 *As an illustration, we apply the map ψ to the damage language $\iota(L_{dam})$ in Figure 5.7, where $n = 1$. To simplify the illustration, we assume that an attacker can, but prefers not to, change events c and d. The outcomes of applying mapping ψ and ν are depicted in Figure 5.8.*

Next, we determine all control pattern sequences in the plant **G** that may be used by a smart attack. Let $p : (\Sigma_o^\epsilon \times \Gamma)^* \to \Gamma^*$ be a mapping, where

- $p(\epsilon) := \epsilon$;

- $(\forall s(\sigma, \gamma) \in (\Sigma_o^\epsilon \times \Gamma)^+) \, p(s(\sigma, \gamma)) := p(s)\gamma.$

Let $\Upsilon_G : L(\mathbf{G}) \times \Sigma^* \times \Gamma \to \{0, 1\}$ be a Boolean map, where for each $(s, t, \gamma) \in L(\mathbf{G}) \times \Sigma^* \times \Gamma$,

$$\Upsilon_G(s, t, \gamma) = 1 \iff st \in L(\mathbf{G}) \wedge t \in \gamma^*.$$

For each $\gamma \in \Gamma$, let

$$B(\gamma) := \begin{cases} \{(\epsilon, \gamma)\}^* & \text{if } \gamma \cap \Sigma_{uo} \neq \varnothing, \\ \{\epsilon\} & \text{otherwise.} \end{cases}$$

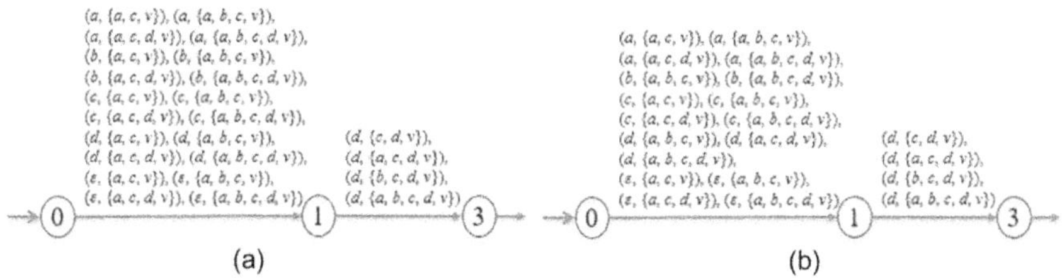

Figure 5.8 $\psi(\iota(L(\mathbf{G})))$ (a), $\nu(\psi(\iota(L(\mathbf{G}))))$ (b).

Let $\zeta : L(\mathbf{G}) \to 2^{(\Sigma_o^\epsilon \times \Gamma)^*}$ be a total mapping, where

- $\zeta(\epsilon) := (\cup_{\gamma \in \Gamma : \gamma \cap \Sigma_{uo} \neq \varnothing} \{(\epsilon, \gamma)\}^+) \bigcup (\cup_{\gamma \in \Gamma : \gamma \subseteq \Sigma_o} \{(\epsilon, \gamma)\})$;

- For all $s \in (\Sigma_{uo}^* \Sigma_o)^*$ and $t \in \Sigma_{uo}^* \Sigma_o^\epsilon$ with $st \in L(\mathbf{G})$,

$$\zeta(st) := \left\{ \begin{array}{ll} \zeta(s) & \text{if } P_o(t) = \epsilon, \\ M & \text{otherwise,} \end{array} \right.$$

where

$$M := \bigcup_{w \in \zeta(s) : \Upsilon_G(s,t,p(w)^\uparrow) = 1} \bigcup_{\gamma' \in \Gamma} \{w(P_o(t), \gamma')\} B(\gamma').$$

We call $\zeta(L(\mathbf{G}))$ the *augmented closed behavior* of $\mathbf{G}$. Let $g : (\Sigma_o^\epsilon \times \Gamma)^* \to \Sigma_o^*$ be a mapping, where

- $g(\epsilon) := \epsilon$;

- $(\forall \mu(\sigma, \gamma) \in (\Sigma_o^\epsilon \times \Gamma)^+) \, g(\mu(\sigma, \gamma)) := g(\mu) P_o(\sigma)$.

The *augmented marked behavior* of $\mathbf{G}$ induced by ζ is defined as $\zeta(L(\mathbf{G})) \cap g^{-1}(P_o(L_m(\mathbf{G})))$.

This definition of ζ indicates that, except for control patterns generated initially, i.e., when $s = \epsilon$, each control pattern will be changed only after an observable event is received, i.e., when $st \in \Sigma^* \Sigma_o \cap L(\mathbf{G})$. This matches the definition of a supervisor S that changes its output only when a new observation is received. In addition, if a control pattern γ contains unobservable events, it will be contained in a self-loop of the augmented event (ϵ, γ), i.e., $\{(\epsilon, \gamma)\}^*$, denoting that the control pattern γ may be used more than once by the plant, as long as no new observable event has been received. Again, this matches the Ramadge-Wonham supervisory control paradigm, where execution of any unobservable transition allowed by the current control pattern will not change the current control pattern - recall that in a finite-state automaton realization of S, unobservable events are self-looped at relevant states.

Example 5.4 *As an illustration, we apply ζ to the plant model $L(\mathbf{G})$ depicted in Figure 5.6. Part of the outcome is depicted in Figure 5.9. Because the total state set is $X \times \Sigma_o^\epsilon \times \Gamma$, which is too big to be*

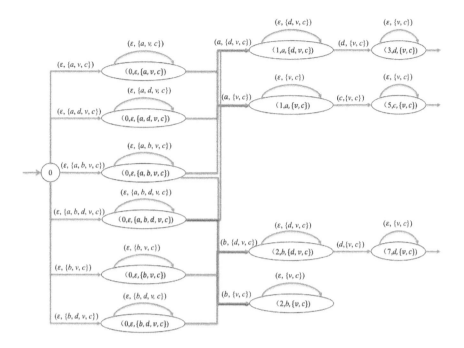

Figure 5.9 The model of $\zeta(L(\mathbf{G}))$.

shown entirely in the picture, we only include states that have at least one future extension, unless they are marker states (i.e., states $(3, d, \{v, c\})$, $(5, c, \{v, c\})$ and $(7, d, \{v, c\})$), except for one blocking state $(2, b, \{v, c\})$, which is left there for an illustration purpose that will be explained shortly. The marker states in Figure 5.9 denote the augmented marked behavior of $\mathbf{G}$ in Figure 5.6.

Till now, we have provided sufficient means to describe all risky pairs, which are captured by $\nu(\psi(\iota(L_{\text{dam}})))$ at the attacker's demand side, and $\zeta(L(\mathbf{G}))$ at the plant's supply side. To avoid such risky pairs, we only need to remove $p^{-1}(p(\nu(\psi(\iota(L_{\text{dam}})))))(\Sigma_o^\epsilon \times \Gamma)^*$ from $\zeta(L(\mathbf{G}))$. The reason why we concatenate $(\Sigma_o^\epsilon \times \Gamma)^*$ at the end of $p^{-1}(p(\nu(\psi(\iota(L_{\text{dam}})))))$ is to denote all possible augmented strings that may contain some strings in $p^{-1}(p(\nu(\psi(\iota(L_{\text{dam}})))))$ as prefix substrings. Thus, all safe supervisory control pattern sequences shall be contained in $\hat{H} := \zeta(L(\mathbf{G})) - p^{-1}(p(\nu(\psi(\iota(L_{\text{dam}})))))(\Sigma_o^\epsilon \times \Gamma)^*$ in order to prevent any sequence of control patterns from being used by an attacker.

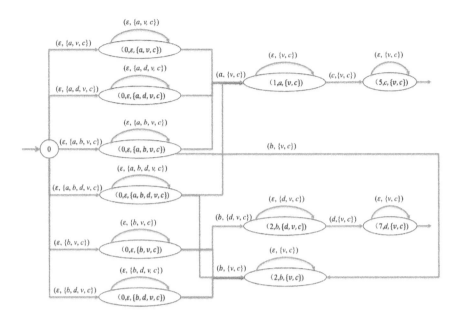

Figure 5.10 The model of $\hat{H}$.

Example 5.5 *Figure 5.10 depicts the outcome of subtracting risky control pattern sequences $p^{-1}(p(\nu(\psi(\iota(L_{dam})))))(\Sigma_o^\epsilon \times \Gamma)^*$ from (part of) $\zeta(L(\mathbf{G}))$ shown in Figure 5.9. It is clear that there cannot be any sequence of control patterns $\gamma_1\gamma_2\ldots\gamma_l$ such that $a \in \gamma_1$ and $d \in \gamma_2$.*

To extract a proper supervisor from $\hat{H}$, we need a few more technical preparations. Let $H := \overline{\hat{H}} \subseteq (\Sigma_o^\epsilon \times \Gamma)^*$ be the prefix closure of $\hat{H}$. All tuples $(\sigma, \gamma) \in \Sigma_o \times \Gamma$ are considered to be controllable, except for tuples $\{\epsilon\} \times \Gamma$. We introduce the concept of conditional controllability inspired by the standard notion of controllability in Ref. [18].

Definition 5.2 A sublanguage $L \subseteq H$ is *conditionally controllable* with respect to $\zeta(L(\mathbf{G}))$ and $\{\epsilon\} \times \Gamma$, if $(\overline{L} - \{\epsilon\})(\{\epsilon\} \times \Gamma) \cap \zeta(L(\mathbf{G})) \subseteq \overline{L}.\square$

In other words, as long as (ϵ, γ) is not defined at the beginning, i.e., $(\epsilon, \gamma) \notin \zeta(L(\mathbf{G}))$, it should not be disabled, if it follows a non-empty string $s \in \overline{L}$. We can briefly explain the motivation as follows. If an event (ϵ, γ) does not appear at the beginning, by the definition of $\zeta(L(\mathbf{G}))$ and subsequently that of H, it must be incurred by another string $s(\sigma, \gamma)$ such that $\gamma \cap \Sigma_{uo} \neq \varnothing$ – clearly, we can stop (σ, γ), if $\sigma \neq \epsilon$, by not choosing γ; but after γ is chosen and some unobservable event allowed by γ occurs, the same control pattern γ will continuously remain active, i.e., (ϵ, γ) will still be allowed, until a new observation is generated, leading to a new control pattern. But the situation is different initially, as we can directly disable the control pattern γ, thus stop the event (ϵ, γ). It is clear that conditional controllability is also closed under set union.

Let $\mathcal{C}(\zeta(L(\mathbf{G})), H)$ be the set of all prefix-closed sublanguages of H, which is conditionally controllable with respect to $\zeta(L(\mathbf{G}))$ and $\{\epsilon\} \times \Gamma$. It is clear that the supremal conditionally controllable sublanguage in $\mathcal{C}(\zeta(L(\mathbf{G})), H)$ under the partial order of set inclusion exists. We denote this unique sublanguage as $\mathcal{S}_* := \sup\mathcal{C}(\zeta(L(\mathbf{G})), H)$. Notice that $\mathcal{S}_*$ contains no sequence of control patterns that may be used by a smart attack to inflict damage. Later, we will show that $\mathcal{S}_*$ contains all feasible supervisors that are resilient to SSAs, as long as such a supervisor exists. We now introduce techniques to extract a feasible resilient supervisor out of $\mathcal{S}_*$, if it exists. To this end, we introduce a few more concepts.

Let $f : \mathcal{S}_* \to 2^X$ be a mapping, where

- For all $(\epsilon, \gamma) \in \mathcal{S}_*$,

$$f(\epsilon, \gamma) := \{x \in X | (\exists t \in \gamma^* \cap \overline{\Sigma_{uo}^* \Sigma_o}) \xi(x_0, t) = x\};$$

- For all $s \in \mathcal{S}_*$ and $(\sigma, \gamma) \in \Sigma_o^\epsilon \times \Gamma$ with $s(\sigma, \gamma) \in \mathcal{S}_*$, if $\sigma = \epsilon$, then $f(s(\sigma, \gamma)) := f(s)$; otherwise,

$$f(s(\sigma, \gamma)) := \{x \in X | (\exists t \in \gamma^* \cap \overline{\Sigma_{uo}^* \Sigma_o})(\exists x' \in f(s))\xi(x', \sigma t) = x\}.$$

The map f essentially associates each string $s \in \mathcal{S}_*$ with the corresponding set of all possible states of $\mathbf{G}$ reachable after s via a given control pattern γ. Let $h : \mathcal{S}_* \to 2^X$ be the marking coreachability map associated with the plant $\mathbf{G}$, where for each $s = (\epsilon, \gamma_0)(\sigma_1, \gamma_1) \ldots (\sigma_n, \gamma_n) \in \mathcal{S}_*$ with $n \in \mathbb{N}$,

- $f(s) \cap X_m = \varnothing \Rightarrow h(s) = \varnothing$;

- If $f(s) \cap X_m \neq \varnothing$, then let $\varrho : 2^X \times \Gamma \to 2^X$, where

$$(\forall U \in 2^X)(\forall \gamma \in \Gamma) \, \varrho(U, \gamma) := \{x \in X | (\exists t \in \gamma^* \cap \overline{\Sigma_{uo}^* \Sigma_o})(\exists x' \in U) \xi(x, t) = x'\},$$

and $h(s) := \cup_{i=0}^n U_i$, where

- $U_n := \varrho(f(s) \cap X_m, \gamma_n);$
- $(\forall i \in \{0, \ldots, n-1\}) \, U_i := \varrho(U_{i+1}, \gamma_i).$

Definition 5.3 A resilient supervisor candidate $\mathcal{L} \subseteq \mathcal{S}_*$ is *nonblocking* with respect to $\mathbf{G}$, if for all $s \in \mathcal{L}$,

$$f(s) \subseteq \bigcup_{t \in \mathcal{L}: s \leq t} h(t).$$

$\square$

Definition 5.4 A sublanguage $\mathcal{L} \in \mathcal{C}(\zeta(L(\mathbf{G})), H)$ is a *nonblocking resilient supervisor candidate* if for all $s \in \mathcal{L}$,

1. $(\forall t \in g^{-1}(g(s)) \cap \mathcal{L}) p(t)^\uparrow = p(s)^\uparrow;$

2. $g(En_{\mathcal{L}}(s)) = P_o(p(s^\uparrow)) \cap g(En_{\zeta(L(\mathbf{G}))}(s));$

3. $\mathcal{L}$ is nonblocking with respect to $\mathbf{G}$. $\square$

Notice that $t \in g^{-1}(g(s)) \cap \mathcal{L}$ means that $g(s) = g(t)$, and $p(t)^\uparrow = p(s)^\uparrow$ means that the incurred control patterns by $g(t)$ and $g(s)$ are the same. Thus, the first condition in Definition 5.4 essentially states that all observably identical strings must lead to the same control pattern – consequently, any silent transition ϵ cannot generate any new control pattern other than the current one. The second condition states that an "observable" event $\sigma \in \Sigma_o^\epsilon$ is allowed by $\mathcal{L}$, i.e., $\sigma \in g(En_{\mathcal{L}}(s))$, if and only if it is allowed by the control pattern incurred by s, i.e., $\sigma \in P_o(p(s^\uparrow))$, and also allowed by $L(\mathbf{G})$, i.e., $\sigma \in g(En_{\zeta(L(\mathbf{G}))}(s)))$. The last condition refers to nonblockingness of $\mathcal{L}$.

Example 5.6 *As an illustration, we calculate* $sup\mathcal{C}(\zeta(L(\mathbf{G})), H)$ *and remove all states that violate either one of the conditions of Definition 5.4. Figure 5.11 depicts the outcome. We can see that the state* $(2, b, \{v, c\})$ *in Figure 5.11 needs to be removed because it is blocking, violating the third condition in Definition 5.4. In addition,*

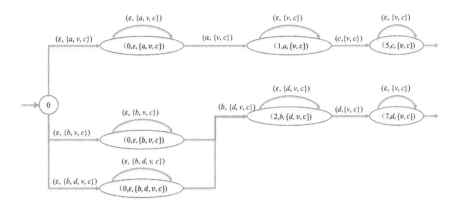

Figure 5.11   All nonblocking resilient supervisor candidates of $\mathcal{S}_*$.

states $(0, \epsilon, \{a, b, v, c\})$ and $(0, \epsilon, \{a, b, d, v, c\})$ and $(0, \epsilon, \{a, d, v, c\})$ in Figure 5.11 also need to be removed because they clearly violate the second condition of Definition 5.4, as the event b is defined in control patterns $\{a, b, v, c\}$ and $\{a, b, d, v, c\}$ of states $(0, \epsilon, \{a, b, v, c\})$ and $(0, \epsilon, \{a, b, d, v, c\})$, respectively, but no outgoing transitions containing b are allowed at these two states in H, even though these transitions are allowed in $\zeta(L(\mathbf{G}))$, and event d is defined in the control pattern $\{a, d, v, c\}$ of state $(0, \epsilon, \{a, d, v, c\})$, but no outgoing transition containing d is allowed in H, even though such a transition is allowed in $\zeta(L(\mathbf{G}))$.

We now state the following theorem, which is the first step toward solving the decidability problem of the existence of a supervisor resilient to SSAs.

Theorem 5.2 Given a plant $\mathbf{G}$ and a damage language $L_{\mathrm{dam}} \subseteq L(\mathbf{G})$, let $\mathcal{S}_*$ be defined above. Then there exists a supervisor $S : P_o(L(\mathbf{G})) \to \Gamma$ such that $(\mathbf{G}, S)$ is not attackable w.r.t. L_{dam}, iff there exists a nonblocking resilient supervisor candidate $\mathcal{L} \subseteq \mathcal{S}_*$.

Proof

1. *We first show the IF part. Assume that there exists a nonblocking resilient supervisor candidate $\mathcal{L} \subseteq \mathcal{S}_*$. For each $s \in P_o(L(\mathbf{G}))$, if $s \notin g(\mathcal{L})$ then let $S(s) := \Sigma_{uc}$; otherwise, for any $u \in g^{-1}(s) \cap \mathcal{L}$, let $S(s) := [p(u)]^\uparrow$. For the latter case, we first show that*

$S(s)$ is well defined. Assume that it is not true, then there exist $u_1, u_2 \in g^{-1}(s) \cap \mathcal{L}$ such that $u_1 \neq u_2$ and $[p(u_1)]^{\uparrow} \neq [p(u_2)]^{\uparrow}$. But this violates Condition 1 of Definition 5.4, thus, contradicts our assumption that $\mathcal{L}$ is a nonblocking resilient supervisor candidate. So S must be well defined, that is, for each $s \in P_o(L(\boldsymbol{G}))$, $S(s)$ is uniquely defined.

Secondly, since $[p(u)]^{\uparrow}$ is a control pattern for $u \in g^{-1}(s) \cap \mathcal{L}$, it is clear that $S(s) \in \Gamma$. Since S maps all strings observably identical to the same control pattern, we know that $L(S/G)$ is observable. Finally, by the third condition of Definition 5.4, it is clear that $\mathcal{L}$ is nonblocking. By the construction of $\mathcal{L}$, and the second condition of Definition 5.4, where for all $\hat{s} \in \mathcal{L}$,

$$g(En_{\mathcal{L}}(\hat{s})) = P_o(p(\hat{s}^{\uparrow})) \cap g(En_{\zeta(L(\boldsymbol{G}))}(\hat{s})),$$

we can show that $g(\mathcal{L}) = P_o(L(S/G))$. Thus, by the third condition of Definition 5.4, we have that S is a nonblocking supervisory control map. Clearly, S does not allow any weak sensor attack damage. Thus, it is resilient to any smart sensor attack, regardless of whether the attack is a strong or weak one.

2. We now show the ONLY IF part. Assume that there exists a supervisor S, which does not allow any smart sensor attack. Since each strong attack is also a weak attack, we will only need to consider weak sensor attacks. We define the following language $\mathcal{L}$ induced from S:

   i. $\epsilon \in \mathcal{L}$;

   ii. $(\epsilon, S(\epsilon)) \in \mathcal{L}$;

   iii. For all $s \in \mathcal{L}$, and $\sigma' \in P_o(p(s)^{\uparrow})$ and $\gamma \in \Gamma$,

   $$(\sigma', \gamma) \in En_{\zeta(L(\boldsymbol{G}))}(s) \Rightarrow s(\sigma', S(g(s)\sigma')) \in \mathcal{L};$$

   iv. All strings in $\mathcal{L}$ are generated in Steps (1)-(3).

Clearly, $\mathcal{L} \subseteq \zeta(L(\boldsymbol{G}))$. Because V is a resilient supervisor, by Theorem 5.1 we know that $\mathcal{L} \subseteq H$ - otherwise, there must exist a smart weak attack. By the construction of $\mathcal{L}$, we know that $\mathcal{L}$ is conditionally controllable with respect to $\zeta(L(\boldsymbol{G}))$ and $\{\epsilon\} \times \Gamma$. Thus, $\mathcal{L} \in$

$C(\zeta(L(\mathbf{G})), H)$, namely, $\mathcal{L} \subseteq S_*$. Since S is a nonblocking supervisor, we can check that the first and last conditions in Definition 5.4 hold. Since $\mathcal{L} \subseteq \zeta(L(\mathbf{G}))$, we know that $g(En_{\mathcal{L}}(s)) \subseteq g(En_{\zeta(L(\mathbf{G}))}(s))$. By Steps (iii)-(iv), we know that $g(En_{\mathcal{L}}(s)) \subseteq P_o(p(s^\uparrow))$. Thus, we have $g(En_{\mathcal{L}}(s)) \subseteq P_o(p(s^\uparrow)) \cap g(En_{\zeta(L(\mathbf{G}))}(s))$. On the other hand, by Step (iii), we know that $g(En_{\mathcal{L}}(s)) \supseteq P_o(p(s^\uparrow)) \cap g(En_{\zeta(L(\mathbf{G}))}(s))$. Thus, we finally have

$$g(En_{\mathcal{L}}(s)) = P_o(p(s^\uparrow)) \cap g(En_{\zeta(L(\mathbf{G}))}(s)),$$

which means the second condition of Definition 5.4 holds. Thus, $\mathcal{L}$ is a nonblocking resilient supervisor candidate, which completes the proof.

∎

As an illustration, we can check that any marked sequence in Figure 5.11 is a nonblocking resilient supervisor candidate. For example, take a look at the sublanguage $\mathcal{L} := \{(\epsilon, \{a, v, c\})\}^+ \{(a, \{v, c\})\} \{(\epsilon, \{v, c\})\}^* \{(c, \{v, c\})\} \{(\epsilon, \{v, c\})\}^*$. We can check that $\mathcal{L}$ is conditional controllable with respect to $\zeta(L(\mathbf{G}))$ and $\{\epsilon\} \times \Gamma$. Thus, $\mathcal{L} \in C(\zeta(L(\mathbf{G})), H)$. In addition, $\mathcal{L}$ is nonblocking and satisfies conditions in Definition 5.4. Thus, $\mathcal{L}$ is a nonblocking resilient supervisor candidate of S_*. By Theorem 5.2, we know that there must exist a resilient supervisor S that does not allow any smart sensor attack. Based on the construction shown in the proof of Theorem 5.2, the corresponding supervisor is $S(\epsilon) := \{a, v, c\}$, $S(a) := \{v, c\}$ and $S(ac) := \{v, c\}$. For any other observable string $s \in P_o(L(\mathbf{G}))$, we simply set $S(s) := \Sigma_{uc}$.

Theorem 5.2 indicates that, to decide whether there exists a nonblocking supervisor that disallows SSAs, we only need to decide whether there exists a nonblocking resilient supervisor candidate $\mathcal{L} \subseteq S_*$. Next, we shall discuss how to determine the existence of such a language $\mathcal{L}$.

5.6 DECIDABILITY OF EXISTENCE OF SUPERVISOR RESILIENT TO SMART SENSOR ATTACKS

In the previous section, we present a sufficient and necessary condition for the existence of a resilient supervisor. However, the computability issue is not addressed. In this section, we discuss how to compute all those sets and languages introduced in the previous section, and eventually show how to decide the existence of a resilient supervisor, i.e., to decide when that sufficient and necessary condition mentioned in Theorem 5.2 holds for a given plant $\mathbf{G}$ and a regular damage language L_{dam}.

We first discuss how to compute $\iota(L_{\text{dam}})$. As shown in Section 5.4, let $D = (W, \Sigma, \kappa, w_0, W_m)$ recognize L_{dam}, i.e., $L_m(D) = L_{\text{dam}}$. We construct another finite-state automaton $D_\iota := (W, \Sigma \times \Gamma, \kappa_\iota, w_0, W_m)$, where $\kappa_\iota : W \times \Sigma \times \Gamma \to W$ is the (partial) transition map such that for each $(w, \sigma, \gamma) \in W \times \Sigma \times \Gamma$ and $w' \in W$,

$$\kappa_\iota(w, \sigma, \gamma) = w' \iff \sigma \in \gamma \wedge \kappa(w, \sigma) = w'.$$

Proposition 5.1 $\iota(L_{\text{dam}}) = L_m(D_\iota)$.

Proof *It is clear from the construction of D_ι.* ◼

Next, we describe how to calculate $\psi(\iota(L_{\text{dam}}))$. Let $D_\psi = (W, (\Sigma \cup \Delta_n) \times \Gamma, \kappa_\psi, w_0, W_m)$, where $\kappa_\psi : W \times (\Sigma \cup \Delta_n) \times \Gamma \to W$ is the (partial) transition map such that for each $(w, u, \gamma) \in W \times (\Sigma \cup \Delta_n) \times \Gamma$ and $w' \in W$, we have $\kappa_\psi(w, u, \gamma) = w'$ if one of the following holds:

- $u \in \Sigma_{uo} \wedge \kappa_\iota(w, u, \gamma) = w'$;

- $u \in \Delta_n \wedge (\exists \sigma \in \Sigma_o) \kappa_\iota(w, \sigma, \gamma) = w'$.

Proposition 5.2 $\psi(\iota(L_{\text{dam}})) = L_m(D_\psi)$.

Proof *By the construction of D_ψ and the definition of ψ, the proposition follows.* ◼

Next, we describe how to calculate $\nu(\psi(\iota(L(\mathbf{G}))))$ by modifying D_ψ. For each transition $\kappa_\psi(w, u, \gamma) = w'$, if $u \in \Delta_n$ and $|u| \geq 2$, we make the following changes to D_ψ. Assume that $u = \sigma_1 \ldots \sigma_r$ with $r \in \mathbb{N}$ and $\sigma_i \in \Sigma_o$ ($i \in \{1, \ldots, r\}$) and $\sigma_r \in \gamma$. We create $r - 1$ new states $\tilde{w}_1, \ldots, \tilde{w}_{r-1}$ such that for each sequence $\gamma_1 \ldots \gamma_{r-1} \in \Gamma^*$ with $\sigma_i \in \gamma_i$ ($i = 1, \ldots, r - 1$), we define $\kappa_\psi(w, \sigma_1, \gamma_1) = \tilde{w}_1$, $\kappa_\psi(\tilde{w}_i, \sigma_{i+1}, \gamma_{i+1}) = \tilde{w}_{i+1}$ ($i = 1, \ldots, r - 2$) and $\kappa_\psi(\tilde{w}_{r-1}, \sigma_r, \gamma) = w'$. Add newly created states to the state set W of D_ψ and new transitions to κ_ψ. Continue this process until all transitions are processed. Let the final finite-state automaton be D_ν.

Proposition 5.3 $\nu(\psi(\iota(L_{\mathrm{dam}}))) = L_m(D_\nu)$.

Proof *By the construction of D_ν and the definition of ν, the proposition follows.* ∎

Next, we will show how to compute $\zeta(L(\mathbf{G}))$. We construct a nondeterministic finite-state automaton $G_\zeta := (X \times \Sigma_o^\epsilon \times \Gamma, \Sigma_o^\epsilon \times \Gamma, \xi_\zeta, (x_0, \epsilon, \Sigma), X_m \times \Sigma_o^\epsilon)$, where

$$\xi_\zeta : X \times \Sigma_o^\epsilon \times \Gamma \times \Sigma_o^\epsilon \times \Gamma \to 2^{X \times \Sigma_o^\epsilon \times \Gamma}$$

is the nondeterministic transition map such that

- For all $\gamma \in \Gamma$, $\xi_\zeta(x_0, \epsilon, \Sigma, \epsilon, \gamma) := \{(x_0, \epsilon, \gamma)\}$;

- For all $(x, \sigma, \gamma) \in X \times \Sigma_o^\epsilon \times \Gamma - \{(x_0, \epsilon, \Sigma)\}$, and $(\sigma', \gamma') \in \Sigma_o^\epsilon \times \Gamma$, we have that

  - if $\sigma' = \epsilon$ and $\gamma' = \gamma$ and $\gamma \cap \Sigma_{uo} \neq \varnothing$, then

    $$\xi_\zeta(x, \sigma, \gamma, \epsilon, \gamma) = \{(x, \sigma, \gamma)\};$$

  - if $\sigma' \in \Sigma_o$, then

    $$\xi_\zeta(x, \sigma, \gamma, \sigma', \gamma') := \{(x', \sigma', \gamma') \in X \times \Sigma_o^\epsilon \times \Gamma \mid (\exists u \in P_o^{-1}(\sigma') \cap \gamma^* \cap \Sigma_{uo}^* \Sigma_o) \xi(x, u) = x'\}.$$

Example 5.7 *To illustrate the construction procedure for G_ζ, a small example is depicted in Figure 5.12, where $\Sigma = \{a, b, c, v\}$, $\Sigma_c = \{a\}$ and $\Sigma_o = \{a, b, c\}$. Thus, there are only two control patterns $\gamma_1 = \{a, b, v, c\}$ and $\gamma_2 = \Sigma_{uc} = \{b, v, c\}$. The outcome of G_ζ is shown in Figure 5.12, where nondeterministic transitions occur at both (augmented) states $(1, a, \{b, v, c\})$ and $(1, a, \{a, b, v, c\})$.*

Proposition 5.4 $\zeta(L(\mathbf{G})) = L(G_\zeta)$.

Proof *By the definition of ζ and the construction of G_ζ, it is clear that $\zeta(L(\mathbf{G})) \subseteq L(G_\zeta)$. So we only need to show that $L(G_\zeta) \subseteq \zeta(L(\mathbf{G}))$. We use induction. At the initial state (x_0, ϵ, Σ), for each $\gamma \in \Gamma$, if $\gamma \cap \Sigma_{uo} \neq \varnothing$, we have $\xi_\zeta(x_0, \epsilon, \Sigma, \epsilon, \gamma) = \{(x_0, \epsilon, \gamma)\}$ and $\xi_\zeta(x_0, \epsilon, \gamma, \epsilon, \gamma) = \{(x_0, \epsilon, \gamma)\})$, namely $\{(\epsilon, \gamma)\}^+ \subseteq L(G_\zeta)$. By the definition of $\zeta(L(\mathbf{G}))$, we know that $\{(\epsilon, \gamma)\}^+ \subseteq \zeta(L(\mathbf{G}))$. If $\gamma \cap \Sigma_{uo} = \varnothing$, then we have*

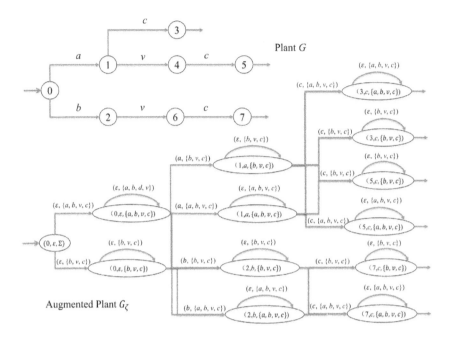

Figure 5.12 A plant **G** and the corresponding G_ζ.

$\xi_\zeta(x_0, \epsilon, \Sigma, \epsilon, \gamma) = \{(x_0, \epsilon, \gamma)\}$, *namely* $(\epsilon, \gamma) \in L(G_\zeta)$. *By the definition of* $\zeta(L(G))$, *we know that* $(\epsilon, \gamma) \in \zeta(L(G))$. *Thus, the base case holds. Assume that* $s \in \zeta(L(G)) \cap L(G_\zeta)$, *and* $s(\sigma, \gamma) \in L(G_\zeta)$, *we need to show that* $s(\sigma, \gamma) \in \zeta(L(G))$. *If* $\sigma = \epsilon$, *then since* $s(\sigma, \gamma) \in L(G_\zeta)$, *we know that* $\gamma = p(s)^\uparrow$ *and* $\gamma \cap \Sigma_{uo} \neq \varnothing$. *Since* $s \in \zeta(L(G))$ *and* $p(s)^\uparrow = \gamma$ *and* $\gamma \cap \Sigma_{uo} \neq \varnothing$, *we know that* $s(\epsilon, \gamma) \in \zeta(L(G))$. *If* $\sigma \in \Sigma_o$, *then clearly there exists* $tu \in L(G)$ *such that* $g(s) = P_o(t)$ *and* $u \in P_o^{-1}(\sigma) \cap p(s)^* \cap (\Sigma_{uo}^*\Sigma_o)^*$. *Clearly,* $s \in \zeta(t)$ *and* $P_o(u) = \sigma \neq \epsilon$. *Thus, by the definition of* $\zeta(L(G))$, *we know that* $s(P_o(u), \gamma) = s(\sigma, \gamma) \in \zeta(L(G))$. *Thus, the induction holds, which completes the proof.* ■

Notice that in G_ζ, except for being at the initial state (x_0, ϵ, Σ), no transition between two different states can be unobservable.

Since the map p introduced before is a projection, it is not difficult to check that $\hat{H} = \zeta(L(G)) - p^{-1}(p(\nu(\psi(\iota(L_{\text{dam}})))))(\Sigma_o^\epsilon \times \Gamma)^*$ is regular, as both $\zeta(L(G))$ and $\nu(\psi(\iota(L_{\text{dam}})))$ are shown to be regular. Thus, its prefix closure $H := \overline{\hat{H}}$ is also regular. Let the alphabet be $\Sigma_o^\epsilon \times \Gamma$ and the uncontrollable alphabet be $\{\epsilon\} \times \Gamma$. Since G_ζ is nondeterministic, H

can be recognized by a nondeterministic automaton, without masking out necessary marking information inherited from $\mathbf{G}$, which will be used later. By using a synthesis algorithm similar to the one proposed in Refs. [13,14], which is realized in Ref. [39], we can show that $S_* = \sup\mathcal{C}(\zeta(L(\mathbf{G})), H)$ is also regular, and generated by a nondeterministic finite-state automaton $\mathcal{H} := (Q, \Sigma_o^\epsilon \times \Gamma, \Xi, q_0, Q_m)$, where $Q = X \times \Sigma_o^\epsilon \times \Gamma \times R$ and $Q_m = X_m \times \Sigma_o^\epsilon \times \Gamma \times R$ with R being the state set of the recognizer of $p^{-1}(p(\nu(\psi(\iota(L_{\mathrm{dam}})))))(\Sigma_o^\epsilon \times \Gamma)^*$. That is $S_* = L(\mathcal{H})$. Next, we will develop a computational method to determine whether a nonblocking resilient supervisor candidate in S_* exists.

To handle partial observation induced by g, we undertake the following subset-construction style operation on $\mathcal{H}$. Let $\mathcal{P}(\mathcal{H}) = (Q_\mathcal{P}, \Sigma_o^\epsilon \times \Gamma, \Xi_\mathcal{P}, q_{0,\mathcal{P}}, Q_{m,\mathcal{P}})$, where

- $Q_\mathcal{P} := \Sigma_o^\epsilon \times 2^Q \times Q$, $Q_{m,\mathcal{P}} := \Sigma_o^\epsilon \times 2^Q \times Q_m$;

- $q_{0,\mathcal{P}} := (\epsilon, \{q \in Q | (\exists t \in g^{-1}(\epsilon))q \in \Xi(q_0, t)\}, q_0)$;

- The transition map $\Xi_\mathcal{P} : Q_\mathcal{P} \times \Sigma_o^\epsilon \times \Gamma \to 2^{Q_\mathcal{P}}$ is defined as follows: for each $(\sigma, U, q) \in Q_\mathcal{P}$ and $(\sigma', \gamma) \in \Sigma_o^\epsilon \times \Gamma$, if $\sigma' = \epsilon$, then

$$\Xi_\mathcal{P}(\sigma, U, q, \epsilon, \gamma) := \{\sigma\} \times \{U\} \times \Xi(q, \epsilon, \gamma);$$

otherwise, we have

$$\Xi_\mathcal{P}(\sigma, U, q, \sigma', \gamma) := \{\sigma'\} \times \Xi(U, \sigma', \gamma) \times \Xi(q, \sigma', \gamma),$$

where

$$\Xi(U, \sigma', \gamma) := \{\hat{q} \in Q | (\exists \tilde{q} \in U)(\exists t \in g^{-1}(P_o(\sigma')))\hat{q} \in \Xi(\tilde{q}, t)\}.$$

Remark 5.2 *It is clear that $L(\mathcal{P}(\mathcal{H})) = L(\mathcal{H}) = S_*$. In addition, since all unobservable transitions in G_ζ are selflooped at relevant states, by the construction of S_*, we can check that the recognizer $\mathcal{H}$ also selfloops all unobservable transitions. Due to this property, we have $\Xi_\mathcal{P}(\sigma, U, q, \epsilon, \gamma) := \{\sigma\} \times \{U\} \times \Xi(q, \epsilon, \gamma)$ in the definition of $\mathcal{P}(\mathcal{H})$, where $\Xi(q, \epsilon, \gamma)$ either equals $\{q\}$ or $\varnothing$ in $\mathcal{H}$.*

Example 5.8 *To illustrate the construction procedure for $\mathcal{P}(\mathcal{H})$, assume that in Example 3 depicted in Figure 5.13, $\mathcal{H} = G_\zeta$. After*

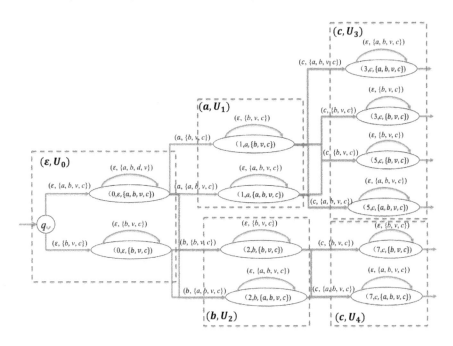

Figure 5.13 The model of $\mathcal{P}(\mathcal{H})$.

applying the construction procedure for $\mathcal{P}(\mathcal{H})$, the outcome is depicted in Figure 5.13, where

$$
\begin{aligned}
U_0 &= \{q_{0,\mathcal{P}}, (0, \epsilon, \{a, b, v, c\}), (0, \epsilon, \{b, v, c\})\};\\
U_1 &= \{(1, a, \{a, b, v, c\}), (1, a, \{b, v, c\})\};\\
U_2 &= \{(2, b, \{a, b, v, c\}), (2, b, \{b, v, c\})\};\\
U_3 &= \{(3, c, \{a, b, v, c\}), (3, c, \{b, v, c\}), (5, c, \{a, b, v, c\}),\\
&\quad (5, c, \{b, v, c\})\};\\
U_4 &= \{(7, c, \{a, b, v, c\}), (7, c, \{b, v, c\})\}.
\end{aligned}
$$

Definition 5.5 Given $\mathcal{P}(\mathcal{H})$, a reachable sub-automaton $\Omega = (Q_\Omega \subseteq Q_\mathcal{P}, \Sigma_o^\epsilon \times \Gamma, \Xi_\Omega, q_{0,\mathcal{P}}, Q_{m,\Omega} \subseteq Q_{m,\mathcal{P}})$ of $\mathcal{P}(\mathcal{H})$ is *control feasible* if the following conditions hold:

1. For all $q = (\sigma, U, x, \sigma, \gamma, r) \in Q_\Omega$ with $q \neq q_{0,\mathcal{P}}$,

$$
(\forall \gamma' \in \Gamma)\, \xi_\zeta(x, \sigma, \gamma, \epsilon, \gamma') \neq \varnothing \Rightarrow \Xi_\Omega(q, \epsilon, \gamma') \neq \varnothing;
$$

2. For all $(\sigma, U, x_1, \sigma, \gamma_1, r_1), (\sigma, U, x_2, \sigma, \gamma_2, r_2) \in Q_\Omega$, we have $\gamma_1 = \gamma_2$;

3. For each $q = (\sigma, U, x, \sigma, \gamma, r) \in Q_\Omega$,

$$g(En_\Omega(q)) = P_o(\gamma) \cap g(En_{G_\zeta}(x, \sigma, \gamma));$$

4. For all $(\sigma, U, q) \in Q_\Omega$ and $\mu \in \Sigma_o^\epsilon \times \Gamma$, if $\Xi_\Omega(\sigma, U, q, \mu) \neq \varnothing$, then for all $(\sigma, U, q') \in Q_\mathcal{P}$,

$$\Xi_\Omega(\sigma, U, q', \mu) = \Xi_\mathcal{P}(\sigma, U, q', \mu) \subseteq Q_\Omega;$$

5. Ω is co-reachable. □

The first condition in Definition 5.5 essentially states that in Ω no uncontrollable transitions allowed by G_ζ shall be disabled, which is similar to the concept of *state controllability* in Ref. [13] that handles nondeterministic transitions. Based on the construction of $\mathcal{P}(\mathcal{H})$, if (ϵ, γ') is allowed at state $q = (\sigma, U, x, \sigma, \gamma, r)$ in Ω, then $\gamma' = \gamma$ and $\Xi_\Omega(q, \epsilon, \gamma) = \{q\}$. The second condition states that all strings observably identical in $L(\Omega)$ must result in the same control pattern. The third condition states that, for any state in Ω, an observable event is allowed at state q if and only if it is allowed both by the plant G_ζ and the corresponding control pattern γ associated with q. The fourth condition is similar to the concept of *state observability* in Ref. [13] to handle nondeterminism, which requires that all states in $\mathcal{P}(\mathcal{H})$ reachable by strings observably identical to some string in $L(\Omega)$, must be included in Ω. The last condition is self-explained.

Example 5.9 *As an illustration, Figure 5.14 depicts one choice of Ω derived from $\mathcal{P}(\mathcal{H})$ in Example 5.3. We can see that clearly no self-looped uncontrollable events are disabled. So the first condition in Definition 5.5 holds. Due to the second condition in Definition 5.5, in U_0 we choose to keep $\gamma = \{a, b, v, c\}$, and thus, only states $q_{0,\mathcal{P}}$ and $(\epsilon, U_0, 0, \epsilon, \{a, b, v, c\})$ will be kept in Ω. Similarly, in U_1 the control pattern $\gamma = \{b, v, c\}$ is chosen; in U_2 the control pattern $\gamma = \{a, b, v, c\}$ is chosen; in U_3 the pattern $\gamma = \{a, b, v, c\}$ is chosen; and in U_4 the pattern $\gamma = \{b, v, c\}$ is chosen. Due to the third condition in Definition 5.5, we can see that in U_0 both outgoing transitions $(a, \{b, v, c\})$ and $(b, \{a, b, v, c\})$ of state $(\epsilon, U_0, 0, \epsilon, \{a, b, v, c\})$ must be chosen in Ω, as*

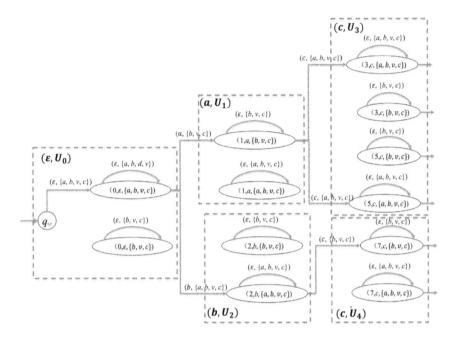

Figure 5.14 A model containing one Ω.

both events a and b are allowed by the control pattern $\{a, b, v, c\}$ and the augmented plant G_ζ. In U_1, due to the fourth condition in Definition 5.5, both nondeterministic outgoing transitions $(c, \{a, b, v, c\})$ toward $(c, U_3, 3, c, \{a, b, v, c\})$ and $(c, U_3, 5, c, \{a, b, v, c\})$ must be allowed in Ω. Clearly, all reachable states in Ω is co-reachable. Thus, after removing all unreachable states in Figure 5.14, the remaining structure Ω is a control feasible sub-automaton of $\mathcal{P}(\mathcal{H})$ in Figure 5.13. The corresponding supervisory control map $V : P_o(L(G)) \rightarrow \Gamma$ can be derived as follows: $S(\epsilon) := \{a, b, v, c\}$, $S(a) := \{b, v, c\}$, $S(b) := \{a, b, v, c\}$, $S(ac) := \{a, b, v, c\}$ and $S(bc) := \{b, v, c\}$. Similarly, we can check that in Figure 5.14, each marked trajectory leads to one control feasible sub-automaton Ω, which satisfies all conditions in Definition 5.5.

Theorem 5.3 Let $\mathcal{P}(\mathcal{H})$ be constructed as shown above. Then there exists a nonblocking resilient supervisor candidate of $\mathcal{S}_*$ if and only if there exists a control feasible reachable sub-automaton of $\mathcal{P}(\mathcal{H})$.

Proof

1. *To show the IF part, assume that Ω is a control feasible reachable sub-automaton of $\mathcal{P}(\mathcal{H})$. Let $\mathcal{L} := L(\Omega)$. By condition (1) of Definition 5.5, we know that $\mathcal{L}$ is conditionally controllable with respect to $\zeta(L(G))$ and $\{\epsilon\} \times \Gamma$. Thus, $\mathcal{L} \in \mathcal{C}(\zeta(L(G)), H)$. For all $s \in \mathcal{L}$ and $t \in g^{-1}(g(s)) \cap \mathcal{L}$, let $(\sigma, U, x_1, \sigma, \gamma_1, r_1), (\sigma, U, x_2, \sigma, \gamma_2, r_2) \in Q_\Omega$ be induced by s and t with $\sigma = g(s)^\uparrow = g(t)^\uparrow$. Then by condition (2) of Definition 5.5, we have $\gamma_1 = \gamma_2$. Thus, the first condition in Definition 5.4 holds. In addition, we have*

$$En_{\mathcal{L}}(s) := \bigcup_{q=(g(s)^\uparrow, U, x, g(s)^\uparrow, \gamma, r) \in \Xi_\Omega(q_{0,\mathcal{P}}, s)} En_\Omega(q).$$

By condition (3) of Definition 5.5, we have $g(En_\Omega(q)) = P_o(\gamma) \cap g(En_{G_\zeta}(x, g(s)^\uparrow, \gamma))$, by condition (4) of Definition 5.5, we have

$$\bigcup_{(\sigma, U, x, \sigma, \gamma, r) \in \Xi_\Omega(q_{0,\mathcal{P}}, s)} En_{G_\zeta}(x, \sigma, \gamma) = En_{\zeta(L(G))}(s),$$

where $\sigma = g(s)^\uparrow$. Thus, we conclude that $g(En_{\mathcal{L}}(s)) = P_o(p(s^\uparrow)) \cap g(En_{\zeta(L(G))}(s))$, namely the second condition of Definition 5.4 holds. Finally, since Ω is co-reachable, and together with condition (4) of Definition 5.5, we know that $\mathcal{L}$ is nonblocking. Thus, by Definition 5.4, $\mathcal{L}$ is a nonblocking resilient supervisor candidate of $\mathcal{S}_*$.

2. *To show the ONLY IF part, assume that there exists a nonblocking resilient supervisor candidate $\mathcal{L} \subseteq \mathcal{S}_*$. We need to show that there exists a control feasible sub-automaton Ω of $\mathcal{P}(\mathcal{H})$. We construct a sub-automaton $\mathcal{P}(\mathcal{H})_{\mathcal{L}} := (Q_{\mathcal{L}}, \Sigma_o^\epsilon \times \Gamma, \Xi_{\mathcal{L}}, q_{0,\mathcal{P}}, Q_{m,\mathcal{L}})$, where*

$$Q_{\mathcal{L}} := \{q \in Q_{\mathcal{P}} | (\exists s \in \mathcal{L}) q \in \Xi_{\mathcal{P}}(q_{0,\mathcal{P}}, s)\},$$

and $Q_{m,\mathcal{L}} := Q_{\mathcal{L}} \cap Q_{m,\mathcal{P}}$. The transition map $\Xi_{\mathcal{L}}$ is the restriction of $\Xi_{\mathcal{P}}$ over $Q_{\mathcal{L}}$.

Let Ω be the sub-automaton $\mathcal{P}(\mathcal{H})_{\mathcal{L}}$. Since $\mathcal{L}$ is a supervisor candidate, by the first condition of Definition 5.4, we have the *following property:*

$$(\forall s \in \mathcal{L})\{[p(t)]^\uparrow \,|\, t \in g^{-1}(g(s)) \cap \mathcal{L}\} = \{p(s)^\uparrow\}. \qquad (*)$$

By the construction of $\mathcal{P}(\mathcal{H})$, we know that for each state reachable by s, say $(g(s)^\uparrow, U_s, q_s)$, and each state reachable by $t \in g^{-1}(g(s)) \cap \mathcal{L}$, say $(g(t)^\uparrow, U_t, q_t)$, we have $U_s = U_t$. Thus, if $q_s = (x_s, g(s)^\uparrow, \gamma_s, r_s)$ and $q_t = (x_t, g(t)^\uparrow, \gamma_t, r_t)$, by the property $(*)$, we have $\gamma_s = \gamma_t$, which means the second condition of Definition 5.5 holds. Based on the construction of Ω, it is also clear that the condition (1) of Definition 5.5 holds because $\mathcal{P}(\mathcal{H})_\mathcal{L}$ is conditionally controllable due to the conditional controllability of $\mathcal{L}$. Because $\mathcal{P}(\mathcal{H})_\mathcal{L}$ is derived from a language $\mathcal{L}$, the fourth condition of Definition 5.5 holds for $\mathcal{P}(\mathcal{H})_\mathcal{L}$. In addition, since $\mathcal{L}$ is a resilient supervisor candidate, by the second condition of Definition 5.4, we know that the third condition of Definition 5.5 holds. Finally, since $\mathcal{L}$ is nonblocking, based on Definition 5.3, we know that each state in Ω must be co-reachable. This completes the proof that Ω is indeed control feasible. ■

The complexity of computing $\mathcal{P}(\mathcal{H})$ is $O(|Q_\mathcal{P}|^2|\Sigma_o^\epsilon||\Gamma|)$. To determine the existence of a control feasible sub-automaton of $\mathcal{P}(\mathcal{H})$, in the worst case we need to check each sub-automaton. There are $2^{|Q_\mathcal{P}|}$ sub-automata. For each sub-automaton Ω, whose state set is $Q_\Omega \subseteq Q_\mathcal{P}$, we need to check all four conditions defined in Definition 5.5, whose complexity is $O(|Q_\Omega|^2 + |Q_\Omega||\Sigma_o^\epsilon||\Gamma|)$. Typically, we have $|Q_\mathcal{P}| \gg |\Sigma_o^\epsilon||\Gamma|$ and $2^{|Q_\mathcal{P}|} \gg |Q_\mathcal{P}|^3$. The final complexity of finding a control feasible sub-automaton is $O(2^{|Q_\mathcal{P}|})$. Notice that $|Q_\mathcal{P}| = |\Sigma_o^\epsilon|2^{|Q|}|Q|$, where $|Q| = |X||\Sigma_o^\epsilon||\Gamma||R|$ with $|R| = 2^{|W|+n|\Delta n|}$. The final complexity is $O(2^{|\Sigma_o^\epsilon|2^{|X||\Sigma_o^\epsilon||\Gamma|2^{|W|+n|\Delta n|}}|X||\Sigma_o^\epsilon||\Gamma|2^{|W|+n|\Delta n|}})$.

Theorem 5.4 Given a plant **G** and a damage language $L_{\text{dam}} \subseteq L(\mathbf{G})$, it is decidable whether there exists a nonblocking supervisor S such that the closed-loop system $(\mathbf{G}, S)$ is not attackable with respect to L_{dam}.

Proof *By Theorem 5.2, there exists a nonblocking supervisor which disallows any regular smart sensor attack with respect to L_{dam} if and only if there exists a nonblocking resilient supervisor candidate $\mathcal{L} \subseteq S_*$. By Theorem 5.3, we know that there exists a nonblocking resilient* *supervisor candidate if and only if there exists a control feasible sub-automaton of $\mathcal{P}(\mathcal{H})$, which recognizes $\mathcal{S}_*$. Since there exists a finite number of sub-automata in $\mathcal{P}(\mathcal{H})$, the existence of a control feasible sub-automaton of $\mathcal{P}(\mathcal{H})$ is decidable. Thus, the existence of a nonblocking supervisor which disallows any regular smart sensor attack with respect to L_{dam} is decidable.* ■

It is interesting to point out that, in general, there are typically many choices of a control feasible sub-automaton Ω, leading to possibly many resilient supervisors. It is unfortunate that the most permissive resilient supervisor in terms of set inclusion of closed-loop behaviors typically does not exist. For example, there are up to three different supervisory control maps depicted in Figure 5.11, leading to two non-compatible maximally permissive supervisors: one generates the closed-loop behavior of $L(S_1/G) = \overline{\{avc\}}$ and the other one generates $L(S_2/G) = \overline{\{bvd\}}$. It is an interesting question whether the structure $\mathcal{P}(\mathcal{H})$ could be used to directly synthesize a maximally permissive nonblocking resilient supervisor, as it conceptually contains all resilient supervisors.

5.7 CONCLUSIONS

Although in Chapter 2 and some early works [55,56], the concept of SSAs was introduced, and syntheses of an SSA and a supervisor resilient to SSAs were presented, it has not been shown whether the existence of a nonblocking supervisor resilient to all SSAs is decidable, as the synthesis algorithm presented in Chapter 2 and [56] does not guarantee to find a resilient supervisor, even though it may exist. In this chapter, we have first shown that the existence of a regular smart weak sensor attack is decidable, and in case it exists, it can be synthesized. By identifying risky pairs that describe how a legal sequence of control patterns may be used by a sensor attack to inflict weak damage, Theorem 5.1 states that there exists a smart weak sensor attack if and only if there exists at least one risky pair. Notice that this result is valid, regardless of whether the attack model is regular, i.e., representable by a finite-state automaton. With this key idea, to ensure the existence of a supervisor resilient to SSAs, we only need to make sure that there should be no risky pairs. We have shown that all risky pairs can be identified and removed from the plant behaviors, via a genuine encoding scheme, upon which a verifiable sufficient and necessary condition is presented to ensure the existence of a nonblocking supervisor resilient to SSAs. This establishes the result that the existence of a supervisor resilient to all SSAs is decidable. Finally, the presented decision process renders a synthesis algorithm for a resilient supervisor, whenever it exists, which has never been addressed in any existing works.

The decidability result established in this chapter may shed light on future research on cyberattack-related resilient synthesis, e.g., to decide existence of a resilient supervisor for smart actuator attacks or smart attacks with observations different from those of the supervisor, which are gaining more and more attention recently. This decidability result allows us to focus more on computational efficiency related to SSAs.

CHAPTER 6

System Vulnerability Analysis via Attack Model Reduction

In Chapter 5, it is shown that the existence of a supervisor resilient to all smart sensor attacks is decidable, and in case such a resilient supervisor exists, it can be computed. However, the whole solution strategy leverages on existing sensors, assuming that many of them might be compromised. Such a passive attack defense strategy in many cases renders no solution if some key assets or sensor data are compromised. It would be interesting and potentially important to know which sensor data are critical for the existence of a successful SSA, upon which extra efforts could be spent to prevent those sensor data from being compromised, thus, eliminating effectively any SSA. We call this a *proactive defense strategy*. The key to the success of this strategy is to effectively identify key assets to protect. In this chapter, we will address this problem by making use of model reduction techniques. The main idea of model reduction is to remove redundant transition information from the attack model while retaining the same attack capability by keeping necessary attack information and the corresponding transition sequences - the latter reveals key observable events exploitable by an attacker that ensure the availability of control patterns to form risk pairs, mentioned in Chapter 5, whose presence determines the existence of an SSA. We call such observable events *key assets* that should NOT be compromised by an SSA. More explicitly, given a supervisor S and a smart sensor attack model A, another smart attack model A' is called *attack equivalent* to A with respect to S, if the resulting compromised supervisor $S \circ A'$ is control equivalent to the original compromised supervisor $S \circ A$. We aim to find A' with a much smaller FSA realization, with a belief that a simplified and ideally minimum-state attack model can reveal all necessary observation sequences for a successful SSA. Our solution strategy is to transform the attack model reduction problem into a classical supervisor reduction problem [15,136], whose effectiveness is illustrated in an example.

6.1   INTRODUCTION TO SUPERVISOR REDUCTION

Before we introduce attack model reduction, we first recall existing works on supervisor reduction. In supervisory control theory (SCT) [12,18], the control problem associated with a discrete-event system (DES) is to enforce controllable and nonblocking behavior of the plant that is admissible by the specification. When applying SCT to a real application, there are two basic questions that require a user to answer, that is, are we doing the right thing, and are we doing things in the right way. The first question is about the correctness of the plant and requirement models. The second is about the correctness of supervisor synthesis, which, if computational complexity is not a concern, has been adequately answered by SCT researchers. When computational complexity is indeed a concern, several efficient synthesis approaches have been proposed in the literature, e.g., [13,14,127,129], which can ensure correct behaviors of the closed-loop system with low computational complexity. The first question, on the other hand, has been a long-standing hurdle for SCT to be readily adopted by the industry because so far there is no efficient way to identify potential errors in plant models or requirement models. The current practice is to synthesize a supervisor based on a given plant model and requirements. An empty supervisor usually indicates a fault either in the model or in requirements; this should prompt the system designer to undertake model or requirement updates. The current SCT and its relevant tools can assist the designer to quickly locate the problems in the model that lead to emptiness of the supervisor. The real challenge is how to determine whether the plant model and requirements are correct when the supervisor synthesis returns a non-empty supervisor. In this case, it usually requires not only syntactic correctness but also semantic correctness, i.e., the designer has to understand the true meaning and impact of every transition in the synthesized supervisor. Thus, to make a supervisor small enough for a designer to understand its function becomes important.

A supervisor carries two types of information: the key information at each state for event enabling/disabling and marking, and the information that tracks the evolution of the plant. The latter may contain some redundancy because the plant itself also carries such evolution information. In principle, it is possible to remove redundant transitional information from the supervisor, which will not interfere with the first kind of information, i.e., a reduced supervisor can still ensure the same control capability as that of the original supervisor. This is the key idea used in Vaz and Wonham's paper on supervisor reduction [128], which relies on the concept of *control cover*. A control cover is a collection of subsets of states in a supervisor, in which the states of each subset are "control consistent" with respect to event enabling/disabling and state marking; the exact meaning will be explained later. The authors proved two reduction theorems and proposed a corresponding (exponential time) reduction algorithm. To overcome the computational complexity involved in supervisor reduction, Su and Wonham made a significant extension in Ref. [15,136] by first relaxing the concept of control cover, then providing a polynomial-time reduction algorithm based on a special type of cover called *control congruence*, and finally showing that the minimal supervisor problem (MSP) of computing a supervisor with minimal state size is NP-hard. A polynomial-time lower bound estimation algorithm provided in Ref. [15] has indicated that in many instances minimal supervisors can be achieved in polynomial time by using control congruence. Since then, this reduction algorithm has been used with gratifying results. One important application of supervisor reduction is in supervisor localization [124], which aims to create a control-equivalent distributed implementation of a given centralized supervisor.

The supervisor reduction theory proposed in Ref. [15] rests on two basic assumptions: (1) only full observation is considered; (2) the supervisor under consideration represents a sublanguage of the plant, which can be easily satisfied by applying supremal synthesis. Since then, many questions have been raised by users. For example, can we apply supervisor reduction to partially reduced supervisors (which may not necessarily represent sublanguages of a given plant) and can we apply supervisor reduction in cases with partial observation? Some results have been reported in the literature about the second question, see e.g., [126]. The main objective of supervisor reduction is to ensure control equivalence between the original supervisor and a reduced supervisor. The fundamental questions are (1) **Q1:** what information ensures control equivalence, even under partial observation, and (2) **Q2:** what information determines the state size of a reduced supervisor, which is the main performance index of supervisor reduction. These two questions have been successfully answered in Ref. [135], whose solution idea will be reviewed in this chapter. Basically, for each feasible supervisor **S** of a plant **G**, that is, **S** does not disable uncontrollable events and always issues the same control command after receiving strings that are not distinguishable based on observations, there always exists a feasible supervisor **SUPER** derivable from the linguistic definition of *uncertainty subset construction* [17]. **SUPER** has the "universal" property that any feasible supervisor that is control equivalent to **S** with respect to **G**, and non-redundant with respect to **S** (i.e. without superfluous transitions), can be projected from **SUPER** via a suitable control cover on its state space, namely is a "quotient" of **SUPER** with respect to this cover. This result will answer our first question **Q1**. After that, we define a preorder $\preceq$ (referred to as "leanness") on feasible supervisors by using key information about event enabling/disabling and state marking such that for any two control equivalent supervisors $\mathbf{S}_1$ and $\mathbf{S}_2$ with respect to **G**, if $\mathbf{S}_1$ is leaner than $\mathbf{S}_2$, i.e., $\mathbf{S}_1 \preceq \mathbf{S}_2$, then the minimal reduced supervisor induced by a minimal control cover on $\mathbf{S}_1$ is no bigger than the one induced by a minimal control cover on $\mathbf{S}_2$. This result provides an answer to the second question **Q2**. As a direct consequence of this result, as long as control equivalence holds, a feasible supervisor under full observation always results in a reduced supervisor no bigger than the one induced from a supervisor under partial observation. The theory is independent of the specific way of achieving observability, for instance via the property of normality [11] or of relative observability [125], or by direct search [11] - the effect of such a choice is lumped into the property of control feasibility, which states that a feasible supervisor must apply the same control law to all transitional sequences which cannot be distinguished based on observations.

6.2 PRELIMINARIES

Given a plant $\mathbf{G} = (X, \Sigma, \xi, x_0, X_m)$, recall that a *(feasible) supervisor of $\mathbf{G}$ under $P_o : \Sigma^* \to \Sigma_o^*$* can be represented as a finite state automaton $\mathbf{S} = (Z, \Sigma, \delta, z_0, Z_m)$ such that

- **Control existence:**

$$(\forall s \in L(\mathbf{G} \wedge \mathbf{S}))(\forall \sigma \in \Sigma_{uc})\, s\sigma \in L(\mathbf{G}) \Rightarrow s\sigma \in L(\mathbf{S}).$$

- **Control feasibility:**

$$(\forall s, s' \in L(\mathbf{S}))\, P_o(s) = P_o(s') \Rightarrow \delta(z_0, s) = \delta(z_0, s').$$

- **Marking feasibility:**

$$(\forall z \in Z_m)(\exists s \in L_m(\mathbf{G} \wedge \mathbf{S}))\, \delta(z_0, s) = z.$$

The first property says that a supervisor can only disable controllable events, thus, all uncontrollable events allowed by the plant $\mathbf{G}$ must be allowed by the supervisor $\mathbf{S}$. This property can be ensured by enforcing controllability [12] on the closed-loop system behaviors. The second property says that a supervisor will issue the same (enabling) control command to strings which are observationally identical under P_o, that is, the supervisor may change its control command only when an observable event is received, or equivalently, all unobservable events can only be selflooped at relevant states, and any transition between two different states must be observable. This property guarantees implementation feasibility of the supervisor, and can be ensured by enforcing *observability* [11] on the closed-loop system behaviors.[1] The last property states that any marker state in the supervisor $\mathbf{S}$ must be reachable by a string $s \in L_m(\mathbf{G} \wedge \mathbf{S})$, namely there is no redundant marking information in **S**. The closed-loop behavior of the system is denoted by two languages: the closed behavior $L(\mathbf{G} \wedge \mathbf{S}) = L(\mathbf{G}) \cap L(\mathbf{S})$ and the marked behavior $L_m(\mathbf{G} \wedge \mathbf{S}) = L_m(\mathbf{G}) \cap L_m(\mathbf{S})$. A supervisor **S** satisfying the properties of control existence, control feasibility and marking feasibility can be computed by the following simple procedure.

6.2.1 Procedure of Synthesis of Feasible Supervisors

- **Step 1**: Compute, by any method, a controllable observable sublanguage $K \subseteq L_m(\mathbf{G})$. For instance, TCT [38] can compute controllable and normal (or relatively observable) sublanguages and SuSyNA [39] can compute controllable and normal sublanguages.

- **Step 2**: **Uncertainty Subset Construction** (Chapter 6, [17]). Let $\equiv_K$ be the *Nerode equivalence relation* for K, i.e., for all $s, s' \in \overline{K}$,

$$s \equiv_K s' \iff (\forall u \in \Sigma^*)[su \in K \iff s'u \in K].$$

Let $[s]_K := \{s' \in \overline{K} | s \equiv_K s'\}$ the equivalence class of $s \in \overline{K}$ in the quotient $\overline{K}/\equiv_K = \{[s]_K | s \in \overline{K}\}$. Let $\simeq$ be the equivalence relation on $\overline{K}$ defined by

$$(\forall s, s' \in \overline{K}) \, s \simeq s' \iff \{[t]_K | t \in P_o^{-1}(P_o(s)) \cap \overline{K}\} = \{[t']_K | t' \in P_o^{-1}(P_o(s')) \cap \overline{K}\}.$$

Compute $\mathbf{S} = (Z, \Sigma, \delta, z_0, Z_m)$, where $Z := \overline{K}/\simeq$, $Z_m := \{z \in Z | z \cap K \neq \varnothing\}$, $z_0 := [\epsilon]_\simeq$ and the transition function $\delta : Z \times \Sigma \rightarrow Z$ is induced in the natural way (see Ref. [17]), i.e., for all $z, z' \in Z$ and for all $\sigma \in \Sigma$,

$$\delta(z, \sigma) = z' \iff (\exists s \in z, s' \in z') \, s\sigma = s'.$$

It is straightforward to check that **S** is feasible and qualifies as a proper supervisor for **G** that synthesizes K; namely $K = L_m(\mathbf{G} \wedge \mathbf{S})$ and $\overline{K} = L(\mathbf{G} \wedge \mathbf{S})$. A similar procedure called P-supervisor Synthesis and Standard Realization in Ref. [2] can also achieve the same goal, which essentially relies on the automaton subset construction algorithm [130].

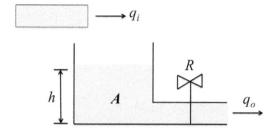

Figure 6.1 A single-tank system.

Example 6.1 *We will use the single-tank system of Figure 6.1 introduced in Chapter 2 as a running example. To make it convenient for readers, we repeat relevant system models below. The whole system consists of a water supply source whose supply rate q_i is a constant (for simplicity), a tank (A), and a control valve (R) at the bottom of the tank controlling the outgoing flow rate q_o, whose value depends on the valve opening and the water level h. We assume that the valve can only be fully open or fully closed, and in case of a full opening, the water level h can only go down. The water level h can be measured; its value change triggers one of the following predefined events: $h = L$, $h = M$, $h = H$, and $h = EH$, which denote that the water level is changed to low, medium, high, extremely high, respectively. The plant model **G** of the system is depicted in Figure 6.2, where the alphabet Σ consists exactly of the events shown in the figure. The actions of opening the valve ($q_o = 1$) and closing the valve ($q_o = 0$) are controllable but unobservable, and all water level events are observable*

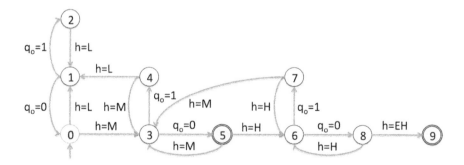

Figure 6.2 Automaton model of the plant **G**.

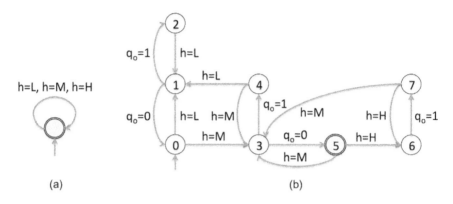

Figure 6.3 Models of a requirement E (a) and the controllable and observable sublanguage K (b).

but uncontrollable. In the model, a shaded double circle denotes a marker state, i.e., states 5 and 9 in Figure 6.2. Assume that we do not want the water level to become extremely high, i.e., the event $h = EH$ should not occur. To prevent state 9 from being reached, we bring in requirement E shown in Figure 6.3, whose alphabet is $\{h{=}L, h{=}M, h{=}H, h{=}EH\}$, but the event $h = EH$ is prohibited from occurring. A controllable and observable sublanguage, i.e., a closed-loop behavior

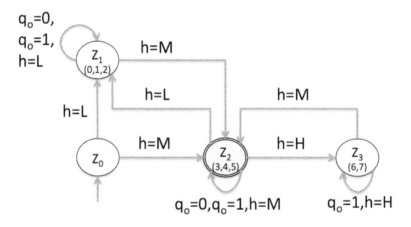

Figure 6.4 A feasible supervisor **S**.

$K = L_m(\mathbf{G} \wedge \mathbf{S})$, can be synthesized by using the standard Ramadge-Wonham supervisory control paradigm, which is also depicted in Figure 6.3. The corresponding feasible supervisor $\mathbf{S}$ via the uncertainty subset construction on K is depicted in Figure 6.4. We can see that in $\mathbf{S}$ all unobservable events are selflooped at some states, and transitions between different states are all labeled by observable events.

For a plant $\mathbf{G}$, there may exist more than one supervisor that ensures the closed-loop system behavior to be contained in a predefined requirement language $E \subseteq \Sigma^*$. Two supervisors $\mathbf{S}_1$ and $\mathbf{S}_2$ of $\mathbf{G}$ are *control equivalent* [15] if $L(\mathbf{G} \wedge \mathbf{S}_1) = L(\mathbf{G} \wedge \mathbf{S}_2)$ and $L_m(\mathbf{G} \wedge \mathbf{S}_1) = L_m(\mathbf{G} \wedge \mathbf{S}_2)$. Let $\mathcal{F}(\mathbf{G}, \mathbf{S})$ be the collection of all feasible supervisors of $\mathbf{G}$ under partial observation P_o, which are control equivalent to a given supervisor $\mathbf{S}$. It is desirable to find one supervisor $\mathbf{S}_* \in \mathcal{F}(\mathbf{G}, \mathbf{S})$ such that for all $\mathbf{S}' \in \mathcal{F}(\mathbf{G}, \mathbf{S})$ we have $|\mathbf{S}_*| \leq |\mathbf{S}'|$, i.e., the supervisor $\mathbf{S}_*$ has the minimum number of states. It has been shown in Ref. [15] that, unfortunately, finding $\mathbf{S}_*$ based on the concept of *control covers* is NP-hard, even for a supervisor under full observation. Each control cover is a collection of subsets of states in $\mathbf{S}$, in which the states of each subset are "control consistent", to be defined shortly. Thus, by grouping those compatible states of $\mathbf{S}$ together, we may get a new supervisor $\mathbf{S}'$ such that (1) $\mathbf{S}'$ is control equivalent to $\mathbf{S}$; (2) $|\mathbf{S}'| \leq |\mathbf{S}|$. In the next two sections, we investigate which information is responsible for control consistency, and which for size reduction.

6.3 INFORMATION FOR CONTROL EQUIVALENCE

Given a plant $\mathbf{G} = (X, \Sigma, \xi, x_0, X_m)$ and a feasible supervisor $\mathbf{S} = (Z, \Sigma, \delta, z_0, Z_m)$, at each state $z \in Z$ there are four items of information shown below:

- Let $En_{\mathbf{S}} : Z \to 2^\Sigma$ with

$$z \mapsto En_{\mathbf{S}}(z) := \{\sigma \in \Sigma | \delta(z, \sigma)!\}$$

  be the ($\mathbf{S}$-)enabled event set at state $z \in Z$.

- Let $D_{\mathbf{S}} : Z \to 2^\Sigma$ with

$$z \mapsto D_S(z) := \{\sigma \in \Sigma | \neg\delta(z, \sigma)! \wedge (\exists s \in L(G)) \, s\sigma \in \\ L(G) \wedge \delta(z_0, s) = z\}$$

be the (**S**-)disabled event set at state $z \in Z$.

- Let $M_{\mathbf{S}} : Z \to \{\text{true}, \text{false}\}$ with

$$z \mapsto M_{\mathbf{S}}(z) := \text{true if } (\exists s \in L_m(\mathbf{G} \wedge \mathbf{S})) \, \delta(z_0, s) = z$$

  be the **S**-marking indicator at state $z \in Z$.

- Let $T_{\mathbf{S}} : Z \to \{\text{true}, \text{false}\}$ with

$$z \mapsto T_{\mathbf{S}}(z) := \text{true if } (\exists s \in L_m(\mathbf{G})) \, \delta(z_0, s) = z$$

  be the **G**-marking indicator at state $z \in Z$.

The (**S**−)enabled event sets can be easily obtained by simply checking the transition structure of **S**. To determine the other sets for each state $z \in Z$, we can first construct the meet $\mathbf{G} \wedge \mathbf{S}$, and then check each state pair (x, z) in the meet associated with the state $z \in Z$. Compared with relevant definitions in Ref. [15], the only change is made to the concept of **S**-marking indicator, which requires that $M_{\mathbf{S}}(z) = \text{true}$ iff z is reachable by a string $s \in L_m(\mathbf{G} \wedge \mathbf{S})$, instead of simply requiring $z \in Z_m$ as in Ref. [15], because here it is not necessary that $L_m(\mathbf{S}) \subseteq L_m(\mathbf{G})$.

Example 6.2 *As an illustration, we revisit the supervisor **S** for the single-tank system depicted in Figure 6.4. By computing the meet $\mathbf{G} \wedge \mathbf{S}$ we obtain the transition structure recognizing K shown in the right-hand picture of Figure 6.3. From that structure we get the following:*

- $Ens(z_0) = \{h{=}L, h{=}M\}$, $D_{\mathbf{S}}(z_0) = \varnothing$, $M_{\mathbf{S}}(z_0) = false$, $T_{\mathbf{S}}(z_0) = false$,

- $Ens(z_1) = \{q_0{=}0, q_0{=}1, h{=}L, h{=}M\}$, $D_{\mathbf{S}}(z_1) = \varnothing$, $M_{\mathbf{S}}(z_1) = false$, $T_{\mathbf{S}}(z_1) = false$,

- $Ens(z_2) = \{q_0{=}0, q_0{=}1, h{=}L, h{=}M, h{=}H\}$, $D_{\mathbf{S}}(z_2) = \varnothing$, $M_{\mathbf{S}}(z_2) = true$, $T_{\mathbf{S}}(z_2) = true$,

- $Ens(z_3) = \{q_0{=}1, h{=}M, h{=}H\}$, $D_{\mathbf{S}}(z_3) = \{q_0{=}0\}$, $M_{\mathbf{S}}(z_3) = false$, $T_{\mathbf{S}}(z_3) = false$.

Let $\mathcal{R} \subseteq Z \times Z$ be a binary relation, where $(z, z') \in \mathcal{R}$ iff the following two properties hold:

1. $En_\mathbf{S}(z) \cap D_\mathbf{S}(z') = En_\mathbf{S}(z') \cap D_\mathbf{S}(z) = \varnothing$,

2. $T_\mathbf{S}(z) = T_\mathbf{S}(z') \Rightarrow M_\mathbf{S}(z) = M_\mathbf{S}(z')$.

We call $\mathcal{R}$ the *binary compatibility relation* over Z. The first condition requires that no event enabled at one state can be disabled at the other state. The second condition requires that both states must have the same marking status, if they are reachable by strings from the marked behavior of $\mathbf{G}$. Notice that $\mathcal{R}$ is reflexive and symmetric, but needn't be transitive, namely is a *tolerance* but not an equivalence relation. Any two states satisfying $\mathcal{R}$ may potentially be merged together, if their suffix behaviors are "compatible", which is precisely captured in the following concept. Let I be a finite index set. The subscript m below denotes marking; it is not an element of I.

Definition 6.1 A collection $\mathcal{C} = \{(Z_i, i)|Z_i \subseteq Z \wedge i \in I\}$ is a *control cover* on $\mathbf{S}$ if

1. $\cup_{i \in I} Z_i = Z$, $(\forall (Z_i, i), (Z_j, j) \in 2^Z \times I) \, i = j \Rightarrow Z_i = Z_j$,

2. $(\forall i \in I) \, Z_i \neq \varnothing \wedge (\forall z, z' \in Z_i) \, (z, z') \in \mathcal{R}$,

3. $(\forall i \in I)(\forall \sigma \in \Sigma)(\exists j \in I)[(\forall z \in Z_i)\delta(z, \sigma)! \Rightarrow \delta(z, \sigma) \in Z_j]$.

$\mathcal{C}$ is *minimal* if for all other control covers $\mathcal{C}'$ of Z we have $|\mathcal{C}| \leq |\mathcal{C}'|$. $\square$

The definition of a control cover ensures that any two different elements in the cover must have distinct index values from I. But it is possible that $Z_i = Z_j$ when $i \neq j$. Because $\mathcal{C} := \{(\{z\}, z)|z \in Z\}$ is trivially a control cover, we know that $\mathbf{S}$ is non-empty if and only if there exists a non-empty control cover $\mathcal{C}$ of $\mathbf{S}$. Given a control cover $\mathcal{C} = \{(Z_i, i)|Z_i \subseteq Z \wedge i \in I\}$ on $\mathbf{S}$, we construct an induced supervisor $\mathbf{S}_\mathcal{C} = (I, \Sigma, \kappa, i_0, I_m)$, where $i_0 \in I$ such that $z_0 \in Z_{i_0}$, $I_m := \{i \in I|Z_i \cap Z_m \neq \varnothing\}$, and $\kappa : I \times \Sigma \rightarrow I$ is the partial transition map such that for each $i \in I$ and $\sigma \in \Sigma$, $\kappa(i, \sigma) := j$ if j is chosen to satisfy the following property:

$$(\exists z \in Z_i)\delta(z, \sigma) \in Z_j \wedge [(\forall z' \in Z_i) \, \delta(z', \sigma)! \Rightarrow \delta(z', \sigma) \in Z_j];$$

otherwise, $\kappa(i, \sigma)$ is not defined. In general, there may exist more than one choice of j with the above property. An arbitrary selection among multiple choices will be adopted to ensure a deterministic transitional structure for $\mathbf{S}_\mathcal{C}$.

Theorem 6.1 Let $\mathbf{S} = (Z, \Sigma, \delta, z_0, Z_m)$ be a feasible supervisor for a plant $\mathbf{G} = (X, \Sigma, \xi, x_0, X_m)$, and let $\mathcal{C} = \{(Z_i, i) | Z_i \subseteq Z \wedge i \in I\}$ be a control cover on $\mathbf{S}$, and $\mathbf{S}_\mathcal{C}$ be an induced supervisor from $\mathcal{C}$. Then $\mathbf{S}_\mathcal{C}$ is a feasible supervisor, which is control equivalent to $\mathbf{S}$.

Proof

1. *We first claim that $L_m(\mathbf{G} \wedge \mathbf{S}) \subseteq L_m(\mathbf{G} \wedge \mathbf{S}_\mathcal{C})$. Let $s \in L_m(\mathbf{G} \wedge \mathbf{S})$. If $s = \epsilon$, then $z_0 \in Z_m$. Since $z_0 \in Z_{i_0}$, we have $Z_{i_0} \cap Z_m \neq \varnothing$. Therefore $i_0 \in I_m$, namely $\epsilon \in L_m(\mathbf{S}_\mathcal{C})$. Let $s = \sigma_0 \ldots \sigma_k$ $(k > 0)$. Because $\delta(z_0, \sigma_0)!$, $\delta(z_0, \sigma_0\sigma_1)!, \ldots, \delta(z_0, \sigma_0\sigma_1 \ldots \sigma_k)!$, we have $\delta(z_0, \sigma_0)!$ and $\delta(z_j, \sigma_j)!$ with $z_{j+1} = \delta(z_0, \sigma_0 \ldots \sigma_j)$, $j = 1, \ldots, k$. Since $\{Z_i | i \in I\}$ is a control cover on Z, by Definition 1 and the definition of κ we have: for all $j : 0 \leq j \leq k$,*

$$(\exists i_j, i_{j+1} \in I) z_j \in Z_{i_j} \wedge z_{j+1} \in Z_{i_{j+1}} \wedge \kappa(i_j, \sigma_j) = i_{j+1}.$$

Therefore, $\kappa(i_0, s)!$. Since $s \in L_m(\mathbf{G} \wedge \mathbf{S})$, we have $\kappa(i_0, s) \in I_m$. Therefore $s \in L_m(\mathbf{G} \wedge \mathbf{S}_\mathcal{C})$, namely

$$L_m(\mathbf{G} \wedge \mathbf{S}) \subseteq L_m(\mathbf{G} \wedge \mathbf{S}_\mathcal{C}).$$

By taking the prefix closure on both sides, and recalling that $\overline{L_m(\mathbf{G} \wedge \mathbf{S})} = L(\mathbf{G} \wedge \mathbf{S})$, we have

$$L(\mathbf{G} \wedge \mathbf{S}) \subseteq L(\mathbf{G} \wedge \mathbf{S}_\mathcal{C}).$$

2. *For the reverse inclusion, let $s \in L(\mathbf{G} \wedge \mathbf{S}_\mathcal{C})$. If $s = \epsilon$ then, as $L(\mathbf{G} \wedge \mathbf{S}) \neq \varnothing$, $s \in L(\mathbf{G} \wedge \mathbf{S})$. Suppose $s = \sigma$. Then $\kappa(i_0, s)!$, so there are $z \in Z_{i_0}$ and $z' \in Z$ such that $\delta(z, \sigma) = z'$, namely $\sigma \in En_{\mathbf{S}}(z)$. By the definition of the control cover $\mathcal{C}$, $\sigma \notin D_{\mathbf{S}}(z_0)$, so either $\delta(z_0, \sigma)!$ or*

$$(\forall t \in \Sigma^*) \delta(z_0, t) = z_0 \Rightarrow t\sigma \notin L(\mathbf{G}).$$

But since $s = \sigma \in L(\mathbf{G} \wedge \mathbf{S}_\mathcal{C})$, we have $\epsilon s \in L(\mathbf{G})$ and $\delta(z_0, \epsilon) = z_0$. Thus, we conclude that $\delta(z_0, \sigma)!$, namely $s \in L(\mathbf{G} \wedge \mathbf{S})$. Of course, by the definition of the control cover $\mathcal{C}$, there follows $\delta(z_0, \sigma) = z' \in Z_{i'}$ for some $i' \in I$. In general, let $s = \sigma_0\sigma_1 \ldots \sigma_k$. Repeating the foregoing argument k-fold, we see that $s \in L(\mathbf{G} \wedge \mathbf{S}_\mathcal{C})$ implies $s \in L(\mathbf{G} \wedge \mathbf{S})$. This shows that $L(\mathbf{G} \wedge \mathbf{S}_\mathcal{C}) \subseteq L(\mathbf{G} \wedge \mathbf{S})$.

3. Let $s \in L_m(\boldsymbol{G} \wedge \boldsymbol{S}_\mathcal{C})$. As shown above, $\delta(z_0, s)!$ with $\delta(z_0, s) = z \in \kappa(i_0, s)$. Since $\kappa(i_0, s) \in I_m$, there exists $z' \in Z_{\kappa(i_0,s)} \cap Z_m$, namely $M_{\boldsymbol{S}}(z') = true$. By the definition of feasible supervisor, we know that there is $s' \in L_m(\boldsymbol{G} \wedge \boldsymbol{S})$ such that $\delta(z_0, s') = z'$, namely $T_{\boldsymbol{S}}(z') = true$. At the same time, $s \in L_m(\boldsymbol{G} \wedge \boldsymbol{S}_\mathcal{C})$ implies $T_{\boldsymbol{S}}(z) = true$. By definition of control cover $\mathcal{C}$, we get $M_{\boldsymbol{S}}(z) = M_{\boldsymbol{S}}(z') = true$, namely $\delta(z_0, s) = z \in Z_m$, and $s \in L_m(\boldsymbol{G} \wedge \boldsymbol{S})$, as required.

So far we have shown that $L(\boldsymbol{G} \wedge \boldsymbol{S}) = L(\boldsymbol{G} \wedge \boldsymbol{S}_\mathcal{C})$ and $L_m(\boldsymbol{G} \wedge \boldsymbol{S}) = L_m(\boldsymbol{G} \wedge \boldsymbol{S}_\mathcal{C})$. Finally, we need to show that $\boldsymbol{S}_\mathcal{C}$ is a feasible supervisor, namely the conditions of control existence and control feasibility must hold. The control existence condition obviously holds because the construction of $\boldsymbol{S}_\mathcal{C}$ from $\boldsymbol{S}$ does not disable more events than $\boldsymbol{S}$ does. Since $\boldsymbol{S}$ is feasible, namely the control existence condition holds, we know that this condition must hold for $\boldsymbol{S}_\mathcal{C}$. For the second condition of control feasibility, notice that, by the definition of control cover $\mathcal{C}$, unobservable events selflooped at certain states in $\boldsymbol{S}$ are also selflooped at appropriate states in $\boldsymbol{S}_\mathcal{C}$. Thus, the control feasibility condition holds for $\boldsymbol{S}_\mathcal{C}$. Since $\boldsymbol{S}$ is marking feasible, it is not difficult to check that $\boldsymbol{S}_\mathcal{C}$ must also be marking feasible, which completes the proof. ■

Theorem 5.4 indicates that we can start with any given plant $\boldsymbol{G}$ and feasible supervisor $\boldsymbol{S}$ to generate another feasible supervisor $\boldsymbol{S}'$, which is control equivalent to $\boldsymbol{S}$ with respect to $\boldsymbol{G}$, by applying the aforementioned construction induced by a properly chosen control cover on $\boldsymbol{S}$. Of special interest is the fact that we do not need to know how $\boldsymbol{S}$ was obtained in the first place. Thus, we have a unified way of undertaking supervisor reduction regardless of whether $\boldsymbol{S}$ is under full observation or partial observation. As an illustration, we revisit the single-tank system, whose feasible supervisor $\boldsymbol{S}$ is depicted in Figure 6.4. Based on the aforementioned analysis about those four sets, i.e., $En_{\boldsymbol{S}}(z)$, $D_{\boldsymbol{S}}(z)$, $M_{\boldsymbol{S}}(z)$ and $T_{\boldsymbol{S}}(z)$, we can check that the set $\mathcal{C} := \{(\{z_0, z_1, z_2\}, 1), (\{z_3\}, 2)\}$ is a control cover, where $I = \{1, 2\}$. The resulting induced supervisor $\boldsymbol{S}_\mathcal{C}$ is depicted in Figure 6.5. We can easily check that $\boldsymbol{S}_\mathcal{C}$ is control equivalent to $\boldsymbol{S}$ with respect to $\boldsymbol{G}$. From $\boldsymbol{S}_\mathcal{C}$ we can see that what $\boldsymbol{S}$ really does is preventing the valve from being closed when the water level is high, which matches our expectation perfectly.

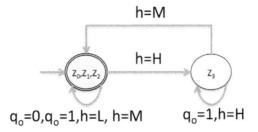

Figure 6.5 An induced supervisor $\mathbf{S}_C$.

Next, we will present a result similar to the Generalized Quotient Theorem in Ref. [15].

Definition 6.2 Given a plant $\mathbf{G}$ and a feasible supervisor $\mathbf{S}$, let $\mathbf{S}' = (Z', \delta', \Sigma, z_0', Z_m')$ be another feasible supervisor of $\mathbf{G}$. Then $\mathbf{S}'$ is *non-redundant* with respect to $\mathbf{S}$ if the following hold:

1. $(\forall z \in Z')(\forall \sigma \in \Sigma)\delta'(z, \sigma)! \Rightarrow (\exists s \in L(\mathbf{G} \wedge \mathbf{S})) s\sigma \in L(\mathbf{G} \wedge \mathbf{S}) \wedge \delta'(z_0', s) = z$,

2. $(\forall z \in Z_m')(\exists s \in L_m(\mathbf{G} \wedge \mathbf{S})) \delta'(z_0', s) = z$. $\qquad\square$

Definition 6.2 indicates that each transition in a non-redundant supervisor $\mathbf{S}'$ must belong to a string in the closed behavior $L(\mathbf{G} \wedge \mathbf{S})$, and every marker state in $\mathbf{S}'$ must be reachable by a string in the marked behavior $L_m(\mathbf{G} \wedge \mathbf{S})$. Both synthesis tools TCT and SuSyNA can be used to compute a non-redundant feasible supervisor.

Definition 6.3 Given two finite-state automata $\mathbf{G}_A = (X_A, \Sigma, \xi_A, x_{A,0}, X_{A,m})$, $\mathbf{G}_B = (X_B, \Sigma, \xi_B, x_{B,0}, X_{B,m})$, we say that $\mathbf{G}_B$ is the image of $\mathbf{G}_A$ under the DES-isomorphism $\theta : X_A \to X_B$ if

1. θ is bijective,

2. $\theta(x_{A,0}) = x_{B,0}$ and $\theta(X_{A,m}) = X_{B,m}$,

3. for all $x, x' \in X_A$ amd for all $\sigma \in \Sigma$,

$$\xi_A(x, \sigma) = x' \Rightarrow \xi_B(\theta(x), \sigma) = \theta(x'),$$

4. for all $x \in X_B$ and for all $\sigma \in \Sigma$,

$$\xi_B(x, \sigma)! \Rightarrow \xi_A(\theta^{-1}(\{x\}), \sigma)!. \qquad \square$$

Definition 6.3 states that an automaton $\mathbf{G}_A$ is DES-isomorphic to another automaton $\mathbf{G}_B$ if $\mathbf{G}_A$ and $\mathbf{G}_B$ are identical up to state relabeling, i.e., every state in $\mathbf{G}_A$ maps to a unique state in $\mathbf{G}_B$, in particular, the initial state of $\mathbf{G}_A$ maps to the initial state of $\mathbf{G}_B$, each marker state of $\mathbf{G}_A$ maps to a marker state of $\mathbf{G}_B$, each marker state in $\mathbf{G}_B$ must have one marker state in $\mathbf{G}_A$ as a pre-image, each transition in $\mathbf{G}_A$ corresponds to one transition in $\mathbf{G}_B$, and each transition in $\mathbf{G}_B$ has one transition in $\mathbf{G}_A$ as the pre-image.

Given a plant $\mathbf{G}$ and a feasible supervisor $\mathbf{S}$, by computing the meet of $\mathbf{G}$ and $\mathbf{S}$, i.e., $\mathbf{G} \wedge \mathbf{S}$, we can obtain the closed-loop (closed and marked) behaviors. By applying the uncertainty subset construction shown in Procedure 1 to $\mathbf{G} \wedge \mathbf{S}$ with respect to $P_o : \Sigma^* \to \Sigma_o^*$, we can derive a feasible supervisor, say **SUPER**, which is control equivalent to $\mathbf{S}$. The following result shows that any non-redundant feasible supervisor, which is control equivalent to $\mathbf{S}$ with respect to $\mathbf{G}$, can be constructed from **SUPER** by using a suitable control cover on $\mathbf{S}$. It is an extension of the Generalized Quotient Theorem stated in Ref. [15] to more generally defined feasible supervisors, and clearly shows the "universality" of control covers.

Theorem 6.2 [Extended Quotient Theorem]
Given a feasible supervisor $\mathbf{S}$ of a plant $\mathbf{G}$, let **SUPER** be constructed as above. Then for any non-redundant feasible supervisor **SIMSUP** with respect to $\mathbf{S}$, which is control equivalent to $\mathbf{S}$ with respect to $\mathbf{G}$, there exists a control cover $\mathcal{C}$ on **SUPER** and an induced feasible supervisor $\mathbf{S}_{\mathcal{C}}$ such that $\mathbf{S}_{\mathcal{C}}$ is DES-isomorphic to **SIMSUP**.

Proof *With* $\mathbf{SUPER} = (Z, \Sigma, \delta, z_0, Z_m)$ *and* $\mathbf{SIMSUP} = (Y, \Sigma, \eta, y_0, Y_m)$, *for each* $y \in Y$, *let*

$$Z(y) := \{z \in Z | (\exists s \in L(\mathbf{G} \wedge \mathbf{S}) \delta(z_0, s) = z \wedge \eta(y_0, s) = y\}$$

and define $\mathcal{C} := \{(Z(y), y) | y \in Y\}$. *We now check that* $\mathcal{C}$ *is a control cover on* $\mathbf{SUPER}$.

By non-redundancy of $\mathbf{SIMSUP}$, *we have* $Z(y) \neq \varnothing$ *for all* $y \in Y$. *Since* $\mathbf{SUPER}$ *is obtained by the uncertainty subset construction, for* each $z \in Z$, there is $s \in L(\boldsymbol{G} \wedge \boldsymbol{S}) = L(\boldsymbol{G} \wedge \boldsymbol{SIMSUP})$ with $\delta(z_0, s) = z$ and $\eta(y_0, s)!$. Hence, $z \in Z(\eta(y_0, s))$. Thus, $\mathcal{C} = \{(Z(y), y) | y \in Y\}$ covers Z.

Next, fix $y \in Y$ and let $a, b \in Z(y)$ with $\sigma \in En_{\boldsymbol{SUPER}}(a)$. We need to show that $\sigma \notin D_{\boldsymbol{SUPER}}(b)$. Since $\boldsymbol{SUPER}$ is constructed via the uncertainty subset construction, we know that for all $s \in L(\boldsymbol{G} \wedge \boldsymbol{S})$ such that $\delta(z_0, s) = a$, there exists $s' \in P_o^{-1}(P_o(s)) \cap L(\boldsymbol{G} \wedge \boldsymbol{S})$ such that $s'\sigma \in L(\boldsymbol{G} \wedge \boldsymbol{S})$. In addition, $\delta(z_0, s') = a$. Since $a \in Z(y)$, there exists $\hat{s} \in L(\boldsymbol{G} \wedge \boldsymbol{S})$ such that $\delta(z_0, \hat{s}) = a$ and $\eta(y_0, \hat{s}) = y$. Thus, we know that there exists $\hat{s}' \in P_o^{-1}(P_o(\hat{s})) \cap L(\boldsymbol{G} \wedge \boldsymbol{S})$ such that $\hat{s}'\sigma \in L(\boldsymbol{G} \wedge \boldsymbol{S})$ and $\delta(z_0, \hat{s}') = a$. Since $\boldsymbol{SIMSUP}$ is a feasible supervisor, we know that $\eta(y_0, \hat{s}') = y$. Thus, $\eta(y, \sigma)!$. Since $b \in Z(y)$, there exists $t \in L(\boldsymbol{G} \wedge \boldsymbol{S})$ such that $\delta(z_0, t) = b$ and $\eta(y_0, t) = y$. If there exists $t'\sigma \in L(G)$ such that $\delta(z_0, t') = b$, we know that there must exist $\hat{t} \in P_o^{-1}(P_o(t)) \cap L(\boldsymbol{G} \wedge \boldsymbol{S})$ such that $\hat{t}\sigma \in L(G)$, $\delta(z_0, \hat{t}) = b$ and, because $\boldsymbol{SIMSUP}$ is a feasible supervisor, we have $\eta(y_0, \hat{t}) = y$. Since $\hat{t}\sigma \in L(G \wedge \boldsymbol{SIMSUP}) = L(G \wedge \boldsymbol{SUPER})$, we know that $\delta(b, \sigma)!$. Thus, $\sigma \notin D_{\boldsymbol{SUPER}}(b)$, namely $En_{\boldsymbol{SUPER}}(a) \cap D_{\boldsymbol{SUPER}}(b) = \varnothing$, as required.

Next, we show that

$$T_{\boldsymbol{SUPER}}(a) = T_{\boldsymbol{SUPER}}(b) \Rightarrow M_{\boldsymbol{SUPER}}(a) = M_{\boldsymbol{SUPER}}(b).$$

To this end, let $y \in Y$ and $a, b \in Z(y)$ with $M_{\boldsymbol{SUPER}}(a) \neq M_{\boldsymbol{SUPER}}(b)$. Without loss of generality, assume that $M_{\boldsymbol{SUPER}}(a) = true$ and $M_{\boldsymbol{SUPER}}(b) = false$. Since $M_{\boldsymbol{SUPER}}(a) = true$, there exists $s \in L_m(\boldsymbol{G} \wedge \boldsymbol{S})$ such that $\delta(z_0, s) = a$. Thus, $T_{\boldsymbol{SUPER}}(a) = true$. Since $a \in Z(y)$, we know that there exists $s' \in L(\boldsymbol{G} \wedge \boldsymbol{S})$ such that $\delta(z_0, s') = a$ and $\eta(y_0, s') = y$. Thanks to the uncertainty subset construction, we know that there exists $\hat{s} \in P_o^{-1}(P_o(s')) \cap L_m(\boldsymbol{G} \wedge \boldsymbol{S})$ such that $\delta(z_0, \hat{s}) = a$ and, because $\boldsymbol{SIMSUP}$ is a feasible supervisor, we have $\eta(y_0, \hat{s}) = y$. This means $y \in Y_m$. Since $b \in Z(y)$, for all $t \in L(\boldsymbol{G} \wedge \boldsymbol{S})$ with $\delta(z_0, t) = b$, thanks to the uncertainty subset construction and the fact that $\boldsymbol{SIMSUP}$ is a feasible supervisor, we can deduce that there exists $\hat{t} \in L(\boldsymbol{G} \wedge \boldsymbol{S})$ such that $\delta(z_0, \hat{t}) = b$, $\eta(y_0, \hat{t}) = y$ and $t \in L_m(G) \iff \hat{t} \in L_m(G)$. Since $M_{\boldsymbol{SUPER}}(b) = false$, we know that $\hat{t} \notin L_m(\boldsymbol{G} \wedge \boldsymbol{S}) = L_m(G \wedge \boldsymbol{SIMSUP})$. Since $y \in Y_m$, we deduce that $\hat{t} \notin L_m(G)$. Thus, $t \notin L_m(G)$. Since t is arbitrarily chosen, we know that $T_{\boldsymbol{SUPER}}(b) = false$. Thus, we have

$$M_{\textbf{SUPER}}(a) \neq M_{\textbf{SUPER}}(b) \Rightarrow T_{\textbf{SUPER}}(a) \neq T_{\textbf{SUPER}}(b),$$

or equivalently,

$$T_{\textbf{SUPER}}(a) = T_{\textbf{SUPER}}(b) \Rightarrow M_{\textbf{SUPER}}(a) = M_{\textbf{SUPER}}(b).$$

Finally, we need to show that for each $y \in Y$ and $\sigma \in \Sigma$, there exists $y' \in Y$ such that

$$(\forall z \in Z(y))\delta(z,\sigma)! \Rightarrow \delta(z,\sigma) \in Z(y').$$

Let $z \in Z(y)$ and $\delta(z,\sigma)!$. Clearly, there exists $s \in L(\textbf{G} \wedge \textbf{S})$ such that $s\sigma \in L(\textbf{G} \wedge \textbf{S})$ and $\delta(z_0, s) = z$. By using an argument similar to the above, we know that there exists $s' \in P_o^{-1}(P_o(s)) \cap L(\textbf{G} \wedge \textbf{S})$ such that $\delta(z_0, s') = z$, $\eta(y_0, s') = y$, and $s'\sigma \in L(\textbf{G} \wedge \textbf{S})$. Clearly, $\eta(y,\sigma)!$. Thus, $\delta(z,\sigma) \in Z(\eta(y,\sigma))$, as required.

So far we have shown that $\mathcal{C} = \{(Z(y), y)|y \in Y\}$ is a control cover on $\textbf{SUPER}$. Let $\textbf{S}_{\mathcal{C}} := (Y, \Sigma, \kappa, y_0, Y_m)$ be induced from $\mathcal{C}$, where

$$(\forall y \in Y)(\forall \sigma \in \Sigma)\,\kappa(y,\sigma) := \begin{cases} \eta(y,\sigma) & \text{if } \eta(y,\sigma)!, \\ \text{undefined} & \text{otherwise.} \end{cases}$$

For any $y \in Y$ and $\sigma \in \Sigma$, assume that there exists $z \in Z(y)$ such that $\delta(z,\sigma)!$. For all $z' \in Z(y)$, we know that there exists $s \in L(\textbf{G} \wedge \textbf{S})$ such that $\delta(z_0, s) = z'$ and $\eta(y_0, s) = y$. If $\delta(z', \sigma)!$, by the construction of $\textbf{SUPER}$ we know that there must exist $s' \in \Sigma^*$ and $u \in \Sigma_{uo}^*$ such that $P_o(s) = P_o(s')$, $\delta(z_0, s'u) = z'$ and $s'u\sigma \in L(G \wedge \textbf{SUPER}) = L(\textbf{G} \wedge \textbf{S}) \subseteq L(\textbf{SIMSUP})$ (owing to the control equivalence of $\textbf{SIMSUP}$ to $\textbf{S}$). Since $\textbf{SIMSUP}$ is feasible, by the control feasibility property and the fact that $P_o(s) = P_o(s')$, we know that $\eta(y_0, s) = \eta(y_0, s') = y$. Since $s'u\sigma \in L(\textbf{SIMSUP})$, by the control feasibility property and the fact that $u \in \Sigma_{uo}^*$, we know that $\eta(y_0, s'u\sigma) = \eta(y, u\sigma) = \eta(y,\sigma)$. Thus, $\delta(z',\sigma) = \delta(z_0, s'u\sigma) \in Z(\eta(y,\sigma))$. This means, if there exists $z \in Z(y)$ such that $\delta(z,\sigma)!$, then

$$(\forall z' \in Z(y))[\delta(z',\sigma)! \Rightarrow \delta(z',\sigma) \in Z(\eta(y,\sigma))].$$

By Theorem 19 we know that $\textbf{S}_{\mathcal{C}}$ is a feasible supervisor, which is control equivalent to $\textbf{S}$ with respect to $\textbf{G}$. In addition, there exists a *natural bijective mapping between the state set Y of $\textbf{SIMSUP}$ and the state set Y of $\textbf{S}_C$ with respect to the control cover $\mathcal{C}$,*

$$\theta : Y \to Y : y \mapsto \theta(y) := y.$$

Thus, $\textbf{S}_C$ is DES-isomorphic to $\textbf{SIMSUP}$, which completes the proof.
■

Up to now we have developed a general theory on supervisor reduction, which unifies both the full observation case and the partial observation case. It is clear that the concrete way of ensuring observability in a feasible supervisor is not important in achieving control equivalence during supervisor reduction. Knowledge of the plant $\textbf{G}$ and a feasible supervisor $\textbf{S}$ will be sufficient for us to construct a feasible supervisor, which is control equivalent to $\textbf{S}$, and optimistically has a (significantly) smaller size.

6.4 INFORMATION DETERMINING REDUCTION EFFICIENCY

Our case studies indicate that a supervisor with full observation usually allows a much higher reduction ratio than that allowed by a supervisor with partial observation. An interesting question is what causes such a discrepancy. In this section we propose an answer to this question, and explain the actual effects of partial observation on supervisor reduction.

Given a plant $\textbf{G}$ and a feasible supervisor $\textbf{S}$, each feasible supervisor $\textbf{S}' \in \mathcal{F}(\textbf{G}, \textbf{S})$ carries four pieces of critical information captured by $(En_{\textbf{S}'}, D_{\textbf{S}'}, M_{\textbf{S}'}, T_{\textbf{S}'})$. We define a preorder "$\preceq$" among elements of $\mathcal{F}(\textbf{G}, \textbf{S})$,[2] where for all $S_i = (Z_i, \Sigma, \delta_i, z_{i,0}, Z_{i,m}) \in \mathcal{F}(\textbf{G}, \textbf{S})$ $(i = 1, 2)$, we say $\textbf{S}_1$ is *leaner than* $\textbf{S}_2$, denoted as $\textbf{S}_1 \preceq \textbf{S}_2$, if for all $s \in L(\textbf{G} \wedge \textbf{S})$ we have

- $En_{\textbf{S}_1}(\delta_1(z_{1,0}, s)) \subseteq En_{\textbf{S}_2}(\delta_2(z_{2,0}, s))$,

- $D_{\textbf{S}_1}(\delta_1(z_{1,0}, s)) \subseteq D_{\textbf{S}_2}(\delta_2(z_{2,0}, s))$,

- $M_{\textbf{S}_1}(\delta_1(z_{1,0}, s)) = \text{true} \Rightarrow M_{\textbf{S}_2}(\delta_2(z_{2,0}, s)) = \text{true}$,

- $T_{\textbf{S}_1}(\delta_1(z_{1,0}, s)) = \text{true} \Rightarrow T_{\textbf{S}_2}(\delta_2(z_{2,0}, s)) = \text{true}$.

In words, $\textbf{S}_1$ is leaner than $\textbf{S}_2$ if for each pair of states z_1 in $\textbf{S}_1$ and z_2 in $\textbf{S}_2$ reachable by the same string in $L(\textbf{G} \wedge \textbf{S})$, the enabled and disabled event sets at z_1 are subsets of those at z_2; and, if the values of the **S**-marking indicator and the **G**-marking indicator at z_1 are both true, then those values at z_2 are also true. Informally speaking, each string $s \in L(\mathbf{G} \wedge \mathbf{S})$ carries two types of information. Type 1: information associated with **S** only, i.e., the set of enabled events $\psi(s) := \{\sigma \in \Sigma | s\sigma \in L(\mathbf{G} \wedge \mathbf{S})\}$ and the set of disabled events $\lambda(s) := \{\sigma \in \Sigma | s\sigma \in L(G) \wedge s\sigma \notin L(S)\}$. Type 2: information associated with all strings that reach the same state as that reached by **S**, e.g., z_1 in $\mathbf{S}_1$ above, i.e., the set of enabled events at the state reached by s, e.g., $En_{\mathbf{S}_1}(z_1)$, and the set of disabled events at the state reached by s, e.g., $D_{\mathbf{S}_1}(z_1)$. It is clear that $\psi(s) \subseteq En_{\mathbf{S}_1}(z_1)$ and $\lambda(s) \subseteq D_{\mathbf{S}_1}(z_1)$. In other words, when the plant **G** executes the string s, the supervisor $\mathbf{S}_1$ allows more events specified by $En_{\mathbf{S}_1}(z_1) - \psi(s)$ and disables more events specified by $D_{\mathbf{S}_1}(z_1) - \lambda(s)$, owing to the need for ensuring control feasibility. Such extra enabled/disabled events are clearly redundant for s. If $\mathbf{S}_1 \preceq \mathbf{S}_2$, we know that $En_{\mathbf{S}_1}(z_1) - \psi(s) \subseteq En_{\mathbf{S}_2}(z_2) - \psi(s)$, and $D_{\mathbf{S}_1}(z_1) - \lambda(s) \subseteq D_{\mathbf{S}_2}(z_2) - \lambda(s)$, that is, $\mathbf{S}_1$ carries less redundant information (or equivalently, is leaner) than $\mathbf{S}_2$ does. Although such redundant information does not affect control equivalence of relevant supervisors, it does affect the state-size reduction ratio, when we construct a reduced supervisor based on a control cover.

The example of Figure 6.6 illustrates preorder over control equivalent feasible supervisors. The alphabet of the plant **G** is $\Sigma = \{a, b, c, d_1, d_2, e\}$, $\Sigma_c = \{d_1, d_2\}$, and all events are observable for the sake of simplicity. It is not difficult to check that $\mathbf{S}_1$ and $\mathbf{S}_2$ are control equivalent - they both disable events d_1 and d_2 after executing the event c. To check that $\mathbf{S}_1$ is leaner than $\mathbf{S}_2$, we only need to check those conditions for two strings $s = \epsilon$ and $s = c$ because for other strings in $L(\mathbf{G} \wedge \mathbf{S})$, $\mathbf{S}_1$ and $\mathbf{S}_2$ are the same. For $s = \epsilon$, we have $z_1 = 0$ in $\mathbf{S}_1$ and $z_2 = 0$ in $\mathbf{S}_2$. Clearly, $En_{\mathbf{S}_1}(z_1) = \{a, b, c\} = En_{\mathbf{S}_1}(z_2)$, and $D_{\mathbf{S}_1}(z_1) = \emptyset \subseteq \{d_1, d_2\} = D_{\mathbf{S}_2}(z_2)$. In addition, we can check that $M_{\mathbf{S}_1}(z_1) = false$ and $M_{\mathbf{S}_2}(z_2) = true$, and $T_{\mathbf{S}_1}(z_1) = false$ and $T_{\mathbf{S}_2}(z_2) = true$. Thus, those conditions hold for $s = \epsilon$. For $s = c$ we have $z_1 = 3$ in $\mathbf{S}_1$ and $z_2 = 0$ in $\mathbf{S}_2$. Clearly, $En_{\mathbf{S}_1}(z_1) = \emptyset \subseteq En_{\mathbf{S}_1}(z_2) = \{a, b, c\}$, and $D_{\mathbf{S}_1}(z_1) = \{d_1, d_2\} = D_{\mathbf{S}_2}(z_2)$. In addition, we can check that $M_{\mathbf{S}_1}(z_1) = true = M_{\mathbf{S}_2}(z_2)$, and $T_{\mathbf{S}_1}(z_1) = true = T_{\mathbf{S}_2}(z_2)$. Thus, we conclude that $\mathbf{S}_1$ is leaner than $\mathbf{S}_2$.

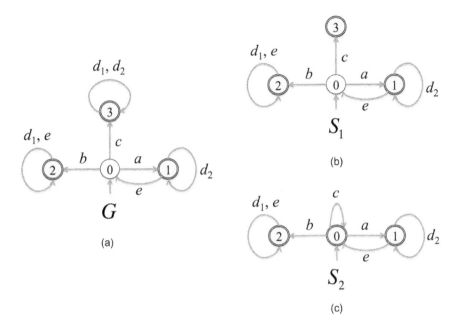

Figure 6.6 A plant **G** (a), supervisors **S**₁ (b) and **S**₂ (c).

Theorem 6.3 Given a plant **G** and a feasible supervisor **S**, let **SUPER** be the same as that stated in Theorem 6.1. Then for all $S' \in \mathcal{F}(G, S)$, we have **SUPER** $\preceq$ **S**′.

Proof Let $SUPER = (\hat{Z}, \Sigma, \hat{\delta}, \hat{z}_0, \hat{Z}_m)$ and $S' = (Z', \Sigma, \delta', z_0', Z_m')$. Let $s \in L(G \wedge S)$. Recall that **SUPER** is obtained by applying the uncertainty subset construction on $G \wedge S$. Thus, we know that the following properties hold:

(a) $(\forall \sigma \in En_{SUPER}(\hat{\delta}(\hat{z}_0, s)))(\exists s' \in L(G \wedge S)) s'\sigma \in L(G \wedge S) \wedge \hat{\delta}(\hat{z}_0, s') = \hat{\delta}(\hat{z}_0, s)$,
   i.e., no transition in **SUPER** is redundant.

(b) $(\forall s', s'' \in L(G \wedge S)) P_o(s') = P_o(s'') \Rightarrow \hat{\delta}(\hat{z}_0, s') = \hat{\delta}(\hat{z}_0, s'')$,
   i.e., strings with the same projected image with respect to P_o reach the same state.

(c) for any two strings $s', s'' \in L(G \wedge S)$, if $\hat{\delta}(\hat{z}_0, s') = \hat{\delta}(\hat{z}_0, s'')$, then

$$\{\sigma \in \Sigma | (\exists t \in L(G \wedge S) \cap P_o^{-1}(s')) t\sigma \in L(G \wedge S)\} = \{\sigma' \in \Sigma | (\exists t' \in L(G \wedge S) \cap P_o^{-1}(s'')) t'\sigma' \in L(G \wedge S)\},$$

i.e., for any event $\sigma \in \Sigma$, there exists a string $t \in L(\boldsymbol{G} \wedge \boldsymbol{S}) \cap P_o^{-1}(s')$ such that σ is enabled after t iff there exists a string $t' \in L(\boldsymbol{G} \wedge \boldsymbol{S}) \cap P_o^{-1}(s'')$ such that σ is enabled after t'.

Let $z := \hat{\delta}(\hat{z}_0, s)$. Thus, we know that

$$En_{\boldsymbol{SUPER}}(\hat{\delta}(\hat{z}_0, s))$$

$$= \cup_{s' \in L(\boldsymbol{G} \wedge \boldsymbol{S}): \hat{\delta}(\hat{z}_0, s') = z} \{\sigma \in \Sigma | s'\sigma \in L(\boldsymbol{G} \wedge \boldsymbol{S})\} \text{ by Property (a)}$$

$$= \cup_{s' \in L(\boldsymbol{G} \wedge \boldsymbol{S}): \hat{\delta}(\hat{z}_0, s') = z} \{\sigma \in \Sigma | (\exists t \in L(\boldsymbol{G} \wedge \boldsymbol{S})) t\sigma$$

$$\in L(\boldsymbol{G} \wedge \boldsymbol{S}) \wedge P_o(s') = P_o(t)\}$$

$$\text{by Property (b)}$$

$$= \{\sigma \in \Sigma | (\exists s' \in L(\boldsymbol{G} \wedge \boldsymbol{S})) s'\sigma \in L(\boldsymbol{G} \wedge \boldsymbol{S}) \wedge P_o(s) = P_o(s')\}$$

$$\text{by Property (c)}$$

$$\subseteq \{\sigma \in \Sigma | (\exists s' \in L(\boldsymbol{S}') P_o(s) = P_o(s') \wedge s'\sigma \in L(\boldsymbol{S}')\}$$

$$\text{as } L(\boldsymbol{G} \wedge \boldsymbol{S}) \subseteq L(\boldsymbol{S}') \text{ and } \boldsymbol{S}' \text{ is feasible}$$

$$= En_{\boldsymbol{S}'}(\delta'(z_0', s))$$

Thus, $En_{\boldsymbol{SUPER}}(\hat{\delta}(\hat{z}_0, s)) \subseteq En_{\boldsymbol{S}'}(\delta'(z_0', s))$.

To show that $D_{\boldsymbol{SUPER}}(\hat{\delta}(\hat{z}_0, s)) \subseteq D_{\boldsymbol{S}'}(\delta'(z_0', s))$, let $\sigma' \in D_{\boldsymbol{SUPER}}(\hat{\delta}(\hat{z}_0, s))$ and $z := \hat{\delta}(\hat{z}_0, s)$. Then $\neg\hat{\delta}(z, \sigma')!$ but there exists $s'\sigma' \in L(G)$ such that $\hat{\delta}(\hat{z}_0, s') = z$. Clearly, $s' \in L(\boldsymbol{G} \wedge \boldsymbol{S})$ but $s'\sigma' \notin L(S)$. In addition, by definition of the uncertainty subset construction, we can choose s' in such a way that $P_o(s) = P_o(s')$. Thus, we know that

$$\sigma' \in \{\sigma \in \Sigma | (\exists s' \in L(\boldsymbol{G} \wedge \boldsymbol{S})) \, s'\sigma \in L(G) \wedge P_o(s) = P_o(s') \wedge s'\sigma \notin L(S)\},$$

which means $D_{\boldsymbol{SUPER}}(z) \subseteq \{\sigma \in \Sigma | (\exists s' \in L(\boldsymbol{G} \wedge \boldsymbol{S})) \, s'\sigma \in L(G) \wedge P_o(s) = P_o(s') \wedge s'\sigma \notin L(S)\}$. Thus, we have

$$D_{\boldsymbol{SUPER}}(z)$$

$$\subseteq \{\sigma \in \Sigma | (\exists s' \in L(\boldsymbol{G} \wedge \boldsymbol{S})) \, s'\sigma \in L(G) \wedge P_o(s) = P_o(s') \wedge s'\sigma \notin L(S)\}$$

$$\subseteq \{\sigma \in \Sigma | (\exists s' \in L(\boldsymbol{G} \wedge \boldsymbol{S}')) \, s'\sigma \in L(G) \wedge s'\sigma \notin L(\boldsymbol{S}') \wedge \delta'(z_0', s) = \delta'(z_0', s')\}$$

$$\text{because } L(\boldsymbol{G} \wedge \boldsymbol{S}) = L(\boldsymbol{G} \wedge \boldsymbol{S}')$$

$$= D_{\boldsymbol{S}'}(\delta'(z_0', s))$$

Assume that $M_{\boldsymbol{SUPER}}(\hat{\delta}(\hat{z}_0, s)) = \text{true}$. Then $s \in L_m(\boldsymbol{G} \wedge \boldsymbol{S}) = L_m(\boldsymbol{G} \wedge \boldsymbol{S}')$, which means $M_{\boldsymbol{S}'}(\delta'(z_0', s)) = \text{true}$. Assume that $T_{\mathbf{SUPER}}(\hat{\delta}(\hat{z}_0, s)) = true.$ *Then* $s \in L_m(G),$ *which means* $T_{S'}(\delta'(z'_0, s)) = true.$ *Thus, we have* $\mathbf{SUPER} \preceq \mathbf{S'}.$ ■

Theorem 6.3 indicates that for all feasible supervisors in $\mathcal{F}(\mathbf{G}, \mathbf{S})$, **SUPER** has the leanest information which still ensures control equivalence. The interesting point is that for any feasible supervisor $\mathbf{S'} \in \mathcal{F}(\mathbf{G}, \mathbf{S})$, we can construct **SUPER** by applying the uncertainty subset construction on $\mathbf{G} \wedge \mathbf{S'}$, namely we can always obtain the leanest feasible supervisor, which is control equivalent to **S** with respect to **G**. Nevertheless, the size of **SUPER** could be large for a practical application. Thus, supervisor reduction may be directly applied to any feasible supervisor $\mathbf{S'} \in \mathcal{F}(\mathbf{G}, \mathbf{S})$. The following result indicates that the state size of a reduced supervisor solely depends on the leanness of the key information specified by those four functions - the leaner the information, the smaller the reduced state size.

Theorem 6.4 Given a plant **G** and a feasible supervisor **S**, let $\mathbf{S}_1, \mathbf{S}_2 \in \mathcal{F}(\mathbf{G}, \mathbf{S})$ be non-redundant with respect to **S**, and assume that $\mathbf{S}_1 \preceq \mathbf{S}_2$. Let $\mathcal{C}_1$ and $\mathcal{C}_2$ be minimal control covers of $\mathbf{S}_1$ and $\mathbf{S}_2$, respectively. Then we have $|\mathcal{C}_1| \leq |\mathcal{C}_2|$.

Proof *Let* $S_j = (Z_j, \Sigma, \delta_j, z_{j,0}, Z_{j,m})$ $(j = 1, 2)$, *and* $\mathcal{R}_j \subseteq Z_j \times Z_j$ *the binary compatibility relation over* Z_j. *Let* $\mathcal{C}_2 = \{(Z_{2,i}, i) | Z_{2,i} \subseteq Z_2 \wedge i \in I_2\}$ *be a minimal control cover on* $\mathbf{S}_2$. *By Definition 6.1 we know that*

1. $(\forall i \in I_2) Z_{2,i} \neq \varnothing \wedge (\forall z, z' \in Z_{2,i}) (z, z') \in \mathcal{R}_2$,

2. $(\forall i \in I_2)(\forall \sigma \in \Sigma)(\exists j \in I_2)[(\forall z \in Z_{2,i})\delta_2(z, \sigma)! \Rightarrow \delta_2(z, \sigma) \in Z_{2,j}]$.

Since $\mathbf{S}_2$ *is non-redundant with respect to* $\mathbf{S}$, *we can derive that for each* $z \in Z_2$ *there exists* $s \in L(\mathbf{G} \wedge \mathbf{S})$ *such that* $\delta_2(z_{2,0}, s) = z$. *For each* $(Z_{2,i}, i) \in \mathcal{C}_2$, *let*

$$\mathcal{L}(Z_{2,i}) := \{s \in L(\mathbf{G} \wedge \mathbf{S}) | \delta_2(z_{2,0}, s) \in Z_{2,i}\} \cup (\Sigma^* \setminus L(G)).$$

We can easily check that

$$En_{\mathbf{S}_2}(Z_{2,i}) = \cup_{z \in Z_{2,i}} En_{\mathbf{S}_2}(z) = \{\sigma \in \Sigma | s\sigma \in L(\mathbf{G} \wedge \mathbf{S}) \wedge s \in \mathcal{L}(Z_{2,i})\}.$$

Since $\mathbf{S}_1, \mathbf{S}_2 \in \mathcal{F}(\mathbf{G}, \mathbf{S})$, *we know that* $\mathcal{L}(Z_{2,i}) \cap L(G) \subseteq L(\mathbf{G} \wedge \mathbf{S}_2) = L(\mathbf{G} \wedge \mathbf{S}_1)$. *Let*

$$\hat{\mathcal{C}}_1 := \{(Z_{1,i}, i) | Z_{1,i} \subseteq Z_1 \wedge$$
$$[(\forall z \in Z_1)\, z \in Z_{1,i} \iff (\exists s \in \mathcal{L}(Z_{2,i}))\delta_1(z_{1,0}, s) = z] \wedge i \in I_2\}.$$

We now show that $\hat{\mathcal{C}}_1$ is a control cover of $\boldsymbol{S}_1$. First, we show that $\{Z_{1,i} | i \in I_2\}$ is a cover of Z_1. To see this, notice that $\cup_{i \in I_2} \mathcal{L}(Z_{2,i}) \cap L(G) = L(\boldsymbol{G} \wedge \boldsymbol{S}) = L(G \wedge \boldsymbol{S}_2) = L(G \wedge \boldsymbol{S}_1)$. Since $\boldsymbol{S}_1$ is also non-redundant with respect to $\boldsymbol{S}$, we know that $\{Z_{1,i} | i \in I_2\}$ must be a cover of Z_1. It is obvious that, for all $(Z_{1,i}, i), (Z_{1,j}, j) \in \hat{\mathcal{C}}_1$, we have that $i = j$ implies $Z_{1,i} = Z_{1,j}$.

To show that $\hat{\mathcal{C}}_1$ is a control cover of $\boldsymbol{S}_1$, we need to show that the remaining Conditions 2-3 stated in Definition 1 hold. To check Condition 2, for each $(Z_{1,i}, i) \in \hat{\mathcal{C}}_1$ and for all $z_1, z_1' \in Z_{1,i}$, we know that there exist $s, s' \in \mathcal{L}(Z_{2,i})$ such that $\delta_1(z_{1,0}, s) = z_1$ and $\delta_1(z_{1,0}, s') = z_1'$. On the other hand, let $z_2 = \delta_2(z_{2,0}, s)$ and $z_2' = \delta_2(z_{2,0}, s')$. Since $\boldsymbol{S}_1 \preceq \boldsymbol{S}_2$, we know that

- $En_{\boldsymbol{S}_1}(z_1) \subseteq En_{\boldsymbol{S}_2}(z_2)$ and $D_{\boldsymbol{S}_1}(z_1) \subseteq D_{\boldsymbol{S}_2}(z_2)$,

- $M_{\boldsymbol{S}_1}(z_1) = true \Rightarrow M_{\boldsymbol{S}_2}(z_2) = true$,

- $T_{\boldsymbol{S}_1}(z_1) = true \Rightarrow T_{\boldsymbol{S}_2}(z_2) = true$,

and

- $En_{\boldsymbol{S}_1}(z_1') \subseteq En_{\boldsymbol{S}_2}(z_2')$ and $D_{\boldsymbol{S}_1}(z_1') \subseteq D_{\boldsymbol{S}_2}(z_2')$,

- $M_{\boldsymbol{S}_1}(z_1') = true \Rightarrow M_{\boldsymbol{S}_2}(z_2') = true$,

- $T_{\boldsymbol{S}_1}(z_1') = true \Rightarrow T_{\boldsymbol{S}_2}(z_2') = true$.

Since $(z_2, z_2') \in \mathcal{R}_2$, we have

- $En_{\boldsymbol{S}_2}(z_2) \cap D_{\boldsymbol{S}_2}(z_2') = En_{\boldsymbol{S}_2}(z_2') \cap D_{\boldsymbol{S}_2}(z_2) = \varnothing$,

- $T_{\boldsymbol{S}_2}(z_2) = T_{\boldsymbol{S}_2}(z_2') \Rightarrow M_{\boldsymbol{S}_2}(z_2) = M_{\boldsymbol{S}_2}(z_2')$.

Thus, we can easily conclude that

$$En_{\boldsymbol{S}_1}(z_1) \cap D_{\boldsymbol{S}_1}(z_1') = En_{\boldsymbol{S}_1}(z_1') \cap D_{\boldsymbol{S}_1}(z_1) = \varnothing.$$

To show that

$$T_{\boldsymbol{S}_1}(z_1) = T_{\boldsymbol{S}_1}(z_1') \Rightarrow M_{\boldsymbol{S}_1}(z_1) = M_{\boldsymbol{S}_1}(z_1'),$$

it is clear that if $T_{S_1}(z_1) = T_{S_1}(z_1') = false$, then by the definition of M_{S_1} we know that $M_{S_1}(z_1) = M_{S_1}(z_1') = false$. So we only need to show that when $T_{S_1}(z_1) = T_{S_1}(z_1') = true$, we have $M_{S_1}(z_1) = M_{S_1}(z_1')$. Suppose otherwise. Then without loss of generality, let $M_{S_1}(z_1) = true$ and $M_{S_1}(z_1') = false$. Since $M_{S_1}(z_1') = false$ and $T_{S_1}(z_1') = true$, we can conclude that $M_{S_2}(z_2') = false$ due to the control equivalence of S_1 and S_2. But on the other hand, since $S_1 \preceq S_2$, we know that $M_{S_1}(z_1) = true$ implies that $M_{S_2}(z_2) = true$. Thus, we have $T_{S_2}(z_2) = T_{S_2}(z_2') = true$, $M_{S_2}(z_2) = true$, and $M_{S_2}(z_2') = false$, which contradicts our assumption that

$$T_{S_2}(z_2) = T_{S_2}(z_2') \Rightarrow M_{S_2}(z_2) = M_{S_2}(z_2').$$

Thus, we can only have $M_{S_1}(z_1) = M_{S_1}(z_1')$, which means $(z_1, z_1') \in \mathcal{R}_1$.

To see that Condition 3 is satisfied, for each $i \in I_2$, $\sigma \in \Sigma$, we know that there exists $j \in I_2$ such that

$$(\forall z \in Z_{2,i})\delta_2(z, \sigma)! \Rightarrow \delta_2(z, \sigma) \in Z_{2,j}.$$

For each $z' \in Z_{1,i}$, if $\delta_1(z', \sigma)!$, there are two cases. Case 1: there exists $s \in \mathcal{L}(Z_{2,i})$ such that $\delta_1(z_{1,0}, s) = z'$ and $s\sigma \in L(G \wedge S)$. Since $\delta_2(z_{2,0}, s) = z'' \in Z_{2,i}$ and $\delta_2(z'', \sigma)!$, we know that $s\sigma \in \mathcal{L}(Z_{2,j})$. Thus, $\delta_1(z', \sigma) \in Z_{1,j}$. Case 2: for all $s' \in \mathcal{L}(Z_{2,i})$ with $\delta_1(z_{1,0}, s') = z'$, we have $s'\sigma \notin L(G \wedge S)$. Then clearly $s'\sigma \notin L(G)$ because otherwise the first condition of control cover will be violated. Thus, we still have that $s'\sigma \in \mathcal{L}(Z_{2,j})$. Thus, $\delta_1(z', \sigma) \in Z_{1,j}$. So in either case, we can conclude that

$$(\forall z \in Z_{1,i})\delta_1(z, \sigma)! \Rightarrow \delta_1(z, \sigma) \in Z_{1,j},$$

which completes our proof that $\hat{\mathcal{C}}_1$ is a control cover of S_1.

Clearly, $|\hat{\mathcal{C}}_1| = |\mathcal{C}_2|$. On the other hand, if $\mathcal{C}_1$ is a minimal control cover of S_1, we know that $|\mathcal{C}_1| \leq |\hat{\mathcal{C}}_1|$. Thus, we can conclude that $|\mathcal{C}_1| \leq |\mathcal{C}_2|$. ■

As an illustration, in the example depicted in Figure 6.6 we know that $S_1 \preceq S_2$. We can easily compute $\hat{S}_1$ and $\hat{S}_2$, which are minimal feasible supervisors control equivalent to S_1 and S_2, respectively. The results are shown in Figure 6.7. To show that $\hat{S}_1$ is minimal, we notice that any feasible supervisor, which is control equivalent to S_1,

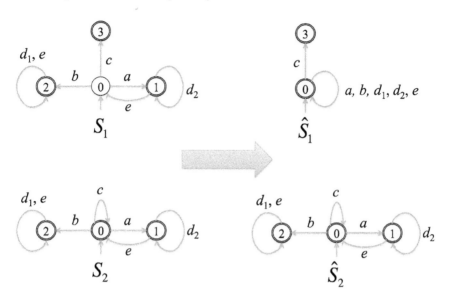

Figure 6.7 Reduced supervisors $\hat{S}_1$ (right top) and $\hat{S}_2$ (right bottom).

needs to have at least two different control patterns, i.e., to disable d_1 and d_2 together (at state 3 in $\mathbf{G}$), and to disable neither of them (at the remaining states in $\mathbf{G}$). Thus, it must have at least two states. Since $\hat{S}_1$ has precisely two states, it is a minimal supervisor. But it is not the unique one because we can check that the cover $\mathcal{C} = \{(\{0,3\},1),(\{1,2\},2)\}$ with $I = \{1,2\}$ is also a control cover of $\mathbf{S}_1$, whose induced supervisor is different from $\hat{S}_1$ and has two states. To see that $\hat{S}_2$ is minimal, with the same argument as before, we know that any feasible supervisor, which is control equivalent to $\mathbf{S}_2$, must have at least two states. But we can check manually that none of the covers of $\mathbf{S}_2$, whose size is 2, is a control cover of $\mathbf{S}_2$. Thus, the size of any control cover of $\mathbf{S}_2$ must be at least 3, which means $\mathbf{S}_2$ is the smallest one, which cannot be reduced further. It is clear that $|\hat{S}_1| = 2 < |\hat{S}_2| = 3$, which matches the conclusion made in Theorem 6.4.

With Theorem 6.3 and Theorem 6.4 we are able to answer the question: among all feasible supervisors that are control equivalent, which one will lead to a minimal reduced supervisor, and for any two control equivalent feasible supervisors, which one will result in a smaller reduced supervisor. As one simple application of these results, we can explain why a supervisor under full observation results in a smaller reduced supervisor than a supervisor under partial observation can achieve when they are control equivalent. More explicitly, given a plant $\mathbf{G}$ and a feasible supervisor S_f, if $L_m(\mathbf{G} \wedge \mathbf{S}_f)$ happens to be observable with respect to (G, P_o) [11] for some observable alphabet $\Sigma_o \subseteq \Sigma$, then there exists another feasible supervisor S_p under partial observation, which is derivable from S_f via the uncertainty subset construction, such that S_p is control equivalent to S_f with respect to $\mathbf{G}$, namely $L(\mathbf{G} \wedge \mathbf{S}_f) = L(\mathbf{G} \wedge \mathbf{S}_p)$ and $L_m(\mathbf{G} \wedge \mathbf{S}_f) = L_m(\mathbf{G} \wedge \mathbf{S}_p)$. But notice that S_f and S_p work under different observation scenarios. The point of interest is that the same supervisor reduction procedure can be applied to both S_f and S_p. We have the following result.

Corollary 6.1 Given a plant $\mathbf{G}$, let S_f and S_p be constructed above. Assume that S_f is DES-isomorphic to $\mathbf{G} \wedge S_f$ and S_p is DES-isomorphic to the outcome of the uncertainty subset construction of $\mathbf{G} \wedge S_p$. Let **SIMSUP**$_f$ and **SIMSUP**$_p$ be the minimal reduced supervisors of S_f and S_p respectively, based on the control cover construction. Then we have $|\mathbf{SIMSUP}_f| \leq |\mathbf{SIMSUP}_p|$.

Proof *Since S_f is DES-isomorphic to $\mathbf{G} \wedge S_f$ and S_p is DES-isomorphic to the uncertainty subset construction of $\mathbf{G} \wedge S_p$, both S_f and S_p are the leanest supervisors of those under full and partial observation, respectively. Since S_f and S_p are control equivalent with respect to $\mathbf{G}$, it is not difficult to check that for all $s \in L(\mathbf{G} \wedge S_f) = L(\mathbf{G} \wedge S_p)$, we have the following results:*

1. *$En_{S_f}(\delta_f(z_{f,0}, s)) \subseteq En_{S_p}(\delta_p(z_{p,0}, s))$*
   $= \cup_{s' \in P_o^{-1}(P_o(s)) \cap L(\mathbf{G} \wedge S_p)} En_{S_f}(\delta_f(z_{f,0}, s')),$

2. *$D_{S_f}(\delta_f(z_{f,0}, s)) \subseteq D_{S_p}(\delta_p(z_{p,0}, s)) =$*
   $\cup_{s' \in P_o^{-1}(P_o(s)) \cap L(\mathbf{G} \wedge S_p)} D_{S_f}(\delta_f(z_{f,0}, s')),$

3. *$M_{S_f}(\delta_f(z_{f,0}, s)) = M_{S_p}(\delta_p(z_{p,0}, s)),$*

4. *$T_{S_f}(\delta_f(z_{f,0}, s)) = T_{S_p}(\delta_p(z_{p,0}, s)).$*

Thus, we can derive that $S_f \preceq S_p$, which by Theorem 6.4 implies that the minimal control covers $\mathcal{C}_f$ of S_f and $\mathcal{C}_p$ of S_p satisfy $|\mathcal{C}_f| \leq |\mathcal{C}_p|$. Thus, by Theorem 1, we know that $|\mathbf{SIMSUP}_f| \leq |\mathbf{SIMSUP}_p|$. ■

Corollary 6.1 shows that, for two control equivalent feasible supervisors, the one under full observation is always leaner than the one under partial observation; thus, the former supervisor always results in a (typically much) smaller reduced supervisor than the one under partial observation can achieve. For example, in Figure 6.6, no matter whether the event c is observable or unobservable, the closed-loop behavior $L_m(\mathbf{G} \wedge \mathbf{S})$ is always controllable and observable; thus, $\mathbf{S}_1$ and $\mathbf{S}_2$ depicted in Figure 6.6 can be considered as supervisors under full observation and partial observation, respectively. It is clear that the supervisor $\mathbf{S}_1$ under full observation results in a smaller reduced supervisor $\hat{S}_1$, which is control equivalent to $\mathbf{S}_1$. By a quick check on $\mathbf{S}_1$ and $\mathbf{S}_2$ we can see that strings in $\mathbf{S}_2$ reaching the state 0 carry event enabling/disabling information for both states 0 and 3 in $\mathbf{S}_1$, making $\mathbf{S}_1$ leaner than $\mathbf{S}_2$, i.e., $\mathbf{S}_1 \preceq \mathbf{S}_2$. Because of such "redundant" information at the state 0 in $\mathbf{S}_2$, it is impossible to merge the state 0 with any other states in $\mathbf{S}_2$ to generate a smaller supervisor.

6.5 IDENTIFYING SYSTEM VULNERABILITY VIA ATTACK MODEL REDUCTION

Previously, we have explained how to preserve and illustrate critical control patterns by removing redundant transitional information in the supervisor. We will follow the same spirit and identify critical observations vital for the existence of a smart sensor attack (SSA). In contrast to a mapping-based modeling of SSA introduced in Chapter 2, here, we will present an event-relabeling-based automaton modeling framework, which attains some modeling inspiration from [131,133] on networked control. For any set Λ, we introduce two sets: $\Lambda^{\#} = \{\lambda^{\#} | \lambda \in \Lambda\}$ and $\Lambda^{\mathrm{com}} = \{\lambda^{\mathrm{com}} | \lambda \in \Lambda\}$, which denote relabeled copies of Λ with superscript "#" and "com" attached to each element in Λ, respectively.

Let the plant be $\mathbf{G} = (X, \Sigma, \xi, x_0, X_d)$, where $X_d \subseteq X$ is the marker state set, denoting a set of damage states, and the supervisor be $\mathbf{S} = (Z, \Sigma, \delta, z_0, Z_m = Z)$. Basically, $\mathbf{S}$ should not stop any uncontrollable event and should not issue any new control pattern (or command) without receiving a new observation, that is:

- $(\forall z \in Z)(\forall \sigma \in \Sigma_{uc})\delta(z,\sigma)!$,

- $(\forall z \in Z)(\forall \sigma \in \Sigma_{uo})\delta(z,\sigma)! \Rightarrow \delta(z,\sigma) = z$.

Example 6.3 *We adopt the water tank example depicted in Example 6.1. Unlike the plant model **G** depicted in Figure 6.2, the simplified models of the plant **G** and the supervisor **S** are shown in Figure 6.8 (a) and (b), respectively. The state marked red is the damage state of **G**. Double-edged circles are marker states. $\Sigma_o = \Sigma = \{L, H, EH, close, open\}$. $\Sigma_c = \{close, open\}$. It can be checked that the supervisor given in Figure 6.8 (b) is a safe one, that is, could prevent the plant from reaching the damage state.*

Next, we present a transformation construction procedure [63], based on which we are able to view a sensor attacker as a new supervisor for a new surrogate plant. As described in Chapter 2, a sensor attacker will replace an intercepted plant output event, observable by the attacker, with a "fake" observable event. We assume that the attacker can only observe events in $\Sigma_{o,a} \subseteq \Sigma_o$ and can only make changes to events in $\Sigma_{s,a} \subseteq \Sigma_{o,a}$. In Chapter 2, we adopt a language-based framework. In This chapter, due to a need for automaton reduction, we introduce a new automaton-based sensor attack model introduced in Refs. [63,83]. We first describe each component model.

6.5.1 Sensor Attack Constraint Model

To capture the attack capabilities of the sensor attacker, we construct a sensor attack constraint model $\mathbf{AC} = (Q_{ac}, \Sigma_{ac}, \xi_{ac}, q_{ac}^{init})$, where

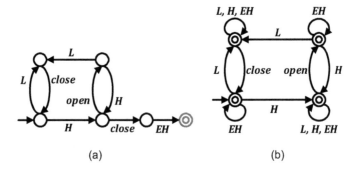

(a)   (b)

Figure 6.8 (a) Plant; (b) supervisor.

$Q_{ac} = \{q_{ac}^{\text{init}}, q^{\text{obs}}\}$, $\Sigma_{ac} = \Sigma \cup \Sigma_{s,a}^{\#}$ and $\xi_{ac} : Q_{ac} \times \Sigma_{ac} \to Q_{ac}$. The (partial) transition function ξ_{ac} is defined as follows:

1. $(\forall \sigma \in \Sigma \setminus \Sigma_{s,a}) \xi_{ac}(q_{ac}^{\text{init}}, \sigma) = q_{ac}^{\text{init}}$;

2. $(\forall \sigma \in \Sigma_{s,a}) \xi_{ac}(q_{ac}^{\text{init}}, \sigma) = q^{\text{obs}}$;

3. $(\forall \sigma \in \Sigma_{s,a}) \xi_{ac}(q^{\text{obs}}, \sigma^{\#}) = q_{ac}^{\text{init}}$.

In the event set, any event $\sigma^{\#} \in \Sigma_{s,a}^{\#}$ denotes the compromised event $\sigma \in \Sigma_{s,a}$ sent by the sensor attacker, which means that the supervisor could only receive the attacked copy $\sigma^{\#}$ instead of σ. In the later model construction about supervisor, we also carry out the event relabelling on $\Sigma_{s,a}$ to encode the feature that the supervisor could only react to $\Sigma_{s,a}^{\#}$ instead of $\Sigma_{s,a}$, which allows us to capture the sensor attack effects. In the following text, we refer to $\mathbf{C}_{ac} = (\Sigma_{s,a}^{\#}, \Sigma_{o,a} \cup \Sigma_{s,a}^{\#})$ as the attacker's control constraint, that is, the sensor attacker could only disable events in $\Sigma_{s,a}^{\#}$ and observe events in $\Sigma_{o,a} \cup \Sigma_{s,a}^{\#}$, and $(\Sigma_{o,a}, \Sigma_{s,a})$ as the attack constraint.

Example 6.4 *In the water tank example, $\Sigma_{o,a} = \{L, H, EH, close, open\}$. $\Sigma_{s,a} = \{L, H, EH\}$. Then the constructed sensor attack constraint is illustrated in Figure 6.9, where an attacker could modify the sensor reading to $L^{\#}$ or $H^{\#}$ or $EH^{\#}$ only after it intercepts an event, L or H or EH.*

Next, we perform the following operations to transform a supervisor under an attack.

> *Step 1: Supervisor bipartization.* We firstly carry out a bipartization transformation on supervisor $\mathbf{S}$ to explicitly encode the control command sending phase [63,64]. For any supervisor $\mathbf{S}$, the procedure to construct a bipartite supervisor $BT(\mathbf{S}) = (Q_{bs}, \Sigma_{bs}, \xi_{bs}, q_{bs}^{\text{init}})$ is given as follows:

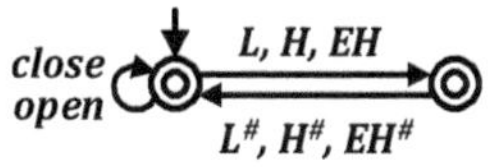

Figure 6.9 Sensor attack constraint $\mathbf{AC}$.

(a) $Q_{bs} = Q_s \cup Q_s^{\text{com}} = Q_s \cup \{q^{\text{com}} \mid q \in Q_s\}$, where $q \in Q_s$ is a reaction state ready to observe any event in $\Gamma(q)$, and $q^{\text{com}} \in Q_s^{\text{com}}$ is a control state corresponding to q, which is ready to issue the control command denoted by $\Gamma(q) \in \Gamma$.

(b) $\Sigma_{bs} = \Sigma \cup \Gamma$

(c) i. $(\forall q^{\text{com}} \in Q_s^{\text{com}})\, \xi_{bs}(q^{\text{com}}, \Gamma(q)) = q$.

ii. $(\forall q \in Q_s)(\forall \sigma \in \Sigma_{uo})\, \xi_s(q, \sigma)! \Rightarrow \xi_{bs}(q, \sigma) = \xi_s(q, \sigma)$.

iii. $(\forall q \in Q_s)(\forall \sigma \in \Sigma_o)\, \xi_s(q, \sigma)! \Rightarrow \xi_{bs}(q, \sigma) = (\xi_s(q, \sigma))^{\text{com}}$.

(d) $q_{bs}^{\text{init}} = (q_s^{\text{init}})^{\text{com}}$

Step 2: Attack actions encoding. For a transformed bipartite supervisor $BT(\mathbf{S})$, we need to relabel any event $\sigma \in \Sigma_{s,a}$ to $\sigma^{\#}$, in order to capture the setting that the supervisor can only receive the attacked copy $\sigma^{\#}$ of the original event σ. The generated new model is called the bipartite supervisor under attack $BT(\mathbf{S})^A = (Q_{bs,a}, \Sigma_{bs,a}, \xi_{bs,a}, q_{bs,a}^{\text{init}})$, whose construction procedure is given as follows:

(a) $Q_{bs,a} = Q_{bs} \cup \{q^{\text{no,covert}}\} = Q_s \cup Q_s^{\text{com}} \cup \{q^{\text{no,covert}}\}$

(b) $\Sigma_{bs,a} = \Sigma \cup \Sigma_{s,a}^{\#} \cup \Gamma$

(c) The (partial) transition mapping $\zeta_{bs,a}$ is defined as follows:

i. $(\forall q, q' \in Q_s)(\forall \sigma \in \Sigma_{s,a})\, \xi_{bs}(q, \sigma) = q' \Rightarrow \xi_{bs,a}(q, \sigma^{\#}) = q' \wedge \xi_{bs,a}(q, \sigma) = q$.

ii. $(\forall q, q' \in Q_{bs})(\forall \sigma \in (\Sigma - \Sigma_{s,a}) \cup \Gamma)\, \xi_{bs}(q, \sigma) = q' \Rightarrow \xi_{bs,a}(q, \sigma) = q'$.

iii. $(\forall q \in Q_s)(\forall \sigma \in \Sigma_{s,a})\neg\xi_{bs}(q, \sigma)! \Rightarrow \xi_{bs,a}(q, \sigma^{\#}) = q^{\text{no,covert}}$.

iv. $(\forall q \in Q_s)(\forall \sigma \in \Sigma_o - \Sigma_{s,a})\neg\xi_{bs}(q, \sigma)! \Rightarrow \xi_{bs,a}(q, \sigma) = q^{\text{no,covert}}$.

(d) $q_{bs,a}^{\text{init}} = q_{bs}^{\text{init}}$

In the (partial) transition function $\xi_{bs,a}$, defined at Step (c.i), (1) all the transitions labelled by events in $\Sigma_{s,a}$ are replaced with the copies in $\Sigma_{s,a}^{\#}$, denoted by $\xi_{bs,a}(q, \sigma^{\#}) = q'$, and (2) the transitions labelled by events in $\Sigma_{s,a}$ and originally defined in $BT(\mathbf{S})$ at state q would become self-loops since these events can be fired and are unobservable to the supervisor, denoted by $\xi_{bs,a}(q, \sigma) = q$. At Step (c.ii), all the other transitions, labelled by events in $(\Sigma - \Sigma_{s,a}) \cup \Gamma$, are retained. Steps (c.iii) and (c.iv) encode the covertness-violation situations, that is, the attacker is discovered.

Example 6.5 *In the water tank example, since* $\Sigma = \{L, H, EH, close,$ *open*$\}$ *and* $\Sigma_c = \{close, open\}$, *we have* $\Gamma = \{v_1, v_2, v_3, v_4\}$, *where* $v_1 = \{L, H, EH\}$, $v_2 = \{L, H, EH, close\}$, $v_3 = \{L, H, EH, open\}$ *and* $v_4 = \{L, H, EH, close, open\}$. *Then the transformed supervisor under attack is constructed as shown in Figure 6.10. We shall take the initial state as an instance to briefly explain this model: When the system initiates, the supervisor would issue the initial control command* v_1, *then it would only react to the event* $L^{\#}$, $H^{\#}$ *and* $EH^{\#}$ *instead of* L, H *and* EH *(denoted by self-loop transitions) due to the relabeling effects of sensor attack. In addition, the event close and open are not supposed to occur and be observed by the supervisor after the sending of* v_1, *so once close or open happens, the model would transit to the state* $q^{no,covert}$, *meaning that the attacker is discovered.*

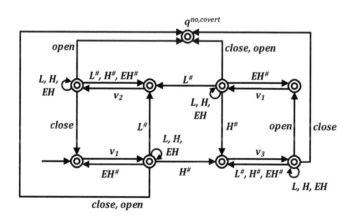

Figure 6.10 Transformed supervisor under attack.

6.5.2 Command Execution Model

It is constructed to describe how each individual event from a control command received by the plant to be chosen and executed at the plant [63,64], which is denoted as $\mathbf{CE} = (Q_{ce}, \Sigma_{ce}, \xi_{ce}, q_{ce}^{\text{init}})$, where $Q_{ce} = \{q^\gamma | \gamma \in \Gamma\} \cup \{q_{ce}^{\text{init}}\}$, $\Sigma_{ce} = \Gamma \cup \Sigma$ and $\xi_{ce} : Q_{ce} \times \Sigma_{ce} \to Q_{ce}$. The (partial) transition function ξ_{ce} is defined as follows:

1. For any $\gamma \in \Gamma$, $\xi_{ce}(q_{ce}^{\text{init}}, \gamma) = q^\gamma$.

2. For any $\sigma \in \gamma \cap \Sigma_{uo}$, $\xi_{ce}(q^\gamma, \sigma) = q^\gamma$.

3. For any $\sigma \in \gamma \cap \Sigma_o$, $\xi_{ce}(q^\gamma, \sigma) = q_{ce}^{\text{init}}$.

With such a command execution automaton and the bipartite supervisor construction procedure, the control equivalence could also be formulated as follows: two supervisors $\mathbf{S}_1$ and $\mathbf{S}_2$ are control equivalent if

- $P_\Sigma(L(\mathbf{G} \times \mathbf{CE} \times BT(\mathbf{S}_1))) = P_\Sigma(L(\mathbf{G} \times \mathbf{CE} \times BT(\mathbf{S}_2)))$,

- $P_\Sigma(L_m(\mathbf{G} \times \mathbf{CE} \times BT(\mathbf{S}_1))) = P_\Sigma(L_m(\mathbf{G} \times \mathbf{CE} \times BT(\mathbf{S}_2)))$,

where $P_\Sigma : (\Sigma \cup \Gamma)^* \to \Sigma^*$.

Example 6.6 *For the water tank example, the constructed command execution automaton is shown in Figure 6.11.*

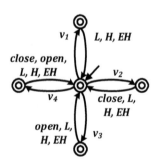

Figure 6.11 Command execution automaton **CE**.

6.5.3 Sensor Attacker Model

The sensor attack model is a finite state automaton $\mathbf{A} = (Q_a, \Sigma_a = \Sigma \cup \Sigma^{\#}_{s,a}, \xi_a, q^{init}_a)$ [63,83], where all states are marked. The actual details of the attack automaton $\mathbf{A}$ is not important. We only need to assume that it fulfills the goal of converting each intercepted observable event into a "fake" observable event. The closed-loop system is $\mathbf{G} \times \mathbf{CE} \times BT(\mathbf{S})^{\mathbf{A}} \times \mathbf{A}$. In this work, the sensor attack model $\mathbf{A}$ is known and we assume it is covert, that is, the supervisor would not discover the sensor information inconsistency by comparison with the closed behavior of the closed-loop system in the absence of attack, which could be generated from models of the plant and supervisor. Our goal in this work is to compute a reduced attack model with a simplified attack logic for $\mathbf{A}$ to reveal all the necessary observation sequences that ensure a covert and damage inflicting sensor attack.

Example 6.7 *For the water tank example, in Figure 6.12, we illustrate a covert damage-nonblocking sensor attacker $\mathbf{A}$ that is synthesized in Ref. [63]. The closed-loop system under attack $\mathbf{G} \times \mathbf{CE} \times BT(\mathbf{S})^{A} \times \mathbf{A}$ is shown in Figure 6.13. We can see that undesirable behaviors can appear under the attack.*

Based on the component models presented previously, the closed-loop system under sensor attack is $\mathbf{B} = \mathbf{G} \times \mathbf{CE} \times BT(\mathbf{S})^{A} \times \mathbf{A} = (Q_b, \Sigma_b, \xi_b, q^{init}_b, Q_{b,m})$. We could then view $\mathbf{G} \times \mathbf{CE} \times BT(\mathbf{S})^{A}$ as a new plant and the sensor attacker $\mathbf{A}$ as a new supervisor over the control constraint $\mathbf{C}_{ac}$, which completes the transformation procedure

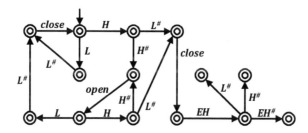

Figure 6.12 Sensor attack model **A**.

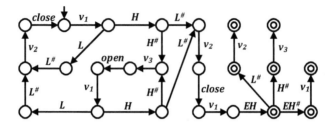

Figure 6.13 Closed-loop system under attack $\mathbf{G} \times \mathbf{CE} \times BT(\mathbf{S})^A \times \mathbf{A}$.

from a sensor attacker to a new supervisor for a new surrogate plant in the Ramadge-Wonham supervisory control problem.

Definition 6.4 Compromised Supervisor under Sensor Attack
Given a plant $\mathbf{G}$, a supervisor $\mathbf{S}$ and a sensor attacker $\mathbf{A}$, $BT(S)^A \times \mathbf{A}$ is the compromised supervisor under sensor attack $\mathbf{A}$ for $\mathbf{G}$.

Definition 6.5 Attack Equivalence
Given a plant $\mathbf{G}$, a supervisor $\mathbf{S}$ and an attack constraint $(\Sigma_{o,a}, \Sigma_{s,a})$, two sensor attackers $\mathbf{A}$ and $\mathbf{A}'$ over $(\Sigma_{o,a}, \Sigma_{s,a})$ are attack equivalent on $(\mathbf{G}, \mathbf{S})$ if

- $L(\mathbf{G} \times \mathbf{CE} \times BT(\mathbf{S})^A \times \mathbf{A}) = L(\mathbf{G} \times \mathbf{CE} \times BT(\mathbf{S})^A \times \mathbf{A}')$,

- $L_m(\mathbf{G} \times \mathbf{CE} \times BT(\mathbf{S})^A \times \mathbf{A}) = L_m(\mathbf{G} \times \mathbf{CE} \times BT(\mathbf{S})^A \times \mathbf{A}')$.

That is, two compromised supervisors under sensor attack $BT(\mathbf{S})^A \times \mathbf{A}$ and $BT(\mathbf{S})^A \times \mathbf{A}'$ are control equivalent on the plant $\mathbf{G}$.

In this work, given a plant $\mathbf{G}$, a supervisor $\mathbf{S}$, a sensor attacker $\mathbf{A}$ and an attack constraint $(\Sigma_{o,a}, \Sigma_{s,a})$, we need to find a reduced sensor attack model $\mathbf{A}'$ such that $\mathbf{A}$ and $\mathbf{A}'$ over $(\Sigma_{o,a}, \Sigma_{s,a})$ are attack equivalent on $(\mathbf{G}, \mathbf{S})$. Based on the above-analyzed transformation result, we could naturally transform the attack model reduction problem to the supervisor reduction problem [15,135]. The detailed attack model reduction procedure is presented as follows: Firstly, we shall define the following two[3] pieces of information[4] regarding the enabled event set and disabled event set w.r.t. any state of $\mathbf{A}$.

- Let $En_{\mathbf{A}} : Q_a \to 2^{\Sigma_a}$ with

$$q \mapsto En_{\mathbf{A}}(q) := \{\sigma \in \Sigma_a | \xi_a(q, \sigma)!\}$$

be the ($\mathbf{A}$-)enabled event set at state $q \in Q_a$.

- Let $D_{\mathbf{A}} : Q_a \to 2^{\Sigma_a}$ with

$$q \mapsto D_{\mathbf{A}}(q) := \{\sigma \in \Sigma_a | \neg \xi_a(q, \sigma)! \wedge (\exists s \in L(\mathbf{G} \times \mathbf{CE} \times BT(\mathbf{S})^A)) s\sigma \in L(\mathbf{G} \times \mathbf{CE} \times BT(\mathbf{S})^A) \wedge \xi_a(q_a^{\text{init}}, s) = q\}$$

be the (**A**-)disabled event set at state $q \in Q_a$.

Let $\mathcal{R} \subseteq Q_a \times Q_a$ be a binary relation, where $(q, q') \in \mathcal{R}$ if the following property[5] hold: $En_{\mathbf{A}}(q) \cap D_{\mathbf{A}}(q') = En_{\mathbf{A}}(q') \cap D_{\mathbf{A}}(q) = \emptyset$. We call $\mathcal{R}$ the *binary compatibility relation* over Q_a [135]. This condition requires that no event enabled at one state can be disabled at the other state. For any two states satisfying $\mathcal{R}$, they may potentially be merged together, if their suffix behaviors are "compatible", which could be captured in the following definition. Let I be a finite index set.

Definition 6.6 A collection $\mathcal{C} = \{(Q_{a,i}, i) | Q_{a,i} \subseteq Q_a \wedge i \in I\}$ is a *control congruence* [15] on **A** if

1. $\bigcup_{i \in I} Q_{a,i} = Q_a$, $(\forall (Q_{a,i}, i), (Q_{a,j}, j) \in 2^{Q_a} \times I) i = j \Rightarrow Q_{a,i} = Q_{a,j} \wedge i \neq j \Rightarrow Q_{a,i} \cap Q_{a,j} = \emptyset$,

2. $(\forall i \in I) Q_{a,i} \neq \emptyset \wedge (\forall q, q' \in Q_{a,i})(q, q') \in \mathcal{R}$,

3. $(\forall i \in I)(\forall \sigma \in \Sigma_a)(\exists j \in I)[(\forall q \in Q_{a,i}) \xi_a(q, \sigma)! \Rightarrow \xi_a(q, \sigma) \in Q_{a,j}]$.

Condition 1 requires that $\mathcal{C}$ is a partition on Q_a, i.e., $Q_{a,i}$ and $Q_{a,j}$ are pairwise disjoint. Condition 2 requires that each state pair in $Q_{a,i}$ should have consistent control actions, and Condition 3 requires that the set of states that can be reached from any state in $Q_{a,i}$ by a one-step transition σ is covered by some $Q_{a,j}$.

Given a control congruence $\mathcal{C} = \{(Q_{a,i}, i) | Q_{a,i} \subseteq Q_a \wedge i \in I\}$ on **A**, we shall construct an induced sensor attacker $\mathbf{A}_{\mathcal{C}} = (I, \Sigma_a, \kappa, i_0)$, where

- $i_0 \in I$ such that $q_a^{\text{init}} \in Q_{a,i_0}$

- $\kappa : I \times \Sigma_a \to I$ is the (partial) transition function such that for each $i \in I$ and $\sigma \in \Sigma_a$, $\kappa(i, \sigma) := j$ if j is chosen to satisfy the following property: there exists $q \in Q_{a,i}$ such that $\xi_a(q, \sigma) \in Q_{a,j}$ and

$$(\forall q' \in Q_{a,i})\xi_a(q', \sigma)! \Rightarrow \xi_a(q', \sigma) \in Q_{a,j}$$

otherwise, κ is not defined.

Theorem 6.5 Given a sensor attacker $A = (Q_a, \Sigma_a = \Sigma \cup \Sigma^{\#}_{s,a}, \xi_a, q_a^{\text{init}})$ for a closed-loop system, consisting of a plant $G = (Q, \Sigma, \xi, q^{\text{init}}, Q_d)$ and a supervisor $S = (Q_s, \Sigma, \xi_s, q_s^{\text{init}})$, let $\mathcal{C} = \{(Q_{a,i}, i)|Q_{a,i} \subseteq Q_a \wedge i \in I\}$ be a control congruence on A, and $A_{\mathcal{C}}$ be an induced sensor attacker from $\mathcal{C}$. Then $A_{\mathcal{C}}$ is attack equivalent to A.

Proof *We need to show $L(G \times CE \times BT(S)^A \times A) = L(G \times CE \times BT(S)^A \times A_{\mathcal{C}})$ and $L_m(G \times CE \times BT(S)^A \times A) = L_m(G \times CE \times BT(S)^A \times A_{\mathcal{C}})$. Based on the above-analyzed transformation result, that is, viewing $G \times CE \times BT(S)^A$ as a new plant and the sensor attacker A as a new supervisor, we just need to prove the following result: Given a supervisor $A = (Q_a, \Sigma_a = \Sigma \cup \Sigma^{\#}_{s,a}, \xi_a, q_a^{\text{init}})$ for a plant $G \times CE \times BT(S)^A$, and a control congruence $\mathcal{C} = \{(Q_{a,i}, i)|Q_{a,i} \subseteq Q_a \wedge i \in I\}$ on A, an induced supervisor $A_{\mathcal{C}}$ from $\mathcal{C}$ is control equivalent to A. To prove it, we could directly follow Theorem 15 in Section 6.1 or the proof of* Proposition 2.1 *in Ref. [15].* ■

Next, to accomplish the sensor attack model reduction, let $\mathcal{C} := \{[q] \subseteq Q_a|q \in Q_a \wedge q \in [q]\}$ be a control congruence on A, initially set to be $(\forall q \in Q_a)[q] := \{q\}$, then we could directly adopt a polynomial-time algorithm, named as *Reduction algorithm (RA)*, in Ref. [15] to generate a new control congruence, whose induced minimum sensor attack $A_{\mathcal{C}}$ is unique [15]. The complexity of this algorithm is $O(|Q_a|^4)$ [15].

Example 6.8 *We shall continue the water tank example. By adopting the developed attack model reduction technique on the attack model A illustrated in Figure 6.12, we could obtain the reduced attack model A', which is shown in Figure 6.14.*

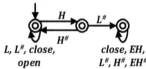

Figure 6.14 Reduced sensor attack model A'.

We can see that A in Figures 6.12 has 14 states and the reduced model A' only has three states. Thus, the compression ratio [15] is $\frac{14}{3} \approx 4.67$, which numerically verifies the effectiveness of the attack model reduction method. It can be checked that 3 is already the lower bound estimate [15] for the size of the state set of a minimal sensor attack which is attack equivalent to A. It is clear that the attack model A is complex and not easy for designers to grasp the attack logic. However, after the attack model reduction, the reduced model A' convincingly reveals the key observation sequence that could induce the damage infliction, that is, to lead to the occurrence of the event EH (water level becomes extremely high), once the sensor attacker receives H, it should alter it into $L^{\#}$. Then, based on the model S, the supervisor would issue the control command $v_2 = \{L, H, EH, close\}$ under the fake sensor information $L^{\#}$, and the valve is closed, resulting in that the water level finally becomes extremely high, meaning the damage infliction goal is achieved. Consequently, to prevent any smart sensor attack on this water tank system, it is clear that the key asset to be protected is the sensor that reports the water level value of L. Otherwise, a smart sensor attack is unavoidable.

6.6 CONCLUSIONS

This chapter addresses a potentially interesting question, that is, which sensors are critically important for a potential attacker to exploit in order to deploy a smart sensor attack, which is introduced in Chapter 2. With this knowledge, it will allow a system designer to be fully aware of critical sensor assets in a target system and take necessary precautionary actions, if needed, to prevent smart sensor attacks. It turns out that this problem can be transformed into a standard supervisor reduction problem, which aims to synthesize a new and possibly simplified supervisor that is, however, control equivalent to an originally given supervisor. To handle attack model reduction, by creating some necessary augmented component models, we can convert an originally given closed-loop system model $(\mathbf{G}, \mathbf{S})$ into a new model closed-loop system model $(\mathbf{G} \times \mathbf{CE} \times BT(\mathbf{S})^A, \mathbf{A})$, where we treat $\mathbf{G} \times \mathbf{CE} \times BT(\mathbf{S})^A$ as a plant and $\mathbf{A}$ as a "supervisor", which aims to bring the new plant into damage states. With this treatment, a slightly revised supervisor reduction procedure, which ignores all marking indicator information, can be applied to generate a (significantly) simplified attack model $\mathbf{A}'$, which, due to a much smaller number of states, may potentially reveal necessary sensor attack actions. That is, at which state and with which plant observable output a sensor attack is necessary in order to ensure the existence of a smart attack. It should be reminded that, due to the preservation of attack equivalence property, a reduced attack model $\mathbf{A}'$ is a strong (or weak) attack model if and only if the original model $\mathbf{A}$ is a strong (or weak) attack model.

This chapter introduces a new automaton-based modeling framework that can capture explicitly the impact of sensor event alterations by using event relabeling, instead of using more subtle transducers introduced in Chapter 2. This new framework is potentially more comprehensible at the price of modeling complexity. We will adopt such an event-relabeling-based modeling framework again in Chapter 7, when we introduce a new defense strategy.

Notes

1. Various properties such as normality [11] or relative observability [125] can achieve observability
2. A *preorder* is reflexive and transitive but not necessarily antisymmetric.
3. Marking indicators (M and T), defined in Refs. [15,135], are not needed in the attack model reduction procedure. The reason is that: The marked behavior of a compromised closed-loop system is $L_m(\mathbf{G} \times \mathbf{CE} \times BT(\mathbf{S})^A \times \mathbf{A}) = L(\mathbf{G} \times \mathbf{CE} \times BT(\mathbf{S})^A \times \mathbf{A}) \times L_m(G)$. Thus, to preserve the marked behavior before and after attack model reduction, we only need to preserve the closed behavior $L(\mathbf{G} \times \mathbf{CE} \times BT(\mathbf{S})^A \times \mathbf{A})$ of the compromised closed-loop system, which means the marking information is not needed for attack model reduction. In the original supervisor reduction work, if the supervisor is prefix closed, by the condition of $M(x) = M(x') \Rightarrow T(x) = T(x')$, equivalent states of the supervisor must have the same marking affiliation in the plant, which is certainly not necessary in our attack model reduction method. The underlying theoretical reason behind this difference is that the supervisor reduction framework does not assume the marked behavior of the closed-loop system to be $L_m(G)$-closed, which however holds true for the attack model reduction.
4. The enabled event set and disabled event set are different from those in Refs. [15,135] as we are now dealing with a sensor attack model (new supervisor) w.r.t. a new surrogate plant.
5. Due to the reason explained in endnote 1, the condition about the consistency in terms of marking states required in Refs. [15,135] would naturally hold for the attack model reduction procedure.

CHAPTER 7

Supervisor Obfuscation against Smart Actuator Attacks

In this chapter, we propose and address the problem of supervisor obfuscation against smart actuator attacks introduced previously. Unlike what we have done in Chapter 2 against smart sensor attacks by removing all possible risky pairs from the plant model, we propose a method to obfuscate the control command output of an (insecure) supervisor so that it is impossible for any smart actuator attacker to properly identify a plant state and successfully initiate an enabling attack while ensuring control equivalence between the given supervisor and a new one derived from obfuscation. Our proposed obfuscation method over a given closed-loop system involves two steps. In the first step, we apply an algorithm to encode all possible ways of artificially adjusting some control patterns of a given supervisor, while ensuring control equivalence between any resulting obfuscated supervisor and the original one. This step reduces clarity of the control command encoded at each supervisor state, making an actuator attacker have less information to estimate the current state of the plant. After that, in the second step, we apply a novel synthesis algorithm to determine whether there exists at least one obfuscated supervisor that does not permit any smart actuator attack. By identifying a necessary and sufficient condition to ensure the existence of a smart actuator attack, we show

DOI: 10.1201/9781003333883-9

that the previously mentioned two-step algorithm terminates in a finite number of steps and its outcome can decide the existence of a smart actuator attack, which successfully answers the decidability question. Following the same spirit of technical development in the previous chapters, we will first use a language-based framework to clearly illustrate the theoretical intuition and then apply an automaton-based framework for computation.

7.1 INTRODUCTION

In Chapter 5, we have introduced resilient supervisory control against smart sensor attacks. However, how to handle smart actuator attacks introduced in Chapter 3 is still open. In this chapter, we propose a specific approach called *supervisor obfuscation*. The basic idea was first introduced in Ref. [71], where, by deliberately obscuring some control command information, while ensuring control equivalence, a supervisor will not provide sufficient information for any smart actuator attack to confidently identify a state, where an enablement attack can be covertly carried out.

As mentioned in previous chapters, there has been a large volume of research on robust supervisory control, e.g., see Refs. [54,74,77,78,86,95–100] for supervisor synthesis that satisfies a set of design requirements against a given attack model. In Refs. [29,50–53,75,76,101–103,134] the authors study diagnostic methods against attacks that may compromise system detectability or diagnosability. For example, [29,50,51,53,76,101,102,134] simply disable controllable events after the attack is detected before the system may go to some undesirable state. References [104,105] design transition protecting policies to guarantee the behavior or deadline requirement. References [87,106] synthesize secret protection strategies to ensure that any sequence satisfies a given security level. Reference [107] introduces a new mechanism to determine which supervisor should be active at a given time to defend against sensor attacks. Reference [108] identifies events that should be protected for a manufacturing system to ensure safe operations. Reference [109,133] synthesize supervisors to satisfy liveness or mutual exclusion constraints under sensor attacks. Reference [110] proposes a robust corrective control scheme for input/state asynchronous sequential machines (ASMs) under actuator attacks.

Reference [37] designs a defender to optimize a min-max performance criterion in the context of a computer network. Reference [111] constructs a monitoring system to transit between normal and fallback operations.

In contrast to those existing works, the proposed method in this chapter starts with a given closed-loop system $(\mathbf{G}, S)$. The goal is to transform the supervisor S to a new supervisor S', which, although control equivalent to S, deliberately obscures some key control information at certain states that is critical for the existence of a successful smart actuator attack. To achieve this goal, we first present a sufficient and necessary condition to ensure the existence of a smart actuator attack, upon which we can identify key state information that permits a smart actuator attack. By removing such information, we will guarantee that no smart actuator attacks will exist. Recall that, in Chapter 2, we present a sufficient and necessary condition to permit a smart sensor attack, which relies on the concept of a risky pair that describes a possible match between what sequence of control patterns a smart sensor attack needs to fulfill a successful attack and what sequence of control patterns a given supervisor can provide. By eliminating such risky pairs, we can ensure that no smart sensor attacks will exist. We will follow the same footprint and derive a condition that describes what information is required by a smart actuator attack. It turns out that a smart actuator attack consists of two key ingredients: a *state estimate* derived from a standard observer based on observable plant outputs and supervisory control commands, and a *risky state set*, which contains all states where an enablement attack will take the plant $\mathbf{G}$ to a state that can eventually reach a damage state uncontrollably. A state estimate becomes a *covert risky state estimate* if, firstly, this state estimate contains at least one risky state and, secondly, by enabling an attackable event defined at that risky state, if the plant $\mathbf{G}$ is at the risky state, then damage is inevitable; if the plant $\mathbf{G}$ is not at that risky state, the enabled event will not take the plant to another non-damage-reaching state disallowed by the supervisor, that is, the miscalculated enablement attack will not reveal the existence of an actuator attack. We can show that, for each given closed-loop system $(\mathbf{G}, S)$, there exists a smart (weak) actuator attack if and only if there exists at least one covert risky state estimate. The good news is that, for a given $(\mathbf{G}, S)$, the set of all covert risky state estimates is finite and identifiable. Thus, we can easily decide whether there exists a smart actuator attack. If the answer is *yes*, we have a resilient supervisor S against all possible smart actuator attacks. However, if the answer is *no*, the question is whether we can find another control equivalent supervisor S' such that $(\mathbf{G}, S')$ does not contain any covert risky state estimate. For this purpose, we propose an obfuscation method to derive S' from S, and show that this obfuscation method can identify one control equivalent S', as long as it exists. This result answers one fundamental decidability question: given a closed-loop system $(\mathbf{G}, S)$, is it decidable whether there exists another obfuscated supervisor S', which is control equivalent to S, such that S' is resilient against all smart actuator attacks. As a by-product, this result also suggests one algorithm to compute one such resilient supervisor, if it exists.

Because we target at resilient supervisory control against ALL SMART actuator attacks, this sets our proposed framework apart from existing works on defense against actuator attacks, e.g., [54,74,77,78, 86,95–100], which either considers resilience against only one specific smart attack, or against the worst-case attack, which is not smart (i.e., covert). Our methodology idea is also different from those existing works based on fault diagnosis, e.g., [29,50–53,75,76,101–103,134], which essentially consider worst-case attacks that are not smart (i.e., covert). With a similar argument, our framework is also different from those studied in Refs. [37,87,104–111,133]. Our framework relies on one modeling technique to encode all possible insertions of redundant control commands in a given supervisor that could guarantee control equivalence while providing all obfuscation means. In a loose sense, the aim of this encoding strategy for encoding different supervisors bears some similarity to several existing works, e.g., [43,93,112,113]. However, the All Inclusive Controller in Refs. [43,112] contains all the supervisors satisfying a certain safety specification, and the All Inclusive Controller for Opacity in Ref. [113] contains all the supervisors enforcing opacity, which are different from attack-resilient control equivalent supervisors considered in this chapter.

This chapter is organized as follows. We recall the preliminaries in Section 7.2. In Section 7.3, a language-based framework is provided to explain the intuition behind the problem setup and solution strategy. In Section 7.4, we introduce an automaton-based system architecture and the problem formulation. The main idea of our proposed solution methodology is summarized in Section 7.5. Section 7.6 constructs the behavior-preserving structure to encode all the control equivalent supervisors. Section 7.7 introduces how to synthesize obfuscated supervisors and shows the decidability result. Finally, conclusions are drawn in Section 7.8. A running example is given throughout the chapter.

7.2 PRELIMINARIES

Recall that $\mathbb{N}$ denotes the set of natural numbers. For any two natural numbers $m, n \in \mathbb{N}$ with $m \leq n$, let $[m : n] := \{m, m+1, \ldots, n\}$. Let $\mathcal{P}_j(s)$ denote the prefix of length j of s. By default, $\mathcal{P}_0(s) = \varepsilon$. Let $s[i]$ denote the i-th element in s.

Given a finite state automaton $\mathbf{G} = (X, \Sigma, \xi, x_0, X_m)$, the "unobservable reach" of the state $x \in X$ under the subset of events $\Sigma' \subseteq \Sigma$ is given by

$$UR_{\mathbf{G}, \Sigma \setminus \Sigma'}(x) := \{x' \in X | (\exists s \in (\Sigma \setminus \Sigma')^*) x' = \xi(x, s)\}.$$

For each $W \subseteq X$, $UR_{\mathbf{G}, \Sigma \setminus \Sigma'}(W) := \bigcup_{x \in W} UR_{\mathbf{G}, \Sigma \setminus \Sigma'}(x)$. Let $\mathscr{P}_{\Sigma'}(\mathbf{G}) := (2^X, \Sigma, \psi, UR_{\mathbf{G}, \Sigma \setminus \Sigma'}(x_0))$ be an FSA, where the transition function $\delta : 2^X \times \Sigma \to 2^X$ is defined as follows:

1. For any $W \in 2^X$ and $\sigma \in \Sigma'$, $\psi(W, \sigma) := UR_{\mathbf{G}, \Sigma \setminus \Sigma'}(\xi(W, \sigma))$.

2. For any $W \in 2^X$ and $\sigma \in \Sigma \setminus \Sigma'$,

$$[(\exists x \in W) \xi(x, \sigma)!] \Rightarrow \psi(W, \sigma) = W.$$

For $\mathbf{G}$, after removing the states in $X' \subseteq X$ and the transitions associated with the states in X', the generated automaton is denoted as $\mathbf{G}^{X \setminus X'}$.

7.3 SMART ACTUATOR ATTACK – AN INSIGHT VIEW

Given a closed-loop system $(\mathbf{G}, S)$, where $S : L(\mathbf{G}) \to \Gamma$ is a supervisor, as introduced in Chapter 1 and Chapter 2. Let $D \subseteq X$ be the *damage state set* and $L_{\mathrm{dam}} := \{s \in L(\mathbf{G}) | \xi(x_0, s) \in D\}$ be a *damage language*.

Assume that $\Sigma_{o,a} \subseteq \Sigma_o$ is the set of observable events that can be seen by an actuator attacker, which may not be necessarily the same as Σ_o that is observable by the supervisor S. We use $P_{o,a} : \Sigma^* \to \Sigma_{o,a}^*$ to denote the corresponding natural projection. Let $\Sigma_{c,a} \subseteq \Sigma_c$ denote the set of controllable events, whose occurrences can be disabled or enabled by an attack. An actuator attacker can obtain two pieces of observation information: one from the observation channel and one from the control channel. Let $\Omega := \Sigma_{o,a}^\epsilon \times \Gamma$. We define a new projection mapping $\pi_S : P_o(L(\mathbf{G})) \to \Omega^*$, where

1. $\pi_S(\epsilon) := (\epsilon, S(\epsilon))$,

2. $(\forall s\sigma \in P_o(L(\mathbf{G})))\pi_S(s\sigma) := \pi_S(s)(P_{o,a}(\sigma), S(s\sigma))$.

Example 7.1 *As a simple illustration, if the plant $\mathbf{G}$ generates one observation sequence, say $abc \in P_o(L(\mathbf{G}))$ and the corresponding control patterns triggered by this sequence is $S(\epsilon) = \gamma_\epsilon$, $S(a) = \gamma_a$, $S(ab) = \gamma_b$ and $S(abc) = \gamma_c$. Assume that an actuator attacker cannot see event b, i.e., $b \notin \Sigma_{o,a}$. Then $\pi_S(abc) = (\epsilon, \gamma_\epsilon)(a, \gamma_a)(P_{o,a}(b), \gamma_b)(c, \gamma_c) = (\epsilon, \gamma_\epsilon)(a, \gamma_a)(\epsilon, \gamma_b)(c, \gamma_c)$.*

Let $\theta_1 : \Omega^* \to (\Sigma_{o,a}^\epsilon)^*$ and $\theta_2 : \Omega^* \to \Gamma^*$ be two projections, where for each string $\mu = (\sigma_1, \gamma_1) \ldots (\sigma_n, \gamma_n) \in \Omega^*$, $\theta_1(\mu) = \sigma_1 \ldots \sigma_n$ and $\theta_2(\mu) = \gamma_1 \ldots \gamma_n$. Recall that for any string, say ν, we use $\nu^\uparrow$ to denote its last event; and by default, $\epsilon^\uparrow = \epsilon$.

A *(nondeterministic) actuator attack* on S is modeled as a mapping $A_c : \pi_S(P_o(L(\mathbf{G}))) \to 2^\Gamma$, where for all $\mu \in \pi_S(P_o(L(\mathbf{G})))$,

$$A_c(\mu) \subseteq \{\gamma' \in \Gamma | (\exists W \subseteq \Sigma_{c,a})\gamma' = (\theta_2(\mu)^\uparrow \setminus \Sigma_{c,a}) \cup W\}.$$

That is, A_c takes each observation sequence μ in $\pi_S(P_o(L(\mathbf{G}))) \subseteq \Omega^*$ and may replace each attackable controllable event in the last control pattern contained in μ, that is, $\theta_2(\mu)^\uparrow \in \Gamma$, with a subset of attackable controllable events $W \subseteq \Sigma_{c,a}$, and leave other events in γ intact. We assume that A_c can "block" transmission of any control pattern sent by supervisor S from reaching the plant. The definition allows A_c to send $\emptyset$ as a control pattern, when $\Sigma_{c,a} = \Sigma$, namely all events are disabled.

The effect of an actuator attack A_c on a given supervisor $S :$ $P_o(L(\mathbf{G})) \to \Gamma$ can be captured by the following mapping $A_c \circ S :$ $P_o(L(\mathbf{G})) \to 2^\Gamma$, where

$$(\forall t \in P_o(L(\mathbf{G})))A_c \circ S(t) := A_c(\pi_S(t)).$$

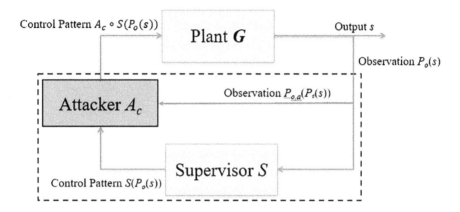

Figure 7.1 General architecture for actuator attack.

We call $A_c \circ S$ a *compromised* supervisory control with respect to (S, A_c). The general architecture for actuator attack is depicted in Figure 7.1.

The closed and marked behaviors of the closed-loop compromised system $A_c \circ S/\mathbf{G}$, that is, $L(A_c \circ S/\mathbf{G})$ and $L_m(A_c \circ S/\mathbf{G})$, are defined as follows:

1. $\epsilon \in L(A_c \circ S/\mathbf{G})$;

2. For all $t \in L(A_c \circ S/\mathbf{G})$ and $\sigma \in \Sigma$,

   $$t\sigma \in L(\mathbf{G}) \wedge (\exists \gamma \in A_c \circ S(P_o(t)))\sigma \in \gamma \Rightarrow t\sigma \in L(A_c \circ S/\mathbf{G}),$$

3. All strings in $L(A_c \circ S/\mathbf{G})$ are generated in Steps (1) and (2),

4. $L_m(L(A_c \circ S/\mathbf{G})) = L(A_c \circ S/\mathbf{G}) \cap L_m(\mathbf{G})$.

   Let $\Sigma_{c,a,o} := \Sigma_{c,a} \cap \Sigma_o$ and $\Sigma_{c,a,uo} := \Sigma_{c,a} \cap \Sigma_{uo}$.

Definition 7.1 A given closed-loop system $(\mathbf{G}, S)$ is *attackable* if there exists a non-empty actuator attack A_c such that the following properties hold:

1. **Covertness**: Attack moves by A_c must be covert to S, i.e.,

   $$L(A_c \circ S/\mathbf{G}) \subseteq L(S/\mathbf{G}) \cup \overline{L(S/\mathbf{G})\Sigma_{c,a,uo}^*\Sigma_{c,a,o}} \cap L_{\text{dam}} \quad (7.1)$$

namely the supervisor will not see any unexpected event enablement from A_c, except for the last observable enablement attack that incurs damage.

2. **Damage infliction**: Given the damage language L_{dam}, either one of the following properties hold:

- Strong Damage Infliction (SDI)

$$L(A_c \circ S/\mathbf{G}) = \overline{L(A_c \circ S/\mathbf{G}) \cap L_{\text{dam}}}, \qquad (7.2)$$

namely A_c will always be able to cause $\mathbf{G}$ to generate forbidden behaviors.

- Weak Damage Infliction (WDI)

$$L(A_c \circ S/\mathbf{G}) \cap L_{\text{dam}} \neq \emptyset, \qquad (7.3)$$

namely A_c will possibly cause $\mathbf{G}$ to generate forbidden behaviors.

A_c is a *Smart Actuator Attack* of $(\mathbf{G}, S)$ with respect to L_{dam}. □

Our covertness definition requires an actuator attack to be unnoticeable by the supervisor S, except for the last enablement attack, which, if observable, can be discovered by the supervisor. However, in this case, by the damage infliction property, the closed-loop behavior will reach a damage state, which is too late for the supervisor to take any rectification action.

Given two smart actuator attacks $A_{c,1}$ and $A_{c,2}$ of $(\mathbf{G}, S)$ with respect to L_{dam}, let $A_{c,1} \cup A_{c,2}$ denote the join of two mappings, i.e., for all $t \in P_{o,a}(L(\mathbf{G}))$ and $\gamma \in \Gamma$, $A_{c,1} \cup A_{c,2}(t, \gamma) := A_{c,1}(t, \gamma) \cup A_{c,2}(t, \gamma)$. We can show the following result.

Proposition 7.1 Given a closed-loop system $(\mathbf{G}, S)$ with $L_{\text{dam}} \subseteq L(\mathbf{G})$ being a damage language, let $\{A_{c,i} | i \in I\}$ be a collection of smart strong (or weak) actuator attacks of $(\mathbf{G}, S)$ with respect to L_{dam}, where I is an index set, not necessarily finite. Then $\cup_{i \in I} A_{c,i}$ is also a smart strong (or weak) actuator attack of $(\mathbf{G}, S)$ with respect to L_{dam}.

Proof *By applying the definition of $\cup_{i \in I} A_{c,i}$, since each $A_{c,i}$ satisfies those three properties of smart actuator attack, we can check that all three properties (7.1)–(7.3) also hold for $\cup_{i \in I} A_{c,i}$.* ∎

Let $\mathcal{A}(\mathbf{G}, S, L_{\text{dam}})$ be the collection of all smart strong (or weak) actuator attacks of $(\mathbf{G}, S)$ with respect to L_{dam}. We introduce a partial order "$\preceq$" on $\mathcal{A}(\mathbf{G}, S, L_{\text{dam}})$ such that

$$(\forall A_{c,1}, A_{c,2} \in \mathcal{A}(\mathbf{G}, S, L_{\text{dam}}))A_{c,1} \preceq A_{c,2} \iff L(A_{c,1} \circ S/\mathbf{G})$$
$$\subseteq L(A_{c,2} \circ S/\mathbf{G}).$$

Then by Proposition 7.1, we know that

$$A_{c,\text{sup}} := \cup_{A_c \in \mathcal{A}(\mathbf{G},S,L_{\text{dam}})} A_c \in \mathcal{A}(\mathbf{G}, S, L_{\text{dam}}).$$

Clearly, for all $A_c \in \mathcal{A}(\mathbf{G}, S, L_{\text{dam}})$, we have $A_c \preceq A_{c,\text{sup}}$, namely $A_{c,\text{sup}}$ is the least restrictive smart actuator attack, which will be called the *supremal smart (strong or weak) actuator attack* of $(\mathbf{G}, S)$ with L_{dam}.

Next, we try to derive a sufficient and necessary condition to ensure the existence of a smart weak actuator attack. Since each smart strong actuator attack must also be a smart weak actuator attack, by eliminating all smart weak attacks, we can ensure robustness against all smart actuator attacks.

Definition 7.2 Given a closed-loop system $(\mathbf{G}, S)$ with a damage language $L_{\text{dam}} \subseteq L(\mathbf{G}) \backslash L(S/\mathbf{G})$, a string $s \in L(S/\mathbf{G})$ is *attack feasible* if

1. $\{s\}\Sigma_{c,a,uo}^* \Sigma_{c,a,o} \cap (L(\mathbf{G}) \backslash L(S/\mathbf{G})) \subseteq L_{\text{dam}}$;

2. $(\forall t \in L(S/\mathbf{G}))\pi_S(P_o(t)) = \pi_S(P_o(s)) \Rightarrow (\forall u \in \Sigma_{c,a,uo}^* \Sigma_{c,a,o})$
   $[su \in L_{\text{dam}} \Rightarrow tu \notin L(\mathbf{G}) \backslash (L(S/\mathbf{G}) \cup L_{\text{dam}})]$. □

That is, a string s in the (legal) closed-loop behavior $L(S/\mathbf{G})$ is attack feasible, if, firstly, whenever an observable attackable event, after a sequence of unobservable attackable events, can take s out of the legal behavior $L(\mathbf{G}) \backslash L(S/\mathbf{G})$, then the resulting strings must be damage strings; and secondly, if for any other legal string t, which is observably identical to s with respect to π_S, if s can be extended to a damage string via a string u, then, as long as t can be extended by u in the plant $\mathbf{G}$, this extension tu must not be an illegal string but not causing damage - otherwise, it will violate the covertness property. The existence of an attack feasible string suggests one covert (weak) actuator attack. We have the following result.

Theorem 7.1 Given a closed-loop system $(\mathbf{G}, S)$ and a damage language $L_{\mathrm{dam}} \subseteq L(\mathbf{G}) \setminus L(S/\mathbf{G})$, there exists a smart weak actuator attack of $(\mathbf{G}, S)$ with respect to L_{dam} if and only if $L(S/\mathbf{G})$ contains one attack feasible string.

Proof

1. *We first show the ONLY IF part. Assume that there exists a smart weak actuator attack A_c. Then by Property (7.1), we know that*

$$L(A_c \circ S/\mathbf{G}) \subseteq L(S/\mathbf{G}) \cup \overline{L(S/\mathbf{G})\Sigma^*_{c,a,uo}\Sigma_{c,a,o} \cap L_{dam}},$$

   namely, for any string $s \in L(S/\mathbf{G})$ and any $t \in L(S/\mathbf{G})$ with $\pi_S(P_o(t)) = \pi_S(P_o(s))$, if there exists $u \in \Sigma^*_{c,a,uo}\Sigma_{c,a,o}$ such that $su \in L_{dam}$ and $tu \in L(\mathbf{G})$, then since $P_o(su) = P_o(tu)$ and $su \in L_{dam}$, we have that, either $tu \in L(S/\mathbf{G})$, or $tu \in \cup L_{dam}$. This means that s is attack feasible, which means $L(S/\mathbf{G})$ contains one attack feasible string.

2. *Next, we show the IF part. Assume that $L(S/\mathbf{G})$ contains one attack feasible string. We construct an actuator attack $A_c : P_o(L(\mathbf{G})) \rightarrow 2^\Gamma$ as follows. Let $t \in L(S/\mathbf{G})$ be the attack feasible string. Clearly, there exists $u \in \Sigma^*_{c,a,uo}\Sigma^\epsilon_{c,a,o}$ such that $tu \in L(S/\mathbf{G})\Sigma^*_{c,a,uo}\Sigma^\epsilon_{c,a,o} \cap L_{dam}$. Then for all $s \in P_o(L(\mathbf{G}))$,*

$$A_c(\pi_S(P_o(s))) := \begin{cases} S(P_o(s)) & \text{if } s \in P_o(L(S/\mathbf{G})) \setminus P_o(\{t\}); \\ S(P_o(t)) \cup \{\sigma \in \Sigma_{c,a} | \sigma \in u\} & \text{if } s = P_o(t); \\ \text{undefined} & \text{otherwise} \end{cases}$$

   Clearly, A_c is well defined. We can check that $L(A_c \circ S/\mathbf{G}) = L(S/\mathbf{G}) \cup \overline{\{t\}\Sigma^*_{c,a,uo}\Sigma_{c,a,o} \cap L(\mathbf{G})}$. Since t is an attack feasible string, we know that

$$\overline{\{t\}\Sigma^*_{c,a,uo}\Sigma_{c,a,o} \cap L(\mathbf{G})} \subseteq L(S/\mathbf{G}) \cup \overline{L(S/\mathbf{G})\Sigma^*_{c,a,uo}\Sigma_{c,a,o} \cap L_{dam}},$$

   namely, the covertness property (7.1) in Definition 7.1 holds. In addition,

$$tu \in L(A_c \circ S/\boldsymbol{G}) \cap L_{dam},$$

namely, $L(A_c \circ S/\boldsymbol{G}) \cap L_{dam} \neq \emptyset$. Property (7.3) holds. Thus, A_c is a smart weak attack, which completes the proof. ■

With Theorem 7.1, one immediate question is how to decide whether there exists an attack feasible string in $L(S/\boldsymbol{G})$. This will be discussed in subsequent sections when we introduce automaton-based models and computational procedures, where we will show that the existence of an attack feasible string is decidable, and furthermore, the existence of a supervisor S that does not permit any attack feasible strings, namely S is resilient against any smart actuator attack, is decidable.

Example 7.2 *Given a closed-loop system $(\boldsymbol{G}, S)$ shown in Figure 7.2, where $\Sigma = \{a, a', b, c, d\}$, $\Sigma_o = \{a, c, d\}$, $\Sigma_{o,a} = \{a, c\}$, $\Sigma_c = \{a, a', c, d\}$ and $\Sigma_{c,a} = \{a'\}$, assume that L_{dam} is the set of all strings hitting state 8. The supervisor S simply disables transitions labeled by event a' in $\boldsymbol{G}$. We can check that there are the following control patterns generated by S:*

$$\gamma_\epsilon = S(\epsilon) = \{a, b\}, \gamma_a = S(a) = \{b, c\}, \gamma_c = S(ac) = \{a, b, d\},$$
$$\gamma_d = S(acd) = \{b\}.$$

The closed-loop behavior $L(S/\boldsymbol{G})$ is depicted in the left picture of Figure 7.3. The right picture of Figure 7.3 shows an augmented version of $L(S/\boldsymbol{G})$, where each transition is labeled by a 2-tuple (σ, γ_σ) with $\sigma \in \Sigma_o$. The unobservable transition such as $(1, b, 3)$ is relabeled as ϵ because no control pattern will be generated by S. We specifically add a new state 0 in order to include the initial control pattern generation

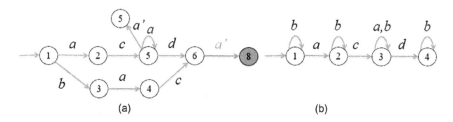

(a)   (b)

Figure 7.2 Plant $\boldsymbol{G}$ (a) and Supervisor S (b).

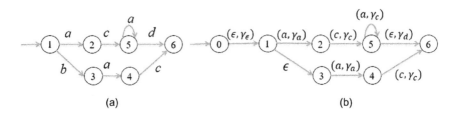

Figure 7.3 A closed-loop system (a) and its augmented model (b).

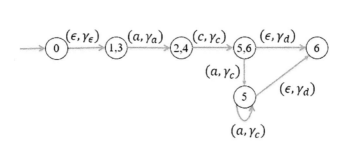

Figure 7.4 An observer based on π_S.

$(\epsilon, \gamma_\epsilon)$. *With this augmented model whose alphabet is Ω, we can apply π_S on $L(S/G)$. The outcome is depicted in Figure 7.4. We can check that string acd is an attack feasible string in $L(S/G)$. To see this, we can check the state estimates captured by the observer shown in Figure 7.4. After string ac takes place, the attacker can estimate that the current system state is either 5 or 6. However, if, without any event observation, the attacker receives a control command γ_d, namely (ϵ, γ_d) takes place, the attacker is certain that event d must have occurred and state 6 is reached, even though d is unobservable to the attacker. After that, the attacker can safely enable attackable event a'. Since acd is one attack feasible string, by Theorem 7.1, we know that a smart weak actuator A_c exists, whose function is defined as follows:*

$$
\begin{aligned}
A_c(\pi_S(\epsilon)) &= A_c((\epsilon, \gamma_\epsilon)) = S(\epsilon) \\
A_c(\pi_S(a)) &= A_c((\epsilon, \gamma_\epsilon)(a, \gamma_a)) = S(a) \\
A_c(\pi_S(ac)) &= A_c((\epsilon, \gamma_\epsilon)(a, \gamma_a)(c, \gamma_c)) = S(ac) \\
A_c(\pi_S(acd)) &= A_c((\epsilon, \gamma_\epsilon)(a, \gamma_a)(c, \gamma_c)(\epsilon, \gamma_d)) = S(acd) \cup \{a'\}
\end{aligned}
$$

In case that there does exist one attack feasible string, the question is "can we modify S to make such an attack feasible string disappear".

One possible solution is to use supervisor obfuscation, *which essentially derives a new supervisor S', which is control equivalent to S as described in Chapter 6, such that, under $\pi_{S'}$, there is no attack feasible string, no matter what an actuator attack may do. We will use the above example to illustrate the idea of supervisor obfuscation.*

We apply supervisor reduction algorithm introduced in Chapter 6 on the closed-loop system (G, S), and a control equivalent supervisor S' is depicted in Figure 7.5, where, after event c occurs, only the control pattern $\gamma_c = \{a, b, d\}$ will be generated and the subsequent control pattern $\gamma_d = \{b\}$ is removed. We can check that $L(S/G) = L(S'/G)$ and $L_m(S/G) = L_m(S'/G)$. The resulting closed-loop system (G, S') and its augmented model is depicted in Figure 7.6, where, the original compound observation (ϵ, γ_d) in Figure 7.3 is replaced by (ϵ, γ_c), as an actuator attacker cannot see the occurrence of event d and the control command is the same as γ_c in S'. After applying $\pi_{S'}$ on $L(S'/G)$, the resulting state observer is depicted in Figure 7.7. We can see that the attacker still manages to distinguish state 5 and state 6 based on the compound observation sequence $\pi_{S'}(acd) = (\epsilon, \gamma_\epsilon)(a, \gamma_a)(c, \gamma_c)(\epsilon, \gamma_c)$. Thus, it is covert for the attacker to enable event a' after state 6

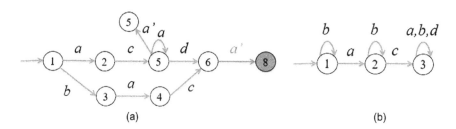

(a)   (b)

Figure 7.5 Plant G (a) and a control equivalent supervisor S' (b).

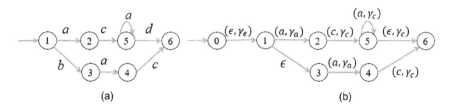

(a)   (b)

Figure 7.6 A closed-loop system (a) and its augmented model (b).

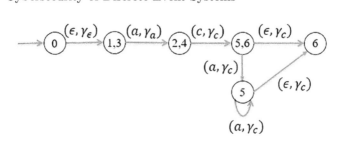

Figure 7.7 An observer based on $\pi_{S'}$.

is reached. In this case, string acd is still an attack feasible string in $(\mathbf{G}, S')$. If we carefully check the observer based on $\pi_{S'}$, we can see that, although the attacker cannot see event d and the control pattern γ_d is replaced by γ_c, based on the knowledge about the plant model $\mathbf{G}$, the attacker knows that the compound observation (ϵ, γ_c) can only be generated by the occurrence of event d in the plant. In this case, the supervisor obfuscation fails to generate an attack-resilient supervisor, which is equivalent to S. The fundamental question is **whether the existence of such a supervisor S', control equivalent to S and disallowing any attack feasible string, is decidable.** *If this question can be answered, basically, we can answer the ultimate question* **whether it is possible to apply supervisor obfuscation on $(\mathbf{G}, S)$ to ensure non-existence of any smart actuator attacks.** *By using a method introduced in the subsequent sections, we can check that the closed-loop system depicted in Figure 7.2 does not permit an attack-resilient supervisor against all smart actuator attacks.*

7.4 COMPONENT MODELS AND PROBLEM FORMULATION

In this section, we present an automaton model of each system component, based on which we formulate our target problem. We rephrase the attack architecture shown in Figure 7.1 in a deployment-feasible manner, as depicted in Figure 7.8, where an extra module is inserted to capture command channel properties, similar to what we do in Chapter 6, which will be explained below.

The plant is modeled as a finite state automaton $\mathbf{G} = (X, \Sigma, \xi, x_0, X_d)$, where X_d is the set of damage states. The supervisor is modeled as a finite state automaton $\mathbf{S} = (Z, \Sigma, \delta, z_0, Z_m = Z)$. Recall

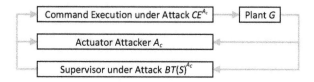

Figure 7.8 Supervisory control architecture under actuator attack.

that the control command issued by $\mathbf{S}$ at state $z \in Z$ is defined to be $\Gamma(z) := En_{\mathbf{S}}(z) \cup \Sigma_{uc} \subseteq \Gamma$.

Next, we follow a similar modeling strategy illustrated in Section 6.6 in Chapter 6 and perform a bipartization transformation on $\mathbf{S}$ such that the observation reception phase and control command sending phase are explicitly modeled, while the control function remains the same as $\mathbf{S}$. The transformed structure is called a *bipartite supervisor* [64], denoted by $\mathbf{BT}(\mathbf{S}) = (Q_{bs}, \Sigma_{bs}, \xi_{bs}, q_{bs}^{init})$, where:

- $Q_{bs} = Z \cup Z^{com}$, where $Z^{com} = \{q^{com} \mid q \in Z\}$.

- $q_{bs}^{init} = (z_0)^{com}$

- $\Sigma_{bs} = \Sigma \cup \Gamma$

- ξ_{bs} is defined as:

  1. $(\forall q^{com} \in Z^{com}) \, \xi_{bs}(q^{com}, \Gamma(q)) = q$.
  2. $(\forall q \in Z)(\forall \sigma \in \Sigma_{uo}) \, \delta(q, \sigma)! \Rightarrow \xi_{bs}(q, \sigma) = q$.
  3. $(\forall q \in Z)(\forall \sigma \in \Sigma_o) \, \delta(q, \sigma)! \Rightarrow \xi_{bs}(q, \sigma) = (\delta(q, \sigma))^{com}$.

In the state set Q_{bs}, any $q \in Z$ is a reaction state ready to observe any event in $\Gamma(q)$, and any $q^{com} \in Z^{com}$ is a control state corresponding to q, which is ready to issue the control command $\Gamma(q)$. Thus, the initial state is $(z_0)^{com}$. For ξ_{bs}, (1) at any control state q^{com}, a control command $\Gamma(q)$ should be issued, which leads to a reaction state q (Case 1), and (2) at any reaction state q, any unobservable event, if defined in $\mathbf{S}$, is a self-loop (Case 2), and any observable event, if defined in $\mathbf{S}$, would lead to a control state $(\delta(q, \sigma))^{com}$ (Case 3).

For the bipartite supervisor $\mathbf{BT}(\mathbf{S})$, we now model the effect of actuator attacks on $\mathbf{BT}(\mathbf{S})$ by constructing the bipartite supervisor under attack, denoted by $\mathbf{BT}(\mathbf{S})^{\mathbf{A}} = (Q_{bs}^a, \Sigma_{bs}^a, \xi_{bs}^a, q_{bs}^{a,init})$, where:

- $Q_{bs}^a = Q_{bs} \cup \{q^{\text{detect}}\}$

- $q_{bs}^{a,\text{init}} = q_{bs}^{\text{init}}$

- $\Sigma_{bs}^a = \Sigma \cup \Gamma$

- ξ_{bs}^a is defined as:

  1. $(\forall q, q' \in Q_{bs}^a)(\forall \sigma \in \Sigma \cup \Gamma)\xi_{bs}(q,\sigma) = q' \Rightarrow \xi_{bs}^a(q,\sigma) = q'$
  2. $(\forall q \in Z)(\forall \sigma \in \Sigma_{c,a,uo})\neg\xi_{bs}(q,\sigma)! \Rightarrow \xi_{bs}^a(q,\sigma) = q$
  3. $(\forall q \in Z)(\forall \sigma \in \Sigma_{c,a,o})\neg\xi_{bs}(q,\sigma)! \Rightarrow \xi_{bs}^a(q,\sigma) = q^{\text{detect}}$

In the state set Q_{bs}^a, a new state q^{detect} is added, denoting the situation where the actuator attack is detected. For ξ_{bs}^a, Case 1 retains all the transitions defined in $\mathbf{BT(S)}$. In Case 2, for any reaction state $q \in Z$, the transitions labeled by unobservable and attackable events in $\Sigma_{c,a,uo}$, which are not defined at the state q in $\mathbf{BT(S)}$, are added. In Case 3, for any reaction state $q \in Z$, the transitions labeled by observable and attackable events, which are not defined at the state q in $\mathbf{BT(S)}$, would lead to the state q^{detect}, with the interpretation that the supervisor has received some observation that should not have occurred based on the supervisor structure, i.e., the actuator attacker is detected.

To explicitly encode the phase from receiving a control command in Γ to executing an event in Σ at the plant, we construct the command execution automaton [64] $\mathbf{CE} = (Q_{ce}, \Sigma_{ce}, \xi_{ce}, q_{ce}^{init})$, where

- $Q_{ce} = \{q^\gamma | \gamma \in \Gamma\} \cup \{q_{ce}^{init}\}$

- $\Sigma_{ce} = \Gamma \cup \Sigma$

- ξ_{ce} is defined as:

  1. $(\forall \gamma \in \Gamma)\xi_{ce}(q_{ce}^{init}, \gamma) = q^\gamma$
  2. $(\forall \gamma \in \Gamma)(\forall \sigma \in \gamma \cap \Sigma_o)\xi_{ce}(q^\gamma, \sigma) = q_{ce}^{init}$
  3. $(\forall \gamma \in \Gamma)(\forall \sigma \in \gamma \cap \Sigma_{uo})\xi_{ce}(q^\gamma, \sigma) = q^\gamma$

The above command execution automaton $\mathbf{CE}$ is an unattacked model, i.e., the event execution always follows the unmodified control command based on $\mathbf{CE}$. We need to encode the impact of all possible actuator attacks into $\mathbf{CE}$ to build the model for the command execution process under attack, denoted by $\mathbf{CE^A} = (Q_{ce}^a, \Sigma_{ce}^a, \xi_{ce}^a, q_{ce}^{a,\text{init}})$, where

- $Q_{ce}^a = Q_{ce}$

- $q_{ce}^{a,\text{init}} = q_{ce}^{\text{init}}$

- $\Sigma_{ce}^a = \Gamma \cup \Sigma$

- ξ_{ce}^a is defined as:

  1. $(\forall q, q' \in Q_{ce}^a)(\forall \sigma \in \Sigma \cup \Gamma)\xi_{ce}(q,\sigma) = q' \Rightarrow \xi_{ce}^a(q,\sigma) = q'$
  2. $(\forall \gamma \in \Gamma)(\forall \sigma \in \Sigma_{c,a,o})\neg\xi_{ce}(q^\gamma,\sigma)! \Rightarrow \xi_{ce}^a(q^\gamma,\sigma) = q_{ce}^{a,\text{init}}$
  3. $(\forall \gamma \in \Gamma)(\forall \sigma \in \Sigma_{c,a,uo})\neg\xi_{ce}(q^\gamma,\sigma)! \Rightarrow \xi_{ce}^a(q^\gamma,\sigma) = q^\gamma$

For ξ_{ce}^a, Case 1 retains all the transitions defined in **CE**. In Case 2 and Case 3, the attack effects are encoded. For any state q^γ, the transitions labeled by attackable events, which are not defined at the state q^γ in **CE**, are added, where the observable events would lead to the initial state q_{ce}^{init} (Case 2), and the unobservable events would lead to self-loop transitions (Case 3).

An actuator attacker is modeled as a finite state automaton $\mathbf{A_c} = (Q_a, \Sigma_a, \xi_a, q_a^{\text{init}})$, where $\Sigma_a = \Sigma \cup \Gamma$. Let $\Sigma_{a,uc} := \Sigma_a - \Sigma_{c,a}$ and $\Sigma_{a,uo} := \Sigma_a - (\Sigma_{o,a} \cup \Gamma)$. To match the previous language description, there are two conditions that need to be satisfied by $\mathbf{A_c}$:

- ($\mathbf{A_c}$-controllability) $(\forall q \in Q_a)(\forall \sigma \in \Sigma_{a,uc})\xi_a(q,\sigma)!$,

- ($\mathbf{A_c}$-observability) $(\forall q \in Q_a)(\forall \sigma \in \Sigma_{a,uo})\xi_a(q,\sigma) \Rightarrow \xi_a(q,\sigma) = q$.

$\mathbf{A_c}$-controllability states that the attacker can only disable events in $\Sigma_{c,a}$. $\mathbf{A_c}$-observability states that the attacker can only make a state change after observing an event in $\Sigma_{o,a} \cup \Gamma$. In the following text, we shall refer to $(\Sigma_{o,a}, \Sigma_{c,a})$ as the attack constraint, and $\mathcal{C}_{ac} = (\Sigma_{c,a}, \Sigma_{o,a} \cup \Gamma)$ as the attacker's control constraint. The model of $\mathbf{A_c}$ is nondeterministic in terms of making attack decisions as it allows multiple attack choices upon each observation.

As shown in Figure 7.8, the closed-loop system under attack can be modeled as the parallel composition of the above-constructed component models, denoted by $\mathbf{CLS^A} = \mathbf{G} \times \mathbf{CE^A} \times \mathbf{BT(S)^A} \times \mathbf{A_c} = (Q_{cls}^a, \Sigma_{cls}^a, \xi_{cls}^a, q_{cls}^{a,\text{init}}, Q_{cls,m}^a)$.

Definition 7.3 Given $\mathbf{G}$, $\mathbf{BT(S)^A}$ and $\mathbf{CE^A}$, an actuator attacker $\mathbf{A_c}$ is *covert* against $\mathbf{S}$ if any state in $\{(q_g, q_{ce}^a, q_{bs}^a, q_a) \in Q_{cls}^a | q_g \notin X_d \wedge q_{bs}^a = q^{\text{detect}}\}$ is unreachable in $\mathbf{CLS^A}$. □

The concept of covertness introduced in Definition 7.3 matches the language-based covertness definition introduced previously in Definition 7.1, where the violation of covertness means there exists an observable string s that is observably deviated from what is expected by the supervisor after an observable enablement attack move, i.e., q^{detect} is reached, but has not reached a damage state, i.e., $q_g \notin X_d$. This concept is different from the one about smart sensor attacks introduced in Refs. [56,94]). The notion of covertness depends on the monitoring mechanism used. Definition 7.3 means that we rely on the supervisor and plant structure to monitor attacks.

Definition 7.4 Given $\mathbf{G}$, $\mathbf{BT(S)^A}$ and $\mathbf{CE^A}$, an actuator attacker $\mathbf{A_c}$ is said to be *damage-reachable* against $\mathbf{S}$ if $L_m(\mathbf{CLS^A}) \neq \emptyset$. □

Definition 7.5 Given $\mathbf{G}$, a supervisor $\mathbf{S}$ is said to be *resilient* if there does not exist any covert and damage-reachable actuator attacker $\mathbf{A_c}$ against $\mathbf{S}$. □

Definition 7.6 Given $\mathbf{G}$ and $\mathbf{S}$, a supervisor $\mathbf{S'}$ ($\mathbf{BT(S')}$) is said to be *control equivalent* to $\mathbf{S}$ ($\mathbf{BT(S)}$) if $L(\mathbf{G} \times \mathbf{S}) = L(\mathbf{G} \times \mathbf{S'})$ ($P_{\Sigma}(L(\mathbf{G} \times \mathbf{CE} \times \mathbf{BT(S)})) = P_{\Sigma}(L(\mathbf{G} \times \mathbf{CE} \times \mathbf{BT(S')}))$). □

Definition 7.7 Given $\mathbf{G}$ and $\mathbf{S}$, a supervisor $\mathbf{S'}$ is said to be an *obfuscated supervisor* for $\mathbf{S}$ if $\mathbf{S'}$ is resilient and control equivalent to $\mathbf{S}$. □

Definition 7.8 Given $\mathbf{G}$, $\mathbf{S}$, and a covert damage-reachable actuator attacker $\mathbf{A_c}$ against $\mathbf{S}$, any $s \in L_m(\mathbf{G} \times \mathbf{CE^A} \times \mathbf{BT(S)^{A_c}} \times \mathbf{A_c})$ is a *covert damage string* for $\mathbf{S}$. □

We can check that each attack feasible string mentioned in Section 7.3 is a covert damage string. However, not every covert damage string is an attack feasible string. Based on Theorem 7.1, we can see that, for each closed-loop system $(\mathbf{G}, \mathbf{S})$, there exists a non-empty covert damage string set if and only if there exists at least one attack feasible string. For this reason, in the subsequent treatment, we will mainly focus on the emptiness of each covert damage strings set, for the sake of computation. We now formulate our problem in an automaton-based framework.

Proposition 7.2 Given a closed-loop system $(\mathbf{G}, \mathbf{S})$, determine whether there exists an obfuscated supervisor for $\mathbf{S}$. □

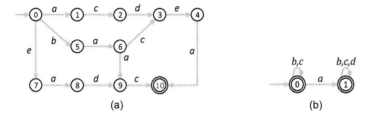

Figure 7.9 (a) **G**. (b) **S**.

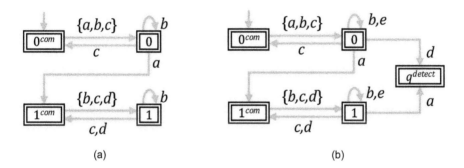

Figure 7.10 (a) **BT(S)**. (b) **BT(S)**$^\mathbf{A}$.

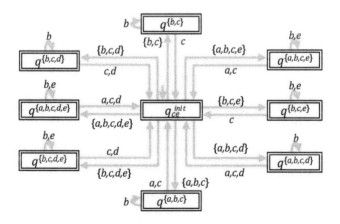

Figure 7.11 **CE**

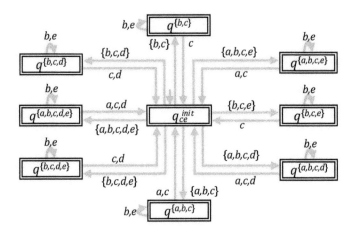

Figure 7.12 **CE$^{\mathbf{A}}$**

Example 7.3 *Consider the plant* **G** *and supervisor* **S** *shown in Figure 7.9.* $\Sigma = \{a, b, c, d, e\}$. $\Sigma_o = \{a, c, d\}$. $\Sigma_{uo} = \{b, e\}$. $\Sigma_c = \{a, d, e\}$. $\Sigma_{uc} = \{b, c\}$. $\Sigma_{o,a} = \{b, c, d, e\}$. $\Sigma_{c,a} = \{a, d, e\}$. *The damage state is state 10, i.e.,* $X_d = \{10\}$. *We have* $L(\mathbf{G} \times \mathbf{S}) = \overline{\{acd, bac\}}$. *Figure 7.10 illustrates* **BT(S)**, **BT(S)$^{\mathbf{A}}$**. *Figure 7.11 illustrates* **CE**, *and to Figure 7.12 depicts* **CE$^{\mathbf{A}}$**.

We can see that **S** is non-resilient as covert and damage-reachable actuator attackers exist, e.g., enabling event e after the initial control command $\{a, b, c\}$.

7.5 MAIN IDEA OF SOLUTION METHODOLOGY

Before proceeding further, we first present the high-level idea, as illustrated in Figure 7.13. In Step 1 (Section 7.6), based on **G**, **S**, and **CE**, we construct the behavior-preserving structure **BPNS** to exactly encode all the control equivalent bipartite supervisors. In Step 2 (Section 7.7.1), based on **G**, **CE$^{\mathbf{A}}$** and **BPNS$^{\mathbf{A}}$**, which is the version of **BPNS** under attack, we synthesize $\hat{\mathbf{A}}_{\mathbf{c}}$ to encode all the covert damage strings. In Step 3 (Section 7.7.2), based on **G**, **CE$^{\mathbf{A}}$**, **BPNS$^{\mathbf{A}}$** and $\hat{\mathbf{A}}_{\mathbf{c}}$, we prune from **BPNS$^{\mathbf{A}}$** those illegal control commands leading to damage infliction to generate **S$_{\mathbf{0}}^{\mathbf{A}}$**. In Step 4 (Section 7.7.3), we iteratively prune from **S$_{\mathbf{0}}$** (the non-attacked version of **S$_{\mathbf{0}}^{\mathbf{A}}$**) those states

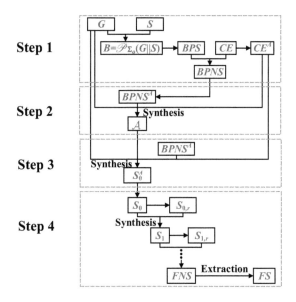

Figure 7.13 The procedure of the proposed solution methodology.

where there is no control command defined upon each observation and generate **FNS**, which exactly encodes all the obfuscated supervisors. Finally, we extract one supervisor **FS** from **FNS**, which is the solution.

7.6 BEHAVIOR-PRESERVING STRUCTURE CONSTRUCTION

In this section, we explain how to construct the behavior-preserving structure that encodes all the control equivalent bipartite supervisors.

7.6.1 Equivalent Behavior Computation

Firstly, we compute $\mathbf{G} \times \mathbf{S}$, which is the closed-loop system under $\mathbf{S}$ in the absence of attacks. Recall that for any supervisor $\mathbf{S}'$, we have $L(\mathbf{BT}(\mathbf{S}')) \subseteq \overline{(\Gamma\Sigma_{uo}^*\Sigma_o)^*}$ and any unobservable event defined in $\mathbf{BT}(\mathbf{S}')$ is a self-loop transition. Since we need to construct a structure to encode all the control equivalent bipartite supervisors, we conduct a subset construction $\mathbf{B} = \mathscr{P}_{\Sigma_o}(\mathbf{G} \times \mathbf{S}) = (Q_b, \Sigma_b = \Sigma, \xi_b, q_b^{\text{init}})$, where $|Q_b| \leq 2^{|X| \times |Z|}$. By construction, $\mathbf{B}$ is built upon the observer [2] of $\mathbf{G} \times \mathbf{S}$ by adding self-loops labeled by the unobservable events that could occur at each state of the observer of $\mathbf{G} \times \mathbf{S}$. It can be checked

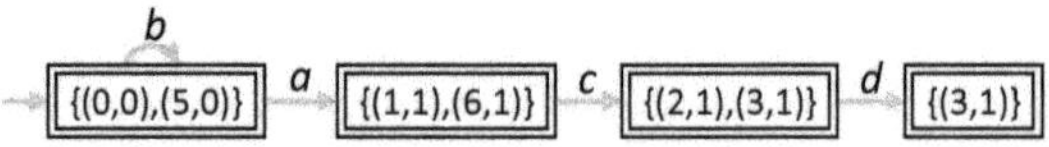

Figure 7.14 The computed automaton **B**.

that, for any $(q_g, q_s), (q_g', q_s') \in q \in Q_b$, we have $q_s = q_s'$ since all the unobservable events in Σ_{uo} are self-loops in **S**. Thus, for any $q_1, q_2 \in Q_b$ and any $\sigma \in \Sigma_o$ such that $\xi_b(q_1, \sigma) = q_2$, where $q_{1,s}$ ($q_{2,s}$, respectively) is the supervisor state in the state q_1 (q_2, respectively), we have (1) the state of the supervisor **S** transits from $q_{1,s}$ to $q_{2,s}$ upon the observation of σ, and (2) $En_B(q_2)$ contains all the events that could happen at **G** when **S** issues the corresponding control command at the state $q_{2,s}$. Consequently, based on the structure **B**, we could find all the feasible control commands with respect to each observation, which would be realized later in Section 7.6.2.

Example 7.4 *Given* **G** *and* **S** *shown in Figure 7.9, the automaton* **B** *is shown in Figure 7.14.*

7.6.2 Feasible Control Commands Completion

Based on $\mathbf{B} = \mathscr{P}_{\Sigma_o}(\mathbf{G} \times \mathbf{S})$, we generate a bipartite structure similar to $\mathbf{BT(S)}$, where upon each observation in **B**, we add all the feasible control commands, under which the closed-behavior of the closed-loop system $L(\mathbf{G} \times \mathbf{S})$ is preserved. We call such a structure the bipartite behavior-preserving structure, denoted by $\mathbf{BPS} = (Q_{bps}, \Sigma_{bps}, \xi_{bps}, q_{bps}^{init})$, where

- $Q_{bps} = Q_b \cup Q_b^{com} \cup \{q^{dump}\}$, where $Q_b^{com} = \{q^{com} | q \in Q_b\}$

- $q_{bps}^{init} = (q_b^{init})^{com}$

- $\Sigma_{bps} = \Sigma \cup \Gamma$

- ξ_{bps} is defined as:

  1. $(\forall q \in Q_b)(\forall \gamma \in \Gamma) \mathcal{C}_1 \wedge \mathcal{C}_2 \Rightarrow \xi_{bps}(q^{com}, \gamma) = q$, where
     i. $\mathcal{C}_1 := En_B(q) \subseteq \gamma$
     ii. $\mathcal{C}_2 := (\forall (q_g, q_s) \in q) En_G(q_g) \cap \gamma \subseteq En_B(q)$

2. $(\forall q \in Q_b)(\forall \sigma \in \Sigma_{uo})\xi_b(q,\sigma)! \Rightarrow \xi_{bps}(q,\sigma) = q$

3. $(\forall q \in Q_b)(\forall \sigma \in \Sigma_o)\xi_b(q,\sigma)! \Rightarrow \xi_{bps}(q,\sigma) = (\xi_b(q,\sigma))^{com}$

4. $(\forall q \in Q_b)(\forall \sigma \in \Sigma_{uo})\neg\xi_b(q,\sigma)! \Rightarrow \xi_{bps}(q,\sigma) = q$

5. $(\forall q \in Q_b)(\forall \sigma \in \Sigma_o)\neg\xi_b(q,\sigma)! \Rightarrow \xi_{bps}(q,\sigma) = q^{dump}$

6. $(\forall \sigma \in \Sigma \cup \Gamma)\xi_{bps}(q^{dump},\sigma) = q^{dump}$

In the state set Q_{bps}, any state $q^{com} \in Q_b^{com}$ is a control state corresponding to state q, which is ready to issue the control command, and any state q in Q_b is a reaction state, which is ready to receive an observation. After a control command is issued at a control state q^{com}, **BPS** transits to a reaction state q. The state q^{dump} denotes the situation when an event $\sigma \in \Sigma_o$, which is not defined at the state $q \in Q_b$ in $\mathbf{B} = \mathscr{P}_{\Sigma_o}(\mathbf{G} \times \mathbf{S})$, occurs at the state q in **BPS**. The initial state of **BPS** is thus the initial control state, denoted by $q_{bps}^{init} = (q_b^{init})^{com}$. Next, we explain the definition of ξ_{bps}. Case 1 adds any feasible control command γ that can be issued at any control state q^{com} to preserve the control equivalence. The criteria for adding $\gamma \in \Gamma$ at the state q^{com} contains two conditions: (1) The sending of γ should make sure that all the events in $En_{\mathbf{B}}(q)$ would occur at the plant $\mathbf{G}$ once γ is received, denoted by the condition $\mathcal{C}_1 := En_{\mathbf{B}}(q) \subseteq \gamma$; (2) According to the way of constructing $\mathbf{B} = \mathscr{P}_{\Sigma_o}(\mathbf{G} \times \mathbf{S})$, any state $q \in Q_b$ such that $(\exists t \in \Sigma_o^*)\xi_b(q_b^{init},t) = q$ already contains all the possible estimated states of the plant $\mathbf{G}$ with respect to the observation sequence t. Henceforth, for any possible plant state q_g in the state q, the sending of γ should make sure that any event that might be executed at the state q_g under γ would not go beyond $En_{\mathbf{B}}(q)$, denoted by the condition $\mathcal{C}_2 := (\forall(q_g,q_s) \in q)En_{\mathbf{G}}(q_g) \cap \gamma \subseteq En_{\mathbf{B}}(q)$. The conditions $\mathcal{C}_1$ and $\mathcal{C}_2$ together enforce that at the control state q^{com}, any control command γ satisfying these two conditions would enable the plant to execute exactly those events in $En_{\mathbf{B}}(q)$. Case 2 and Case 3 retain all the transitions defined in $\mathbf{B}$, similar to the construction of $\mathbf{BT(S)}$. Next, we explain why we add Case 4 and Case 5. Our goal is to construct a structure to include all the control equivalent bipartite supervisors. By construction, for any bipartite supervisor, after a control command is issued at a control state, all the events in this control command should be defined. Since Case 1 adds all the possible control commands that ensure control equivalence, we do the following operations:

1. Firstly, for any reaction state $q \in Q_b$ in **BPS**, we carry out Case 4 and Case 5 to complete all the transitions labeled by events in Σ that are not defined at the state $q \in Q_b$ in **B**. The completed unobservable events lead to self-loop transitions. The completed observable events result in transitions to the state q^{dump}, where any control command is defined. Since these completed observable events do not occur under control commands defined at the control state q^{com}, the control equivalence will not be violated no matter which command is issued at the state q^{dump}.

2. Then we use **CE** to refine the above-constructed structure to get all bipartite control equivalent supervisors, which will be explained in Section 7.6.3.

In Case 6, since **BPS** has transited from some state $q \in Q_b$ to the state q^{dump}, we can safely add self-loop transitions labeled by the events in Γ at the state q^{dump} without affecting the control equivalence. We also add self-loop transitions labeled by the events in Σ at the state q^{dump} for the later structure refinement.

Example 7.5 *Based on* **B** *shown in Figure 7.14, the constructed* **BPS** *is illustrated in Figure 7.15. At the initial control state* $\{(0,0),(5,0)\}^{com}$, *(1) according to* $\mathcal{C}_1$ *of Case 1, we have* $En_{\mathbf{B}}(\{(0,0),(5,0)\}) = \{a,b\} \subseteq \gamma$, *and (2) according to* $\mathcal{C}_2$ *of Case*

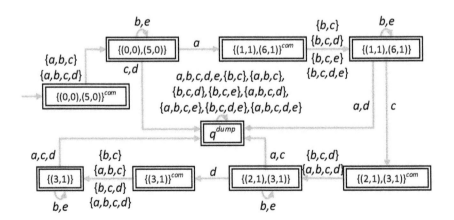

Figure 7.15 Bipartite behavior-preserving structure **BPS**.

1, we have $En_{\mathbf{G}}(0) = \{a, b, e\} \cap \gamma \subseteq En_{\mathbf{B}}(\{(0,0), (5,0)\}) = \{a, b\}$ and $En_{\mathbf{G}}(5) = \{a\} \cap \gamma \subseteq En_{\mathbf{B}}(\{(0,0), (5,0)\}) = \{a, b\}$. Thus, the control commands satisfying C_1 and C_2 are $\{a, b, c\}$ and $\{a, b, c, d\}$. Hence, there are two transitions labeled by $\{a, b, c\}$ and $\{a, b, c, d\}$ from the initial state to the reaction state $\{(0,0), (5,0)\}$. At the state $\{(0,0), (5,0)\}$, according to Case 2 and Case 3, there are two transitions labeled by event b, which is a self-loop, and event a, which leads to the state $(\xi_b(\{(0,0), (5,0)\}, a)^{com} = \{(1,1), (6,1)\}^{com}$. According to Case 4, a transition labeled by unobservable event e is added at the state $\{(0,0), (5,0)\}$. According to Case 5, two transitions labeled by observable events c and d are added at the state $\{(0,0), (5,0)\}$, which lead to the state q^{dump}. We can check that c and d would not occur under the initial command $\{a, b, c\}$ and $\{a, b, c, d\}$.

7.6.3 Structure Refinement

Although the constructed **BPS** contains all the feasible control commands that could ensure the control equivalence upon each observation, it does not exactly encode all the control equivalent bipartite supervisors due to the completion operations in Cases 4–6 of ξ_{bps}. Notice that **CE** encodes all the bipartite supervisors.[1] Since **BPS** and **CE** have the same set of events, we know that all transitions are forced to be synchronized in **BPS** $\times$ **CE**. Thus, we carry out the refinement on **BPS** by computing **BPS** $\times$ **CE**. We call **BPS** $\times$ **CE** the bipartite behavior-preserving command-nondeterministic[2] supervisor, denoted by $\mathbf{BPNS} = \mathbf{BPS} \times \mathbf{CE} = (Q_{\mathrm{bpns}}, \Sigma_{\mathrm{bpns}} = \Sigma \cup \Gamma, \xi_{\mathrm{bpns}}, q_{\mathrm{bpns}}^{\mathrm{init}})$, where $Q_{\mathrm{bpns}} = (Q_b \cup Q_b^{\mathrm{com}} \cup \{q^{\mathrm{dump}}\}) \times Q_{ce} = (Q_b \cup Q_b^{\mathrm{com}} \cup \{q^{\mathrm{dump}}\}) \times (\{q^{\gamma} | \gamma \in \Gamma\} \cup \{q_{ce}^{\mathrm{init}}\})$. According to the structure of **BPS** and **CE**, we know that $Q_{\mathrm{bpns}} = ((Q_b \cup \{q^{\mathrm{dump}}\}) \times \{q^{\gamma} | \gamma \in \Gamma\}) \dot{\cup} ((Q_b^{\mathrm{com}} \cup \{q^{\mathrm{dump}}\}) \times \{q_{ce}^{\mathrm{init}}\})$. Thus, we have $|Q_{\mathrm{bpns}}| \leq (2^{|X| \times |Z|} + 1) \times |\Gamma| + 2^{|X| \times |Z|} + 1 = (2^{|X| \times |Z|} + 1)(|\Gamma| + 1)$. For convenience, we call $Q_{\mathrm{bpns}}^{\mathrm{rea}} := (Q_b \cup \{q^{\mathrm{dump}}\}) \times \{q^{\gamma} | \gamma \in \Gamma\}$ the set of reaction states since any event, if defined at these states, belongs to Σ, and we call $Q_{\mathrm{bpns}}^{\mathrm{com}} := (Q_b^{\mathrm{com}} \cup \{q^{\mathrm{dump}}\}) \times \{q_{ce}^{\mathrm{init}}\}$ the set of control states since any event, if defined at these states, belongs to Γ. Thus, $Q_{\mathrm{bpns}} = Q_{\mathrm{bpns}}^{\mathrm{rea}} \dot{\cup} Q_{\mathrm{bpns}}^{\mathrm{com}}$.

Example 7.6 *Based on* **BPS** *shown in Figure 7.15 and* **CE** *shown in Figure 7.11. (a), part of the computed* **BPNS** *is illustrated in Figure 7.16. At the initial control state* $(\{(0,0), (5,0)\}^{com}, q_{ce}^{init})$, *two*

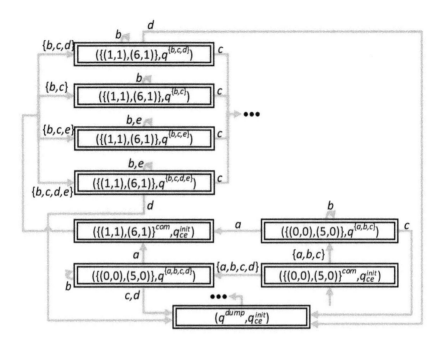

Figure 7.16 Bipartite behavior-preserving command-nondeterministic supervisor **BPNS**.

control commands $\{a, b, c\}$ and $\{a, b, c, d\}$ are defined, which means that a control equivalent supervisor could issue either $\{a, b, c\}$ or $\{a, b, c, d\}$ when the system initiates. If $\{a, b, c\}$ is issued, then **BPNS** *will transit to state $(\{(0, 0), (5, 0)\}, q^{\{a,b,c\}})$, where according to the structure of a bipartite supervisor, unobservable event b is a self-loop transition, and observable events a and c lead to two control states $(\{(1, 1), (6, 1)\}^{com}, q_{ce}^{init})$ and $(q^{dump}, q_{ce}^{init})$. Note that at the control state $(q^{dump}, q_{ce}^{init})$, any command could be issued without violating the control equivalence since the event c leading to $(q^{dump}, q_{ce}^{init})$ would never occur under the issued initial command $\{a, b, c\}$ according to the structure of* **G**.

Lemma 7.1 *Given* **G** *and* **S**, *for any supervisor* **S'**, *we have $L(\mathbf{G} \times \mathbf{S}) = L(\mathbf{G} \times \mathbf{S'})$ iff $L(\mathscr{P}_{\Sigma_o}(\mathbf{G} \times \mathbf{S})) = L(\mathscr{P}_{\Sigma_o}(\mathbf{G} \times \mathbf{S'}))$.*

Proof *(If) Firstly, it can be checked that $L(\mathscr{P}_{\Sigma_o}(\mathbf{G} \times \mathbf{S})) \subseteq L(\mathscr{P}_{\Sigma_o}(\mathbf{G}) \times \mathscr{P}_{\Sigma_o}(\mathbf{S})) = L(\mathscr{P}_{\Sigma_o}(\mathbf{G}) \times \mathbf{S})$. Next, we prove that $L(\mathbf{G} \times$*

S) $\subseteq L(\mathbf{G} \times \mathbf{S}')$. Thus, we need to show that for any $t \in L(\mathbf{G} \times \mathbf{S})$, we have $t \in L(\mathbf{G} \times \mathbf{S}')$. Since $t \in L(\mathbf{G} \times \mathbf{S})$, we have $t \in L(\mathbf{G})$ and $t \in L(\mathbf{S})$. Thus, to prove $t \in L(\mathbf{G} \times \mathbf{S}') = L(\mathbf{G}) \cap L(\mathbf{S}')$, we only need to show $t \in L(\mathbf{S}')$. Since $t \in L(\mathbf{G} \times \mathbf{S}) \subseteq L(\mathscr{P}_{\Sigma_o}(\mathbf{G} \times \mathbf{S}))$, we have $t \in L(\mathscr{P}_{\Sigma_o}(\mathbf{G} \times \mathbf{S})) = L(\mathscr{P}_{\Sigma_o}(\mathbf{G} \times \mathbf{S}')) \subseteq L(\mathscr{P}_{\Sigma_o}(\mathbf{G}) \times \mathbf{S}') = L(\mathscr{P}_{\Sigma_o}(\mathbf{G})) \cap L(\mathbf{S}')$, which implies that $t \in L(\mathbf{S}')$. Thus, $L(\mathbf{G} \times \mathbf{S}) \subseteq L(\mathbf{G} \times \mathbf{S}')$. By the same way, we could prove that $L(\mathbf{G} \times \mathbf{S}') \subseteq L(\mathbf{G} \times \mathbf{S})$. Hence, $L(\mathbf{G} \times \mathbf{S}) = L(\mathbf{G} \times \mathbf{S}')$.

(Only if) The necessity is straightforward. ■

Proposition 7.3 Given $\mathbf{G}$ and $\mathbf{S}$, for any supervisor $\mathbf{S}' = (Z', \Sigma, \delta', z_0')$ such that $L(\mathbf{G} \times \mathbf{S}) = L(\mathbf{G} \times \mathbf{S}')$, we have $L(\mathbf{BT}(\mathbf{S}')) \subseteq L(\mathbf{BPNS})$.

Proof *Since $L(\mathbf{BT}(\mathbf{S}')) \subseteq L(\mathbf{CE})$ and $L(\mathbf{BPNS}) = L(\mathbf{BPS}) \cap L(\mathbf{CE})$, to prove $L(\mathbf{BT}(\mathbf{S}')) \subseteq L(\mathbf{BPNS})$, we only need to show that $L(\mathbf{BT}(\mathbf{S}')) \subseteq L(\mathbf{BPS})$. Thus, we need to prove for any $t \in L(\mathbf{BT}(\mathbf{S}'))$, we have $t \in L(\mathbf{BPS})$. We adopt the mathematical induction to prove this result. The base case is: $t = \varepsilon$. Clearly, $\varepsilon \in L(\mathbf{BT}(\mathbf{S}'))$ and $\varepsilon \in L(\mathbf{BPS})$. Next, the induction hypothesis is that: for any $t \in L(\mathbf{BT}(\mathbf{S}'))$, we have $t \in L(\mathbf{BPS})$, when $|t| = k$. Then we show that for any $t\sigma \in L(\mathbf{BT}(\mathbf{S}'))$, we have $t\sigma \in L(\mathbf{BPS})$. For convenience, we denote $\mathbf{BT}(\mathbf{S}') = (Q_{bs'}, \Sigma \cup \Gamma, \xi_{bs'}, q_{bs'}^{init})$. By construction, we have $L(\mathbf{BT}(\mathbf{S}')) \subseteq \overline{(\Gamma \Sigma_{uo}^* \Sigma_o)^*}$, and then the verification can be divided into the following two cases:*

1. *$\sigma \in \Gamma$. For convenience, we denote $\sigma = \gamma \in \Gamma$. Based on the structure of $\mathbf{BT}(\mathbf{S}')$, we have $t \in (\Gamma \Sigma_{uo}^* \Sigma_o)^*$. Then we have the following two subcases:*

   1. *$\xi_{bps}(q_{bps}^{init}, t) = q^{dump}$. Based on Case 6 of ξ_{bps} of $\mathbf{BPS}$, we have $En_{\mathbf{BPS}}(\xi_{bps}(q_{bps}^{init}, t)) = \Gamma \cup \Sigma$. Thus, it holds that $t\gamma \in L(\mathbf{BPS})$.*

   2. *$\xi_{bps}(q_{bps}^{init}, t) \neq q^{dump}$. We show that at the state $\xi_{bps}(q_{bps}^{init}, t)$, γ satisfies the conditions $\mathcal{C}_1$ and $\mathcal{C}_2$ presented in Case 1 of ξ_{bps}. Since $L(\mathbf{G} \times \mathbf{S}) = L(\mathbf{G} \times \mathbf{S}')$, we have $L(\mathbf{B}) = L(\mathscr{P}_{\Sigma_o}(\mathbf{G} \times \mathbf{S})) = L(\mathscr{P}_{\Sigma_o}(\mathbf{G} \times \mathbf{S}')) \subseteq L(\mathbf{S}')$. Thus, we have $En_{\mathbf{B}}(\xi_b(q_b^{init}, P(t))) \subseteq En_{\mathbf{S}'}(\delta'(z_0', P(t))) = \gamma$, which satisfies $\mathcal{C}_1$. For $\mathcal{C}_2$, it requires that $(\forall(q_g, q_s) \in \xi_b(q_b^{init}, P(t)))En_{\mathbf{G}}(q_g) \cap$*

$En_{\mathbf{S'}}(\delta'(z_0', P(t))) \subseteq En_{\mathbf{B}}(\xi_b(q_b^{init}, P(t)))$, which clearly holds; otherwise, we know that there exists $(q_g, q_s) \in \xi_b(q_b^{init}, P(t))$ such that $En_{\mathbf{G}}(q_g) \cap En_{\mathbf{S'}}(\delta'(z_0', P(t))) \not\subseteq En_{\mathbf{B}}(\xi_b(q_b^{init}, P(t)))$, and then we have $L(\mathscr{P}_{\Sigma_o}(\mathbf{G} \times \mathbf{S})) \neq L(\mathscr{P}_{\Sigma_o}(\mathbf{G} \times \mathbf{S'}))$, implying that $L(\mathbf{G} \times \mathbf{S}) \neq L(\mathbf{G} \times \mathbf{S'})$ based on Lemma 7.1, which causes the contradiction.

2. $\sigma \in \Sigma$. By construction, there exists $t_1 \in (\Gamma\Sigma_{uo}^*\Sigma_o)^*$, $\gamma \in \Gamma$ and $t_2 \in (\gamma \cap \Sigma_{uo})^*$ such that $t = t_1\gamma t_2 \in L(\mathbf{BPS})$ and $\sigma \in \gamma$. Then we have the following two subcases:

   1. $\xi_{bps}(q_{bps}^{init}, t) = q^{dump}$. Based on Case 6 of ξ_{bps} of $\mathbf{BPS}$, we have $En_{\mathbf{BPS}}(\xi_{bps}(q_{bps}^{init}, t)) = \Gamma \cup \Sigma$. Thus, it holds that $t\sigma \in L(\mathbf{BPS})$.

   2. $\xi_{bps}(q_{bps}^{init}, t) \neq q^{dump}$. Clearly, $\xi_{bps}(q_{bps}^{init}, t_1\gamma)$ is a reaction state. According to Case 2 and Case 4 of ξ_{bps} of $\mathbf{BPS}$, we have $\xi_{bps}(q_{bps}^{init}, t_1\gamma) = \xi_{bps}(q_{bps}^{init}, t_1\gamma t_2)$, which is still a reaction state. In addition, by construction, any event in Σ is defined at any reaction state, we have $t\sigma = t_1\gamma t_2\sigma \in L(\mathbf{BPS})$.

Based on the above analysis, in any case, we have $t\sigma \in L(\mathbf{BPS})$, which completes the proof. ∎

Proposition 7.4 Given $\mathbf{G}$ and $\mathbf{S}$, for any supervisor $\mathbf{S'} = (Z', \Sigma, \delta', z_0')$ such that $L(\mathbf{G} \times \mathbf{S}) \neq L(\mathbf{G} \times \mathbf{S'})$, we have $L(\mathbf{BT}(\mathbf{S'})) \not\subseteq L(\mathbf{BPNS})$.

Proof Since $L(\mathbf{G} \times \mathbf{S}) \neq L(\mathbf{G} \times \mathbf{S'})$, based on Lemma 7.1, we have $L(\mathbf{B}) = L(\mathscr{P}_{\Sigma_o}(\mathbf{G} \times \mathbf{S})) \neq L(\mathscr{P}_{\Sigma_o}(\mathbf{G} \times \mathbf{S'})) = L(\mathbf{B'})$, where $\mathbf{B'} = \mathscr{P}_{\Sigma_o}(\mathbf{G} \times \mathbf{S'}) = (Q_{b'}, \Sigma, \xi_{b'}, q_{b'}^{init})$. Then we know that there exists $t \in \Sigma_o^* \cap L(\mathbf{B}) \cap L(\mathbf{B'})$ such that for any $i \in [0 : |t| - 1]$, the following conditions are satisfied:

C1) $En_{\mathbf{B}}(\xi_b(q_b^{init}, \mathcal{P}_i(t))) \subseteq En_{\mathbf{S'}}(\delta'(z_0', \mathcal{P}_i(t)))$

C2) for all $(q_g, q_s) \in \xi_b(q_b^{init}, \mathcal{P}_i(t))$,

$$En_{\mathbf{G}}(q_g) \cap En_{\mathbf{S'}}(\delta'(z_0', \mathcal{P}_i(t))) \subseteq En_{\mathbf{B}}(\xi_b(q_b^{init}, \mathcal{P}_i(t)))$$

C3) $En_{\mathbf{B}}(\xi_b(q_b^{init}, t)) \not\subseteq En_{\mathbf{S'}}(\delta'(z_0', t)) \vee (\exists(q_g, q_s) \in \xi_b(q_b^{init}, t))$ $En_{\mathbf{G}}(q_g) \cap En_{\mathbf{S'}}(\delta'(z_0', t)) \not\subseteq En_{\mathbf{B}}(\xi_b(q_b^{init}, t))$

Next, we consider two strings $u = \gamma_0 t[1]\gamma_1 \ldots t[|t| - 1]\gamma_{|t|-1}t[|t|]$ ($u = \varepsilon$ if $t = \varepsilon$) and $u\gamma_{|t|}$, where for any $i \in [0 : |t|]$, we have $\gamma_i = En_{\mathbf{S}'}(\delta'(z_0', \mathcal{P}_i(t)))$. Since $t \in \Sigma_o^* \cap L(\mathbf{B}) \cap L(\mathbf{B}')$, we know that $t \in L(\mathbf{S}')$. Thus, for any $j \in [1 : |t|]$, it holds that $t[j] \in \gamma_{j-1}$. By construction, we have $u \in L(\mathbf{BT}(\mathbf{S}'))$. Next, we prove that $u \in L(\mathbf{BPS})$ by mathematical induction. For convenience, we denote $u = c_1 \ldots c_{|t|}$, where $c_i = \gamma_{i-1}t[i]$. The base case is to prove $c_1 = \gamma_0 t[1] \in L(\mathbf{BPS})$. If $t = \varepsilon$, then $u = \varepsilon$, which means that $c_1 = \varepsilon \in L(\mathbf{BPS})$. Next, we only consider $t \neq \varepsilon$. Since $t \in L(\mathscr{P}_{\Sigma_o}(\mathbf{G} \times \mathbf{S}))$, we have $t[1] \in L(\mathscr{P}_{\Sigma_o}(\mathbf{G} \times \mathbf{S}))$. In addition, since the condition C1) and C2) hold, we know that for Case 1 of ξ_{bps} of $\mathbf{BPS}$, the condition $\mathcal{C}_1$ and $\mathcal{C}_2$ are satisfied for γ_0 at the state $(q_b^{init})^{com}$ in $\mathbf{BPS}$. Thus, $\gamma_0 t[1] \in L(\mathbf{BPS})$ and the base case holds. The induction hypothesis is $c_1 \ldots c_k = \gamma_0 t[1]\gamma_1 \ldots \gamma_{k-1}t[k] \in L(\mathbf{BPS})$ and we need to prove $c_1 \ldots c_{k+1} = \gamma_0 t[1]\gamma_1 \ldots \gamma_{k-1}t[k]\gamma_k t[k + 1] \in L(\mathbf{BPS})$, where the hypothesis holds for $k \leq |t|-2$. It can be checked that $\mathbf{BPS}$ would transit to the state $(\xi_b(q_b^{init}, t[1] \ldots t[k]))^{com}$ via the string $c_1 \ldots c_k$. Thus, we need to check whether the condition $\mathcal{C}_1$ and $\mathcal{C}_2$ in Case 1 of ξ_{bps} of $\mathbf{BPS}$ are satisfied for γ_k at the state $(\xi_b(q_b^{init}, t[1] \ldots t[k]))^{com}$. Clearly, these two conditions hold as it is a special case of C1) and C2) when $i = k$. Thus, $u \in L(\mathbf{BPS})$. Since $\mathbf{BPNS} = \mathbf{BPS} \times \mathbf{CE}$ and $t[j] \in \gamma_{j-1}$ ($j \in [1 : |t|]$), we know that $u \in L(\mathbf{BPNS})$.

Finally, we prove that $u\gamma_{|t|} \in L(\mathbf{BT}(\mathbf{S}'))$ and $u\gamma_{|t|} \notin L(\mathbf{BPS})$. By construction, $u\gamma_{|t|} \in L(\mathbf{BT}(\mathbf{S}'))$. Since the condition C3) holds, we know that for $\mathbf{BPS}$, at the state $q^{com} = (\xi_b(q_b^{init}, t))^{com} = \xi_{bps}(q_{bps}^{init}, u)$, it holds that either $En_{\mathbf{B}}(q) \not\subseteq En_{\mathbf{S}'}(\delta'(z_0', t)) = \gamma_{|t|}$ or $(\exists(q_g, q_s) \in q)En_{\mathbf{G}}(q_g) \cap En_{\mathbf{S}'}(\delta'(z_0', t)) = En_{\mathbf{G}}(q_g) \cap \gamma_{|t|} \not\subseteq En_{\mathbf{B}}(q)$, i.e., the conditions $\mathcal{C}_1$ and $\mathcal{C}_2$ in Case 1 of ξ_{bps} of $\mathbf{BPS}$ are not satisfied for the state $q^{com} = \xi_{bps}(q_{bps}^{init}, u)$, rendering that $u\gamma_{|t|} \notin L(\mathbf{BPS})$ and thus $u\gamma_{|t|} \notin L(\mathbf{BPNS})$, which completes the proof. ■

In the following text, we shall denote by $\mathscr{S}$ the set of all the supervisors (satisfying controllability and observability), and $\mathscr{S}_e(\mathbf{S}) := \{\mathbf{S}' \in \mathscr{S} | L(\mathbf{G} \times \mathbf{S}) = L(\mathbf{G} \times \mathbf{S}')\}$ the set of supervisors that are control equivalent to $\mathbf{S}$.

Theorem 7.2 $\displaystyle\bigcup_{\mathbf{S}' \in \mathscr{S}_e(\mathbf{S})} L(\mathbf{BT}(\mathbf{S}')) = L(\mathbf{BPNS})$.

Proof *Based on Proposition 7.3, we have LHS $\subseteq$ RHS. Next, we prove RHS $\subseteq$ LHS. Thus, we need to show that for any $t \in L(\mathbf{BPNS})$, we have $t \in$ LHS. We adopt the contradiction and assume that $t \notin$ LHS. Thus, we know that there exists a supervisor $\hat{S}$ such that $L(\mathbf{G} \times \mathbf{S}) \neq L(\mathbf{G} \times \hat{\mathbf{S}})$ and $t \in L(\mathbf{BT}(\hat{\mathbf{S}})) -$ LHS. Then, without loss of generality, we know that there exists $u \leq t$ such that $u = \gamma_0 t_1 \gamma_1 \ldots t_m \gamma_m$, where $m \in \mathbb{N}$ ($u = \gamma_0$ when $m = 0$) and the following conditions are satisfied: for all $i \in [1 : m]$ with $m \geq 1$,*

1. *$t_i \in (\gamma_{i-1} \cap \Sigma_{uo})^* (\gamma_{i-1} \cap \Sigma_o)$.*
   For convenience, we denote $t^{obs} = t_1^\uparrow \ldots t_m^\uparrow$, and $t^{obs} = \varepsilon$ for $m = 0$.

2. *$En_\mathbf{B}(\xi_b(q_b^{init}, \mathcal{P}_{i-1}(t^{obs}))) \subseteq \gamma_{i-1}$.*

3. *$(\forall (q_g, q_s) \in \xi_b(q_b^{init}, \mathcal{P}_{i-1}(t^{obs}))) En_\mathbf{G}(q_g) \cap \gamma_{i-1} \subseteq En_\mathbf{B}(\xi_b(q_b^{init}, \mathcal{P}_{i-1}(t^{obs})))$.*

4. *$En_\mathbf{B}(\xi_b(q_b^{init}, t^{obs})) \not\subseteq \gamma_m \vee (\exists (q_g, q_s) \in \xi_b(q_b^{init}, t^{obs})) En_\mathbf{G}(q_g) \cap \gamma_m \not\subseteq En_\mathbf{B}(\xi_b(q_b^{init}, t^{obs}))$*

Thus, $\mathcal{C}_1 \wedge \mathcal{C}_2$ is not satisfied for the command γ_m at the state $(\xi_b(q_b^{init}, t^{obs}))^{com}$ in Case 1 of ξ_{bps} of $\mathbf{BPS}$. Thus, $u \notin L(\mathbf{BPS})$ and $t \notin L(\mathbf{BPS})$, which causes the contradiction. Hence, $t \in$ LHS, which completes the proof. ■

Based on Theorem 7.2, **BPNS** exactly encodes all the control equivalent bipartite supervisors.

7.7 SYNTHESIS OF OBFUSCATED SUPERVISORS

In this section, we present a method to synthesize obfuscated supervisors based on $BPNS$.

7.7.1 Identification of Covert Damage Strings

To maintain control equivalence, any obfuscated supervisor cannot change the behaviors of the closed-loop system. Thus, to find obfuscated supervisors from **BPNS**, we need to prune those illegal control commands, which requires us to first identify the covert damage strings. However, **BPNS** only contains the control equivalent supervisors in the absence of attacks. Hence, we need to encode the impact of all possible actuator attacks into **BPNS** to build the model under attack, denoted by $\mathbf{BPNS^A} = (Q^a_{\text{bpns}}, \Sigma^a_{\text{bpns}}, \xi^a_{\text{bpns}}, q^{a,\text{init}}_{\text{bpns}})$, where

- $Q^a_{\text{bpns}} = Q_{\text{bpns}} \cup \{q^{\text{detect}}_{\text{bpns}}\} = Q^{\text{rea}}_{\text{bpns}} \cup Q^{\text{com}}_{\text{bpns}} \cup \{q^{\text{detect}}_{\text{bpns}}\}$

- $q^{a,\text{init}}_{\text{bpns}} = q^{\text{init}}_{\text{bpns}}$

- $\Sigma^a_{\text{bpns}} = \Sigma \cup \Gamma$

- ξ^a_{bpns} is defined as:

  1. $(\forall q, q' \in Q^a_{\text{bpns}})(\forall \sigma \in \Sigma \cup \Gamma)\xi_{\text{bpns}}(q,\sigma) = q' \Rightarrow \xi^a_{\text{bpns}}(q,\sigma) = q'$

  2. $(\forall q \in Q^{\text{rea}}_{\text{bpns}})(\forall \sigma \in \Sigma_{c,a,uo})\neg\xi_{\text{bpns}}(q,\sigma)! \Rightarrow \xi^a_{\text{bpns}}(q,\sigma) = q$

  3. $(\forall q \in Q^{\text{rea}}_{\text{bpns}})(\forall \sigma \in \Sigma_o)\neg\xi_{\text{bpns}}(q,\sigma)! \Rightarrow \xi^a_{\text{bpns}}(q,\sigma) = q^{\text{detect}}_{\text{bpns}}$

The construction procedure of **BPNS^A** from **BPNS** is similar to that of generating **BT(S)^A** from **BT(S)**. When an unexpected observation is received (Case 3), **BPNS^A** reaches the state $q^{\text{detect}}_{\text{bpns}}$. We have the following results.

Proposition 7.5 Given **G** and **S**, for any supervisor $\mathbf{S'} = (Z', \Sigma, \delta', z'_0)$ such that $L(\mathbf{G} \times \mathbf{S}) = L(\mathbf{G} \times \mathbf{S'})$, we have $L(\mathbf{BT(S')^A}) \subseteq L(\mathbf{BPNS^A})$.

Proof *We denote* $\mathbf{BT(S')} = (Q_{bs'}, \Sigma \cup \Gamma, \xi_{bs'}, q^{init}_{bs'})$ *and* $\mathbf{BT(S')^A} = (Q^a_{bs'}, \Sigma \cup \Gamma, \xi^a_{bs'}, q^{a,init}_{bs'})$. *We shall show that* $\mathbf{BT(S')^A}$ *is simulated by* $\mathbf{BPNS^A}$. *Let* $R \subseteq Q^a_{bs'} \times Q^a_{bpns} = (Q_{bs'} \cup \{q^{detect}\}) \times (Q_{bpns} \cup \{q^{detect}_{bpns}\})$ *be a relation defined such that 1) for any* $q_1 \in Q_{bs'} \subseteq Q^a_{bs'}$, *any* $q_2 \in Q_{bpns} \subseteq Q^a_{bpns}$ *and any* $t \in L(\mathbf{BT(S')}) \subseteq L(\mathbf{BPNS})$ *such that* $\xi_{bs'}(q^{init}_{bs'}, t) = q_1$ *and* $\xi_{bpns}(q^{init}_{bpns}, t) = q_2$, $(q_1, q_2) \in R$, *and 2)* $(q^{detect}, q^{detect}_{bpns}) \in R$. *We observe that, by construction,* $(q^{a,init}_{bs'}, q^{a,init}_{bpns}) \in R$. *Next, without loss of generality, we consider two states* $q_1 \in Q_{bs'}$ *and* $q_2 \in Q_{bpns}$ *such that* $(q_1, q_2) \in R$. *According to the definition of* R, *we know that there exists* $t \in L(\mathbf{BT(S')}) \subseteq L(\mathbf{BPNS})$ *such that* $\xi_{bs'}(q^{init}_{bs'}, t) = q_1$ *and* $\xi_{bpns}(q^{init}_{bpns}, t) = q_2$. *Since* $L(\mathbf{BT(S')}) \subseteq \overline{(\Gamma\Sigma^*_{uo}\Sigma_o)^*}$, *there are three cases:*

1. $t \in (\Gamma\Sigma_{uo}^*\Sigma_o)^*\Gamma$. *We know that q_1 and q_2 are reaction states, where only events in Σ are defined. Then, for any $\sigma \in \Sigma$ such that $\xi_{bs'}^a(q_1, \sigma) = \hat{q}_1$, by construction, we have $\xi_{bpns}^a(q_2, \sigma)!$ and we denote $\xi_{bpns}^a(q_2, \sigma) = \hat{q}_2$. If $\sigma \in En_{\mathbf{BT(S')}}(q_1)$, then we have $\xi_{bs'}(q_{bs'}^{init}, t\sigma) = \hat{q}_1$ and $\xi_{bpns}(q_{bpns}^{init}, t\sigma) = \hat{q}_2$, i.e., $(\hat{q}_1, \hat{q}_2) \in R$. If $\sigma \notin En_{\mathbf{BT(S')}}(q_1)$, then we have the following two subcases. 1) $\sigma \in \Sigma_{uo}$. Since unobservable events are self-loop transitions, we know that $\hat{q}_1 = q_1$ and $\hat{q}_2 = q_2$, i.e., $(\hat{q}_1, \hat{q}_2) \in R$. 2) $\sigma \in \Sigma_o$. Then we know that $\hat{q}_1 = q^{detect}$ and $\hat{q}_2 = q_{bpns}^{detect}$. In addition, since $(q^{detect}, q_{bpns}^{detect}) \in R$, we still have $(\hat{q}_1, \hat{q}_2) \in R$.*

2. $t \in (\Gamma\Sigma_{uo}^*\Sigma_o)^*\Gamma\Sigma_{uo}^*$. *Since unobservable events are self-loops, this case can be reduced to Case 1.*

3. $t \in (\Gamma\Sigma_{uo}^*\Sigma_o)^*$. *We know that q_1 and q_2 are control states, where only events in Γ are defined. For any $\gamma \in \Gamma$ such that $\xi_{bs'}^a(q_1, \gamma) = \hat{q}_1$, we have $t\gamma \in L(\mathbf{BT(S')}) \subseteq L(\mathbf{BPNS}) \subseteq L(\mathbf{BPNS^A})$, i.e., $\xi_{bpns}^a(q_2, \sigma)!$ and we denote $\xi_{bpns}^a(q_2, \sigma) = \hat{q}_2$. Clearly, $(\hat{q}_1, \hat{q}_2) \in R$ as $\xi_{bs'}(q_{bs'}^{init}, t\gamma) = \hat{q}_1$ and $\xi_{bpns}(q_{bpns}^{init}, t\gamma) = \hat{q}_2$.*

Thus, $\mathbf{BT(S')^A}$ is simulated by $\mathbf{BPNS^A}$, which completes the proof. ■

Theorem 7.3 $\bigcup\limits_{\mathbf{S'} \in \mathscr{S}_e(\mathbf{S})} L(\mathbf{BT(S')^A}) = L(\mathbf{BPNS^A})$.

Proof *Based on Proposition 7.5, we have $L(\mathbf{BT(S')^A}) \subseteq L(\mathbf{BPNS^A})$. Next, we prove $L(\mathbf{BT(S')^A}) \supseteq L(\mathbf{BPNS^A})$, that is, for any $t \in L(\mathbf{BPNS^A})$, we need to show $t \in L(\mathbf{BT(S')^A})$. Then there are two cases:*

1. $t \in L(\mathbf{BPNS})$. *Based on **Theorem 7.2**, we have $t \in \bigcup\limits_{\mathbf{S'} \in \mathscr{S}_e(\mathbf{S})} L(\mathbf{BT(S')})$. Since the construction of $\mathbf{BT(S')^A}$ does not remove any transition defined in $\mathbf{BT(S)}$, we have $t \in LHS$.*

2. $t \notin L(\mathbf{BPNS})$ *but $t \in L(\mathbf{BPNS^A})$. Then we need to prove $t \in LHS$, i.e., for any $n \in [0 : |t|]$, we have $\mathcal{P}_n(t) \in LHS$. We adopt the mathematical induction. For the base case, it clearly holds as $\mathcal{P}_0(t) = \varepsilon \in LHS$. The induction hypothesis is $\mathcal{P}_k(t) \in LHS$, where the hypothesis holds for $k \leq |t| - 2$, and we need to prove $\mathcal{P}_{k+1}(t) := \mathcal{P}_k(t)\sigma \in LHS$. Then there are two subcases:*

a. $\mathcal{P}_k(t) = t_1 \gamma t_2$, where $t_1 \in (\Gamma \Sigma_{uo}^* \Sigma_o)^*$, $\gamma \in \Gamma$, $t_2 \in (\gamma \cap \Sigma_{uo})^*$. Since $\mathcal{P}_k(t) \in LHS$, there exists a supervisor $\mathbf{S}' \in \mathscr{S}_e(\mathbf{S})$ such that $\mathcal{P}_k(t) \in L(\mathbf{BT}(\mathbf{S}')^{\mathbf{A}})$. We denote $\mathbf{BT}(\mathbf{S}')^{\mathbf{A}} = (Q_{bs'}^a, \Sigma \cup \Gamma, \xi_{bs'}^a, q_{bs'}^{a,init})$. By construction, we have

$$En_{\mathbf{BPNS}^{\mathbf{A}}}(\xi_{bpns}^a(q_{bpns}^{a,init}, \mathcal{P}_k(t)))$$
$$= En_{\mathbf{BT}(\mathbf{S}')^{\mathbf{A}}}(\xi_{bs'}^a(q_{bs'}^{a,init}, \mathcal{P}_k(t))).$$

Thus, $\mathcal{P}_{k+1}(t) = \mathcal{P}_k(t)\sigma \in L(\mathbf{BT}(\mathbf{S}')^{\mathbf{A}}) \subseteq LHS$.

b. $\mathcal{P}_k(t) \in (\Gamma \Sigma_{uo}^* \Sigma_o)^*$. In this case, $\sigma \in \Gamma$ because $L(\mathbf{BPNS}^{\mathbf{A}}) \subseteq \overline{(\Gamma \Sigma_{uo}^* \Sigma_o)^*}$. Since the construction of $\mathbf{BPNS}^{\mathbf{A}}$ does not remove from $\mathbf{BPNS}$ any transition that is labeled by an event in Γ and $\mathcal{P}_k(t) \in LHS$, based on Theorem 7.2, there exists a supervisor $\mathbf{S}' \in \mathscr{S}_e(\mathbf{S})$ such that $\mathcal{P}_{k+1}(t) = \mathcal{P}_k(t)\sigma \in L(\mathbf{BT}(\mathbf{S}')^{\mathbf{A}}) \subseteq LHS$.

Thus, we have $t \in L(\mathbf{BT}(\mathbf{S}')^{\mathbf{A}})$, which completes the proof. ■

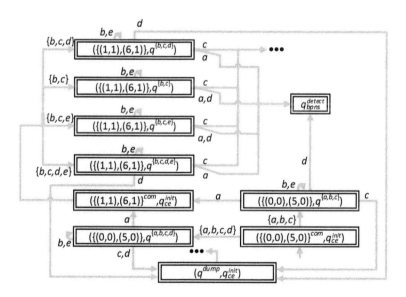

Figure 7.17 Bipartite behavior-preserving command-nondeterministic supervisor under attack $\mathbf{BPNS}^{\mathbf{A}}$.

Example 7.7 *Based on* **BPNS** *shown in Figure 7.16, part of the constructed* **BPNS**^{A} *is illustrated in Figure 7.17. We take the state* $(\{(0,0),(5,0)\}, q^{\{a,b,c\}})$ *as an instance to explain how to construct* **BPNS**^{A}**(S)** *based on* **BPNS(S)**. *According to Case 2 of* ξ^a_{bpns}, *the transition labeled by the unobservable but attackable event e is added, which is a self-loop. According to Case 3 of* ξ^a_{bpns}, *the transition labeled by the observable event d, which is not defined in* **BPNS(S)**, *is added and leads to the state* q^{detect}_{bpns}.

Next, we shall synthesize a structure to encode all the covert damage strings, where each one works for at least one control equivalent supervisor. The procedure is as follows:

Procedure 7.1:

1. Input: **G**, **CE**^{A}, **BPNS**^{A}, and $\mathscr{C}_{ac} = (\Sigma_{c,a}, \Sigma_{o,a} \cup \Gamma)$.

2. Compute **P** = **G** × **CE**^{A} × **BPNS**^{A} = $(Q_\mathcal{P}, \Sigma_\mathcal{P}, \xi_\mathcal{P}, q^{init}_\mathcal{P}, Q_{\mathcal{P},m})$, where $Q_{\mathcal{P},m} = X_d \times Q^a_{ce} \times Q^a_{bpns}$.

3. Generate **P$_r$** = **P**$^{Q_\mathcal{P} - Q_{bad}}$, where

$$Q_{bad} = \{(q, q^a_{ce}, q^a_{bpns}) \in Q_\mathcal{P} | q \notin X_d \wedge q^a_{bpns} = q^{detect}_{bpns}\}.$$

4. Solve a supervisor synthesis problem under partial observation (SSPO) where the plant is **P**, the legal language is $L(\mathbf{P_r})$, and the control constraint is $\mathscr{C}_{ac} = (\{\gamma \in \Gamma | \gamma \cap \Sigma_{c,a} \neq \emptyset\}, \Sigma_{o,a} \cup \Gamma)$. Because all controllable events under consideration here are observable, the supremal solution exists and is denoted as $\hat{\mathbf{A}}_\mathbf{c} = (Q_{\hat{a}}, \Sigma_{\hat{a}}, \xi_{\hat{a}}, q^{init}_{\hat{a}})$.

5. Output: $\hat{\mathbf{A}}_\mathbf{c}$.

We briefly explain **Procedure 7.1**. In Step 2, we generate a new plant **P** = **G** × **CE**^{A} × **BPNS**^{A}. In Step 3, we generate **P$_r$** from **P** by removing states in Q_{bad}, where the covertness is broken, denoted by $q^a_{bpns} = q^{detect}_{bpns}$. In Step 4, we solve a SSPO problem by treating **P** as the plant and $L(\mathbf{P_r})$ as the legal language. We also remark that a resilient supervisor should prevent damage infliction against any covert actuator attack. Thus, we should find covert damage strings that could be used by damage-reachable actuator attackers. Hence, in Step 4, we only need to deal with a synthesis problem that aims only for controllability and observability, without considering nonblockingness. We will show the correctness later.

In the following text, the set of covert and damage-reachable actuator attackers against the supervisor $\mathbf{S}'$ is denoted as $\mathscr{A}(\mathbf{S}')$.

Proposition 7.6 Given $\mathbf{G}$ and $\mathbf{S}$, for any supervisor $\mathbf{S}'$ such that $L(\mathbf{G} \times \mathbf{S}) = L(\mathbf{G} \times \mathbf{S}')$ and any attacker $\mathbf{A_c} \in \mathscr{A}(\mathbf{S}')$, we have $L(\mathbf{G} \times \mathbf{CE^A} \times \mathbf{BT(S')^A} \times \mathbf{A_c}) \subseteq L(\mathbf{G} \times \mathbf{CE^A} \times \mathbf{BPNS^A} \times \mathbf{\hat{A}_c})$.

Proof *We adopt the contradiction and assume that $L(\mathbf{G} \times \mathbf{CE^A} \times \mathbf{BT(S')^A} \times \mathbf{A_c}) \not\subseteq L(\mathbf{G} \times \mathbf{CE^A} \times \mathbf{BPNS^A} \times \mathbf{\hat{A}_c})$. Thus, there exists $t \in \overline{(\Gamma\Sigma_{uo}^*\Sigma_o)^*}$ such that $t \in L(\mathbf{G} \times \mathbf{CE^A} \times \mathbf{BT(S')^A} \times \mathbf{A_c})$ and $t \notin L(\mathbf{G} \times \mathbf{CE^A} \times \mathbf{BPNS^A} \times \mathbf{\hat{A}_c})$. Based on **Proposition 7.5**, we have $t \in L(\mathbf{G} \times \mathbf{CE^A} \times \mathbf{BPNS^A})$ and $t \notin L(\mathbf{\hat{A}_c})$. Then we have the following two cases:*

1. *$t \notin L(\mathbf{P_r})$. By construction, $\mathbf{G} \times \mathbf{CE^A} \times \mathbf{BT(S')^A} \times \mathbf{A_c}$ would reach the state $(q, q_{ce}^a, q_{bs'}^a, q_a)$, where $q_{bs'}^a = q^{detect}$ via the string t, which causes the contradiction as $\mathbf{A_c}$ is covert.*

2. *$t \in L(\mathbf{P_r})$. Since $t \notin L(\mathbf{\hat{A}_c})$, we know that there exists $\hat{t} = \hat{t}'\gamma\sigma_1\sigma_2\ldots\sigma_n\sigma_o \in L(\mathbf{P})$ such that: (1) $(\exists u \leq t)P_{\Sigma_{o,a}\cup\Gamma}(\hat{t}) = P_{\Sigma_{o,a}\cup\Gamma}(u)$, where $P_{\Sigma_{o,a}\cup\Gamma} : (\Sigma \cup \Gamma)^* \rightarrow (\Sigma_{o,a} \cup \Gamma)^*$, (2) $\xi_\mathcal{P}(q_\mathcal{P}^{init}, \hat{t}) \in Q_{bad}$, (3) $\hat{t}^\downarrow = \sigma_o \in (\Sigma_{c,a} - \gamma) \cap \Sigma_o$, and (4) $(\forall i \in [1:n])\sigma_i \in (\gamma \cup \Sigma_{c,a}) \cap \Sigma_{uo}$. Since $P_{\Sigma_{o,a}\cup\Gamma}(\hat{t}) = P_{\Sigma_{o,a}\cup\Gamma}(u)$, we know that $u = t'\gamma\sigma_1'\sigma_2'\ldots\sigma_m'\sigma_o$ such that: (1) $P_{\Sigma_{o,a}\cup\Gamma}(\hat{t}') = P_{\Sigma_{o,a}\cup\Gamma}(t')$, and (2) $(\forall i \in [1:m])\sigma_i' \in (\gamma \cup \Sigma_{c,a}) \cap \Sigma_{uo}$. Since $\sigma_o \in (\Sigma_{c,a} - \gamma) \cap \Sigma_o$, we know that $\mathbf{BPNS^A}$ would reach the state q_{bpns}^{detect} via the string u, implying that $t = u$. Thus, $\xi_\mathcal{P}(q_\mathcal{P}^{init}, t) \in Q_{bad}$, which causes the contradiction with the fact that $t \in L(\mathbf{P_r})$.*

Henceforth, the assumption does not hold, and the proof is completed. ∎

Corollary 7.1 Given $\mathbf{G}$ and $\mathbf{S}$, for any supervisor $\mathbf{S}'$ such that $L(\mathbf{G} \times \mathbf{S}) = L(\mathbf{G} \times \mathbf{S}')$ and any attacker $\mathbf{A_c} \in \mathscr{A}(\mathbf{S}')$, we have $L_m(\mathbf{G} \times \mathbf{CE^A} \times \mathbf{BT(S')^A} \times \mathbf{A_c}) \subseteq L_m(\mathbf{G} \times \mathbf{CE^A} \times \mathbf{BPNS^A} \times \mathbf{\hat{A}_c})$.

Proof *Based on Proposition 7.6, it holds that*

$$L(\mathbf{G} \times \mathbf{CE^A} \times \mathbf{BT(S')^A} \times \mathbf{A_c}) \cap L_m(\mathbf{G}) \subseteq L(\mathbf{G} \times \mathbf{CE^A} \times \mathbf{BPNS^A}$$
$$\times \hat{\mathbf{A}}_{\mathbf{c}}) \cap L_m(\mathbf{G}).$$

Since

$$L_m(\mathbf{G} \times \mathbf{CE^A} \times \mathbf{BT(S')^A} \times \mathbf{A_c}) = L(\mathbf{G} \times \mathbf{CE^A} \times \mathbf{BT(S')^A} \times \mathbf{A_c}) \cap L_m(\mathbf{G})$$

and

$$L_m(\mathbf{G} \times \mathbf{CE^A} \times \mathbf{BPNS^A} \times \hat{\mathbf{A}}_{\mathbf{c}}) = L(\mathbf{G} \times \mathbf{CE^A} \times \mathbf{BPNS^A} \times \hat{\mathbf{A}}_{\mathbf{c}}) \cap L_m(\mathbf{G}),$$

the proof is completed. ■

Theorem 7.4 Let $\mathcal{L} = L_m(\mathbf{G} \times \mathbf{CE^A} \times \mathbf{BPNS^A} \times \hat{\mathbf{A}}_{\mathbf{c}})$. Then

$$\mathcal{L} = \bigcup_{\mathbf{S'} \in \mathscr{S}_e(\mathbf{S})} \bigcup_{\mathbf{A_c} \in \mathscr{A}(\mathbf{S'})} L_m(\mathbf{G} \times \mathbf{CE^A} \times \mathbf{BT(S')^A} \times \mathbf{A_c}).$$

Proof *Based on Corollary 7.1, we have RHS $\subseteq$ LHS. Next, we show LHS $\subseteq$ RHS. We adopt the contradiction and assume LHS $\not\subseteq$ RHS. Then we know that there exists $\varepsilon \neq t \in \overline{(\Gamma\Sigma_{uo}^*\Sigma_o)^*}$ such that $t \in$ LHS and $t \notin$ RHS. Hence, t can be executed in $\mathbf{G}$, $\mathbf{CE^A}$, $\mathbf{BPNS^A}$ and $\hat{\mathbf{A}}_{\mathbf{c}}$, after we lift their alphabets to $\Sigma \cup \Gamma$, and $\mathbf{G}$ reaches the state in X_d via t. Then, based on **Theorem 7.3**, we know that there exists $\mathbf{S'} \in \mathscr{S}_e(\mathbf{S})$ such that $t \in L(\mathbf{BT(S')^A})$. Thus, $t \in L_m(\mathbf{G} \times \mathbf{CE^A} \times \mathbf{BT(S')^A} \times \hat{\mathbf{A}}_{\mathbf{c}})$, i.e., $\hat{\mathbf{A}}_{\mathbf{c}}$ is damage-reachable against $\mathbf{S'}$. In addition, $\hat{\mathbf{A}}_{\mathbf{c}}$ is covert against $\mathbf{S'}$; otherwise, there exists $t' \in L(\mathbf{G} \times \mathbf{CE^A} \times \mathbf{BT(S')^A} \times \hat{\mathbf{A}}_{\mathbf{c}})$ such that $\mathbf{BT(S')^A}$ reaches the state q^{detect} via the string t', which results in that $L(\mathbf{G} \times \mathbf{CE^A} \times \mathbf{BPNS^A} \times \hat{\mathbf{A}}_{\mathbf{c}})$ reaches some state in Q_{bad} via the string t' and the contradiction is caused. Thus, $\hat{\mathbf{A}}_{\mathbf{c}}$ is covert and damage-reachable against $\mathbf{S'}$ and we have $\hat{\mathbf{A}}_{\mathbf{c}} \in \mathscr{A}(\mathbf{S'})$, which means that $t \in$ RHS and this causes the contradiction. Hence, LHS $\subseteq$ RHS, and the proof is completed.* ■

Theorem 7.4 implies that $L_m(\mathbf{G} \times \mathbf{CE^A} \times \mathbf{BPNS^A} \times \hat{\mathbf{A}}_{\mathbf{c}})$ encodes all the covert damage strings, where each one works for at least one control equivalent supervisor.

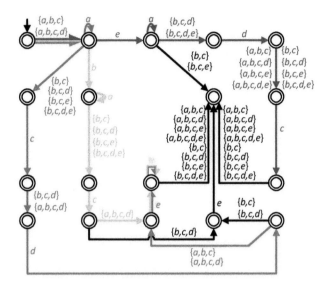

Figure 7.18 The synthesized $\hat{\mathbf{A}}_{\mathbf{c}}$.

Example 7.8 *Based on* **G**, **CE**$^{\mathbf{A}}$ *and* **BPNS**$^{\mathbf{A}}$ *shown in Figure 7.9.* *(a), Figures 7.12. (b) and 7.17, respectively, the synthesized* $\hat{\mathbf{A}}_{\mathbf{c}}$ *by adopting* **Procedure 1** *is illustrated in Figure 7.18. It can be checked that* $\hat{\mathbf{A}}_{\mathbf{c}}$ *encodes three kinds of damage strings (marked in red, green, and blue) that can be exploited by the attacker. We take the red part as an instance. After observing the initial control command* $\{a, b, c\}$ *or* $\{a, b, c, d\}$*, the attacker can carry out the enablement attack to enable the execution of unobservable event* e*, which results in the reuse of initial control command and event* a *is executed. After that, if the supervisor issues a control command containing event* d*, that is, command* $\{b, c, d\}$ *or* $\{b, c, d, e\}$*, then event* d *would be executed, triggering the command sending by the supervisor. Finally, event* c *is executed, causing the damage infliction.*

7.7.2 Pruning of Illegal Control Commands

As stated before, to obtain the obfuscated supervisors from **BPNS**, we need to prune inappropriate transitions labeled by control commands in Γ, which are controllable to the supervisor. Now, since $L_m(\mathbf{G} \times$ $\mathbf{CE}^{\mathbf{A}} \times \mathbf{BPNS}^{\mathbf{A}} \times \hat{\mathbf{A}}_{\mathbf{c}})$ encodes all the covert damage strings based on

Theorem 7.4, the intuitive idea of our methodology is to extract the obfuscated supervisors under attack by treating $\mathbf{BPNS^A}$ as a plant and then performing the synthesis with the guidance of $L_m(\mathbf{G} \times \mathbf{CE^A} \times \mathbf{BPNS^A} \times \hat{\mathbf{A}}_c)$. The detailed methodology is presented as follows:
Procedure 7.2:

1. Input: $\mathbf{G}$, $\mathbf{CE^A}$, $\mathbf{BPNS^A}$, $\hat{\mathbf{A}}_c$, Σ_o and Γ.

2. Compute $\mathbf{P} = \mathbf{G} \times \mathbf{CE^A} \times \mathbf{BPNS^A} \times \hat{\mathbf{A}}_c = (Q_{\mathcal{P}}, \Sigma_{\mathcal{P}} = \Sigma \cup \Gamma, \xi_{\mathcal{P}}, q_{\mathcal{P}}^{\text{init}}, Q_{\mathcal{P},m})$.

3. Construct $\mathbf{P_r} = (Q_{\mathcal{P}_r}, \Sigma_{\mathcal{P}_r}, \xi_{\mathcal{P}_r}, q_{\mathcal{P}_r}^{\text{init}})$ based on $\mathbf{P}$, where

    a. $Q_{\mathcal{P}_r} = (Q_{\mathcal{P}} - Q_{\mathcal{P},m}) \cup \{q^{\text{dump}}\}$

    b. $\Sigma_{\mathcal{P}_r} = \Sigma \cup \Gamma$

    c. $q_{\mathcal{P}_r}^{\text{init}} = q_{\mathcal{P}}^{\text{init}}$

    d. $\xi_{\mathcal{P}_r}$ is defined as:

       i. $(\forall q, q' \in Q_{\mathcal{P}} - Q_{\mathcal{P},m})(\forall \sigma \in \Sigma \cup \Gamma)\xi_{\mathcal{P}}(q, \sigma) = q' \Rightarrow \xi_{\mathcal{P}_r}(q, \sigma) = q'$

       ii. $(\forall q \in Q_{\mathcal{P}} - Q_{\mathcal{P},m})(\forall \sigma \in \Sigma \cup \Gamma)\neg \xi_{\mathcal{P}}(q, \sigma)! \Rightarrow \xi_{\mathcal{P}_r}(q, \sigma) = q^{\text{dump}}$

       iii. $(\forall \sigma \in \Sigma \cup \Gamma)\xi_{\mathcal{P}_r}(q^{\text{dump}}, \sigma) = q^{\text{dump}}$

4. Solve a SSPO problem where the plant is $\mathbf{BPNS^A}$, the legal language is $L(\mathbf{P_r})$, and the control constraint is $(\Gamma, \Sigma_o \cup \Gamma)$. The synthesized supremal solution is denoted as $\mathbf{S_0^A} = (Q_{S_0^A}, \Sigma_{S_0^A} = \Sigma \cup \Gamma, \xi_{S_0^A}, q_{S_0^A}^{\text{init}})$.

5. Output: $\mathbf{S_0^A}$.

In Step 2, we compute $\mathbf{P} = \mathbf{G} \times \mathbf{CE^A} \times \mathbf{BPNS^A} \times \hat{\mathbf{A}}_c$, whose marked behavior encodes all the covert damage strings. Notice that $L_m(\mathbf{P}) \neq \emptyset$ and $Q_{\mathcal{P},m} \neq \emptyset$ according to Theorem 7.4. In Step 3, we construct $\mathbf{P_r}$ based on $\mathbf{P}$. The state set of $\mathbf{P_r}$ is constructed by removing the set of marker states of $\mathbf{P}$ and adding a new state q^{dump}, as shown in Step 3.a. $\xi_{\mathcal{P}_r}$ is defined as follows: (1) for any two states that have not been removed, the transitions between them defined in $\mathbf{P}$ are retained in $\mathbf{P_r}$, as shown in Step 3.d.i, (2) for any state q that has not been removed, we complete the transitions that are not defined at state q in $\mathbf{P}$, which would lead to the newly added state q^{dump}, as shown in Step 3.d.ii, and (3) all the transitions in $\Sigma \cup \Gamma$ are defined at the state q^{dump} in Step 3.d.iii. Since we are only supposed to forbid the execution of the strings that might result in damage infliction, we carry out Step 3.d.ii and Step 3.d.iii such that $\mathbf{P_r}$ specifies all the legal strings. It is noteworthy that, although Step 3.d.ii completes the transitions that are not defined in $\mathbf{P}$ for those states in $Q_{\mathcal{P}} - Q_{\mathcal{P},m}$ and Step 3.d.iii adds self-loops labeled as events in $\Sigma \cup \Gamma$ for the state q^{dump}, $\mathbf{P_r}$ is not a complete automaton because when any state $q \in Q_{\mathcal{P},m}$ is removed from $\mathbf{P_r}$, all the transitions attached to this state q are also removed. In Step 4, we solve a SSPO problem by treating $\mathbf{BPNS^A}$ as the plant and $L(\mathbf{P_r})$ as the legal language. Since $\Gamma \subseteq \Sigma_o \cup \Gamma$, we can always synthesize the supremal solution $\mathbf{S_0^A}$. We remark that the attacked versions of those obfuscated supervisors in $\mathbf{BPNS}$ have been included in $\mathbf{S_0^A}$. We will show the correctness later.

Remark 7.1 *Since $\mathbf{S_0^A}$ is synthesized by treating $\mathbf{BPNS^A}$ as the plant in Step 4 of **Procedure** 2, we consider the case where $\mathbf{S_0^A}$ satisfies that $L(\mathbf{S_0^A}) \subseteq L(\mathbf{BPNS^A})$, following the standard notion of controllability and observability [3] over the control constraint $(\Gamma, \Sigma_o \cup \Gamma)$ with respect to the plant $\mathbf{BPNS^A}$. Without loss of generality, any event in Σ_{uo}, if defined, is a self-loop transition in $\mathbf{S_0^A}$. Thus, $\mathbf{S_0^A}$ is a bipartite structure[3] similar to $\mathbf{BPNS^A}$.*

Example 7.9 *Based on $\mathbf{G}$, $\mathbf{CE^A}$, $\mathbf{BPNS^A}$ and $\hat{\mathbf{A}}_c$ shown in Figure 7.9. (a), Figure 7.12. (b), Figure 7.17 and Figure 7.18, respectively, the synthesized $\mathbf{S_0^A}$ by adopting **Procedure** 2 is illustrated in Figure 7.19. Compared with $\mathbf{BPNS^A}$ shown in Figure 7.17, there are several control commands removed at some control states in $\mathbf{S_0^A}$. For example, after the occurrence of the sequence $\{a, b, c\}/\{a, b, c, d\} \to a \to \{b, c, d\}/\{b, c, d, e\} \to d$, the plant now might execute the string ead due to the enablement attack of unobservable event e. In this case, any control command cannot be issued because the string eadc would cause damage infliction and uncontrollable event c is contained in any control command.*

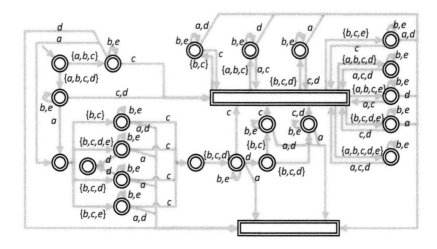

Figure 7.19 The synthesized $\mathbf{S_0^A}$.

7.7.3 Synthesis of Obfuscated Supervisors

The synthesized $\mathbf{S_0^A}$ contains the attacked version of obfuscated (resilient and control equivalent) supervisors. Since the goal is to synthesize the non-attacked version of obfuscated supervisors, we transform $\mathbf{S_0^A}$ to the version in the absence of attacks, denoted as $\mathbf{S_0} = (Q_{S_0}, \Sigma_{S_0}, \xi_{S_0}, q_{S_0}^{\text{init}})$, where

- $Q_{S_0} = Q_{S_0^A}$

- $q_{S_0}^{\text{init}} = q_{S_0^A}^{\text{init}}$

- $\Sigma_{S_0} = \Sigma \cup \Gamma$

- ξ_{S_0} is defined as:

  1. $(\forall q, q' \in Q_{S_0})(\forall \gamma \in \Gamma)\xi_{S_0^A}(q, \gamma) = q' \Rightarrow \xi_{S_0}(q, \gamma) = q'$
  2. $(\forall q, q' \in Q_{S_0})(\forall \gamma \in \Gamma)(\forall \sigma \in \gamma \cap \Sigma_{uo})\xi_{S_0^A}(q, \gamma) = q' \Rightarrow \xi_{S_0}(q', \sigma) = q'$
  3. $(\forall q, q', q'' \in Q_{S_0})(\forall \gamma \in \Gamma)(\forall \sigma \in \gamma \cap \Sigma_o)\xi_{S_0^A}(q, \gamma) = q' \wedge \xi_{S_0^A}(q', \sigma) = q'' \Rightarrow \xi_{S_0}(q', \sigma) = q''$

Briefly speaking, (1) we retain all the transitions labeled by events in Γ that are originally defined in $\mathbf{S_0^A}$, as shown in Case 1, (2) for any state q' such that there exists a transition $\xi_{S_0^A}(q, \gamma) = q'$, we retain the transition labeled by any event in $\gamma \cap \Sigma_{uo}$ ($\gamma \cap \Sigma_o$, respectively), which is a self-loop (leads to a new state q'', respectively), as shown in Case 2 (Case 3, respectively). Then we generate the automaton $Ac(\mathbf{S_0})$. For convenience, in the rest, we shall refer to $Ac(\mathbf{S_0})$ whenever we talk about $\mathbf{S_0}$. By Remark VI.1, $\mathbf{S_0}$ is a bipartite structure and the state set of $\mathbf{S_0}$ could be divided into two disjoint sets $Q_{S_0} = Q_{S_0}^{rea} \dot{\cup} Q_{S_0}^{com}$, where $Q_{S_0}^{rea}$ is the set of reaction states and $Q_{S_0}^{com}$ is the set of control states, satisfying that (1) at any state of $Q_{S_0}^{rea}$, any event in Γ is not defined, (2) at any state of $Q_{S_0}^{rea}$, any event in Σ_{uo}, if defined, leads to a self-loop, and any event in Σ_o, if defined, would lead to a transition to a control state, (3) at any state of $Q_{S_0}^{com}$, any event in Σ is not defined, and (4) at any state of $Q_{S_0}^{com}$, any event in Γ, if defined, would lead to a transition to a reaction state.

Example 7.10 *Based on $\mathbf{S_0^A}$ shown in Figure 7.19, the transformed $\mathbf{S_0}$ is illustrated in Figure 7.20. At the initial state 0 of $\mathbf{S_0}$, according to Case 1 of ξ_{S_0}, we retain the transitions labeled by $\{a, b, c\}$ and $\{a, b, c, d\}$ originally defined in $\mathbf{S_0^A}$. At state 1, according to Case 2 of ξ_{S_0}, the transition labeled by event $b \in \{a, b, c\} \cap \Sigma_{uo}$ is retained, which is a self-loop, and according to Case 3 of ξ_{S_0}, the transitions labeled by events $a, c \in \{a, b, c\} \cap \Sigma_o$ are retained, which would lead to state 2 and state 3, respectively, as defined in $\mathbf{S_0^A}$.*

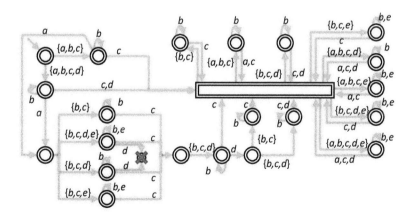

Figure 7.20   The transformed $\mathbf{S_0}$.

Although inappropriate control commands leading to damage infliction have been removed in $\mathbf{S_0}$, we cannot ensure $\mathbf{S_0}$ exactly encodes all the obfuscated supervisors because it is possible that at some control state of $\mathbf{S_0}$, where an observation has just been received, there is no control command defined as a result of the synthesis. Such a phenomenon violates the structure of a bipartite supervisor, where a control command must be defined at any control state according to the construction. Thus, by treating $\mathbf{S_0}$ as a plant, we carry out the following procedure to iteratively remove these newly created bad states until the generated structure satisfies the condition that at least a control command follows any observation.

Procedure 7.3:

1. Input: $\mathbf{S_0}$, Σ_o, and Γ.

2. Let $k := 0$.

3. Compute $Q_{k,\mathrm{del}} := \{q \in Q^{\mathrm{com}}_{S_k} | En_{\mathbf{S_k}}(q) = \emptyset\}$.

4. If $Q_{k,\mathrm{del}} = \emptyset$, then denote $\mathbf{FNS} := \mathbf{S_k}$ and proceed to Step 8; otherwise, i.e., $Q_{k,\mathrm{del}} \neq \emptyset$, then proceed to Step 5.

5. Construct $\mathbf{S_{k,r}} = \mathbf{S_k}^{Q_{S_k} - Q_{k,\mathrm{del}}}$.

6. Solve a SSPO problem where the plant is $\mathbf{S_k}$, the legal language is $L(\mathbf{S_{k,r}})$, and the control constraint is $(\Gamma, \Sigma_o \cup \Gamma)$. The synthesized supremal solution is denoted as $\mathbf{S_{k+1}} = (Q_{S_{k+1}}, \Sigma_{S_{k+1}} = \Sigma \cup \Gamma, \xi_{S_{k+1}}, q^{\mathrm{init}}_{S_{k+1}})$. We also denote $Q_{S_{k+1}} = Q^{\mathrm{rea}}_{S_{k+1}} \dot{\cup} Q^{\mathrm{com}}_{S_{k+1}}$, where $Q^{\mathrm{rea}}_{S_{k+1}}$ is the set of reaction states and $Q^{\mathrm{com}}_{S_{k+1}}$ is the set of control states[4].

7. Let $k \leftarrow k + 1$ and proceed to Step 3.

8. Output: $\mathbf{FNS}$.

In Step 2, we set the counter k to 0. In Step 3, taking the k-th iteration as an instance, we compute the set of control states in $\mathbf{S_k}$, denoted by $Q_{k,\mathrm{del}}$, where any $q \in Q_{k,\mathrm{del}}$ satisfies that there is no control command defined, denoted by $En_{\mathbf{S_k}}(q) = \emptyset$. In Step 4, if $Q_{k,\mathrm{del}} = \emptyset$, then $\mathbf{FNS} := \mathbf{S_k}$ is the desired structure and we output $\mathbf{FNS}$ in Step 8; otherwise, we remove $Q_{k,\text{del}}$ in $\mathbf{S_k}$ to construct $\mathbf{S_{k,r}}$ in Step 5. In Step 6, we solve a SSPO problem by treating $\mathbf{S_k}$ as the plant and $L(\mathbf{S_{k,r}})$ as the legal language. Since $\Gamma \subseteq \Sigma_o \cup \Gamma$, we could always synthesize the supremal solution $\mathbf{S_{k+1}}$. We name the output $\mathbf{FNS}$ of $\mathbf{Procedure}$ $\mathbf{7.3}$ as obfuscated command-nondeterministic supervisor, and denote $\mathbf{FNS} = (Q_{\text{fns}}, \Sigma_{\text{fns}} = \Sigma \cup \Gamma, \xi_{\text{fns}}, q_{\text{fns}}^{\text{init}})$. In addition, we denote $Q_{\text{fns}} = Q_{\text{fns}}^{\text{rea}} \dot\cup Q_{\text{fns}}^{\text{com}}$, where $Q_{\text{fns}}^{\text{rea}}$ is the set of reaction states and $Q_{\text{fns}}^{\text{com}}$ is the set of control states[5].

Remark 7.2 *Similar to Remark VI.1, we consider the case where* $\mathbf{S_{k+1}}$ *satisfies that* $L(\mathbf{S_{k+1}}) \subseteq L(\mathbf{S_k})$, *following the standard notion of controllability and observability [3] over the control constraint* $(\Gamma, \Sigma_o \cup \Gamma)$. *Without loss of generality, any event in* Σ_{uo}, *if defined, is a self-loop transition in* $\mathbf{S_{k+1}}$. *Thus,* $\mathbf{S_{k+1}}$ *is a bipartite structure.*

Proposition 7.7 $L(\mathbf{FNS}) \subseteq L(\mathbf{BPNS})$.

Proof *Firstly, we prove* $L(\mathbf{S_0}) \subseteq L(\mathbf{BPNS})$. *We adopt the contradiction and assume that* $L(\mathbf{S_0}) \not\subseteq L(\mathbf{BPNS})$. *Since* $L(\mathbf{S_0}) \subseteq \overline{(\Gamma\Sigma_{uo}^*\Sigma_o)^*}$ *and* $L(\mathbf{BPNS}) \subseteq \overline{(\Gamma\Sigma_{uo}^*\Sigma_o)^*}$, *we have the following two cases. 1) There exists* $t \in L(\mathbf{S_0}) \cap L(\mathbf{BPNS})$ *and* $\gamma \in \Gamma$ *such that* $t\gamma \in L(\mathbf{S_0})$ *and* $t\gamma \notin L(\mathbf{BPNS})$. *Thus,* $t\gamma \in L(\mathbf{S_0}) \subseteq L(\mathbf{S_0^A}) \subseteq L(\mathbf{BPNS^A})$. *Since the construction of* $\mathbf{BPNS^A}$ *from* $\mathbf{BPNS}$ *does not add any transition labeled by a control command, we have* $t\gamma \in L(\mathbf{BPNS})$, *which causes the contradiction. 2) There exists* $t \in (\Sigma \cup \Gamma)^*$, $\gamma \in \Gamma$, $t' \in (\gamma \cap \Sigma_{uo})^*$ *and* $\sigma \in \Sigma$ *such that* $t\gamma t' \in L(\mathbf{S_0}) \cap L(\mathbf{BPNS})$, $t\gamma t'\sigma \in L(\mathbf{S_0})$ *and* $t\gamma t'\sigma \notin L(\mathbf{BPNS})$. *Thus,* $t\gamma t'\sigma \in L(\mathbf{S_0}) \subseteq L(\mathbf{S_0^A}) \subseteq L(\mathbf{BPNS^A})$. *Based on the construction of* $\mathbf{BPNS^A}$ *from* $\mathbf{BPNS}$, *we have* $\sigma \in \Sigma - \gamma$. *However, this would violate the structure of* $\mathbf{S_0}$, *which causes the contradiction. Thus,* $L(\mathbf{FNS}) \subseteq L(\mathbf{S_0}) \subseteq L(\mathbf{BPNS})$. ∎

Theorem 7.5 $\bigcup\limits_{\mathbf{S'} \in \mathscr{S}_f(\mathbf{S})} L(\mathbf{BT}(\mathbf{S'})) = L(\mathbf{FNS})$, *where* $\mathscr{S}_f(\mathbf{S})$ *denotes* the set of obfuscated supervisors for $\mathbf{S}$.

Proof *Firstly, we prove that the left-hand side (LHS) of the equality stated in the theorem is a subset of the right-hand side (RHS). Thus, we shall show for any* $\mathbf{S'} \in \mathscr{S}_f(\mathbf{S})$, *we have* $L(\mathbf{BT}(\mathbf{S'})) \subseteq L(\mathbf{FNS})$. *Based on* **Proposition 7.5**, *we have* $L(\mathbf{BT}(\mathbf{S'})^\mathbf{A}) \subseteq L(\mathbf{BPNS^A})$. *Next, we prove* $L(\mathbf{BT}(\mathbf{S'})^\mathbf{A}) \subseteq L(\mathbf{S_0^A})$. *We adopt the contradiction and assume* *that $L(\mathbf{BT(S')^A}) \nsubseteq L(\mathbf{S_0^A})$. By synthesis, we know there exists $u \in L(\mathbf{BPNS^A})$, $\gamma \in \Gamma$ and $v \in (\gamma \cup \Sigma_{c,a})^* - \{\varepsilon\}$ such that*

$$u\gamma v \in L_m(\mathbf{P}) \wedge [(\exists t \in L(\mathbf{BT(S')^A}))t\gamma \in L(\mathbf{BT(S')^A}) \wedge$$
$$t\gamma \notin L(\mathbf{S_0^A}) \wedge P_{\Sigma_o \cup \Gamma}(t) = P_{\Sigma_o \cup \Gamma}(u)]$$

*By construction, we have $u\gamma v \in L(\mathbf{BT(S')^A})$, i.e., there exists a covert and damage-reachable actuator attacker against $\mathbf{S'}$, which is contradictory to the fact that $\mathbf{S'}$ is resilient. Thus, $L(\mathbf{BT(S')^A}) \subseteq L(\mathbf{S_0^A})$. Then, it can be checked that $L(\mathbf{BT(S')}) \subseteq L(\mathbf{S_0})$. Next, we prove $L(\mathbf{BT(S')}) \subseteq L(\mathbf{FNS})$. We adopt the contradiction and assume that $L(\mathbf{BT(S')}) \nsubseteq L(\mathbf{FNS})$. Then, according to **Procedure 3**, without loss of generality, we know that there exists $k \geq 0$ such that $L(\mathbf{BT(S')}) \subseteq L(\mathbf{S_k})$ and $L(\mathbf{BT(S')}) \nsubseteq L(\mathbf{S_{k+1}})$. Then we know that there exists $u' \in L(\mathbf{S_k})$, $\gamma'' \in \Gamma$ and $\sigma' \in \gamma \cap \Sigma_o$ such that*

$$En_{\mathbf{S_k}}(\xi_{S_k}(q_{S_k}^{init}, u'\gamma''\sigma')) = \emptyset \wedge$$
$$[(\exists t' \in L(\mathbf{BT(S')}))t'\gamma'' \in L(\mathbf{BT(S')}) \wedge t'\gamma'' \notin L(\mathbf{S_{k+1}}) \wedge$$
$$P_{\Sigma_o \cup \Gamma}(u') = P_{\Sigma_o \cup \Gamma}(t')]$$

Similarly, we have $u'\gamma'' \in L(\mathbf{BT(S')})$, and thus $u'\gamma''\sigma' \in L(\mathbf{BT(S')})$. Since $L(\mathbf{BT(S')}) \subseteq L(\mathbf{S_k})$ and there is always a control command in Γ defined at any control state of $\mathbf{BT(S')}$, we have $En_{\mathbf{S_k}}(\xi_{S_k}(q_{S_k}^{init}, u'\gamma''\sigma')) \neq \emptyset$, which causes the contradiction. Thus, $L(\mathbf{BT(S')}) \subseteq L(\mathbf{FNS})$.

Secondly, we prove that the RHS set is a subset of the LHS set. Thus, we need to show for any $t \in RHS$, we have $t \in LHS$. Firstly, we generate an automaton $\mathbf{T}$ such that $L_m(\mathbf{T}) = t$. Then we compute its subset construction $\mathscr{P}_{\Sigma_o \cup \Gamma}(\mathbf{T}) = (Q_t, \Sigma \cup \Gamma, \xi_t, q_t^{init})$. By construction, we could denote $Q_t = Q_t^{rea} \dot{\cup} Q_t^{com}$, where Q_t^{rea} is the set of reaction states and Q_t^{com} is the set of control states. Then we construct a new automaton $\mathbf{NC} = (Q_{nc}, \Sigma_{nc}, \xi_{nc}, q_{nc}^{init})$, where $Q_{nc} = Q_t \cup \{q^{obs}\} \cup \{q^\gamma | \gamma \in \Gamma\}$, $q_{nc}^{init} = q_t^{init}$, $\Sigma_{nc} = \Sigma \cup \Gamma$, and ξ_{nc} is defined as follows:

1. $(\forall q, q' \in Q_t)(\forall \sigma \in \Sigma \cup \Gamma)\xi_t(q, \sigma) = q' \Rightarrow \xi_{nc}(q, \sigma) = q'$

2. $(\forall q \in Q_t^{rea})(\forall \sigma \in \Sigma_{uo})\neg\xi_t(q, \sigma)! \Rightarrow \xi_{nc}(q, \sigma) = q$

3. $(\forall q \in Q_t^{rea})(\forall \sigma \in \Sigma_o)\neg\xi_t(q, \sigma)! \Rightarrow \xi_{nc}(q, \sigma) = q^{obs}$

4. $(\forall q \in Q_t^{com})En_{\mathscr{P}_{\Sigma_o \cup \Gamma}(\mathbf{T})}(q) = \emptyset \Rightarrow (\forall \gamma \in \Gamma)\xi_{nc}(q, \gamma) = q^\gamma$

5. $(\forall \gamma \in \Gamma)\xi_{nc}(q^{obs}, \gamma) = q^\gamma$

6. $(\forall \gamma \in \Gamma)(\forall \sigma \in \gamma \cap \Sigma_o)\xi_{ce}(q^\gamma, \sigma) = q^{obs}.$

7. $(\forall \gamma \in \Gamma)(\forall \sigma \in \gamma \cap \Sigma_{uo})\xi_{ce}(q^\gamma, \sigma) = q^\gamma.$

Then we compute $\mathbf{NCS} = \mathbf{NC} \times \mathbf{FNS} = (Q_{ncs}, \Sigma \cup \Gamma, \xi_{ncs}, q_{ncs}^{init})$. *By construction, we denote* $Q_{ncs} = Q_{ncs}^{rea} \dot\cup Q_{ncs}^{com}$, *where* Q_{ncs}^{rea} *is the set of reaction states and* Q_{ncs}^{com} *is the set of control states. Based on* $\mathbf{NCS}$, *we generate a bipartite supervisor, denoted as* $\mathbf{BT} = (Q_{bt}, \Sigma_{bt}, \xi_{bt}, q_{bt}^{init})$, *where* $Q_{bt} = Q_{ncs} = Q_{ncs}^{rea} \dot\cup Q_{ncs}^{com}$, $q_{bt}^{init} = q_{ncs}^{init}$, $\Sigma_{bt} = \Sigma \cup \Gamma$, *and* ξ_{bt} *is defined as follows:*

1. $(\forall q, q' \in Q_{bt})(\forall \sigma \in \Sigma)\xi_{ncs}(q, \sigma) = q' \Rightarrow \xi_{bt}(q, \sigma) = q'$

2. *For any control state* $q \in Q_{ncs}^{com}$, *we randomly pick a control command* $\gamma \in En_{\mathbf{NCS}}(q)$ *and define that: for any reaction state* $q' \in Q_{ncs}^{rea}$, *if* $\xi_{ncs}(q, \gamma) = q'$, *then* $\xi_{bt}(q, \gamma) = q'$ *and for any control command* $\gamma' \in En_{\mathbf{NCS}}(q) - \{\gamma\}$, *we have* $\neg \xi_{bt}(q, \gamma')!$.

Finally, we generate the automaton $Ac(\mathbf{BT})$. *For convenience, we shall still denote* $Ac(\mathbf{BT})$ *as* $\mathbf{BT}$. *Next, we prove that* $\mathbf{BT}$ *is a control equivalent and resilient bipartite supervisor, and* $t \in L(\mathbf{BT})$. *We have the following two facts for* $\mathbf{FNS}$*: (1) at any control state, there is at least one control command defined, which would lead to a reaction state, and (2) at any reaction state which is reached from a control state by a transition labeled as a control command* γ, *all the events in* γ *are defined and any unobservable event would lead to a self-loop and any observable event would lead to a control state. Based on the construction of* $\mathbf{NC}$, *it can be checked that the facts (1) and (2) also hold for* $\mathbf{NC}$. *Since* $\mathbf{NCS} = \mathbf{NC} \times \mathbf{FNS}$, *the facts (1) and (2) also hold for* $\mathbf{NCS}$. *According to the construction of* $\mathbf{BT}$, *where we only define one control command at each control state, we know that the fact (2) holds for* $\mathbf{BT}$, *and there is only one control command defined at any control state of* $\mathbf{BT}$. *Thus,* $\mathbf{BT}$ *is consistent with a bipartite supervisor structure. Next, we firstly prove* $\mathbf{BT}$ *is control equivalent to* $\mathbf{S}$. *We adopt the contradiction and assume that* $\mathbf{BT}$ *is not control equivalent to* $\mathbf{S}$. *Based on* **Proposition 7.4**, *we have* $L(\mathbf{BT}) \not\subseteq L(\mathbf{BPNS})$. *Since* $\mathbf{BT} = \mathbf{NC} \times \mathbf{FNS}$, *we have* $L(\mathbf{BT}) \subseteq L(\mathbf{FNS})$.

Based on **Proposition 7.7**, *we have* $L(\mathbf{BT}) \subseteq L(\mathbf{FNS}) \subseteq L(\mathbf{BPNS})$, *which causes the contradiction. Hence,* **BT** *is control equivalent to* **S**. *Secondly, we prove* **BT** *is resilient. We adopt the contradiction and assume* **BT** *is not resilient. We denote the version of* **BT** *under attack as* $\mathbf{BT^{A_c}}$. *Clearly, we have* $L(\mathbf{BT^{A_c}}) \subseteq L(\mathbf{S_0^A})$. *Since* **BT** *is not resilient, we know that there exists an attacker* $\mathbf{A_c} \in \mathscr{A}(\mathbf{BT})$ *and a string* $t \in L(\mathbf{BT^{A_c}}) \subseteq L(\mathbf{S_0^A})$ *such that* $t \in L_m(\mathbf{G} \times \mathbf{CE^A} \times \mathbf{BT^{A_c}} \times \mathbf{A_c})$. *Based on* **Proposition 7.6**, *we have* $t \in L_m(\mathbf{P}) = L_m(\mathbf{G} \times \mathbf{CE^A} \times \mathbf{BPNS^A} \times \hat{\mathbf{A}}_{\mathbf{c}})$. *By synthesis, we know that* $t \notin L(\mathbf{S_0^A})$, *which causes the contradiction. Thus,* **BT** *is resilient. Finally, we show that* $t \in L(\mathbf{BT})$. *By construction,* $t \in L(\mathbf{NC})$. *Since* $t \in RHS = L(\mathbf{FNS})$ *and* $\mathbf{NCS} = \mathbf{NC} \times \mathbf{FNS}$, *we have* $t \in L(\mathbf{NCS})$. *We adopt the contradiction and assume that* $t \notin L(\mathbf{BT})$. *By construction, there exists* $t' \leq t$ *and* $\gamma \in \Gamma$ *such that (1)* $t'\gamma \leq t$, *(2)* $|En_{\mathbf{NCS}}(\xi_{ncs}(q_{ncs}^{init}, t'))| \geq 2$, *and (3) we do not pick the control command* γ *at the control state* $\xi_{ncs}(q_{ncs}^{init}, t')$ *when we construct* **BT**. *However, by construction, there is only one control command defined at the state* $\xi_{ncs}(q_{ncs}^{init}, t')$, *which causes the contradiction. Thus,* $t \in L(\mathbf{BT})$. *Based on the above analysis,* $\mathbf{BT} \in \mathscr{S}_f(\mathbf{S})$, *and* $t \in L(\mathbf{BT}) \subseteq LHS$. *Thus, the RHS set is a subset of the LHS set, which completes the proof.* ■

Example 7.11 *We shall continue with* $\mathbf{S_0}$ *shown in Figure 7.20, where there exists a control state (marked by a red cross) and there is no control command defined at this state. According to Step 5 of*

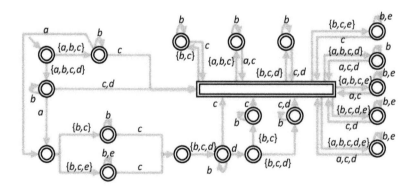

Figure 7.21 The synthesized $\mathbf{S_1}$ (**FNS**).

Procedure 7.3, *we remove this state to generate* $\mathbf{S_{0,r}}$. *By treating* $\mathbf{S_0}$ *as the plant and* $L(\mathbf{S_{0,r}})$ *as the legal language, we synthesize* $\mathbf{S_1}$, *which is illustrated in Figure 7.21. It can be checked that at least a control command is defined at any control state of* $\mathbf{S_1}$, *which means that* $Q_{1,del} = \emptyset$. *Thus, the procedure terminates after the first iteration and outputs* $\mathbf{FNS(S)} := \mathbf{S_1}$.

Theorem 7.6 Given a closed-loop system $(\mathbf{G}, \mathbf{S})$, the existence of an obfuscated supervisor is decidable.

Proof *To prove this result, based on Theorem 7.5, we just need to additionally check whether* **Procedure 7.1**, **Procedure 7.2**, *and* **Procedure 7.3** *could terminate within finite steps. Clearly,* **Procedure 7.1** *and* **Procedure 7.2** *terminate within finite steps. For* **Procedure 7.3**, *in each iteration, since* $\mathbf{S_{k,r}}$ *is generated by removing at least one control state q from the plant* $\mathbf{S_k}$ *and any unobservable event in* Σ_{uo}, *if defined, is a self-loop in* $\mathbf{S_k}$, *we know that* $\mathbf{S_{k+1}}$ *is a substructure of* $\mathbf{S_k}$. *In addition, to satisfy the controllability with respect to the control constraint* $(\Gamma, \Sigma_o \cup \Gamma)$, *at least two states of* $\mathbf{S_k}$ *are removed after synthesis, including the removed control state q and the reaction state* q' *where there exists* $\sigma \in \Sigma_o$ *such that* $\xi_{S_k}(q', \sigma) = q$. *Thus,* **Procedure 7.3** *would iterate Steps 3-7 for at most* $\lfloor \frac{|Q_{S_0}|}{2} \rfloor$ *times, which completes the proof.* ■

The computational complexity of the proposed procedure depends on the complexity of three synthesis steps (**Procedures 7.1–7.3**), and the construction of $\mathbf{S_0}$ from $\mathbf{S_0^A}$. By using the synthesis approach in Refs. [?,3], the complexity of **Procedure 7.1** is no more than $O((|\Sigma| + |\Gamma|)2^{|X| \times |Q_{ce}^a| \times |Q_{bpns}^a|})$, the complexity of **Procedure 7.2** is no more than $O((|\Sigma| + |\Gamma|)2^{|X| \times |Q_{ce}^a| \times |Q_{bpns}^a|^2 \times |Q_{\hat{a}}|})$, and the complexity of **Procedure 7.3** is no more than $O((|\Sigma| + |\Gamma|)|Q_{S_0}|^2)$. The complexity of constructing $\mathbf{S_0}$ from $\mathbf{S_0^A}$ is $O((|\Sigma| + |\Gamma|)|Q_{S_0^A}|)$. Thus, the overall complexity is no more than $O((|\Sigma| + |\Gamma|)(2^{|X| \times |Q_{ce}^a| \times |Q_{bpns}^a|^2 \times |Q_{\hat{a}}|} + |Q_{S_0}|^2))$, where $|Q_{ce}^a| = |\Gamma| + 1$, $|Q_{bpns}^a| \leq (2^{|X| \times |Z|} + 1)(|\Gamma| + 1) + 1$, $|Q_{S_0}| = |Q_{S_0^A}| - 1$, $|Q_{S_0^A}| \leq 2^{|X| \times |Q_{ce}^a| \times |Q_{bpns}^a|^2 \times |Q_{\hat{a}}|}$, $|Q_{\hat{a}}| \leq 2^{|X| \times |Q_{ce}^a| \times |Q_{bpns}^a|}$, and $|\Gamma| = 2^{|\Sigma_c|}$. In summary, the upper bound of the synthesis complexity is double exponential w.r.t. $|X|$, $|Z|$, and $|\Sigma_c|$.

Remark 7.3 *The above analysis of complexity upper bound is not tight. By carefully choosing a proper data structure to record necessary state information, it might be possible to reduce the overall complexity to be exponential in time. This could be an interesting and potentially important topic for future research.*

7.8 CONCLUSIONS

This chapter aims to present a specific way of turning a supervisor not necessarily robust against smart actuator attacks into a control equivalent one, via supervisor obfuscation, that is robust against all smart actuator attacks. The key solution idea is inspired by an insight that a smart weak actuator attack exists if and only if a closed-loop behavior contains no attack feasible string. For each given closed-loop system $(\mathbf{G}, S)$, how to identify all attack feasible strings is relatively straightforward. However, in case the original supervisor S is not robust against smart actuator attacks, it is not obvious how to eliminate attack feasible strings, whose existence depends on the damage language of the plant $\mathbf{G}$ and the corresponding observation capability of a smart actuator attack, captured by the projection π_S. The idea of supervisor obfuscation is to transform S into a control equivalent one S' such that, under a new projection $\pi_{S'}$, previously existing attack feasible strings may disappear, which, based on Theorem 7.1, suggests that there will be no smart actuator attacks. An automaton-based framework is presented, which encodes all attack feasible strings and all supervisors control equivalent to the original one S. Upon such a novel model, specific algorithms are presented to firstly identify all attack feasible strings (with respect to all possible projections $\pi_{s'}$, where S' is control equivalent to S) from the original closed-loop behavior to ensure that no smart actuator attacks exist, and then, to decide whether the remaining safe behaviors permit at least one supervisor, which is control equivalent to the original S. This provides a positive answer to the fundamental question whether the existence of an obfuscated supervisor of the original one is decidable. At the same time, the algorithms also provide a concrete means to extract one robust supervisor via obfuscation, if it exists.

Notes

1. By construction, at the state q_{ce}^{init}, any control command $\gamma \in \Gamma$ is defined and would lead to the state q^γ, where only events in γ are defined. Any unobservable event in γ would lead to a self-loop and any observable event in γ would lead to the initial state q_{ce}^{init}.
2. **BPNS** is deterministic, but command non-deterministic because more than one different control command may be defined at each control state.
3. If we follow our definition of a supervisor and synthesize $\mathbf{S_0^A}$, we could always update $\mathbf{S_0^A} := \mathbf{BPNS^A} \times \mathbf{S_0^A}$ to generate a bipartite structure $\mathbf{S_0^A}$ with $L(\mathbf{S_0^A}) \subseteq L(\mathbf{BPNS^A})$.
4. The division rule is the same as that of $Q_{S_0} = Q_{S_0}^{\text{rea}} \dot\cup Q_{S_0}^{\text{com}}$.
5. The division rule is the same as that of $Q_{S_0} = Q_{S_0}^{\text{rea}} \dot\cup Q_{S_0}^{\text{com}}$.

Bibliography

[1] Morgan, S. (2022). Official annual cybercrime report. *Cybercrime Magazine*.

[2] Cassandra, C., & Lafortune, S. (2008). *Introduction to Discrete Event Systems*, (2nd Ed.), Berlin, Heidelberg: Springer.

[3] Wonham, W. M., & Cai, K. (2019). *Supervisory Control of Discrete-Event Systems*, Berlin, Heidelberg: Springer.

[4] Basilio, J. C., Hadjicostis, C. N., & Su, R. (2021). Analysis and control for resilience of discrete event systems: Fault diagnosis, opacity and cyber security, *Foundations and Trends in Systems and Control*, 8(4):285–443.

[5] Zetter, K. (2014). *Countdown to Zero Day: Stuxnet and the Launch of the World's First Digital Weapon*, New York: Crown Publishing Group.

[6] Langner, R. (2010). Ralph's step-by-step guide to get a crack at stuxnet traffic and behaviour, *OTbase*, https://www.langner.com/2010/09/ralphs-step-by-step-guide-to-get-a-crack-at-stuxnet-traffic-and-behavior. Accessed 8 Oct. 2023.

[7] Stevenson, A. (2015). A hacker group claims it breached over 300 websites and leaked 13,000 people's details online, *Business Insider*, https://www.businessinsider.com/ghostshell-hackers-hack-300-websites. Accessed 8 Oct. 2023.

[8] Merriam-Webster. (2019). *Merriam-Webster Dictionary*, the G. & C. Merriam Co., Springfield, MA.

[9] Milner, R. (1980). *A Calculus of Communicating Systems*, Berlin, Heidelberg: Springer.

[10] Hopcroft, J. E., Motwani, R., & Ullman, J. D. (2001). *Introduction to Automata Theory, Languages, and Computation*, (2nd Ed.), Boston, MA: Addison-Wesley.

[11] Lin, F., & Wonham, W. M. (1988). On observability of discrete-event systems, *Information Sciences*, 44(3):173–198.

[12] Ramadge, P. J., & Wonham, W. M. (1987). Supervisory control of a class of discrete event systems, *SIAM Journal on Control and Optimization*, 25(1):206–230.

[13] Su, R., Van Schuppen, J. H., & Rooda, J. E. (2010). Aggregative synthesis of distributed supervisors based on automaton abstraction, *IEEE Transactions on Automatic Control*, 55(7):1627–1640.

[14] Su, R., Van Schuppen, J. H., & Rooda, J. E. (2012). Maximally permissive coordinated distributed supervisory control of nondeterministic discrete-event systems, *Automatica*, 48(7):1237–1247.

[15] Su, R., & Wonham, W. M. (2004). Supervisor reduction for discrete-event systems, *Journal of Discrete Event Dynamic Systems*, 14(1):31–53.

[16] Wong, K. C. (1998). On the complexity of projections of discrete-event systems, *Proceedings of the 4th International Workshop on Discrete Event Systems*, pp. 201–206, Cagliari, Italy.

[17] Wonham, W. M. (2014). *Supervisory Control of Discrete-Event Systems*. Systems Control Group, Department of ECE, University of Toronto. URL: www.control.utoronto.ca/DES.

[18] Wonham, W. M., & Ramadge, P. J. (1987). On the supremal controllable sublanguage of a given language, *SIAM Journal on Control and Optimization*, 25(3):637–659.

[19] Cardenas, A. A., Amin, S., & Sastry, S. (2008). Secure control: Towards survivable cyber-physical systems, *Proceedings of the 28th International Conference on Distributed Computing Systems Workshops*, pp. 495–500, Beijing, China.

[20] Teixeira, A., Perez, D., Sandberg, H., & Johansson, K. H. (2012). Attack models and scenarios for networked control systems, *Proceedings of the 1st International Conference on High Confidence Networked Systems*, pp. 55–64, Beijing, China.

[21] Bryans, J. W., Koutny, M., & Ryan, P. Y. A. (2005). Modelling opacity using Petri nets, *Electronic Notes in Theoretical Computer Science*, 121:101–115.

[22] Badouel, E., Bednarczyk, M., Borzyszkowski, A., Caillaud, B., & Darondeau, P. (2007). Concurrent secrets, *Journal of Discrete Event Dynamic Systems*, 17(4):425–446.

[23] Saboori, A., & Hadjicostis, C. N. (2007). Notions of security and opacity in discrete event systems, *Proceedings of the 46th IEEE Conference on Decision and Control*, pp. 5056–5061, New Orleans, USA.

[24] Bryans, J. W., Koutny, M., Mazare, L., & Ryan, P. (2008). Opacity generalised to transition systems, *International Journal of Information Security*, 7(6):421–435.

[25] Hadjicostis, C. N. (2020). *Estimation and Inference in Discrete Event Systems*, Berlin, Heidelberg: Springer.

[26] Wu, Y. C., & Lafortune, S. (2014). Synthesis of insertion functions for enforcement of opacity security properties, *Automatica*, 50(5):1336–1348.

[27] Paoli, A., Sartini, M., & Lafortune, S. (2011). Active fault tolerant control of discrete event systems using online diagnostics, *Automatica*, 47(4):639–649.

[28] Thorsley, D., & Teneketzis, D. (2006). Intrusion detection in controlled discrete event systems, *Proceedings of the 45th IEEE Conference on Decision and Control*, pp. 6047–6054, San Diego, USA.

[29] Carvalho, L. K., Wu, Y., Kwong, R., & Lafortune, S. (2016). Detection and prevention of actuator enablement attacks in supervisory control systems, *Proceedings of the 13th International Workshop on Discrete Event Systems*, pp. 298–305, Xi'an, China.

[30] Cherdantseva, Y., Burnap, P., Blyth, A., Eden, P., Jones, K., Soulsby, H., & Stoddart, K. (2016). A review of cyber security risk assessment methods for SCADA systems, *Computers & Security*, 56:1–27.

[31] Colbert, E. J. M., & Kott, A. (2016). Attacks on industrial control systems, *Cyber-Security of SCADA and Other Industrial Control Systems*, 66:95–110.

[32] Fawzi, H., Tabuada, P., & Diggavi, S. (2014). Secure estimation and control for cyber-physical systems under adversarial attacks, *IEEE Transactions on Automatic Control*, 59(6):1454–1467.

[33] Knowles, W., Prince, D., Hutchison, D., Disso, J. F. P., & Jones, K. (2015). A survey of cyber security management in industrial control systems, *International Journal of Critical Infrastructure Protection*, 9:52–80.

[34] Saboori, A., & Hadjicostis, C. N. (2007). Notions of security and opacity in discrete event systems, *Proceedings of the 46th IEEE Conference on Decision and Control*, pp. 5056–5061, New Orleans, USA.

[35] Saboori, A., & Hadjicostis, C. N. (2013). Verification of initial-state opacity in security applications of discrete event systems, *Information Sciences*, 246:115–132.

[36] Jacob, R., Lesage, J., & Faure, J. (2016). Overview of discrete event systems opacity: Models, validation, and quantification, *Annual Reviews in Control*, 41:135–146.

[37] Rasouli, M., Miehling, E., & Teneketzis, D. (2014). A supervisory control approach to dynamic cyber-security, *Proceedings of 2014 International Conference on Decision and Game Theory for Security*, pp. 99–117, Los Angeles, USA.

[38] TCT: A Computation Tool for Supervisory Control Synthesis. http://www.control.utoronto.ca/~wonham/Research.html.

[39] SuSyNA: Supervisor Synthesis for Nondeterministic Automata. http://personal.ntu.edu.sg/rsu/Downloads.html.

[40] Dubreil, J., Darondeau, P., & Marchand, H. (2010). Supervisory control for opacity, *IEEE Transactions on Automatic Control*, 55(5):1089–1100.

[41] Alves, M., Basilio, J. C., da Cunha, A., Carvalho, L. K., & Moreira, M. V. (2014). Robust supervisory control against intermittent loss of observations, *Proceedings of the 12th International Workshop on Discrete Event Systems*, pp. 294–299, Paris, France.

[42] Rohloff, K. (2012). Bounded sensor failure tolerant supervisory control, *Proceedings of the 11th International Workshop on Discrete Event Systems*, pp. 272–277.

[43] Yin, X., & Lafortune, S. (2016). Synthesis of maximally permissive supervisors for partially observed discrete event systems, *IEEE Transactions on Automatic Control*, 61(5):1239–1254.

[44] Lin, F. (1994). Diagnosability of discrete-event systems and its applications, *Journal of Discrete Event Dynamic Systems*, 4(2):197–212.

[45] Sampath, M., Sengupta, R., Lafortune, S., Sinnamohideen, K., & Teneketzis, D. (1995). Diagnosability of discrete-event systems, *IEEE Transactions on Automatic Control*, 40(9):1555–1575.

[46] Contant, O., Lafortune, S., & Teneketzis, D. (2004). Diagnosis of intermittent faults, *Journal of Discrete Event Dynamic Systems*, 14:171–202.

[47] Zaytoon, J., & Lafortune, S. (2013). Overview of fault diagnosis methods for discrete event systems, *Annual Reviews in Control*, 37(2):308–320.

[48] Tsitsiklis, J. N. (1989). On the control of discrete event dynamic systems, *Mathematics of Control Signals and Systems*, 2(2):95–107.

[49] Dibaji, S. M., Pirani, M., Flamholz, D. B., Annaswamy, A. M., Johansson, K. H., & Chakrabortty, A. (2019). A systems and control perspective of CPS security, *Annual Reviews in Control*, 47:394–411.

[50] Lima, P., Alves, M. V., Carvalho, L., & Moreira, M. (2017). Security against network attacks in supervisory control systems, *IFAC-PapersOnLine*, 50(1):12333–12338.

[51] Lima, P., Carvalho, L., & Moreira, M. (2018). Detectable and undetectable network attack security of cyber-physical systems, *IFAC-PapersOnLine*, 51(7):179–185.

[52] Gao, C., Seatzu, C., Li, Z., & Giua, A. (2019). Multiple attacks detection on discrete event systems, *Proceedings of 2019 IEEE International Conference on Systems, Man and Cybernetics*, pp. 2352–2357, Bari, Italy.

[53] Carvalho, L., Wu, Y., Kwong, R., & Lafortune, S. (2018). Detection and mitigation of classes of attacks in supervisory control systems, *Automatica*, 97:121–133.

[54] Wang, Y., & Pajic, M. (2019). Supervisory control of discrete event systems in the presence of sensor and actuator attacks, *Proceedings of the 58th IEEE Conference on Decision and Control*, pp. 5350–5355, Nice, France.

[55] Su, R. (2017). A cyber attack model with bounded sensor reading alterations, *Proceedings of 2017 American Control Conference*, pp. 3200–3205, Seattle, USA.

[56] Su, R. (2018). Supervisor synthesis to thwart cyber attack with bounded sensor reading alterations, *Automatica*, 94:35–44.

[57] Su, R. (2023). On decidability of existence of nonblocking supervisors resilient to smart sensor attacks, *Automatica*, 154:111076.

[58] Meira-Góes, R., Kang, E., Kwong, R., & Lafortune, S. (2017). Stealthy deception attacks for cyber-physical systems, *Proceedings of the 56th IEEE Conference on Decision and Control*, pp. 4224–4230, Melbourne, Australia.

[59] Meira-Góes, R., Kang, E., Kwong, R., & Lafortune, S. (2020). Synthesis of sensor deception attacks at the supervisory layer of cyber-physical systems, *Automatica*, 121:109172.

[60] Meira-Góes, R., Lafortune, S., & Marchand, H. (2021). Synthesis of supervisors robust against sensor deception attacks, *IEEE Transactions on Automatic Control*, 66(10):4990-4997.

[61] Meira-Góes, R., Kwong, R., & Lafortune, S. (2019). Synthesis of sensor deception attacks for systems modeled as probabilistic automata, *Proceedings of 2019 American Control Conference*, pp. 5620–5626, Philadelphia, USA.

[62] Lin, L., Thuijsman, S., Zhu, Y., Ware, S., Su, R., & Reniers, M. (2019). Synthesis of supremal successful normal actuator attackers on normal supervisors, *Proceedings of 2019 American Control Conference*, pp. 5614–5619, Philadelphia, USA.

[63] Lin, L., & Su, R. (2021). Synthesis of covert actuator and sensor attackers, *Automatica*, 130:109714.

[64] Lin, L., Zhu, Y., & Su, R. (2019). Towards bounded synthesis of resilient supervisors, *Proceedings of 58th IEEE Conference on Decision and Control*, pp. 7659–7664, Nice, France.

[65] Lin, L., Tai, R., Zhu, Y., & Su, R. (2021). Observation-Assisted Heuristic synthesis of covert attackers against unknown supervisors, *Journal of Discrete Event Dynamic Systems*, 32:495–520.

[66] Tai, R., Lin, L, & Su, R. (2022). Identification of system vulnerability under a smart sensor attack via attack model reduction, *IEEE Control Systems Letters*, 6:2948–2953.

[67] Tai, R., Lin, L., Zhu, Y., & Su, R. (2024). Synthesis of distributed covert sensor-actuator attacks, *IEEE Transactions on Automatic Control*, DOI: 10.1109/TAC.2023.3339497, Aug. 2024.

[68] Tai, R., Lin, L., & Su, R. (2023). Synthesis of optimal covert sensor-actuator attackers for discrete event systems, *Automatica*, 151:110910.

[69] Tai, R., Lin, L., Zhu, Y., & Su, R. (2023). Synthesis of the supremal covert attacker against unknown supervisors by using observations, *IEEE Transactions on Automatic Control*, 68(6):3453–3468.

[70] Lin, L., Zhu, Y., & Su, R. (2020). Synthesis of covert actuator attackers for free, *Journal of Discrete Event Dynamic Systems*, 30:561–577.

[71] Zhu, Y., Lin, L., & Su, R. (2019). Supervisor obfuscation against actuator enablement attack, *Proceedings of 2019 European Control Conference*, pp. 1760–1765, Naples, Italy.

[72] Tai, R., Lin, L., & Su, R. (2023). On decidability of existence of fortified supervisors against covert actuator attackers, arXiv:2205.02383.

[73] Wu, Y. C., Sankararaman, K. A., & Lafortune, S. (2014). Ensuring privacy in location-based services: An approach based on opacity enforcement, *IFAC Proceedings Volumes*, 47(2):33–38.

[74] Wakaiki, M., Tabuada, P., & Hespanha, J. P. (2019). Supervisory control of discrete-event systems under attacks, *Dynamic Games and Applications*, 9(4):965–983.

[75] Fritz, R., & Zhang, P. (2018). Modeling and detection of cyber attacks on discrete event systems, *IFAC-PapersOnLine*, 51(7):285–290.

[76] Khoumsi, A. (2019). Sensor and actuator attacks of cyber-physical systems: A study based on supervisory control of discrete event systems, *Proceedings of 8th International Conference on Systems and Control*, pp. 176–182, Marrakech, Morocco.

[77] Meira-Goes, R., Marchand, H., & Lafortune, S. (2019). Towards resilient supervisors against sensor deception attacks, *Proceedings of 58th IEEE Conference on Decision and Control*, pp. 5144–5149, Nice, France.

[78] Meira-Goes, R., Lafortune, S., & Marchand, H. (2021). Synthesis of supervisors robust against sensor deception attacks, *IEEE Transactions on Automatic Control*, 66(10):4990–4997.

[79] Meira-Góes, R., Kang, E., Kwong, R., & Lafortune, S. (2017). Stealthy deception attacks for cyber-physical systems, *Proceedings of 56th IEEE Annual Conference on Decision and Control*, pp. 4224—4230, Melbourne, Australia.

[80] Meira-Góes, R., Kang, E., Kwong, R., & Lafortune, S. (2020). Synthesis of sensor deception attacks at the supervisory layer of cyber–physical systems, *Automatica*, 121:109172.

[81] Meira-Góes, R., Kwong, R., & Lafortune, S. (2022). Synthesis of optimal multi-objective attack strategies for controlled systems modeled by probabilistic automata, *IEEE Transactions on Automatic Control*, 67(6):2873–2888.

[82] Lafortune, S., Meira-Góes, R., & Lafortune, S. (2020). Efficient synthesis of sensor deception attacks using observation equivalence-based abstraction, *IFAC-PapersOnLine*, 53(4):28–34.

[83] Lin, L., & Su, R. (2020). Synthesis of covert actuator and sensor attackers as supervisor synthesis, *IFAC-PapersOnLine*, 53(4):1–6.

[84] Lin, L., Tai, R., Zhu, Y., & Su, R. (2021). Heuristic synthesis of covert attackers against unknown supervisors, *Proceedings of 60th IEEE Conference on Decision and Control*, pp. 7003–7008, Austin, USA.

[85] Zhang, Q., Seatzu, C., Li, Z., & Giua, A. (2020). Stealthy sensor attacks for plants modeled by labeled petri nets, *IFAC-PapersOnLine*, 53(4):14–20.

[86] Zheng, S., Shu, S., & Lin, F. (2021). Modeling and control of discrete event systems under joint sensor-actuator cyber attacks, *Proceedings of 6th International Conference on Automation, Control and Robotics Engineering*, pp. 216–220, Dalian, China.

[87] Ma, Z., & Cai, K. (2022). Optimal secret protections in discrete-event systems, *IEEE Transactions on Automatic Control*, 67(6):2816–2828.

[88] Su, R., Van Schuppen, J., & Rooda, J. (2011). The synthesis of time optimal supervisors by using heaps-of-pieces, *IEEE Transactions on Automatic Control*, 57(1):105–118.

[89] Sengupta, R., & Lafortune, S. (1988). An optimal control theory for discrete event systems, *SIAM Journal on control and Optimization*, 36(2):488–541.

[90] Brave, Y., & Heymann, M. (1993). On optimal attraction in discrete-event processes, *Information sciences*, 67(3):245–276.

[91] Marchand, H., Boivineau, O., & Lafortune, S. (2002). On optimal control of a class of partially observed discrete event systems, *Automatica*, 38(11):1935–1943.

[92] Passino K., & Antsaklis, P. J. (1989). On the optimal control of discrete event systems, *Proceedings of 28th IEEE Conference on Decision and Control*, pp. 2713–2718, Tampa, USA.

[93] Arnold, A., Vincent, A., & Walukiewicz, I. (2003). Games for synthesis of controllers with partial observation, *Theoretical Computer Science*, 303(1):7–34.

[94] Su, R. (2023). On decidability of existence of nonblocking supervisors resilient to smart sensor attacks, *Automatica*, 154:111076.

[95] Ma, Z., & Cai, K. (2022). On resilient supervisory control against indefinite actuator attacks in discrete-event systems, *IEEE Control Systems Letters*, 6:2942–2947.

[96] Alves, M. R. C., Pena, P. N., & Rudie, K. (2022). Discrete-event systems subject to unknown sensor attacks, *Discrete Event Dynamic Systems*, 32(1):143–158.

[97] Wang, Y., Li, Y. T., Yu, Z. H., Wu, N. Q., & Li, Z. W. (2021). Supervisory control of discrete-event systems under external attacks, *Information Science*, 562:398–413.

[98] Lima, P. M., Alves, M. V. S., Carvalho, L. K., & Moreira, M. V. (2022). Security of cyber-physical systems: Design of a security supervisor to thwart attacks, *IEEE Transactions on Automation Science and Engineering*, 19(3):1–12.

[99] Wang, Y., & Pajic, M. (2019). Attack-resilient supervisory control with intermittently secure communication, *Proceeding of 58th IEEE*

Annual Conference in Decision and Control, pp. 2015–2020, Melbourne, Australia.

[100] Yao, J., Yin, X., & Li, S. (2020). On attack mitigation in supervisory control systems: A tolerant control approach, *Proceeding of 59th IEEE Annual Confernce in Decision and Control*, pp. 4504–4510, Jeju Island, South Korea.

[101] Wang, Z., Meira-Goes, R., Lafortune, S., & Kwong, R. (2020). Mitigation of classes of attacks using a probabilistic discrete event system framework, *IFAC-PapersOnLine*, 53(4):35–41.

[102] Li, Y., Tong, Y., & Giua, A. (2020). Detection and prevention of cyber-attacks in networked control systems, *Proceedings of 17th International Workshop on Discrete Event Systems*, pp. 7–13, Rio de Janeiro, Brazil.

[103] Fritz, R., Schwarz, P., & Zhang, P. (2019). Modeling of cyber attacks and a time guard detection for ICS based on discrete event systems, *Proceedings of 18th European Control Conference*, pp. 4368–4373, Naples, Italy.

[104] He, Z., Ma, Z., & Tang, W. (2021). Performance safety enforcement in strongly connected timed event graphs, *Automatica*, 128:109605.

[105] He, Z., & Ma, Z. (2021). Performance safety enforcement in stochastic event graphs against boost and slow attacks, *Nonlinear Analysis: Hybrid Systems*, 41:101057.

[106] Matsui, S., & Cai, K. (2019). Secret securing with multiple protections and minimum costs, *Proceedings of 58th IEEE Annual Conference on Decision and Control*, pp. 7635–7640, Melbourne, Australia.

[107] Meira-Góes, R., & Lafortune, S. (2020). Moving target defense based on switched supervisory control: A new technique for mitigating sensor deception attacks, *IFAC-PapersOnLine*, 53(4):317–323.

[108] Jakovljevic, Z., Lesi, V., & Pajic, M. (2021). Attacks on distributed sequential control in manufacturing automation, *IEEE Transactions on Industrial Informatics*, 17(2):775–786.

[109] You, D., Wang, S. G., Zhou, M., & Seatzu, C. (2022). Supervisory control of petri nets in the presence of replacement attacks, *IEEE Transactions on Automatic Control*, 67(3):1466–1473.

[110] Yang, J., & Lee, D. (2021). Robust corrective control against a class of actuator attacks in input/state asynchronous sequential machines, *Journal of the Franklin Institute*, 358(2):1403–1421.

[111] Sakata, K., Fujita, S., & Sawada, K. (2021). Synthesis of resilient third-party monitoring system against cyberattacks via supervisory control, *Proceedings of 2021 IEEE International Conference on Consumer Electronics*, pp. 1–6, Las Vegas, USA.

[112] Yin, X., & Lafortune, S. (2017). Synthesis of maximally-permissive supervisors for the range control problem, *IEEE Transactions on Automatic Control*, 62(8):3914–3929.

[113] Yin, X., & Lafortune, S. (2015). A new approach for synthesizing opacity-enforcing supervisors for partially-observed discrete-event systems, *Proceedings of 2015 American Control Conference*, pp. 377–383, Chicago, USA.

[114] Hopcroft, J. E., & Ullman, J. D. (1979). *Introduction to Automata Theory, Languages, and Computation*, Boston, MA: Addison-Wesley.

[115] Zhu, Y., Lin, L., Ware, S., & Su, R. (2019). Supervisor synthesis for networked discrete event systems with communication delays and lossy events, *Proceedings of 58th IEEE Annual Conference on Decision and Control*, pp. 6730–6735, Melbourne, Australia.

[116] Tai, R., Lin, L., Zhu, Y., & Su, R. (2023). Synthesis of the supremal covert attacker against unknown supervisors by using observations, *IEEE Transactions on Automatic Control*, 68(6):3453–3468.

[117] Lin, L., Zhu, Y., Tai, R., Ware, S., & Su, R. (2022). Networked supervisor synthesis against lossy channels with bounded network delays as non-networked synthesis, *Automatica*, 142:110279.

[118] Rasouli, M., Miehling, E., & Teneketzis, D. (2014). A supervisory control approach to dynamic cyber-security, *Proceedings of 2014 International Conference on Decision and Game Theory for Security*, pp. 99–117, Los Angeles, USA.

[119] Perkins, C., & Muller, G. (2015). Using discrete event simulation to model attacker interactions with cyber and physical security systems, *Procedia Computer Science*, 61:221–226.

[120] Henry, M. H., Layer, R. M., Snow, K. Z., & Zaret, D. R. (2009). Evaluating the risk of cyber attacks on SCADA systems via Petri net analysis with application to hazardous liquid loading operations, *Proceedings of 2009 IEEE Conference on Technologies for Homeland Security*, pp. 607–614, Washington, DC, USA.

[121] Jasiul, B., Szpyrka, M., & Sliwa, J. (2014). Detection and modeling of cyber attacks with Petri nets, *Entropy*, 16:6602–6623.

[122] Feng, L., & Wonham, W. M. (2006). TCT: A computation tool for supervisory control synthesis, *Proceedings of 8th International Workshop Discrete Event Systems*, pp. 388–389, Ann Arbor, USA.

[123] Malik, R., Akesson, K., Flordal, H., & Fabian, M. (2017). Supremica-an efficient tool for large-scale discrete event systems, *IFAC-PapersOnLine*, 50:5794–5799.

[124] Cai, K., & Wonham, W. M. (2010). Supervisor localization: A top-down approach to distributed control of discrete-event systems, *IEEE Transactions on Automatic Control*, 55(3):605–618.

[125] Cai, K., Zhang, R., & Wonham, W. M. (2013). Relative observability of discrete-event systems and its supremal sublanguages, *IEEE Transactions on Automatic Control*, 60(3):659–670.

[126] Zhang, R., & Cai, K. (2016). On supervisor localization based distributed control of discrete-event systems under partial observation, *Proceedings of 2016 American Control Conference*, pp. 764–767, Boston, USA.

[127] Feng, L., & Wonham, W. M. (2008). Supervisory control architecture for discrete-event systems, *IEEE Transactions on Automatic Control*, 53(6):1449–1461.

[128] Vaz, A. F., & Wonham, W. M. (1986). On supervisor reduction in discrete-event systems, *International Journal of Control*, 44(2):475–491.

[129] Mohajerani, S., Malik, R., & Fabian, M. (2014). A framework for compositional synthesis of modular nonblocking supervisors, *IEEE Transactions on Automatic Control*, 59(1):150–162.

[130] Rabin, M. O., & Scott, D. (1959). Finite automata and their decision problems, *IBM Journal of Research and Development*, 3(2):114–125.

[131] Mo, Y., Kim, T. H. J., Brancik, K., Dickinson, D., Lee, H., Perrig, A., & Sinopoli, B. (2012). Cyber-physical security of a smart grid infrastructure, *Proceedings of the IEEE*, 100(1):195–209.

[132] Zhang, H., Cheng, P., Shi, L., & Chen, J. M. (2015). Optimal denial-of-service attack scheduling with energy constraint, *IEEE Transactions on Automatic Control*, 60(11):3023–3028.

[133] You, D., Wang, S., & Seatzu, C. (2022). A liveness-enforcing supervisor tolerant to sensor reading modification attacks, *IEEE Transactions on Systems, Man, and Cybernetics: Systems*, 52(4):2398–2411.

[134] Lima, P. M., Alves, M. V. S., Carvalho, L. K., & Moreira, M. V. (2019). Security against communication network attacks of cyber-physical systems, *Journal of Control, Automation and Electrical Systems*, 30(1):125–135.

[135] Su, R., & Wonham, W. M. (2018). A generalized theory on supervisor reduction, *Proceedings of 57th IEEE Annual Conference on Decision and Control*, pp. 3950–3955, Miami, USA.

[136] Su, R., & Wonham, W. M. (2018). What information really matters in supervisor reduction? *Automatica*, 95:368–377.

[137] Chen, W., Ding, D., Dong, H., & Wei, G. (2019). Distributed resilient filtering for power systems subject to denial-of-service attacks, *IEEE Transactions on Systems, Man, and Cybernetics: Systems*, 49(8):1688–1697.

[138] Xu, Y., Fang, M., Wu, Z. G., Pan, Y. J., Chadli, M., & Huang, T. (2020). Input-based event-triggering consensus of multiagent systems under denial-of-service attacks, *IEEE Transactions on Systems, Man, and Cybernetics: Systems*, 50(4)1455–1464.

[139] Liu, J., Gu, Y., Zha, L., Liu, Y., & Cao, J. (2019). Event-triggered H_∞ load frequency control for multiarea power systems under hybrid

cyber attacks, *IEEE Transactions on Systems, Man, and Cybernetics: Systems*, 49(8):1665–1678.

[140] Zhang, D., & Feng, G. (2019). A new switched system approach to leader-follower consensus of heterogeneous linear multiagent systems with dos attack, *IEEE Transactions on Systems, Man, and Cybernetics: Systems*, 51(2):1258–1266.

[141] Mazare, L. (2004). Using unification for opacity properties, *Proceedings of 2004 Workshop on Issues in the Theory of Security*, pp. 165–176, Nova Scotia, Canada.

[142] Bérard, B., Mullins, J., & Sassolas, M. (2015). Quantifying opacity, *Mathematical Structures in Computer Science*, 25(2):361–403.

[143] Badouel, E., Bednarczyk, M., Borzyszkowski, A., Caillaud, B., & Darondeau, P. (2007). Concurrent secrets, *Discrete Event Dynamic Systems*, 17(4):425–446.

[144] Dubreil, J., Darondeau, P., & Marchand, H. (2008). Opacity enforcing control synthesis, *Proceedings of 9th International Workshop Discrete Event Systems*, pp. 28–35, Gothenburg, Sweden.

[145] Falcone, Y., & Marchand, H. (2015). Enforcement and validation (at runtime) of various notions of opacity, *Discrete Event Dynamic Systems*, 25(4):531–570.

[146] Jacob, R., Lesage, J., & Faure, J. (2016). Overview of discrete event systems opacity: Models validation and quantification, *Annual Reviews in Control*, 41:135–146.

[147] Lafortune, S., Lin, F., & Hadjicostis, C. N. (2018). On the history of diagnosability and opacity in discrete event systems, *Annual Reviews in Control*, 45:257–266.

[148] Takai, S., & Kumar, R. (2009). Verification and synthesis for secrecy in discrete-event systems, *Proceedings of 2009 American Control Conference*, pp. 4741–4746, St. Louis, USA.

[149] Hou, J., Yin, X., Li, S., & Zamani, M. (2019). Abstraction-based synthesis of opacity-enforcing controllers using alternating simulation relations, *Proceedings of 58th IEEE Conference on Decision and Control*, pp. 7653–7658, Nice, France.

[150] Saboori, A., & Hadjicostis, C. N. (2008). Opacity-enforcing supervisory strategies for secure discrete event systems, *Proceedings of 47th IEEE Conference on Decision and Control*, pp. 889–894, Cancun, Mexico.

[151] Saboori, A., & Hadjicostis, C. N. (2012). Opacity-enforcing supervisory strategies via state estimator constructions, *IEEE Transactions on Automatic Control*, 57(5):1155–1165.

[152] Darondeau, P., Marchand, H., & Ricker, L. (2015). Enforcing opacity of regular predicates on modal transition systems, *Discrete Event Dynamic Systems*, 25(1):251–270.

[153] Dubreil, J., Darondeau, P., & Marchand, H. (2008). Opacity enforcing control synthesis, *Proceedings of 9th International Workshop on Discrete Event Systems*, pp. 28–35, Gothenburg, Sweden.

[154] Barcelos, R. J. & Basilio, J. C. (2018). Enforcing current-state opacity through shuffle in event observations, *Proceedings of 14th International Workshop Discrete Event Systems*, pp. 106–111, Sorrento, Italy.

[155] Ji, Y., Wu, Y. C., & Lafortune, S. (2018). Enforcement of opacity by public and private insertion functions, *Automatica*, 93:369–378.

[156] Ji, Y., & Lafortune, S. (2017). Enforcing opacity by publicly known edit functions, *Proceedings of 56th IEEE Conference on Decision and Control*, pp. 4866–4871, Melbourne, Australia.

[157] Ji, Y., Yin, X., & Lafortune, S. (2019). Opacity enforcement using nondeterministic publicly-known edit functions, *IEEE Transactions on Automatic Control*, 64(10):4369–4376.

[158] Ji, Y., Yin, X., & Lafortune, S. (2019). Enforcing opacity by insertion functions under multiple energy constraints, *Automatica*, 108:108476.

[159] Wu, Y. C., & Lafortune, S. (2015). Synthesis of opacity-enforcing insertion functions that can be publicly known, *Proceedings of 54th IEEE Conference on Decision and Control*, pp. 3506–3513, Osaka, Japan.

[160] Mohajerani, S., Ji, Y., & Lafortune, S. (2018). Efficient synthesis of edit functions for opacity enforcement using bisimulation-based abstractions, *Proceedings of 57th IEEE Conference on Decision and Control*, pp. 3573–3578, Miami, USA.

[161] Mohajerani, S., Ji, Y. & Lafortune, S. (2019). Compositional and abstraction-based approach for synthesis of edit functions for opacity enforcement, *IEEE Transactions on Automatic Control*, 65(8):3349–3364.

[162] Falcone, Y., & Marchand, H. (2013). Runtime enforcement of K-step opacity, *Proceedings of 52nd IEEE Conference on Decision and Control*, pp. 7271–7278, Florence, Italy.

[163] Cassez, F., Dubreil, J., & Marchand, H. (2012). Synthesis of opaque systems with static and dynamic masks, *Formal Methods in System Design*, 40(1):88–115.

[164] Yin, X., & Li, S. (2019). Synthesis of dynamic masks for infinite-step opacity, *IEEE Transactions on Automatic Control*, 65(4):1429–1441.

[165] Zhang, B., Shu, S., & Lin, F. (2015). Maximum information release while ensuring opacity in discrete event systems, *IEEE Transactions on Automation Science and Engineering*, 12(3):1067–1079.

[166] Tai, R., Lin, L., Zhu, Y. & Su, R. (2021). Privacy-preserving supervisory control of discrete-event systems via co-synthesis of edit function and supervisor for opacity enforcement and requirement satisfaction, arXiv:2104.04299.

[167] Schulze Darup, M., Alexandru, A. B., Quevedo, D. E., & Pappas, G. J. (2021). Encrypted control for networked systems: An illustrative introduction and current challenges, *IEEE Control Systems Magazine*, 41(3):58–78.

[168] Kogiso, K., & Fujita, T. (2015). Cyber-security enhancement of networked control systems using homomorphic encryption, *Proceedings of 54th IEEE Conference on Decision and Control*, pp. 6836–6843, Osaka, Japan.

[169] Farokhi, F., Shames, I., & Batterham, N. (2017). Secure and private control using semi-homomorphic encryption, *Control Engineering Practice*, 67:13–20.

[170] Kim, J., Shim, H., & Han, K. (2022). Dynamic controller that operates over homomorphically encrypted data for infinite time horizon, *IEEE Transactions on Automatic Control*, 68(2):660–672.

[171] Kim, J., Lee, C., Shim, H., Cheon, J. H., Kim, A., Kim, M., & Song, Y. (2016). Encrypting controller using fully homomorphic encryption for security of cyber-physical systems, *IFAC-PapersOnLine*, 49(22):175–180.

[172] Alexandru, A. B., Morari, M., & Pappas, G. J. (2018). Cloud-based MPC with encrypted data, *Proceedings of 57th IEEE Conference on Decision and Control*, pp. 5014–5019, Miami, USA.

[173] Murguia, C., Farokhi, F., & Shames, I. (2020). Secure and private implementation of dynamic controllers using semihomomorphic encryption, *IEEE Transactions on Automatic Control*, 65(9):3950–3957.

[174] Van Maaren, H., Walsh, T., Biere, A., & Heule, M. (2009). *Handbook of Satisfiability*, (1st Ed.), Amsterdam, Netherlands: IOS Press.

[175] Neider, D. (2012). Computing minimal separating DFAs and regular invariants using SAT and SMT solvers, *Proceedings of 2012 International Symposium on Automated Technology for Verification and Analysis*, pp. 354–369, Thiruvananthapuram, India.

[176] Biere, A., Cimatti, A., Clarke, E. M., Strichman, O., & Zhu, Y. (2003). Bounded model checking, *Advances in Computers*, 58:117–148.

[177] Zhu, Y., Lin, L., Tai, R., & Su, R. (2022). Overview of networked supervisory control with imperfect communication channels, *Journal of Discrete Event Dynamic Systems: Theory and Applications*, 33:25–61.

Index

Note: *Italic* page numbers refer to figures.

a *bipartite supervisor*, denoted by **BT(S)** 213

a *compromised supervisor under A* 133

a *compromised* supervisory control with respect to (S, A) 71

a *compromised* supervisory control with respect to (S, A_c) 205

a *control cover* on **S** 171, 172

a *control congruence* on **A** 195–196

A lean sensor-actuator attack *A* 76

A *(nondeterministic) actuator attack on S* 204

a *non-deterministic compromised supervisor* 35

A prefix-closed sublanguage $L_a \subseteq L(\mathbf{G}_a)$ is *(strong or weak) attack feasible* 84

A resilient supervisor candidate 146, 154

a risky pair (s, t) 138

A *sensor-actuator* attack *A* consists of two sub-attacks 70

a simple single-tank example 40

A sublanguage is a *nonblocking resilient supervisor candidate* 146

A sublanguage $L \subseteq H$ is *conditionally controllable* 144

A supervisor is modeled by a mapping 23

a surrogate of S 104, 115, 118

A_c-controllability 215

A_c-observability 215

an attack and the system are perfectly synchronized 103

an *effective* control pattern of S 79

application-based cyberattack 2

application-based cybersecurity threats 2

attack equivalent on $(\mathbf{G}, \mathbf{S})$ 194

attack feasible 207

attack feasible strings 208–212, 216, 246

attackability 33, 66, 128, 134

augmented closed behavior of **G** 142

augmented marked behavior of **G** 142

behavior oriented 1
behavior-preserving structure,
    denoted by
    BPS 220
bipartite behavior-preserving
    command-
    nondeterministic
    supervisor **BPNS** *224*
bipartite behavior-preserving
    command-
    nondeterministic
    supervisor under attack
    BPNS^{A} *231*

closed behaviour of **G** 20
    augmented closed behavior of
      G 142
    closed behaviour of V/G 24
command channel 3, 6–7, 13–14,
    80, 212
Command Execution Model 192
command execution process
    under attack, denoted by
    CE^{A} 214
compound events 47, 84, 90,
    106, 111
concatenated 17
control patterns (or *control
    commands*) 23
*control unambiguous with respect
    to **G** 116
controllable and *uncontrollable*
    alphabets 23
controllable with respect to **G**
    and Σ_{uc} 25, 26, 36
coreachable 20, 93

DES cybersecurity 4, *16*
*deterministic finite-state
    automaton* (DFSA or
    simply FSA) 19
discrete-event dynamical system
    (DEDS) 2
discrete-event system (DES) 1,
    32, 162

enabled event set 18, 20, 21, 169,
    194, 198
    (**A**-)enabled event set 194
    (**S**-)enabled event set 170
event (or *action*) 17
Extended Quotient Theorem 175

fault diagnosis 3, 12, 33, 61, 202
finite-state weighted
    automaton 22
    weighted FSA 22, 79
free monoid 17
function oriented 1
functional integrity 11

G is called *reachable* 20
G$_{\mathrm{B}}$ is the image of **G**$_{\mathrm{A}}$ under the
    DES-isomorphism 174

information confidentiality 11
input and *output* mappings 37,
    46, 131

L_a is control-integrity
    preserved 85
$L_m(\mathbf{G})$-closed 26, 198
logical conjunction "AND" 18
logical disjunction "OR" 18

marked behavior of **G** 21, 100, 142–143, 171

marker (or final) states 19

meet 22, 170, 175

model a non-deterministic sensor attack as a finite state automaton **A** 37

natural observer 66

natural projection 17, 19, 23, 66, 204

networked control 24, 187

nondeterministic finite-state automaton (NFSA) 21

non-deterministic sensor attack of **G** 34

non-synchronized attack 108, 117–120, 122

obfuscated supervisors 199, 202, 203, 216, 219, 228, 235–238, 240–241, 245–246

observable with respect to **G** and P_o 26, 36

observation channel 3, 13–14, 204

opacity 11–12, 33, 202

parallel composition 1, 21, *22*, 215

(partial) state transition function 19

prefix closed 18, 104, 198

  prefix-closed sublanguages 48, 84, 145

prefix closure 17

(prefix) *normal* 26

prefix substrings 17, 18, 115, 136, 138, 143

Procedure for Supremal Attack Language 56

Procedure for SSA-Robust Supervisor (SSA-RS) 60

Quantified Boolean formulas (QBF) 15

Ramadge-Wonham (RW) 17

Ramadge-Wonham supervisory control architecture *3, 24*

regular expression 18

relatively observable (or $\overline{C}$-*observable*) 26

S' is *non-redundant* with respect to **S** 174

S_1 is leaner than S_2, i.e., $S_1 \preceq S_2$ 164

sensor attack constraint model 188

sensor attacker model 193

smart actuator-attack and supervisor obfuscation
  covertness 206
  (**G**, *S*) is *attackable* 205
  strong damage infliction 206
  weak damage infliction 206

smart sensor-actuator attack (**G**, *S*) is *attackable* 74
  covertness 74
  strong damage infliction 74
  weak damage infliction 75

Smart Sensor-Actuator Attack of (**G**, *S*) with respect to L_{dam} 75

smart sensor attack
  covertness 44
  (**G**, *S*) is *attackable* 44

smart sensor attack
covertness (*cont.*)
strong damage infliction
44, 48
weak damage infliction
44, 48
smart sensor attack (SSA) of
($\mathbf{G}$, S) 44
SQL injection attacks 8–9
SSA-robust supervisor: S is
SSA-robust with respect
to L_{dam} 59
state controllability 155
state observability 155
Stuxnet 4–7
sub-automaton of $\mathbf{G}$ 20
Sun Tse 11
supervisor obfuscation 15, 199,
200, 211–212, 246
supervisor reduction 16, 162–164,
173, 178, 182, 186, 194,
197, 198, 211
supervisory control mapping 24,
26, 38–39
*supremal minimum-weighted
strong attack feasible* 91
*supremal minimum-weighted weak
attack feasible* 94
synchronous product of L_1 and
L_2 19
*Synthesis Procedure for Non-
Synchronized Attack* 117

The automaton $\mathbf{A}$ introduced
above is essentially a
transducer 37
*the binary compatibility relation
over* Q_a 195

the bipartite supervisor under
attack, denoted by
$\mathbf{BT}(\mathbf{S})^A$ 213
the compromised supervisor
under sensor attack $\mathbf{A}$
for $\mathbf{G}$ 194
the existence of a supervisor
resilient to all SSAs is
decidable 160
The impact of a sensor-actuator
attack $A = (\mathbf{A}_s, \mathbf{A}_c)$ 81
The smart attack language D is
supremal 46
the *supremal minimum weighted
smart sensor-actuator
attack* 79
the supremal smart lean
sensor-actuator
attack 77
the supremal smart sensor attack
of the closed-loop system
($\mathbf{G}$, S, L_{dam}) 45
*the supremal smart (strong or
weak) actuator
attack* 207
timeline of major new
frameworks about DES
cybersecurity *16*
trimmed 20
two supervisors $\mathbf{S}_1$ and $\mathbf{S}_2$
of $\mathbf{G}$ are *control
equivalent* 169

weighted smart sensor-actuator
attacks 78
*weighted weak attack feasible
sub-languages* of
$L(\mathbf{G}_a)$ 93